Religious Rights within the Family

It is often asserted that 'A family that prays together, stays together'. But what if a child no longer wishes to pray? This book analyses the law in relation to situations where parents force their children to manifest the parental religion. From thorough examination of international law it argues that, unlike what is generally believed, the human rights regime does not grant parents a right to impose manifestations of their religion on their children. Instead, the author proposes to regard coerced manifestations as a limitation on children's right to freedom of manifestation, based on national laws that give parents rights at the domestic level under principles such as parental responsibility. The book focuses on two aspects of States' positive obligations in this regard. First, the obligation to provide a regulatory framework that can protect children's right to freedom of manifestation, and restricts limitations to those that are proportionate or 'necessary in a democratic society'. Second, to provide access to remedies, which it is argued should consist of access to a family-friendly infrastructure for dispute resolution available to parents and children in conflict over religious manifestation. Both depend heavily on the way States balance power between parents and children at the national level. The book includes three case studies and social research of jurisdictions that offer different perspectives under the principles of parental authority (France), parental responsibility (England) and parental rights (Hong Kong).

Esther Erlings is a Lecturer in Law at Flinders University, Australia. She has published in the areas of human rights (especially those of children), parental responsibility and law, and religion.

ICLARS Series on Law and Religion

The *ICLARS Series on Law and Religion* is a new series designed to provide a forum for the rapidly expanding field of research in law and religion. The series is published in association with the International Consortium for Law and Religion Studies, an international network of scholars and experts of law and religion founded in 2007 with the aim of providing a place where information, data and opinions can easily be exchanged among members and made available to the broader scientific community. The series aims to become a primary source for students and scholars while presenting authors with a valuable means to reach a wide and growing readership.

Series Editors:
Silvio Ferrari, University of Milan, Italy, Russell Sandberg, Cardiff University, UK, Pieter Coertzen, University of Stellenbosch, South Africa, W. Cole Durham, Jr., Brigham Young University, USA, and Tahir Mahmood, Amity International University, India

Other titles in this series:

Religion, Pluralism, and Reconciling Difference
Edited by W. Cole Durham, Jr. and Donlu Thayer

Religious Literacy, Law and History
Perspectives on European Pluralist Societies
Edited by Alberto Melloni and Francesca Cadeddu

Regulating Religion
State Governance of Religious Institutions in South Africa
Helena Van Coller

Religious Rights within the Family
From Coerced Manifestation to Dispute Resolution in France, England and Hong Kong
Esther Erlings

For more information about this series, please visit:

www.routledge.com/ICLARS-Series-on-Law-and-Religion/book-series/ICLARS

Religious Rights within the Family

From Coerced Manifestation to Dispute Resolution in France, England and Hong Kong

Esther Erlings

Routledge
Taylor & Francis Group
LONDON AND NEW YORK

First published 2020
by Routledge
2 Park Square, Milton Park, Abingdon, Oxon OX14 4RN

and by Routledge
605 Third Avenue, New York, NY 10017

First issued in paperback 2020

Routledge is an imprint of the Taylor & Francis Group, an informa business

British Library Cataloguing-in-Publication Data
A catalogue record for this book is available from the British Library

Library of Congress Cataloging-in-Publication Data
Names: Erlings, Esther.
Title: Religious rights within the family : from coerced manifestation to dispute resolution in France, England and Hong Kong / Esther Erlings.
Description: ICLARS series on law and religion. | Abingdon, Oxon ; New York, NY : Routledge, 2020. | Includes index. | Based on author's thesis (doctoral - Chinese University of Hong Kong, 2015).
Identifiers: LCCN 2019012297| ISBN 9781138052185 (hardback) | ISBN 9781315167954 (ebook)
Subjects: LCSH: Parent and child (Law) | Freedom of religion. | Children (International law) | Parent and child (Law)—England. | Parent and child (Law)—France. | Parent and child (Law)—China—Hong Kong. | Freedom of religion—England. | Freedom of religion—France. | Freedom of religion—China—Hong Kong.
Classification: LCC K705 .E75 2020 | DDC 342.08/521441—dc23
LC record available at https://lccn.loc.gov/2019012297

ISBN 13: 978-0-367-72700-0 (pbk)
ISBN 13: 978-1-138-05218-5 (hbk)

Typeset in Galliard
by Swales & Willis Ltd, Exeter, Devon, UK

Contents

Acknowledgements

I would like to start by thanking the people who participated in, or helped facilitate, the research included in this book. Although I cannot mention you by name (for most of you, I do not even know your name), you know who you are.

This book is based on a PhD thesis I wrote at The Chinese University of Hong Kong. During various parts of this journey, Amy Barrow, Eva Pils, Yu Xingzhong and Julie Wallbank had to put up with fair amounts of bad writing, unpolished ideas and Dutch logic. I owe you a great debt of thanks. Other people who have been material to the completion of this book are Olivier Noguera, Peter Barnes, Nicole Tam and the editorial team at Routledge.

Thank you to my family who have been there for me with calls, messages, cards, postal packages and other expressions of love and support. Dank jullie wel.

This book would not exist without the invaluable support of my colleagues and friends. You have made the journey so much better by filling it with dinner parties and tea, challenging conversations, encouraging messages and fits of laughter. Thank you.

I would like to acknowledge Koninklijke Brill, for allowing me to reproduce E. Erlings, Is Anything Left of Children's Rights? How Parental Responsibility Erodes Children's Rights Under English Law. (2016) 24(3) *International Journal of Children's Rights* 624.

Abbreviations

1981 Declaration	Declaration on the Elimination of All Forms of Intolerance and of Discrimination Based on Religion or Belief
ADR	Alternative Dispute Resolution
BORO	Bill of Rights Ordinance
Cass	Cour de Cassation
CC	Conseil Constitutionnel
CDE	Convention against Discrimination in Education
CE	Conseil d'État
CESCR	Committee on Economic, Social and Cultural Rights
CMCoE	Committee of Ministers of the Council of Europe
CmRC	Committee on the Rights of the Child
CoE	Council of Europe
CRC	Convention on the Rights of the Child
CUP	Cambridge University Press
DCSF	Department for Children, Schools and Families
ECHR	European Convention on Human Rights
ECmHR	European Commission on Human Rights
ECtHR	European Court of Human Rights
GA	General Assembly
GMO	Guardianship of Minors Act
HKSAR	Hong Kong Special Administrative Region of the People's Republic of China
HRA	Human Rights Act 1998
HRC	Human Rights Committee
ICCPR	International Covenant on Civil and Political Rights
ICESCR	International Covenant on Economic, Social and Cultural Rights
HKLRC	The Law Reform Commission of Hong Kong
MAE	Mesure d'Assistance Éducative
OUP	Oxford University Press
P1	First Optional Protocol to the European Convention on Human Rights
PACoE	Parliamentary Assembly of the Council of Europe

PCRM	Parentally Coerced Religious Manifestation
PGPCR	Principle Governing Parent Child Relations
PJCO	Protection of Children and Juveniles Ordinance
Special Rapporteur	Special Rapporteur on Freedom of Religion or Belief
The Bill	2015 Children Proceedings (Parental Responsibility) Bill
UDHR	Universal Declaration on Human Rights
UK	United Kingdom
UN	United Nations
UNESCO	United Nations Educational, Scientific and Cultural Organisation
UNHCHR	United Nations High Commissioner for Human Rights

Table of cases and decisions

United Nations

Council of Europe

France

All unreported cases are available via Legifrance.gouv.fr.

England

Hong Kong

Other

Table of legislative documents

Treaties and charters

Declarations

Note Verbale

Travaux Préparatoires

National legislation

France

England

Hong Kong

Other

Table of general comments, resolutions and state reporting

General comments

Committee on Economic, Social and Cultural Rights

Committee on the Rights of the Child

Human Rights Committee

Resolutions and recommendations

United Nations General Assembly

Council of Europe

Parliamentary Assembly

Committee of Ministers

Other CoE

Other

State reporting

Committee on the Rights of the Child

Human Rights Committee

1 Introduction

Children (anyone under 18) are often implicated in manifestations of their parents' religion. In most cases this is a good thing, because parents and children value shared expressions of religion such as prayer, or attendance at religious festivals.[1] Sometimes, however, religious manifestations become contentious. Where this is because manifestations are harmful to children, regulation is generally seen as acceptable (although the question remains what counts as harmful).[2] In other cases, children themselves object to participation in the practice of their parents' religion. It may be that the parental religion is no longer their own, or they interpret it differently. Manifestations then become contentious when parents seek to impose them despite their child's objections. Here the situation is less clear – in practice as much as in law. Whilst international organisations have responded to specific situations of children (allegedly) being forced to manifest the parental religion,[3] and academics have written about various aspects of the child's right to freedom of religion,[4] their right to remain free from religion,[5] and their religious upbringing,[6] no comprehensive analysis of coerced religious manifestations and the relationship between parents and children exists as yet. Different writers have invoked the same human rights to defend diametrically opposed positions with regard to parental control over children's religious practice.[7] Moreover, existing accounts of religion within the parent–child relationship remain at the normative

1 S. Langlaude, *The Right of the Child to Religious Freedom in International Law*. Leiden: Martinus Nijhoff, 2007, 1–35.
2 H. Bielefeldt et al., *Freedom of Religion or Belief: An International Law Commentary*. Oxford: OUP, 2016, 433–6.
3 See 2.6 below.
4 E.g. E. Brems, 'Article 14: The Right to Freedom of Thought, Conscience and Religion', in A. Alen et al. (eds), *A Commentary on the United Nations Convention on the Rights of the Child*. Dordrecht: Martinus Nijhoff Publishers, 2006; Langlaude (2007); A. Scolnicov, *The Right to Religious Freedom in International Law. Between Group Rights and Individual Rights*. Abingdon: Routledge, 2011, ch. 5; Bielefeldt et al. (2016), section 3.4.
5 E.g. M. McAdam, *Freedom from Religion and Human Rights Law*. New York: Routledge, 2018, ch. 5.
6 Especially at national levels, e.g. M.-P. Gil-Rosado, *Les libertes de l'esprit de l'enfant dans les rapports familiaux*. Paris: Défrenois, 2006. R. Taylor, 'Parental Responsibility and Religion', in R. Probert et al. (eds), *Responsible Parents and Parental Responsibility*. Oxford: Hart, 2009, 123–41.
7 See 2.3 below.

level: they ask whether children should have a right to freedom of religion, what that right should look like and how it relates to parental rights. If reference is made to the 'what comes next' question, it is generally in passing only and suggests that children gain access to court to enforce their rights.[8] Commentators do not normally consider whether access to court would truly help children.[9] This book addresses both issues. It provides an in-depth analysis of the law in relation to coerced manifestations ***and*** looks at practical approaches to dispute resolution where such manifestations infringe upon rights. In addition, it seeks to transcend the boundaries between international law, national law and society, because in the field of law and religion, these are closely intertwined (at least on the basis of arguments in this book). International law sets the overarching rules in the form of human rights. National law gives force to human rights at the domestic level and provides the basis for possible limitations. The national level is also where people first seek to enforce their rights through available dispute resolution mechanisms. Society ultimately determines the acceptance and acceptability of human rights, the national (limitation) framework and available dispute resolution mechanisms. In turn, societal values influence national regulation and thereby respect for human rights obligations. With this in mind, the book includes an overview of international law, as well as three case studies (France, England and Hong Kong) that contain an examination of national law and draw on social research conducted in each jurisdiction.

1.1 Parentally coerced religious manifestations

A preliminary question relates to what to call a situation in which parents force their child to manifest the parental religion. It is not a religious manifestation of the parents, because the parents are not acting. Neither is it a religious manifestation of the child, because religious manifestations are based on personal convictions. Some authors have suggested that there is no real difference between religious manifestations and other acts parents may impose,[10] but that ignores that the basis of manifestations is in faith and there is often an added layer of religious or divine command. Moreover, most mundane acts have temporal implications, whereas manifestations tend to be aimed at blessings or eternal salvation. Religious manifestations are therefore distinct, and it is more precise to retain the term. An appropriate phrase to describe the situations with which this book is concerned is therefore 'Parentally Coerced Religious Manifestations', or PCRMs. A PCRM takes place when parents coerce their child to manifest the

8 Langlaude (2007), 60.

9 Unless to reject such access without considering alternatives. See e.g. R.J. Adhar, 'Children's Religious Freedom, Devout Parents and the State', in P.W. Edge and G. Harvey (eds), ***Law and Religion in Contemporary Society***. Aldershot: Ashgate, 2000, 105.

10 See discussions in S.E. Mumford, The Judicial Resolution of Disputes Involving Children and Religion. (1998) 47(1) *International and Comparative Law Quarterly* 117, 133; Taylor (2009), 128, 129.

parental religion. Coercion is not limited to physical constraint. Especially within the family context, it is frequently effectuated through indirect means, such as psychological control,[11] the ignorance and marginalisation of children's views,[12] or other parenting practices that do not involve 'blatant forms of compulsion' but rather present 'indirect forms of control which determine or limit alternative courses of conduct'.[13] This book consequently takes a broad view of coercion for the purposes of PCRMs, limited in particular by the internationally recognised right to 'convince one's neighbour'[14] (or one's child).

Scolnicov has argued that 'the extent to which control of parents over the religious identity of the child is presumed and upheld by law' is notable.[15] The same can be said about children's religious manifestation. Although international and national debates have identified the child as an independent rights-bearer,[16] the primacy of parental rights is still upheld in most of the literature and national law. This is generally based on the presumption that parents have a human right to impose religious manifestations, which can be enforced against States (and indirectly against children).[17] By contrast, the child's right to freedom of manifestation is secondary to this parental right and qualified by considerations of children's competence, maturity, age, the need to give priority to other interests children have, or the possible interference with family unity.[18] It is also often an unenforceable right, because children do not generally have independent access to dispute resolution mechanisms. De Jong aptly describes it as 'the Cinderella of [religious] rights'.[19] If ever the parental and child's own right meet, the situation is regarded as a conflict of human rights governed by the question of whether the parental right should be limited to allow for that of the child.[20]

11 A. Dillen, *Geloof in het Gezin? Ethiek, opvoeding en gezinnen vandaag*. Leuven: Lannoo, 2006, 130, 131.
12 B. Phillips and P. Alderson, Beyond 'Anti-Smacking': Challenging Violence and Coercion in Parent–Child Relationships. (2003) 11(2) *The International Journal of Children's Rights* 175, 179, 182.
13 A. MacDonald, *The Rights of the Child in Law and Practice*. Bristol: Family Law, 2011, 605, 606, quoting *R v Big M Drug Mart* [1985] 1 SCR 295, at [95].
14 *Kokkinakis v Greece* no. 14307/88 (1993) ECtHR Series A 260-A, para 31.
15 A. Scolnicov, The Child's Right to Religious Freedom and Formation of Identity. (2007) 15(2) *International Journal of Children's Rights* 251, 16.
16 See e.g. G. Van Bueren 'Children's Rights: Balancing Traditional Values and Cultural Plurality', in G. Douglas and L. Sebba (eds), *Children's Rghts and Traditional Values*. Aldershot: Dartmouth, 1998, 15.
17 E.g. F. Laroche-Gisserot, *Les droits de l'enfant*. Paris: Dalloz, 1996, 49–52; R. Adhar and I. Leigh, *Religious Freedom in the Liberal State*. Oxford: OUP, 2005, 193; U. Kilkelly, 'The Child's Right to Religious Freedom in International Law: The Search for Meaning', in M.A. Fineman and K. Worthington (eds), *What is Right for Children? The Competing Paradigms of Religion and Human Rights*. Farnham: Ashgate, 2009, 247.
18 This, in various forms, is a recurrent theme in nearly all writing on children's religious rights, including e.g. Adhar (2000); Brems (2006); Langlaude (2007); Kilkelly (2009); MacDonald (2011); Bielefeldt et al. (2016).
19 C.D. de Jong, *The Freedom of Thought, Conscience and Religion or Belief in the United Nations (1946–1992)*. Antwerp: Intersentia–Hart, 2000, 575.
20 See P. Malhaurie and H. Fulchiron, *La famille*. Paris: Defrénois, 2011, 622.

Based on a critical examination of international law, this book concludes to the contrary that there is actually no human right for parents to impose PCRMs. Parents may introduce their children into their religion, and they have some limited rights in education, but these do not amount to a justification for PCRMs. The central right is therefore that of the child to determine their own religious practice (or absence thereof) – a right of equal value and strength as the personal religious rights of adults. States have to protect the child's right, but via their national laws they may pose limitations on its exercise where limitations come within a recognised limitation ground and are proportionate, or 'necessary in a democratic society'. As part of their positive obligations, States should also protect children's rights in private relations. In respect of the family context, this can be done by providing a rights-respecting framework that regulates the relation between parents and children (parental responsibility, authority, etc.), and giving children access to dispute resolution mechanisms when parents violate their rights. It is at this point that States should consider what forms of dispute resolution would help families in conflict over PCRMs. Access to court is an important ultimate remedy, but like in other areas of family law, an argument can be made that (prior) access to Alternative Dispute Resolution (ADR) would be more meaningful to parents and children who continue to share the same front door.

The above indicates the close connection between national and international law. Much depends on States' regulation of the parent–child relation and attitudes towards children's rights at the national level. To explore this further, three case studies examine PCRMs under the principles of parental authority (France), parental responsibility (England),[21] and parental rights (Hong Kong). The jurisdictions further present a mixture of common law (England and Hong Kong) and civil law (France), as well as societies that are traditionally seen as more collective (Hong Kong and France) and individual (England). All three jurisdictions have ratified several human rights treaties, including the *Convention on the Rights of the Child* (CRC)[22], *International Covenant on Civil and Political Rights* (ICCPR)[23], *International Covenant on Economic, Social and Cultural Rights* (ICESCR)[24], and, where relevant, the *European Convention on Human Rights* (ECHR) [25]. The case studies further emphasise the importance of the domestic level, and the difference national principles can make to children's rights. They also reveal a common reluctance, albeit in different forms, to fully protect children's freedom of manifestation.

21 Mostly England and Wales, but for purposes of readability reference is only made to England.

22 1989 *Convention on the Rights of the Child*, Treaty Series, vol. 1577, 1 (20 November 1989).

23 1966 *International Covenant on Civil and Political Rights United Nations*, Treaty Series, vol. 999, 171 (23 March 1976).

24 1966 *International Covenant on Economic, Social and Cultural Rights United Nations*, Treaty Series, vol. 993, 3 (3 January 1976).

25 *European Convention for the Protection of Human Rights and Fundamental Freedoms*, ETS 5 (3 September 1953).

The national legal frameworks are contrasted with findings from exploratory social research on religion within the family and intra-family dispute resolution conducted in the three jurisdictions. That research is not conclusive, but it provides important insights from a range of stakeholders, most importantly children (adolescents) themselves. It consists of questionnaires distributed to students (and in Hong Kong also to parents) asking about their views on, and personal experience with, freedom of religion within the family and conflict resolution with parents. These are personal, sometimes sensitive, matters and it was thought that anonymous questionnaires would elicit more honest responses and a higher participation rate than other types of research, especially in small communities like Hong Kong (there were also some ethics limitations to conducting research with minors overseas). In addition, interviews were conducted with different groups of adults, based on the particular legal framework in each jurisdiction. The interviews were aimed at obtaining opinions of those most likely to influence the acceptability of PCRMs and playing a role in helping children in religious conflict with their parents: teachers in France in view of their important role in education (in the broadest sense), members of religious communities in England due to the hands-off approach the government takes, and family lawyers/mediators in Hong Kong given the state of flux of the law (and questionnaires already being distributed to parents). The choices, and method, are further explained in the introductory sections to the case studies. Substantively, the research paints a picture of children's growing independence and defence of their rights that often stands in stark contrast with national laws.

Following this introduction, Chapter 2 considers whether there is a human right for parents to impose PCRMs under international law and concludes that there is none. Chapter 3 contemplates whether PCRMs can be justified based on interpretations of children's own right to freedom of manifestation. Finding that this is not the case, Chapter 4 then looks at possible limitations on the child's right, particularly under the public order limitation ground. Chapter 5 makes the link from the international to the family level via horizontal effect and States' positive obligations. It reflects on possibilities for children to enforce their rights within the family. Chapters 6, 7 and 8 comprise the case studies of France, England and Hong Kong respectively. Chapter 9 contains a short conclusion.

2 A parental right to impose religious manifestations?

It is often thought – or simply assumed – that international human rights treaties grant parents extensive rights to impose religious manifestations on their children.[1] Yet the actual situation is much more nuanced. Whilst human rights bodies have recognised a parental liberty (sometimes framed as a natural law right)[2] vis-à-vis the State to raise children in the parental religion,[3] international law does not actually support a self-standing parental right to impose parentally coerced religious manifestations (PCRMs). No express rights to coerce religious practice have been included in the text of binding legal instruments and, as explained in this chapter, it is not possible to derive implicit license to impose manifestations from the existing rights parents hold.

This chapter will examine the common propositions that parental rights to impose religious manifestations can be derived from the parental right to determine a child's education (2.1); the parental right to organise religious life within the family (2.2); the parental right to provide direction to the child (2.3); parent's own right to freedom of religion (2.4); and parental rights under non-religion-related provisions (2.5). It scrutinises the text of relevant provisions, their *travaux préparatoires* and further interpretations by treaty bodies to conclude that PCRMs would go contrary to the object, purpose and interpretation of such provisions. The 'relevant provisions' are those adopted by the United Nations (UN) and Council of Europe (CoE). Although a number of other global and regional organisations have also dealt with freedom of religion and manifestation, their provisions on religion and parental rights have been premised on

1 E.g. Laroche-Gisserot (1996), 49–52; Adhar and Leigh (2005), 193; Kilkelly (2009), 247. Even those arguing against parental rights do not question their existence. E.g. J.G. Dwyer, Equality between Adults and Children: Its Meaning, Implications, and Opposition. (2013) 2013(4) *Michigan State Law Review* 1007, 1013, 1014.

2 The European Court of Human Rights (ECtHR) has done so in e.g. *Kjeldsen, Busk Madsen and Pedersen v Denmark*, nos. 5095/71, 5920/72 and 5926/72 (1976) ECtHR Series A 23, para 54; *Appel-Irrgang and Others v Germany* (dec), no. 45216/07 (2009) ECtHR ECHR 2009.

3 E.g. CmRC, *Summary Record of the 387th Meeting, Algeria*. UN Doc. CRC/C/SR.387 (10 September 1997), paras 14, 27; H. Bielefeldt, *Interim Report of the Special Rapporteur on Freedom of Religion or Belief*, UN Doc. A/70/286 (5 August 2015) (Special Rapporteur's Children Report).

and/or reflect standards included in UN documents or the CoE's ECHR (itself largely based on the UN *Universal Declaration on Human Rights* (UDHR))[4]. The European Union's *Charter of Fundamental Rights*, for example, adopts the same structure as the UDHR and ECHR;[5] the Organisation of American States' provision on freedom of religion mirrors that of the UN's ICCPR; [6] and the *African Charter on the Rights and Welfare of the Child* contains a provision on children's freedom of religion and parental guidance similar to Article 14 of the UN CRC.[7] Since there are no significant dissimilarities between these regional documents and those of the UN or CoE that are relevant to PCRMs,[8] discussion will be limited to the law of the UN and CoE.

2.1 The parental right to determine a child's education

The provisions most commonly believed to give parents rights to impose PCRMs in the upbringing of children are those that refer to respect for the liberty or right of parents to ensure the education of their children in accordance with parental convictions.[9] This belief is reinforced because the French versions retain

4 *Universal Declaration on Human Rights*, 217 A (III) (10 December 1948).

5 2000 *Charter of Fundamental Rights of the European Union*, 2012/C 326/02 (26 October 2012), Articles 10 (freedom of religion and manifestation), Article 14 (parental rights in education) and 52 (general limitation clause). See also Council of the European Union, *EU Guidelines on the Promotion and Protection of Freedom of Religion or Belief*. Luxembourg: Foreign Affairs Council, 2013.

6 See 1969 *American Convention on Human Rights*, OAS Treaty series No. 36 1144 UNTS 123 (18 July 1978), Article 12.

7 Article 9 of the 1990 *African Charter on the Rights and Welfare of the Child*, OAU Doc. CAB/LEG/24.9/49 (1990) (29 November 1999). The provision differs slightly: parents have a *duty* which the State must respect to provide guidance and direction in accordance with evolving capacity *and* best interests, *subject to* national laws and policies. See further Article 11 (parental rights in education subject to child's evolving capacities) and the 1981 *African Charter on Human and Peoples' Rights*, OAU Doc. CAB/LEG/67/3 rev. 5, 21 ILM 58 (1982) (21 October 1986), Articles 8 (freedom of conscience, the profession and practice of religion) and 29 (adults' and children's duties to family members). See also the *Conference on Security and Cooperation in Europe Final Act*, Helsinki 1975 14 ILM 1292 (1975) (August 1975), part VII (right to freedom of religion and manifestation) and Article 22 of the 2012 *ASEAN Human Rights Declaration*, (18 November 2012) (unreported) (freedom of thought, conscience and religion – no reference to manifestation).

8 The 2004 *Arab Charter on Human Rights*, 12 International Human Rights Reports 893 (2005) (15 March 2008), Article 30, does grant parents a stronger right to ensure their child's religious education, unqualified by "respect". The CRC negotiations nonetheless indicate that this stronger right is not inspired by parental discretion, but State religion (Islam), which requires that children born of Muslim parents be raised as Muslims, with no possibility to convert. See Langlaude (2007), 118–20; A. Alen and W. Pas, 'The UN Convention on the Rights of the Child's Self-Executing-Character', in E. Verhellen (ed.), *Monitoring Children's Rights*. The Hague: Kluwer, 1996, 181. See also the Organisation of Security and Co-operation in Europe's 2007 *Toledo Guiding Principles on Teaching about Religions and Beliefs in Public Schools* <https://www.osce.org/odihr/29154?download=true> last accessed 10 March 2019, that give a slightly more parent-centred interpretation to parental rights than common under the UN and CoE provisions quoted therein.

9 See e.g. U. Kilkelly, *The Child and the European Convention on Human Rights*. Aldershot: Ashgate, 1999, 72; Langlaude (2007), 86; McAdam (2018), 115–19.

the word *éducation*, which often refers to upbringing rather than formal education (*formation*). Yet, contrary to giving parents broader rights than the English 'education' suggests, the provisions contain more limited parental rights than their text implies. Parental rights in education were drawn up with the dangers of State indoctrination and the elimination of minorities in mind, not as a means for parents to control their child's religious practice. Their scope is therefore very limited.

2.1.1 The United Nations

(1) The Universal Declaration on Human Rights

In the aftermath of the Second World War, negotiations started on a Declaration on Human Rights, later to be transformed into a Covenant on Human Rights.[10] As a declaration, the UDHR does not contain legally binding provisions insofar they have not become part of customary international law. However, Article 26, which states that 'Parents have a prior right to choose the kind of education that shall be given to their children', has since its adoption functioned as the text of reference for later provisions on parental rights in education.[11] Furthermore, the UDHR's *travaux préparatoires* are illuminating on the question of parental rights to impose PCRMs.

At the outset, Article 26 was never meant to give parents rights in education, and even in its current form does not specifically mention religion. Initially, a right for ethnic, linguistic and religious minorities (like those who had been persecuted during the War) to establish and maintain schools was envisaged, but the drafters failed to reach agreement on the inclusion of 'minorities' as France recognises none.[12] It was then proposed that parental rights might offer an alternative.[13] Parental rights were ultimately adopted by amendment after it was agreed that the Declaration would make education compulsory during elementary school age.[14] Compulsory education would place significant power in the hands of the State, and parental rights could offer a buffer against abuse. Since the concern was State indoctrination through the school system as had happened in Nazi Germany,[15] delegates emphasised that parents would not

10 J. Morsink, *Universal Declaration of Human Rights: Origins, Drafting and Intent.* Philadelphia, PA: University of Pennsylvania Press, 1999, 15.

11 E.g. CoE, *Collected Edition of the 'Travaux Préparatoires' of the European Convention on Human Rights.* The Hague: Martinus Nijhoff, 1975–85, Vol. I, 196–9.

12 P. Arajärvi, 'Article 26', in A. Eide and T. Swineheart (eds), *The Universal Declaration of Human Rights: A Commentary.* Oslo: Scandinavian University Press, 1992, 406, 408.

13 A. Eide, 'The Non-Inclusion of Minority Rights: Resolution 217C (III)', in G.S. Alfredsson and A. Eide (eds), *The Universal Declaration of Human Rights: A Common Standard of Achievement.* The Hague: Martinus Nijhoff, 1999, 709–12.

14 Morsink (1999), 265.

15 P. Arajärvi, 'Article 26', in Alfredsson and Eide (1999), 553.

need very extensive rights. Consequently, parents were given 'a' (not 'the') prior right to choose 'the kind of education' (primarily the choice of school) for their children. The result was a provision that concerned itself strictly with formal education instead of upbringing, and on which it was agreed that the right contained therein would not allow parents to oppose non-indoctrinatory education.[16] No rights vis-à-vis children were envisaged.

(2) The International Covenant on Civil and Political Rights

The UDHR did not lead to the adoption of a single, but two covenants: the 1966 ICCPR and the 1966 ICESCR. Both include parental rights in education. The ICESCR does so within the context of the right to education, whilst the ICCPR attaches the rights to freedom of religion in Article 18(1). This makes the latter a more likely candidate for a provision supporting a general parental right to impose PCRMs. Article 18(4) ICCPR states:

> The States Parties to the present Covenant undertake to have respect for the liberty of parents and, when applicable, legal guardians to ensure the religious and moral education of their children in conformity with their own convictions.

The wording is different from that included in the UDHR: parents hold a liberty, but not a right, to ensure their children's moral and religious education (rather than education in full). The liberty, despite being non-derogable,[17] is furthermore restricted by the qualification that States only need to 'undertake' to have 'respect' for it. This indicates a lesser obligation on the part of the State to heed parental wishes than would be the case for an unqualified right.[18] It opens the possibility for States to prioritise children's freedoms and other considerations over parental convictions.[19]

If merely applicable to formal education and not upbringing generally, the right in Article 18(4) ICCPR would be extremely narrow in scope. Yet such narrowness was exactly what the drafters aimed to achieve.[20] Section 4 was not attached to Article 18 to demonstrate a willingness to recognise broader parental

16 Ibid.

17 Human Rights Committee, *General Comment No. 22: The right to freedom of thought, conscience and religion (art. 18)*. UN Doc. CCPR/C/21/Rev.1/Add.4 (30 July 1993), para 8. (General Comment 22).

18 E.g. M.D. Evans, *Religious Liberty and International Law in Europe*. Cambridge: CUP, 1997, 346; Kilkelly (1999), 67; A. Lester and D. Pannick, *Human Rights Law and Practice*. London: Butterworths, 1999, 261.

19 Ibid.

20 M.J. Bossuyt, *Guide to the 'Travaux Préparatoires' of the International Covenant on Civil and Political Rights*. Dordrecht: Martinus Nijhoff, 1987, 368, 369; M. Nowak, *U.N. Covenant on Civil and Political Rights: CCPR Commentary*. Kehl: N.P. Engel, 1993, 410, 431.

rights than under the UDHR, but because attachment to a provision on religion appeared most suitable for want of one on education.[21] In fact, many drafters only very reluctantly agreed to even discuss parental rights in education, which they felt were irrelevant for the ICCPR and only properly belonged in the ICESCR.[22] Barely adopted by a 30:17 majority with 27 abstentions,[23] it has since been confirmed by the Human Rights Committee (HRC) that Article 18(4) relates to education and not upbringing. Within the family context, the right has been linked to parents teaching their children the parental religion, but it is in that respect not broader than the right 'to convince one's neighbour' that parents have by virtue of their personal religious rights.[24]

In keeping with the UDHR, Article 18(4) gives parents a right vis-à-vis the State to challenge indoctrinatory forms of religious and moral education, but nothing more.[25] In *Hartikainen v Finland* the HRC questioned whether atheist parents could be a 'victim' for the purposes of Article 18(4) where they could apply to exempt their children from religious instruction in State schools, and religious education courses were given in a 'neutral and objective way', respecting the convictions of parents though not giving them full effect.[26] Two decades later, the Committee made it clear that Article 18(4) gives parents the right to object to compulsory religious instruction, or other forms of indoctrinatory teaching, but cannot ground a general right for parents to decide on children's religious practice.[27] Moreover, even within education, Article 18(4) does not give parents a clear right to control religious education. The HRC has stated that students should be able to exempt themselves from religious education,[28] and that 'State part[ies] should ensure that every student has the freedom to participate or not to participate in religious education in school'.[29] Article 18(4) ICCPR thus leaves little scope for parents to coerce manifestations within education, and provides no basis for PCRMs beyond that context.

21 Ibid.

22 Ibid.

23 Nowak (1993), 431.

24 HRC (1993), General Comment 22, para 6. See also *Sister Immaculate Joseph and 80 Teaching Sisters of the Holy Cross of the Third Order of Saint Francis in Menzingen of Sri Lanka v Sri Lanka*, no. 1249/2004 (2005) HRC. UN Doc. CCPR/C/85/D/1249/2004, para 7.2.

25 Ibid.; *Hartikainen v Finland*, no. 40/1978 (1981) HRC. UN Doc. CCPR/C/OP/1, para 10.4; *Leirvåg v Norway*, no. 1155/2003 (2004) HRC. UN Doc. CCPR/C/82/D/1155/2003, paras 14.2, 14.3.

26 Phraseology borrowed from the Council of Europe (discussed below). *Hartikainen v Finland*, no. 40/1978 (1981) HRC. UN Doc. CCPR/C/OP/1, paras 10.3, 10.4. See also HRC, *Concluding Observations, Pakistan*. UN Doc. CCPR/C/PAK/CO/1 (23 August 2017), para 34: the State must remove religious bias, incorporate human rights education and regulate religious schools.

27 *Leirvåg v Norway*, no. 1155/2003 (2004) HRC. UN Doc. CCPR/C/82/D/1155/2003, paras 14.2–14.7.

28 HRC, *Concluding Observations, Indonesia*. UN Doc. CCPR/C/IDN/CO/1 (21 August 2013), para 26.

29 HRC, *Concluding Observations, Cyprus*. UN Doc. CCPR/C/CYP/CO/4 (30 April 2015), para 19.

(3) The International Covenant on Economic, Social and Cultural Rights

In line with previous observations that the right in Article 18(4) ICCPR properly belonged in the ICESCR,[30] Article 13(3) ICESCR is an exact copy with the addition that States should also undertake to have respect for the liberty of parents to choose non-public schools for their children that 'conform to such minimum educational standards as may be laid down or approved by the State'. During negotiations, ICESCR delegates repeatedly referred to the right, principle or idea in Article 26(3) UDHR, which they sought to further define, rather than replace with extended parental rights.[31] Some parental rights discussion nonetheless preceded the emergence of a compromise Article that could embrace the rights of children and parents, and the role of the State as the primary education provider. During the Commission on Human Rights' 7th session several delegates emphasised the importance of parental rights in education and 'the natural right of parents' to decide on their child's education.[32] These remarks were met by a reply from the US representative, Mrs Roosevelt, who argued that parental responsibility to choose education existed for the interest of the child and the Covenant, as she would further argue in a subsequent meeting, should reflect that the 'ultimate aim . . . was to safeguard the rights and interests to the child himself'[33].[34] The issue was resolved when the Chairman pointed out that 'the text had been drafted with a view to preventing parents from being forced to send their children to State schools'.[35] Whilst the idea that parents have a role to play in children's religious education was thus recognized during the negotiations, it is also apparent that Article 13 itself contains no far-reaching parental rights.

No cases have tested the boundaries of the right yet, but the Special Rapporteur on Education stressed in 2015 that the parental liberty under Article 13(3) is not unfettered and that States must set minimum standards that respect children's rights.[36] Furthermore, ICESCR General Comment 13 states that education given in an 'unbiased and objective way, respectful of the freedoms of opinion, conscience and expression' is permitted despite parental objections.[37] This suggests that also under the ICESCR parental rights are limited to warding

30 See nn. 20–3 of this chapter.

31 An extensive collection of *travaux préparatoires* documents can be found at <http://hr-travaux.law.virginia.edu/international-conventions/international-covenant-economic-social-and-cultural-rights-icescr>.

32 Commission on Human Rights, *7th Session: Summary Record of the 226th Meeting*. UN Doc. E/CN.4/SR.226 (27 June 1951), 23 (Representative of Lebanon).

33 Commission on Human Rights, *7th Session: Summary Record of the 226th Meeting*. UN Doc. E/CN.4/SR.229 (28 June 1951), 11 (Representative of the United States of America (USA)).

34 See n. 32, 24 (Representative of the USA).

35 Ibid. (Chairman).

36 K. Singh, *Report of the Special Rapporteur on the Right to Education: Protecting the Right to Education Against Commercialization*. UN Doc. A/HRC/29/30 (10 June 2015), paras 47 and 114.

37 Committee on Economic, Social and Cultural Rights (CESCR), *General Comment No. 13: The right to education (art. 13)*. UN Doc. E/C.12/1999/10 (8 December 1999), para 28.

off State indoctrination within the education system. They do not extend to the imposition of PCRMs in that or other contexts, bar, perhaps, attendance at a denominational school to prevent indoctrination.

(4) The Convention Against Discrimination in Education (CDE)

Despite the references made to children's rights during negotiations,[38] on paper the power-balance described in Article 13 ICESCR is mainly one between parents and State. Yet, it was expected that States would ratify the ICCPR and ICESCR twin treaties,[39] in which case States would have to devise an educational framework able to do justice to the religious rights of children (Article 18(1) ICCPR).[40] This appears to be recognised in the CDE, which has no twin treaty. Article 5(b) CDE requires respect for the liberty of parents to choose non-public schools for their children in the same manner as under the ICESCR (subject to minimum standards) and to ensure their children's moral and religious education subject to 'procedures followed in the State for the application of its legislation'. However, the provision equally extends a clear right to freedom of religion to those receiving education, normally children, that is not subject to the parental liberty. Under Article 5(b) 'no person or group of persons should be compelled to receive religious instruction inconsistent with his or their convictions'.

Not only is the parental right therefore subject to requirements laid down by the State, where a child holds different convictions from their parents, it appears that the State should protect these convictions over those of parents.[41] This means that the CDE offers virtually no space for PCRMs, since even the choice of a religious school would be problematic if that implied receiving education contrary to the child's convictions. Like its predecessors and contemporaries, Article 5(b) CDE was included with a view to preventing State indoctrination, not to grant parents broad rights over children.[42]

(5) The 1981 Declaration

The 1981 Declaration on the Elimination of All Forms of Intolerance and of Discrimination Based on Religion or Belief (1981 Declaration),[43] which like the UDHR is non-binding, is the last distinct standard-setting document that refers

38 Above, notes 32–5 and accompanying text.

39 K.J. Partsch, 'Freedom of Conscience and Expression, and Political Rights', in L. Henkin (ed.), *The International Bill of Rights: The Covenant on Civil and Political Rights*. New York: Columbia University Press, 1981, 213.

40 See section 3.1.

41 Brems (2006), 5. See also M. Verheyde, 'Article 28: The Right to Education', in Alen and Pas (2006), 48, 49.

42 H. Cullen, Education Rights or Minority Rights? (1993) 7 *International Journal of Law and the Family* 143, 165.

43 UN General Assembly, *1981 Declaration on the Elimination of All Forms of Intolerance and of Discrimination Based on Religion or Belief*. UN Doc. A/RES/36/55 (25 November 1981).

specifically to parental rights in education.[44] Since the Declaration includes further stipulations related to parental rights within the family (discussed below), Article 5(2) is logically limited to formal education.[45] It states:

> Every child shall enjoy the right to have access to education in the matter of religion or belief in accordance with the wishes of his parents, or as the case may be, legal guardians, and shall not be compelled to receive teaching on religion or belief against the wishes of his parents or legal guardians, the best interests of the child being the guiding principle.

Unlike previous instruments, the 1981 Declaration does not qualify parental rights by a State obligation of respect, but by reference to children's interests. Depending on whether interests are interpreted in a parent-centred or child-centred manner, the provision can either support enhanced parental rights vis-à-vis children or prioritise the child's position when parents seek to impose PCRMs. Whilst pronouncements regarding the Declaration are not always unequivocal,[46] it seems that the latter is probably a more faithful reading of Article 5(2).[47] The Declaration's drafters emphasised the importance (and priority) of children's own rights in the discussion of Article 5, whilst recognising a right for parents to guard against indoctrination.[48] In 2002, Special Rapporteur Amor further lend his approval to a conference document that had described the 'role of parents' as an 'essential factor' in children's education, but equally highlighted the need for education to be compatible with children's rights and interests.[49] Rapporteur Bielefeldt has further highlighted the right of children to opt out of religious instruction without suffering negative repercussions from 'school authorities, *parents* and other children' (emphasis mine).[50] Notably, the two Special Rapporteurs have merged Article 5 of the Declaration with Article 14 CRC to carve out a regime governing children's religious lives.[51] If these

44 Bar the *International Convention on the Protection of Migrant Workers and Members of their Families*, which exactly mirrors Articles 18(4) ICCPR and 13(3) ICESCR and raises no new issues. See also Bielefeldt et al. (2016), 209.

45 Bielefeldt (2015), Special Rapporteur's Children Report, 9.

46 See M. Wiener, 'Interpretation of the 1981 Declaration through the Mandate Practice of the United Nations Special Rapporteur on Freedom of Religion or Belief', in M.D. Evans et al., *The Changing Nature of Religious Rights under International Law*. Oxford: OUP, 2015, 62; Bielefeldt et al. (2016), 204–22.

47 See N. Lerner, 'Toward a Draft Declaration Against Religious Intolerance and Discrimination, in Y. Dinstein (ed.), *Israel Yearbook of Human Rights 1981*. Tel Aviv: Tel Aviv University, 1981, 101.

48 De Jong (2000), 581, 582.

49 A. Amor, *Report Submitted by the Special Rapporteur on Freedom of Religion or Belief.* UN Doc. E/CN.4/2002/73 (14 March 2002), appendix.

50 H. Bielefeldt, *Report of the Special Rapporteur on Freedom of Religion or Belief: Mission to the Republic of Moldova*. UN Doc. A/HRC/19/60/Add.2 (27 January 2012a), para 49.

51 See Bielefeldt (2015), Special Rapporteur's Children Report, para 33; Special Rapporteur Amor in Wiener (2015), 62. See also A. Shaheed, *Report of the Special Rapporteur on Freedom of Religion and Belief.* UN Doc. A/HRC/37/49 (28 February 2018), paras 30, 57, 85, noting that parental rights in education are limited by children's evolving capacities rather than interests.

provisions are indeed compatible, that would mean that the relatively progressive statements of the Commission on the Rights of the Child (CmRC) are equally valid for the purposes of the Declaration. These statements include a reminder for Belgium that children's views must be taken into account when the choice is made between a confessional and non-confessional school;[52] urging of Korea to ensure that children's rights to freedom of religion are not violated in private schools;[53] questioning of Panama on parents making children attend catechism classes;[54] and telling the United Kingdom (UK) that not allowing students under 16 to exempt themselves from religious education and acts of worship in school was contrary to their freedom of manifestation.[55] The effect would thus be that parents need not educate their children in a religious vacuum, but that they cannot coerce religious manifestations as matter of right.[56]

(6) Further Standard Setting

Since the 1990s, the concept of parental rights in (religious) education has disappeared from standard setting at the UN. The right is, for example, conspicuously absent from the Resolution on the Elimination of All Forms of Intolerance,[57] Vienna Declaration and Programme of Action,[58] Universal Declaration on Cultural Diversity,[59] Resolution on Freedom of Religion or Belief,[60] and the four General Assembly resolutions on religion adopted in 2018.[61] Given its frequent misinterpretation, this is probably a sensible development.

52 CmRC, *Summary Record of the 223rd Meeting, Belgium*. UN Doc. CRC/C/SR.223 (08 June 1995), para 25.

53 CmRC, *Concluding Observations (third and fourth reports), Republic of Korea*. UN Doc. CRC/C/KOR/CO/3–4 (02 February 2012), para 38.

54 CmRC, *Summary Record of 355th Meeting, Panama*. UN Doc. CRC/C/SR.355 (17 March 1997), para 12.

55 CmRC, *Summary Record of 2114th Meeting, United Kingdom of Great Britain and Northern Ireland*. UN Doc. CRC/C/SR.2114 (27 May 2016), para 22.

56 Bielefeldt (2015), Special Rapporteur's Children Report, paras 35–8. See also Bielefeldt et al. (2016), 215–19.

57 UN GA, *Resolution 48/128 on the Elimination of All Forms of Intolerance*. UN Doc. A/RES/48/128 (20 December 1993).

58 UN GA, *Vienna Declaration and Programme of Action*. UN Doc. A/CONF.157/23 (12 July 1993).

59 UNESCO, *Universal Declaration on Cultural Diversity* (2 November 2001) <https://www.ohchr.org/en/professionalinterest/pages/culturaldiversity.aspx> last accessed 10 March 2019.

60 UN GA, *Resolution 67/179 on Freedom of Religion or Belief.* UN Doc. A/RES/67/179 (3 April 2013).

61 UN GA, *Resolution 73/128 Enlightenment and Religious Tolerance*. UN Doc. A/Res/73/128 (12 December 2018); *Resolution 73/129 Promotion of Interreligious and Intercultural Dialogue, Understanding and Cooperation for Peace*. UN Doc. A/RES/73/129 (12 December 2018); *Resolution 73/164 Combating Intolerance, Negative Stereotyping, Stigmatization, Discrimination, Incitement to Violence and Violence Against Persons, Based on Religion or Belief.* UN Doc. A/RES/73/164 (17 December 2018); *Resolution 73/176 Freedom of Religion or Belief.* UN Doc. A/RES/73/176 (17 December 2018).

2.1.2 The Council of Europe

When the ECHR opened for signature in 1950, parental rights in education were not included in the document. This was not because such rights had not been discussed; rather they were so controversial that their extended negotiation jeopardised the timely adoption of the entire convention.[62] Several States objected to the inclusion of parental rights per se, or at least to rights going beyond the very confined area of religious instruction in public schools.[63] Following two more years of negotiations, parental rights are now attached to the right to education in Article 2 of the First Protocol to the ECHR (2P1):[64]

> No person shall be denied the right to education. In the exercise of any functions which it assumes in relation to education and to teaching, the State shall respect the right of parents to ensure such education and teaching in conformity with their own religious and philosophical convictions.

Modelled on its UDHR counterpart (Article 26), the article's final scope extends beyond religious instruction, but not beyond formal education. The reference to the functions the State exercises in relation to education and teaching is meant to clarify that e.g. syllabi or aspects of the school system (discipline, religious objects in class, etc.) are covered.[65] Furthermore, whilst there are no limitation grounds attached to the parental right in Article 2P1, it is qualified by an obligation of 'respect'. States can thus give priority to children's rights and interests over those of parents.[66] The ECtHR has indeed ruled that where parental convictions conflict with children's interests, their human dignity or the child's fundamental right to education, the latter prevail.[67] It also found that children's wishes can take priority over parental rights without this undermining respect for such rights.[68]

Like the UN provisions, Article 2P1 was born out of a fear of indoctrination through the school system, not a concern for parental power.[69] The provision has been expressly linked with the State's duty of neutrality and impartiality under Article 9 (Freedom of Religion).[70] Within the educational context the right is

62 CoE (1975–85), Vol. VIII, 4. See also W. Schabas, *The European Convention on Human Rights: A Commentary*. Oxford: OUP, 2015, 989.

63 CoE (1975–85), Vol. I, 196 and Vol. VIII, 24.

64 *Protocol 1 to the European Convention for the Protection of Human Rights and Fundamental Freedoms*, ETS 9 (18 May 1954).

65 CoE (1975–85), Vol. I, 196–9 and Vol. VIII, 24; Schabas (2015), 1002, 1003.

66 Evans (1997), 346; Kilkelly (1999), 67; Lester and Pannick (1999), 261.

67 *Campbell and Cosans v UK*, no. 7743/76 (1982) ECtHR, ECHR A 48, para 36; *Zénon Bernard v Luxembourg* (dec), no. 17187/90 (8 September 1993) ECmHR; *Konrad v Germany* (dec), no. 35504/03 (2006) ECtHR ECHR 2006-XIII.

68 *CJ, JJ and EJ v Poland* (dec), no. 23380/94 (1996) ECmHR DR 84-A, 46.

69 A. Mowbray, *Cases and Materials on the European Convention on Human Rights*. Oxford: OUP, 2007, 968; Schabas (2015), 989.

70 *Lautsi and Others v Italy*, no. 30814/06 (2011) ECtHR (Grand Chamber), ECHR 2011, paras 59, 60.

very narrowly conceived, guided by the landmark case of *Kjeldsen, Busk Madsen and Pedersen v Denmark* on religious objection to compulsory sex education.[71] At the Commission stage, judge Kellberg argued against parental rights to impose PCRMs in education by stating that:

> It is hardly conceivable that the drafters . . . intended that a child up to the formal age of majority shall be under the unfettered powers of its parents . . . And it would of course be wrong to say that a child, who holds another philosophical conviction than his parents, must abide by their decision.[72]

Subsequently, the Court delivered a judgment in which it found that respect for parental rights was solely breached when the State pursued 'an aim of indoctrination'.[73] It held that, if a State provided information and teaching in an 'objective, critical and pluralist manner', parents could not object under Article 2P1.[74] Yet most applications based on parental rights seek to challenge exactly those very aspects of education. In *W and Others v UK*,[75] for example, the applicants complained that their children had not been given places in single-sex schools as per their beliefs regarding (in)equality and attitudes towards sex roles. The Commission rejected the complaints, noting that education in mixed comprehensive schools was provided in an objective, pluralist and critical manner, which was exactly what the applicants were opposed to![76]

The 'objective, critical and pluralist' formula has resulted in a record number of inadmissibility decisions against parents claiming a violation of parental rights.[77] Unless parents can make out indoctrination on the part of State through instruction in a certain religion or belief without the possibility of exemption, the ECtHR has not been willing to find a violation, or even consider the application on its merits.[78] The CoE has also allowed States to prohibit or refuse accreditation

71 *Kjeldsen, Busk Madsen and Pedersen v Denmark*, nos. 5095/71, 5920/72 and 5926/72 (1976) ECtHR Series A 23.

72 *Kjeldsen, Busk Madsen and Pedersen v Denmark* (dec), nos. 5095/71, 5920/72 and 5926/72 (21 March 1975) ECmHR, Separate Opinion judge Kellberg.

73 *Kjeldsen, Busk Madsen and Pedersen v Denmark*, nos. 5095/71, 5920/72 and 5926/72 (1976) ECtHR Series A 23, para 53.

74 Ibid.

75 *W. and D.M., M. and H.I v United Kingdom* (dec), nos. 10228/82 and 10229/82 (1984) DR 37, 96.

76 Ibid.

77 E.g. *V.K. and A.K. v Denmark* (dec), no. 5095/71 (1972) ECmHR Collection 43, 44–56; *Angeleni v Sweden* (dec), no. 10491/83 (1986) ECmHR DR 51, 41; *Jeminez Alonso and Jeminez Merino v Spain* (dec), no. 51188/99 (25 May 2000), ECtHR; *Laduna v Slovakia* (dec), no. 31827/02 (20 October 2010) ECtHR; *Dojan and others v Germany* (dec), nos. 319/08, 2455/08, 7908/10, 8152/10 and 8155/10 (13 September 2013) ECtHR. See also *A.R. and L.R. v Switzerland*, no. 22338/15 (19 December 2017) ECtHR, discussed in 2.5.

78 Indoctrination was found in e.g. *Folgerø and Others v Norway*, no. 15472/02 (2007) ECtHR (Grand Chamber) ECHR 2007-III; *Hasam and Eylem Zengin v Turkey*, no. 1448/04 (3 March 2009), ECtHR; *Mansur Yalçın and others v Turkey*, no. 21163/11 (16 September 2014), ECtHR.

to forms of belief-based education not corresponding with children's interests or facilitating the forced imposition of convictions and religious practice.[79] It would therefore be incongruent to say that Article 2P1 supports a parental right to impose PCRMs, even within the narrow educational context.

Apart from Article 2P1, parental rights in education have not featured in formal CoE standard setting. The 1961 European Social Charter,[80] which furthers the right to education, does not refer to them, and, unlike its international counterpart, neither does the 1995 Framework Convention on National Minorities.[81] Various Resolutions and Recommendations *have* dealt with parental rights in education. These have indicated that the CoE respects the role of parents to provide their children with a religious education and confirmed the right to guard against indoctrination.[82] However, they have simultaneously emphasised that the State should protect children's own rights and interests, and ensure that children receive an objective, critical and pluralistic education that prepares them for democratic citizenship.[83] As under the UN documents, the expectation is that parents will socialise their children, but this recognition stops short of legitimising PCRMs.

2.2 The parental right to organise religious life in the family

The first document to explicitly propose parental rights in relation to religious manifestation outside education is the 1981 Declaration. It was written during the Cold War and negotiations reflected this political context.[84] Western States at the time believed that religion was the best defence against atheist communism,[85] and since they apparently also held the most powerful position in the negotiations,

79 E.g. *Church of X v United Kingdom* (dec), no. 3798/68 (1968) ECmHR Collection 29, 70–80; *Ingrid Jordebo Foundation of Christian Schools and Ingrid Jordebo v Sweden* (dec), no. 11533/85 (1987) ECmHR, DR 51, 125; *Leuffen v Germany* (dec), no. 19844/92 (09 July 1992) ECmHR; *Konrad v Germany* (dec), no. 35504/03 (2006) ECtHR ECHR 2006-XIII.

80 *European Social Charter*, ETS 35 (26 February 1965).

81 *Framework Convention for the Protection of National Minorities*, ETS 157 (1 February 1998). See also the *Revised European Convention on the Adoption of Children (Revised)*, ETS 202 (1 September 2011).

82 E.g. Parliamentary Assembly of the Council of Europe (PACoE), *Recommendation 1121 (1990) on the Rights of Children*, Council of Europe (1 February 1990); Committee of Ministers of the Council of Europe (CMCoE), *Recommendation Rec (2002)12 of the Committee of Ministers to Member States on Education for Democratic Citizenship*, Council of Europe (16 October 2002); PACoE, *Recommendation 1720 (2005) Education and Religion*, Council of Europe (4 October 2005); PACoE, *Resolution 1928 (2013) Safeguarding Human Rights in Relation to Religion and Belief, and Protecting Religious Communities from Violence*, Council of Europe (24 April 2013).

83 Ibid.

84 Evans (1997), 245.

85 Ibid., 233.

the Declaration's text leans heavily towards the favouring of religion and religious upbringing.[86] Of particular importance is Article 5(1), which stipulates:

> The parents . . . of the child have the right to organize the life within the family in accordance with their religion or belief and bearing in mind the moral education in which they believe the child should be brought up.

Other than previous instruments that limit express parental rights to education, the 1981 Declaration refers to parental rights in 'upbringing' and 'life within the family'.[87] In addition, the parental right in upbringing is unqualified: Article 5(1) states that parents have a right, not that the State should respect a parental freedom. The Article does not have an in-built limitation clause either, but restrictions can be conceived through application of Article 5(3) (principles in upbringing) and 5(5) (no-harm principle). The former gives direction as to how children should be brought up – in a spirit of tolerance, friendship, respect, etc. – but fails to include a reference to children's own convictions. Article 5(5) prohibits parents from involving their children in manifestations (coerced or otherwise) that are harmful to their physical or mental health, or full development.[88] The Declaration thus appears to be giving parents wide and strong 'rights' (insofar as that can be said of provisions that are non-binding) that seem applicable vis-à-vis both children and the State.[89] That, however, was not the intention of the Declaration's drafters, or the interpretation the Special Rapporteurs have given to the provision. De Jong has called it 'astonishing' that Article 5 makes no reference to children's rights, because they played an important role in the drafting history.[90] Prior to the provision's adoption, Lerner even referred to Article 5 as concerned with 'the rights of the child'.[91] Delegates notably agreed that in case of parent-child conflict it would be better to give preference to children's rights than to allow parents to 'suppress those views'.[92] While the text of Article 5 thus reads as very parent-centred, the *travaux préparatoires* indicate that the drafters had intended otherwise.

Several Special Rapporteurs have equally touched upon the issue of parental power over children in and outside the family. Although they have acknowledged the special position of parents in relation to children, they have stopped short

86 The communist countries abstained from voting at the Committee stage, but the declaration was eventually adopted by consensus and without vote in the GA: N. Lerner, *Religion, Secular Belief and Human Rights* (2nd ed.). Boston, MA: Martinus Nijhoff Publishers, 2012, 29.

87 See also para 5(4) on parental wishes regarding a child in care.

88 See also Bielefeldt (2015), Special Rapporteur's Children Report, paras 67–73.

89 B.G. Tahzib, *Freedom of Religion or Belief. Ensuring Effective International Legal Protection*. The Hague: Martinus Nijhoff, 1996, 175–9.

90 De Jong (2000), 581, 582.

91 Lerner (1981), 100.

92 De Jong (2000), 581, 582, with reference to a statement by the Swedish delegate (A/C.3/SR.2013, 83).

of recognition of a general parental right to impose PCRMs within the family.[93] Special Rapporteur Jahangir, for example, has argued in favour of protecting minors' autonomy in the face of forced manifestation.[94] Rapporteurs have also used the CRC to give meaning to parental rights,[95] whereas the CRC and its monitoring body are very critical of parental rights that abrogate children's own.[96] In his report on the religious rights of children, Special Rapporteur Bielefeldt, whilst emphasising that parents retain a human rights-based claim to the religious socialisation of their children, argued parents cannot do so 'in an unchangeable way [or] in a manner inconsistent with the evolving capacities of the child'.[97] In 2017, Special Rapporteur Shaheed noted that it was the child's right (and not the parents') to seek and receive guidance and direction, though limitations on children's rights could be imposed as a result of lack of capacity.[98] Contrary to what the text of Article 5 1981 Declaration might suggest, the provision is thus not meant to give parents wide-ranging powers over their children. Whilst fully supporting an appropriate parental role in religious socialisation, the Declaration does not support parental rights to impose PCRMs.

2.3 The parental right to provide direction to the child

Adopted in 1989, the Convention on the Rights of the Child does not make reference to parental rights in education, although the requirement that children be taught respect for their parents (Article 29(c)) would be difficult to reconcile with State indoctrination.[99] The CRC rather takes a novel approach to parental rights by providing for a right to direction in respect of the child's right to religious freedom in Article 14:

1 States Parties shall respect the right of the child to freedom of thought, conscience and religion.
2 States Parties shall respect the rights and duties of the parents and, when applicable, legal guardians, to provide direction to the child in the exercise of his or her right in a manner consistent with the evolving capacities of the child.
3 Freedom to manifest one's religion or beliefs may be subject only to such limitations as are prescribed by law and are necessary to protect public safety, order, health or morals, or the fundamental rights and freedoms of others.

93 E.g. A. Shaheed, *Report of the Special Rapporteur on Freedom of Religion and Belief*. UN Doc. A/HRC/34/50 (17 January 2017), para 51.
94 A. Jahangir, *Civil and Political Rights, Including the Question of Religious Intolerance: Mission to France (18–29 September 2005)*. UN Doc. E/CN.4/2006/5/Add.4 (8 March 2006b), para 99.
95 Bielefeldt (2015), Special Rapporteur's Children Report, para 33; Special Rapporteur Amor in Wiener (2015), 62; Shaheed (2017), para 51.
96 See section 2.3.
97 Bielefeldt (2015), Special Rapporteur's Children Report, para 33.
98 See n. 93.
99 See also Verheyde (2006), 48, 49.

The CRC's distinct formulation proved cause for both euphoria and disappointment amongst children's advocates, divided between those who reasoned that children had been given a genuine right to freedom of religion and parents a right to guidance,[100] and those who felt that children were given a lesser right to freedom of religion than under other instruments whilst parents were granted explicit power to determine their child's religion.[101] These differing opinions were partly inspired by the text adopted, but especially by the negotiations that preceded them. The *travaux préparatoires* of Article 14 are entirely inconclusive as to what was intended by the drafters in respect of parental rights and children's rights to freedom of religion. Opinions differed to such extent that it was decided to remove all particulars from Article 14 for fear it would not be adopted at all.[102] When the provision was finally adopted, its content was so uncertain that reservations and declarations were made by States in favour of parental rights, as well as States prioritising children's rights.[103]

Key to the discussion of PCRMs is respect for the rights and duties of parents to provide direction in the exercise of the child's right under Article 14(2). The right is a qualified one, limited not only by a reference to 'respect', but equally the evolving capacities of the child. Its most contentious part is the reference to 'direction to the child in the exercise of his or her right'.[104] The text suggests an accessory right that only comes into being when the child exercises their right.[105] This would mean that parents have no independent parental right and therefore no right to impose PCRMs irreconcilable with the child's exercise of a freedom. However, some authors have argued against this reading of the provision and in favour of an interpretation that would grant parents standalone rights.[106] In 2016, the CmRC put a stop to the academic debate by adopting the former approach in General Comment 20, which states:

> [A]rticle 14 of the Convention . . . highlights the right of the child to freedom of religion and recognizes the rights and duties of parents and guardians to provide direction to the child in a manner consistent with his or her evolving capacities (see also art. 5). In other words, it is the child who

100 See e.g. G. von Dorsch, *Die Konvention der Vereinten Nationen über die Rechte des Kindes*. Berlin: Duncker & Humblot 1994, 135; Brems (2006), 25. Though see B.C. Hafen and J.O. Hafen, Abandoning Children to their Autonomy: The United Nations Convention on the Rights of the Child. (1996) 37(2) *Harvard International Law Journal* 449, 470 on granting a too wide right to children.

101 E.g. P.E. Veerman, *The Rights of the Child and the Changing Image of Childhood*. Dordrecht: Martinus Nijhoff, 1992, 195; C. Hamilton, *Family, Law and Religion*. London: Sweet & Maxwell, 1995, 144; Alen and Pas (1996), 181; Scolniciv (2011), 160, 161.

102 Langlaude (2007), 118–20.

103 S.L. Detrick, *A Commentary on the United Nations Convention on the Rights of the Child*. The Hague: Martinus Nijhoff, 1999, 248, 249.

104 Bielefeldt et al. (2016), 217.

105 See Brems (2006), 5.

106 Scolnicov (2011), 160, 161; Bielefeldt et al. (2016), 217.

> exercises the right to freedom of religion, not the parent, and the parental role necessarily diminishes as the child acquires an increasingly active role in exercising choice throughout adolescence.[107]

That the CmRC should choose this avenue is unsurprising. Since its inception in 1991, the Committee has made it clear that, whereas parents have an important role to play in the religious upbringing of their children, the right the CRC grants them is additional to the child's and cannot provide a justification for coerced religion or manifestation. On one occasion a Committee member stated that Article 14 was not at variance with a national right of parents to raise their children in their religion, and this is sometimes interpreted as the granting of parental rights over children.[108] That same Committee member, Mr Kolosov, nevertheless noted on another occasion that a law which gave parents a right to determine their child's religious education did not 'correspond fully to article 14 of the Convention, under which parents were entitled to provide *direction* to the child in the exercise of his or her right to freedom of thought, conscience and religion'.[109] These remarks clarify first that there was already an understanding of the additional nature of the parental right in 1996, and second that there is nothing incompatible between parents raising a child in a certain religion and the child enjoying freedom of religion. Incompatibility only arises where parents confuse raising in a religion with imposing their religion and its manifestations.

This is further clarified by the CmRC's pronouncements on Article 14, which have emphasised a full right to freedom of religion for the child with the accessory parental right as mostly one of guidance. Reservations limiting children's rights in favour of parental rights have met with criticism,[110] and the CmRC has on several occasions objected to laws preventing children from choosing their own religion.[111] States must instead take legislative measures to 'guarantee freedom of thought, conscience and religion of all children'.[112] The CmRC has also enquired

107 CmRC, *General Comment No. 20 (2016) on the Implementation of the Rights of the Child During Adolescence*. UN Doc. CRC/C/GC/20 (6 December 2016), para 43. (General Comment 20)

108 CmRC, *Summary Record of the 387th Meeting, Algeria*, UN Doc. CRC/C/SR.387 (10 September 1997), paras 14, 27. See Langlaude (2007), 106.

109 CmRC, *Summary Record of the 277th Meeting, Republic of Korea*, UN Doc. CRC/C/SR.277 (26 January 1996), para 31 (emphasis original).

110 R. Hodgkin and P. Newell, *Implementation Handbook for the Convention on the Rights of the Child* (3rd ed.). New York: United Nations Children's Fund, 2007, 188, 189. See also CmRC, *Concluding Observations (third and fourth reports), Qatar*. UN Doc. CRC/C/QAT/CO/3-4 (22 June 2017), para 5: a reservation subjecting Article 14 to Sharia law is incompatible with the provision's object and purpose.

111 E.g. CmRC, *Summary Record of the 1216th Meeting, Malaysia*. UN Doc. CRC/C/SR.1216 (30 January 2007), para 33. CmRC, *Concluding Observations (third and fourth reports) India*. UN Doc. CRC/C/IND/CO/3-4 (13 June 2014), paras 45, 46.

112 CmRC, *Concluding Observations (second and third reports), Montenegro*. UN Doc. CRC/C/MNE/CO/2-3 (22 June 2018), para 30.

after the acceptance of a child's change of religion by family and society,[113] and whether parents were aware of children's religious rights in raising them.[114] It has urged Member States to review practices in private schools and isolated religious communities to ensure that they did not interfere with children's rights to freedom of religion.[115]

Limiting freedom of manifestation to the age of majority has been deemed contrary to Article 14.[116] The CmRC also found that requiring parental consent for religious practice by minors under 15 was a hindrance to religious freedom.[117] Significantly in respect of PCRMs, the Committee asked Panama at what age children were free to decide to stop catechism classes their parents had obligated them to attend,[118] and told Colombia that '[p]reventing a child from practising a religion or not practising a religion was not in accordance with Articles 12 and Article 14'.[119] It later questioned Djibouti on whether children were able to change religion, asking further how children's religious rights were 'guaranteed in practice' and whether they were tied to parental authority or children's own responsibility.[120]

The CmRC recognises the primary role of parents in children's religious upbringing and has admonished States for not allowing children to practise the parental religion with parents[121] However, the right to direction cannot be interpreted so broadly as to encompass imposition of religion or PCRMs.

113 CmRC, *Summary Record of the 147th Meeting, Chile*. UN Doc. CRC/C/SR.147 (20 April 1994), para 6. See also more generally on a parental right to decide the child's religion: CmRC, *Summary Record of the 136th Meeting, Burkina Faso*. UN Doc. CRC/C/SR.136 (12 April 1994), para 34.

114 CmRC, *Summary Record of the 333rd Meeting, Mauritius*. UN Doc. CRC/C/SR.333 (18 October 1996), para 64 (That the Committee member was referring to children's rights and not to parental rights is clear from para 74).

115 CmRC, *Concluding Observations (third and fourth reports) Republic of Korea*. UN Doc. CRC/C/KOR/CO/3–4 (2 February 2012), para 38; CmRC, *Concluding Observations, Norway*. UN Doc. CRC/C/NOR/CO/4 (29 January 2010), paras 26, 27.

116 E.g. CmRC, *Summary Record of the 299th Meeting, China*. UN Doc. CRC/C/SR.299 (31 May 1996), para 34; CmRC, *Concluding Observations (third and fourth reports), Indonesia*. UN Doc. CRC/C/IND/CO/3–4 (23 June 2014), paras 29, 30. See also CmRC, *Concluding Observations (third to fifth reports), Bhutan*. UN Doc. CRC/C/BTN/CO/3–5 (5 July 2017), para 20: the state must 'ensure to every child the right to practise freely his or her religion or belief'.

117 E.g. CmRC, *Summary Record of the 786th Meeting, Belarus*. UN Doc. CRC/C/SR.786 (24 July 2002), para 70; CmRC, *Summary Record of the 856th Meeting, Iceland*. UN Doc. CRC/C/SR.856 (6 February 2003), para 16.

118 CmRC, *Summary Record of 355th Meeting, Panama*. UN Doc. CRC/C/SR.355 (17 March 1997), para 12.

119 Langlaude (2007), 133 with reference to: CmRC, *Summary Record of the 114th Meeting, Colombia*. UN Doc. CRC/C/SR.114 (7 March 1995), para 28.

120 CmRC, *Summary Record of the 638th Meeting, Djibouti*. UN Doc. CRC/C/SR.638 (7 June 2000), paras 10, 35.

121 See e.g. CmRC, *Concluding Observations (third to fifth reports), Tajikistan*. UN Doc. CRC/C/TJK/CO/3–5 (29 September 2017), para 19.

It appears to be a right to guidance, not control. This is evidenced by General Comment 7, which states that parents 'should be encouraged to offer "direction and guidance" in a child-centred way, through dialogue and example, in ways that enhance young children's capacities to exercise their rights, including their right to freedom of thought, conscience and religion (art. 14)'.[122] If anything, the CmRC has been extremely critical of parental imposition of religion and manifestation. In addition, now that the provision in Article 14(2) has been confirmed to mean that the parental right only comes into being when the child is exercising their own right to freedom of religion, interpreting the parental right as anything that goes beyond guidance would be illogical. It would suggest a compatibility between exercising freedom of religion (by the child) and being coerced in religion (by parents), which is clearly anathema.[123] One could wonder whether the CRC really gives parents a new right at all beyond existing personal rights to convince another person of one's religion through example and discussion.[124]

2.4 Parental rights under parents' religious freedom rights

Critics like Adhar and Leigh[125] have argued that the liberty to impose religious manifestations upon one's children is an aspect of parents' *personal* right to freedom of religion and manifestation as found in e.g. Articles 18 UDHR, 18 ICCPR, 1 1981 Declaration and 9 ECHR. These rights generally provide that everyone has a (non-derogable) right to freedom of thought, conscience and religion (sometimes with an express right to change religions, or not to be coerced in religion), and a freedom to manifest religion or belief in public or private and alone or in community, with manifestation subject to stated limitation grounds such as public order, morals or the rights and freedoms of others. Since many religions emphasise God-given rights over children, the argument goes, parental rights in religion must form part of parents' own right to freedom of religion. Children, on the other hand, are said to have an interest in religion within the family sphere, but no rights that can compete with those of parents.[126] Therefore, parents' own rights to freedom of religion and manifestation provide a justification of PCRMs. However, whilst parents have towards children all religious freedoms they have towards other people, both treaty drafters and treaty bodies have opposed a reading of parents' personal rights that would give parents additional rights over their children.

122 CmRC, *General Comment No. 7 (2005) Implementing child rights in early childhood*. UN Doc. CRC/C/GC/7/Rev.1 (20 September 2006), para 17. (General Comment 7)

123 See 3.1 and 3.2 below.

124 E.g. *Kokkinakis v Greece*, no. 14307/88 (1993) ECtHR Series A 260-A, para 31.

125 Adhar and Leigh (2005), 193. See also K. Wood Colby, When the Family does Not Pray Together: Religious Rights within the Family. (1982) 5 *Harvard Journal of Law and Public Policy* 39, 62; *Re J* [1999] 2 FLR 678 (child's circumcision as part of the father's right to manifestation).

126 Adhar (2000), 94.

(1) The United Nations

During the drafting of the various human rights instruments, the matter of special parental rights was actively discussed, but under no instrument were such rights accepted. The UDHR set the tone by rejecting parental rights as applicable to freedom of religion.[127] A proposed more general provision on parental control over children equally failed to be adopted.[128] Delegates made it clear that parents should not be allowed to obstruct children's own choice and the Russian delegate stated that the idea of parents determining their child's religion 'contradicted the idea of freedom of conscience'.[129] The unwillingness to extend the right in Article 18 UDHR so as to encompass parental rights to coerce religious manifestations has persisted, with the General Assembly failing to include parental rights at all in its most recent resolutions on freedom of religion.[130]

Following up on the UDHR discussion, one of the UDHR and ICCPR's principal drafters, Mr Cassin, vigorously defended the religious rights of children in relation to their parents in an address at the start of the ICCPR negotiations.[131] A subsequent proposal to refer to parental rights in religion was met with such resistance that it was not included in the 1954 Human Rights Commission draft.[132] Delegates rejected every appearance of the non-applicability of full ICCPR rights to children, since human rights had to be equal for everyone.[133] Moreover, there was very strong objection to including third-party rights in an international treaty.[134] The ICCPR's *travaux préparatoires* clearly demonstrate a lack of support for the idea that parents' personal rights can encompass a right to impose PCRMs. The same is true for subsequent interpretations of Article 18 ICCPR. Although General Comment 22 refers to the link between Article 18(4) and the right to teach a religion in Article 18(1), it does not suggest that parents' rights under Article 18(1) are any broader than those of other persons.[135] In addition, the HRC has so far not seen fit to consider any other articles than 18(4) in cases citing parental rights in religious matters.[136]

127 De Jong (2000), 577, 578.

128 See W.A. Schabas, *The Universal Declaration of Human Rights. The Travaux Préparatoires* (Vol. I). Cambridge: CUP, 2013, 102, 124.

129 De Jong (2000), 577, 578, with reference to UN Doc. E/CN.4?AC.1/SR.

130 See n. 61.

131 1949 speech by Cassin in: De Jong (2000), 52.

132 Nowak (1993), 410.

133 See also the opposition to Article 24 ICCPR (Protection of Children). Many delegates opposed this article, because it could detract from the idea that the human rights listed applied to children too. G. van Bueren, *The International Law on the Rights of the Child*. Dordrecht: Martinus Nijhoff Publishers, 1995, 21.

134 Bossuyt (1987), 369.

135 HRC (1993), General Comment 22, para 6.

136 See e.g. *Leirvåg v Norway*, no. 1155/2003 (2004) HRC. UN Doc. CCPR/C/82/D/1155/2003, paras 14.7, 14.8.

Contrary to the UDHR and ICCPR, the question of parental rights under personal rights does not really feature under the 1981 Declaration, as the instrument contains an independent provision on the parental right to organise religious life within the family. If parental rights were included in Article 1, there would not be any need for a separate provision. It is therefore surprising that Rapporteur Bielefeldt has suggested, with reference to Article 18(3) ICCPR, that certain manifestations representing rites of initiation form part of the parental right to freedom of manifestation.[137] It could nonetheless be argued that the rites of initiation Bielefeldt speaks of (those '[w]elcoming the newborn child')[138] are not PCRMs, since they include something that is done to children, at an age where these children presumably lack any understanding of what religion is.[139] The Rapporteur has moreover not generally stated that parents' personal rights include a right to impose PCRMs. Such a right would sit ill with the 1981 Declaration's own *travaux préparatoires* and the rest of the UN human rights regime.[140]

(2) The Council of Europe

Like their counterparts at the UN, the ECHR drafters were resolute on Convention rights not having third-party effect, and parents' personal rights to freedom of religion not including parental rights to determine a child's religion or religious practice.[141] The ECtHR has also explicitly rejected the idea that parents' personal rights to freedom of religion might encompass parental rights to impose manifestations. It has on several occasions declared applications founded on such presumed rights inadmissible.[142] In *Grzelak v Poland*, for example, the Court declared an application claiming that parents' personal rights to freedom of religion had been interfered with when the government restricted religious manifestations carried out by their child inadmissible *ratione personae*.[143] Article 9 (Freedom of Religion) has since been implicated in cases built on a combination of provisions that have carved out a new parental right.[144] However, even under that right, parents cannot impose PCRMs as a matter of personal freedom of religion and manifestation.

137 H. Bielefeldt, *Report of the Special Rapporteur on Freedom of Religion or Belief.* UN Doc. A/HRC/22/51 (24 December 2012c), para 49; Bielefeldt (2015), Special Rapporteur's Children Report, para 41.

138 Bielefeldt (2015), Special Rapporteur's Children Report, para 41.

139 See further 3.3.

140 De Jong (2000), 581, 582.

141 CoE (1975–85), Vol. I, p. 196 and Vol. VIII, p. 4, 24.

142 E.g. *CJ JJ and EJ v Poland* (dec), no. 23380/94 (1996) ECmHR, DR 84-A, 46; *Rupprecht v Spain* (dec), no. 38471/10 (19 February 2013) ECtHR. See also in respect of divorce proceedings: *Deschomets v France* (dec), no. 31956/02 (16 May 2006) ECtHR; *Gineitienė v Lithuania*, no. 20739/05 (27 July 2010) ECtHR, paras 46, 47.

143 *Grzelak v Poland*, no. 7710/02 (15 June 2010) ECtHR, paras 51, 52.

144 See nn. 158–67 and accompanying text.

2.5 Parental rights under non-religion-related provisions

There are international provisions not directly related to religion or education that can impact on religious matters between parents and children and the issue of PCRMs. The most relevant provisions 'unrelated' to religion are those that could grant parents more general rights in relation to their children, capable of covering religious manifestations. As mentioned above, both the UDHR and ICCPR negotiators rejected the idea of third-party effect, including between parents and children. A proposed article on general parental rights under the UDHR was not adopted,[145] and the ICCPR delegates agreed that the Convention was not to give parents any rights over their children.[146] Provisions 'unrelated' to religion holding the potential to include parental rights sanctioning PCRMs are therefore principally found in the CRC and ECHR.

(1) The CRC (UN)

The Convention on the Rights of the Child makes specific mention of respect for parental responsibilities, rights and duties in Article 5, and states that parents have the primary responsibility for the upbringing and development of the child in Article 18. It has therefore been argued that the CRC allows parents to limit children's religious freedom, based in particular on Article 5.[147] Yet, Article 5 is worded in a similar manner to 14(2) and requires that States respect parental responsibilities, rights and duties to provide the child direction and guidance in the child's exercise of their Convention rights in accordance with children's evolving capacities. Hence, the same reasoning applies as provided above in respect of Article 14(2): the parental right is an additional right to guidance that does not detract from the child's own, full right. Or in the words of the CmRC:

> Article 5 states that parents' role is to offer appropriate direction and guidance in 'the exercise by the child of the rights in the . . . Convention'. This applies equally to younger as to older children. . . . Article 5 contains the principle that parents (and others) have the responsibility to continually adjust the levels of support and guidance they offer to a child. . . .
>
> Evolving capacities should be seen as a positive and enabling process, not an excuse for authoritarian practices that restrict children's autonomy and self-expression . . . including [in respect of] . . . their right to freedom of thought, conscience and religion (art. 14).[148]

145 Schabas (2013), 102, 124.
146 Van Bueren (1995), 21.
147 Scolnicov (2011), 160.
148 CmRC (2006), General Comment 7, paras 16, 17. See also CmRC (2016), General Comment 20, para 18.

A right to impose PCRMs can therefore not be derived from Article 5 CRC. Neither can it stem from Article 18 CRC on parents' primary responsibility for the upbringing and development of their children. Hodgkin and Newell note that, although 'article 18 seems to be about parents' rather than about children's rights', the assertion of parents' primacy 'is made in relation to the State, not the child, and the article is about parental responsibilities rather than rights'.[149] It is most commonly associated with matters such as taking children into care, communal upbringing and polygamous families.[150] In its General Comments 7 (Early Childhood) and 20 (Adolescence), the CmRC has expanded on the right as one of primacy for parents to bring up their children, limiting State intervention only to cases where the best interests of the child require it.[151] Yet this primacy is on the basis that 'parents play a crucial role in the achievement of [children's] rights'.[152] The primary responsibility of parents gives them the right and responsibility to raise children. Parents can do so by giving children a religious upbringing, but not in a way that undermines children's own religious rights.[153]

(2) The Council of Europe

The right to family life under Article 8 ECHR has been suggested to support parental rights at the expense of children's independent religious rights.[154] However, family life principally deals with the obligation of States not to sever ties between family members. Where religion plays a role in the context of Article 8, it normally does not do so directly, but through the mediation of Article 14 on non-discrimination.[155] The reasoning in such cases is that ties between parents and children were severed arbitrarily due to discrimination on the grounds of religion or belief. For example, the landmark case of *Hoffmann v Austria*, in which a Jehovah's Witness mother was denied custody of her children, dealt not with a parental right to determine religious upbringing, but with depriving a mother of her children (severing ties) on the sole basis of her religion (discrimination).[156]

149 Hodgkin and Newell (2007), 232.

150 Ibid. See also CmRC, *Concluding Observations, Australia*. UN Doc. CRC/C/AUS/CO/4 (28 August 2012), paras 49, 50.

151 CmRC (2006), General Comment 7, paras 15–21; CmRC (2016), General Comment 20, para 50.

152 CmRC (2006), General Comment 7, para 15.

153 Ibid.

154 Kilkelly (2009), 254. See also J. Murdoch, *Protecting the Right to Freedom of Thought, Conscience and Religion under the European Convention on Human Rights*. Strasbourg: Council of Europe, 2012, 73.

155 See J. Tigchelaar and M. Jonker, How is a Decision Made in Parental Religious Disputes? An Analysis of Determining Factors in Dutch and European Court of Human Rights Case Law. (2016) 12(2) *Utrecht Law Review* 24, 31.

156 *Hoffmann v Austria*, no. 12875/87 (1993) ECtHR Series A 255-C. See also e.g. *Palau-Martinez v France*, no. 64927/01 (2003) ECHR 2003-XII; *Ismailova v Russia*, no. 37614/02 (31 August 2007) ECtHR; *Gineitienė v Lithuania*, no. 20739/05 (27 July 2010) ECtHR; *Mincheva v Bulgaria*, no. 21558/03 (2 September 2010) ECtHR.

As such, it cannot sanction imposed religious practice. Rather, in one of the cases invoking Articles 8 and 14, PCRMs were themselves a reason not to grant a parent custody and the ECtHR upheld this decision.[157]

More recently, the ECtHR has been willing to use Article 8 as a substitute for Article 2P1 in a case where the Member State (Switzerland) had not ratified the First Protocol, on the basis that Article 8 could include the responsibility of parents to educate and raise their children.[158] Though, as such, the court found itself bound by the principles established under 2P1 and held that there could not be a violation of parental rights, unless the State pursued an aim of indoctrination (which it had not).[159] Of greater consequence has been the court's willingness to craft a parental right in religious matters that applies in relation to children on the basis of a combination of provisions, including Article 8. In *Tlapak and Others v Germany*, the court confirmed an earlier finding in *Vojnity v Hungary* that:

> the right to respect for family life and to religious freedom, as enshrined in Articles 8 and 9 of the Convention, together with the right to respect for parents' philosophical and religious convictions in education, as provided for in Article 2 of Protocol No. 1 to the Convention, convey to parents the right to communicate and promote their religious convictions in bringing up their children. While the Court has accepted that this might even occur in an insistent and overbearing manner, it has stressed that it may not expose children to dangerous practices or to physical or psychological harm.[160]

Key to the right are 'communicate and promote' and 'insisting and overbearing manner'. The right is arguably not one to impose PCRMs, but to try and convince the child of the parental religion in a persistent manner. It was developed in the context of a father who lost his access rights after he used access to attempt to convert his son. The ECtHR held that parents have a right to proselytise to their children, unless doing so causes children more than 'mere unease, discomfort or embarrassment'.[161] The right protects 'attempts to transmit [parental] religious beliefs',[162] but not the imposition or submission to a religious practice (in *Tlapak*, the right could not justify religiously motivated caning)[163]. Its significance is in the fact that parents can promote their religion within the protected sphere of the

157 *Deschomets v France* (dec), no. 31956/02 (16 May 2006) ECtHR.

158 *A.R. and L.R. v Switzerland*, no. 22338/15 (19 December 2017) ECtHR, para 26.

159 Ibid., paras 38, 39.

160 *Tlapak and Others v Germany*, nos. 11308/16 and 11344/16 (22 March 2018) ECtHR, para 79 (references omitted). See also *Vojnity v Hungary*, no. 29617/07 (12 February 2013) ECtHR, paras 37–9.

161 *Vojnity v Hungary*, no. 29617/07 (12 February 2013) ECtHR, para 38.

162 Ibid.

163 *Tlapak and Others v Germany*, nos. 11308/16 and 11344/16 (22 March 2018) ECtHR, paras 88–101.

family, where children are effectively a captive audience.[164] Yet it is not a right that otherwise goes beyond that recognised under Article 9 to try to convince others of one's religion[165] – and the tolerance these other parties must practise being confronted with opinions they do not share.[166] It is therefore not a right to force children to manifest the parental religion.[167]

The absence of parental rights regarding children's manifestations does not mean that the ECtHR is hostile towards parents seeking to raise children religiously. *Vojnity v Hungary* rather suggests the contrary. Moreover, the court has sought to find a basis on which parents can involve children in their religion *outside* the written text of the ECHR. It has held on a number of occasions that parents may 'enlighten', 'advise' and 'guide their children on a path in line with the parents' own religious or philosophical convictions' as part of parents' natural functions,[168] in their natural role as educators,[169] or in the discharge of their natural duty to bring up their children.[170] In a series of resolutions and recommendations,[171] the CoE's Parliamentary Assembly and Committee of Ministers have equally indicated that they see a role for parents in their children's religious upbringing (including decision-making whilst children are too young to make their own decisions).[172] This role is nonetheless balanced by the State's task to provide children with a meaningful education that gives them the skills to exercise rights,[173] and children's own rights, which can be invoked and

164 In such situations, proselytising is normally not allowed, especially if there is a power-differential: *Larrisis v Greece*, no. 23372/94 (1998) ECtHTR, Reports 1998-I, paras 47–55.

165 *Kokkinakis v Greece*, no. 14307/88 (1993) ECtHR Series A 260-A, para 31.

166 *Otto Preminger Institut v Austria*, no. 13470/87 (1994), Series A 295-A, para 49.

167 See also *De Souza Ribeiro v France*, no. 22689/07 (2010) ECtHR (Grand Chamber) ECHR 2012, footnote 35: the Convention must be read as a whole, promoting internal consistency. It would be inconsistent to expressly exclude parental rights to coerce under Article 9 but accept them based on that same article in conjunction with Articles 8 and 2P1.

168 *Kjeldsen, Busk Madsen and Pedersen v Denmark*, nos. 5095/71, 5920/72 and 5926/72 (1976) ECtHR Series A 23, para 54; *Çiftçi v Turkey* (dec), no. 71860/01 (17 June 2004) ECtHR; *Konrad v Germany* (dec), no. 35504/03 (2006) ECtHR ECHR 2006-XIII.

169 *Appel-Irrgang and Others v Germany* (dec), no. 45216/07 (2009) ECtHR ECHR 2009

170 *Folgerø and Others v Norway*, no. 15472/02 (2007) ECtHR (Grand Chamber) ECHR 2007-III, para 84.

171 E.g. CMCoE, *Recommendation No. R(84)4 on Parental Responsibilities*, Council of Europe (28 February 1984); CMCoE, *Recommendation Rec (2002)12 of the Committee of Ministers to Member States on Education for Democratic Citizenship*, Council of Europe (16 October 2002); CMCoE, *Recommendation Rec(2006)19 on Policy to Support Positive Parenting*, Council of Europe (13 December 2006); PACoE, *Recommendation 874 (1979) on a European Charter on the Rights of the Child*, Council of Europe (4 October 1979); PACoE, *Resolution 1952 (2013) Children's Right to Physical Integrity*, Council of Europe (1 October 2013); PACoE, *Resolution 2232 (2018) Striking a Balance between the Best Interest of the Child and the Need to Keep Families Together*, Council of Europe (28 June 2018).

172 See PACoE, *Recommendation 1720 (2005) Education and Religion*, Council of Europe (4 October 2005).

173 PACoE, *Resolution 1928 (2013) Safeguarding Human Rights in Relation to Religion and Belief, and Protecting Religious Communities from Violence*, Council of Europe (24 April 2013), para 9.11.

exercised against parents.[174] Ultimately, the CoE's approach is both nuanced and principled: there is acknowledgement of the parental role vis-à-vis the child in matters of religious upbringing, but also a clear rejection of a parental right to impose PCRMs as a matter of parents' human rights.

2.6 The absence of a parental right under international law

As stated in the introduction to this chapter, it is often taken for granted that parents can impose PCRMs as a matter of human rights and questions are seldom raised as to the actual existence of this right. However, whilst the international community has clearly recognised a role for parents in the religious upbringing of their children; establishes parents as those with primary responsibility for children's education and upbringing; and gives parents rights to guard against indoctrination, the various treaties and their subsequent interpretations do not support a parental right to *coerce* children in matters of religious manifestation. Instead of upholding such rights, treaty negotiators and bodies have challenged them, urging States to ensure that parents and other private parties do not undermine the religious freedom of children. It is true that there have been many cases in which parents have asserted parental rights, but parents did not win these cases, unless the State's conduct could be described as indoctrinatory.

Exemplifying the absence of a parental right to impose manifestations is the debate that followed what is known as the 'headscarf-affair'.[175] In 2004, the French government adopted a law banning all 'ostentatious' religious garments and symbols from public schools.[176] Despite the law being framed in general terms to prevent targeting a specific religion, Loi n° 2004-228 aimed to respond to signals that some Muslim girls had been forced to wear headscarves by family members and others.[177] The government argued that a general prohibition to wear religious attire would ensure that these girls could no longer be forced to don a headscarf. It used the same coercion argument to explain why it was justified that other children wearing religious attire (e.g. turbans, kippas or crosses) would equally come within the scope of the law.[178]

174 PACoE, *Recommendation 1121 (1990) on the Rights of Children*, Council of Europe (1 February 1990), para 5.

175 Initially referring to a case involving a prohibition to wear headscarves in school: CE Avis n° 346893, 27 November 1989 *Port de signe d'appartenance à une communauté religieuse*.

176 Loi n° 2004-228 du 15 mars 2004 *encadrant, en application du principe de laïcité, le port de signes ou de tenues manifestant une appartenance religieuse dans les écoles, collèges et lycées publics*.

177 B. Stasi, *Commission de reflexion sur l'application du principe de laïcite dans la République: Rapport au Président de la République*. Paris: La Documentation française, 2003, 45.

178 *Projet de loi relatif à l'application du principe de laïcité dans les écoles, collèges et lycées publics. Exposé des motifs*. Assemblée Nationale N° 1378, 12ième Législature (2004). Reference was also made to the general importance of a secular school environment.

The international community responded in very different – and opposing – ways to the law: some international bodies condoned the law,[179] whereas others offered fierce critique.[180] The ban on religious attire even resulted in a stand-off between the ECtHR which found it to be compatible with human rights[181] and the HRC which held that it was not.[182] Yet, on one matter the international community was united: the idea that parents were allowed to pressure or force the wearing of religious attire was universally rejected.[183] As Special Rapporteur Jahangir noted:

> The law is appropriate insofar as it is intended, in accordance with the principle of the best interests of the child, to protect the autonomy of minors who may be pressured or forced to wear a headscarf or other religious symbols.[184]

None of the international bodies held that parents had a right to determine their children's religious manifestations; reservations were not even made for the rights of parents in respect of younger children. The headscarf affair elicited global agreement on the *absence* of parental rights to coerce the wearing of religious symbols or attire. Whilst parents thus maintain a limited right against the State to protect their children from indoctrination and are the persons primarily responsible for the socialisation of children, express rights or implicit licence to impose PCRMs do not exist under the current global human rights regime.

179 The European Court of Human Rights (ECtHR) has declared all applications in respect of the law inadmissible: *Aktas v France* (dec), no. 43563/08; *Bayrak v France* (dec), no. 14308/08; *Gamaleddyn v France* (dec), no. 18527/08; *Ghazal v France* (dec), no. 29134/08; *Jasvir Singh v France* (dec), no. 25463/08; *Ranjit Singh v France* (dec), no. 27561/08 (all dated 30 June 2009).

180 *Singh v France*, no. 1852/2008 (2013) HRC. UN Doc. CCPR/C/106/D/1852/2008. See also: HRC, *Summary Record of the 1599th Meeting, France*. UN Doc. CCPR/C/SR.1599 (28 July 1997), para 59; CmRC, *Summary Record of the 967th Meeting, France*. UN Doc. CRC/C/SR.967 (10 August 2004), paras 26, 42; CmRC, *Concluding Observations, France*. UN Doc. CRC/C/15/Add.240 (30 June 2004), para 25; CmRC, *Concluding Observations, France*. UN Doc. CRC/C/FRA/CO/4 (22 June 2009), para 45; A. Jahangir, *Civil and Political Rights, Including the Question of Religious Intolerance*. UN Doc. E/CN.4/2006/5 (9 January 2006) (2006a); Jahangir (2006b).

181 See n. 179. The different applications had invoked various ECHR Articles.

182 *Singh v France*, no. 1852/2008 (2013) HRC UN Doc. CCPR/C/106/D/1852/2008 (decided on 18(3)).

183 See nn. 179, 180. See also PACoE, *Resolution 1464 (2005) Women and Religion in Europe*, Council of Europe (4 October 2005), para 7.4: States should ensure that girls are not 'forced to submit to religious codes'.

184 Jahangir (2006b), para 99.

3 Children's right to freedom of manifestation

The previous chapter identified that international law, whilst acknowledging the parental role in religious upbringing, does not give parents a direct or indirect right to impose parentally coerced religious manifestations (PCRMs). However, that is only one side of the coin. If a child's right to freedom of religion and manifestation is not equal to that of adults, or otherwise subordinate to parental wishes, it may still be possible to impose PCRMs without these constituting an interference with the child's right.

In 1998, Van Bueren noted that there was no longer significant disagreement 'over the existence of legal rights for children, it is the content and extent of those rights which is the subject of disagreement'.[1] Recent literature shows that this statement rings as true today as it did back in 1998.[2] Disagreement exists on what is covered by children's rights and, at a more fundamental level, how we should perceive of children's rights. The way we think of rights has consequences for children's ability to hold fundamental rights that allow them to oppose PCRMs. If we e.g. decide that children's rights should be based on their interests and we identify that it is in children's interests to share their parents' religious identity, PCRMs could be justified because they confirm that single identity. Conversely, if we think that children's religious rights should be based on self-determination, then such rights provide a defence against PCRMs, but younger children might not have a claim to such rights as they do not yet have the capacity for religious decision-making. Separately, it has been argued that culture can influence what children's rights are recognized at a given time or place. This chapter addresses these challenges. It starts by surveying children's right to freedom of manifestation at the international level (3.1), and then examines the three challenges of rights theory (the question of what underpins rights) (3.2), competence (the question of whether and when children are competent to make religious decisions) (3.3) and culture (the question of whether culture can and should limit the scope of children's rights) (3.4).

1 Van Bueren (1998), 15.

2 E.g. M. Cowden, *Children's Rights: From Philosophy to Public Policy*. Basingstoke: Palgrave Macmillan, 2016, who discusses both theoretical (Part I) and practical (Part 2) limitations of rights.

3.1 Children's rights under international law

This is not the place for a full overview of children's human rights to freedom of religion and manifestation under international law.[3] It is nonetheless important to highlight some of the background and principles that apply to children's religious rights as they can inform our thinking about rights. The most important aspects are that children have been recognised as holders of religious rights, these rights are justiciable, the core of children's rights to freedom of religion and manifestation is not different from that of adults, and children can exercise their rights against opposing adults.

(1) Children as rights holders

It has been accepted under all the instruments discussed in Chapter 2 (ICCPR, CRC, ECHR, etc.) as in other documents that children, on a practical level, hold rights to freedom of religion and manifestation, which for the most part are unqualified.[4] The 1924 *Geneva Declaration on the Rights of the Child* already determined that '[t]he child must be given the means requisite for its normal development, both materially and spiritually'.[5] Its reference to children's own development and the provision of requisite means, suggests some personal pursuit by children.[6] Further declarations and treaties have recognised the rights of 'everyone' to freedom of religion and manifestation, clarified by delegates during negotiations, and subsequently by treaty bodies, as including children.[7] More recently, the UN General Assembly emphasised that children should be fully recognised as holders of religious rights, by stating that it:

> Stresses that the right to freedom of thought, conscience and religion or belief applies equally to all persons . . . Recognizes with concern the situation of . . . children . . . as regards their ability to freely exercise their right to freedom of religion or belief.[8]

3 For such overview see Langlaude (2007), updated in S. Langlaude Doné and J. Tobin, 'Article 14: The Right to Freedom of Thought, Conscience and Religion', in J. Tobin (ed.), *The UN Convention on the Rights of the Child*. Oxford: OUP (forthcoming).

4 See the discussion throughout Chapter 2. See also Van Bueren (1995), 21; C. Evans, *Freedom of Religion under the European Convention on Human Rights*. Oxford: OUP, 2001, 41, 45.

5 League of Nations, *Geneva Declaration on the Rights of the Child* (26 September 1924) <http://www.un-documents.net/gdrc1924.htm> last accessed 10 March 2019.

6 'Spiritually' here is broader than religion, referring to non-material well-being, including religion. See also UN GA Resolution 1386 (XIV) *Declaration on the Rights of the Child*. UN Doc. A/RES/14/1386 (20 November 1959), principle 2, the child 'shall be given opportunities and facilities, by law and by other means, to enable him to develop physically, mentally, morally, spiritually and socially in a healthy and normal manner and in conditions of freedom and dignity'.

7 Most notably Articles 18 UDHR, 9 ECHR, 18 ICCPR, 1 1981 Declaration. See Chapter 2 and e.g. Bielefeldt (2015), Special Rapporteur's Children Report, paras 38, 79(a).

8 UN General Assembly (GA), *Resolution 67/179 on Freedom of Religion or Belief*. UN Doc. A/RES/67/179 (3 April 2013), paras 2, 8.

In addition to general human rights treaties, some instruments specifically concerned with children have stipulated that children hold rights to freedom of religion and manifestation. The CRC states in Article 14(1) that 'States Parties shall respect the right of the child to freedom of thought, conscience and religion' and that limitations on manifestations are only possible in accordance with the requirements in Art. 14(3).[9] The 1990 *United Nations Rules for the Protection of Juveniles Deprived of their Liberty* stipulate that States should respect 'the religious and cultural beliefs, practices and moral concepts of the juvenile'.[10] Both instruments include the qualification of 'respect', which indicates a lower level of protection than an unqualified right.[11] In the case of the 1990 Rules, that can be explained by the specific situation to which the rules apply (deprivation of liberty) and the combination of beliefs and practices in one rule (practices generally being subject to limitations). With regard to the CRC, it should be kept in mind that only the State and not others can impose limitations, although the State can, of course, delegate this power to parents via concepts like parental responsibility. More importantly, the CRC contains a further provision (Article 41) which states that children enjoy any national or international right that is broader than that included in the CRC. This means that the broadest applicable right to freedom of religion and manifestation should be seen as enforced through the CRC.[12] Provided that there is another provision on freedom of religion in force (and most States will have ratified at least one of the other instruments), the addition of respect has no effect. In any case, the CmRC has not interpreted the rights contained in Article 14 as being of a lesser nature than those contained in other treaties.[13]

(2) Justiciability

In addition to being recognised under international law, children's rights to freedom of religion and manifestation are justiciable. The HRC as well as the ECtHR have accepted cases brought by children to defend their right to freedom of manifestation.[14] Such cases can now equally be pursued under the newly established CRC individual complaints procedure, though amongst the handful of cases brought to date, none have specifically dealt with religious matters.[15]

9 See Langlaude (2007), 129: there is no explicit right to freedom of manifestation, but its existence is derived from applicable limitations.

10 UN GA, Resolution 45/113. UN Doc. A/RES/45/113 (14 December 1990), para 4.

11 See 2.1.1 above.

12 Alen and Pas (1996), 127.

13 E.g. CmRC, *Summary Record of the 786th Meeting, Belarus*, UN Doc CRC/C/SR.786 (24 July 2002), para 70; CmRC, *Concluding Observations (third and fourth reports), India*, UN Doc CRC/C/IND/CO/3–4 (13 June 2014), paras 45, 46. See also Hodgkin and Newell (2007), 188, 189.

14 E.g. *Singh v France*, no. 1852/2008 (2013) HRC, UN Doc. CCPR/C/106/D/1852/2008; *Folgerø and Others v Norway*, no. 15472/02 (2007) ECtHR (Grand Chamber), ECHR 2007-III.

15 Article 14 has once been invoked, but remained substantiated: *M.A.A. v Spain*, no. 2/2015 (2016) CmRC, UN Doc. CRC/C/73/D/2/2015 (Admissibility), para 4.3.

(3) Uniform interpretation

Human rights mechanisms have made no clear distinction between the interpretation of core religious human rights (as opposed to limitations) for children and adults.[16] In both cases, the right itself is posited as protecting individual choice.[17] This is significant in the context of PCRMs, because religious rights tend to emphasise freedom from coercion.[18] The UDHR, for example, commences Article 18 by mentioning freedom of thought, a freedom meant to provide protection against forced adherence to a religion or belief.[19] The provision further includes a right to change religion or belief. This right is particularly relevant for people who automatically became a member of a religion upon birth or during childhood and later wish to renounce adherence and manifestation.[20] The right is also recognised in the ECHR, whose provision on religious freedom mirrors the UDHR's, stating that '[e]veryone has the right to freedom of thought, conscience and religion; this right includes freedom to change his religion or belief and freedom'.

Similar rights in the ICCPR (Article 18) and 1981 Declaration (Article 1) are worded as a right to 'have or adopt' a religion, as a result of diplomatic compromise with States that have a State religion.[21] The HRC has made it clear that to have and adopt a religion 'necessarily entails the freedom to choose a religion or belief, including the right to replace one's current religion or belief with another or to adopt atheistic views'.[22] The ICCPR and 1981 Declaration further contain specific provisions on coercion. Article 18(2) ICCPR stipulates that '[n]o one shall be subject to coercion which would impair his freedom to have or to adopt a religion or belief of his choice'.[23] As a consequence, neither adults nor children should be coerced in a manner that requires or prevents them from having, adopting or changing a religion or (non-religious) belief.[24] The provision does not formally apply to religious manifestation, but Bielefeldt et al. have argued that the lines between the *forum internum* (believing) and *forum externum* (practising) can be blurred.[25] The HRC has indeed found an instance of coercion where a student could not attend tertiary education as a result of a manifestation

16 E.g. see nn. 13, 14; *Rupprecht v Spain* (dec), no. 38471/10 (19 February 2013) ECtHR. See also 2.6 above.

17 Ibid.; CmRC (2006) General Comment 7, para 17; CmRC (2016), General Comment 20, para 43.

18 Compare McAdam (2018), 1, 60.

19 Morsink (1999), 261.

20 See *X v Iceland* (admissibility), ECmHR, Application no. 2525/65 (6 December 1967).

21 Lerner (2012), 20.

22 HRC (1993), General Comment 22, para 5.

23 Article 1(2) 1981 Declaration stipulates: 'No one shall be subject to coercion which would impair his freedom to have a religion or belief of his choice'.

24 Contra S. Joseph and M. Castan, *The International Covenant on Civil and Political Rights. Cases, Materials, and Commentary* (3rd ed.). Oxford: OUP, 2013, 572.

25 Bielefeldt et al. (2016), 85, 93.

(wearing a headscarf).[26] What exactly coercion entails is not defined, though the HRC has suggested that coercion is not limited to physical force and can entail sanctions, restricting access to facilities or benefits, or interference with the right to participation or other convention rights.[27] That finding is especially important for children, since there are many ways to make children feel coerced without physically restraining them, as also explained in Chapter 1.

The international provisions further recognise specific rights to freedom of manifestation that are applicable to children.[28] These rights are nearly always positively formulated as a right to engage in manifestations of various kinds. Only the CDE explicitly recognises an independent right not to be 'compelled' to engage in religious education.[29] However, when read in conjunction with the right to freedom of religion or belief and absence of coercion, a consistent approach would see the right to freedom of manifestation as one to manifest or reject manifestation. This approach has now been taken by various treaty bodies at the global and regional levels.[30] Special Rapporteur Bielefeldt, for example, has stated that:

> With regard to the freedom to manifest one's religion or belief, both the positive and the negative aspects of that freedom must be equally ensured, i.e. the freedom to express one's conviction as well the freedom not to be exposed to any pressure . . . to practice religious or belief activities against one's will.[31]

As a result, 'everyone' (including children) has internationally recognised rights to believe or manifest a religion, or to reject belief and decline manifestation of a religion. In both the case of adults and children, these rights have been defined as rights to follow one's own convictions and decide for oneself on participation.[32]

(4) Opposable rights

Finally, and without getting ahead of the discussion on the potential horizontal effect of human rights in Chapter 5, it is useful to refer to statements that have emphasised that children's exercise of religious rights is not subject to the approval of adults, including parents.[33] Delegates to the UDHR negotiations

26 *Hudoyberganova v Uzbekistan*, no. 931/00 (2005) HRC. UN Doc. CCPR/C/82/D/931/2000. Compare *Türkan v Turkey*, no 2274/2013 (2018) HRC. UN Doc. CCPR/C/123/D/2274/2013/Rev.1, which contained similar facts, but was decided solely on the basis of freedom of manifestation.

27 HRC (1993), General Comment 22, para 5; Lerner (2012), 20.

28 Bielefeldt (2015), Special Rapporteur's Children Report, paras 38, 79(a).

29 Article 5(b) CDE: 'no person or group of persons should be compelled to receive religious instruction inconsistent with his or their convictions'.

30 E.g. CmRC, *Summary Record of the 114th Meeting, Colombia*. UN Doc. CRC/C/SR.114 (7 March 1995), para 28. See Schabas (2015), 428 for an ECtHR overview.

31 H. Bielefeldt, *Report of the Special Rapporteur on Freedom of Religion or Belief*. UN Doc. A/HRC/16/53 (15 December 2010), para 57.

32 See further 3.2 below.

33 See De Jong (2000), 55.

made it clear that parents should not be allowed to obstruct children's own choice.[34] The idea of parents determining their child's religion would '[contradict] the idea of freedom of conscience'.[35] An address at the start of the ICCPR negotiations equally defended the religious rights of children in relation to their parents.[36] That opinion was echoed by the strong resistance to any appearance of subordination of children's rights later in the drafting process.[37] It is further reflected in General Comment 17, which rejects paternalism by family, society and State because 'as individuals, children benefit from all of the civil rights enunciated in the Covenant'.[38]

During the drafting of the 1981 Declaration, the religious rights of children were extensively discussed. It was agreed that, in case of conflict between children's rights-exercise and parental wishes, it would be better to give preference to children's religious rights than to allow parents to 'suppress those views'.[39] This outlook may not have been shared by all negotiators for the subsequent CRC,[40] but it is certainly the stance taken by the CmRC.[41] The Committee has not only held that parental guidance is only relevant where a child exercises their own religious rights,[42] but has regularly questioned States about children's freedom to make their own religion-related decisions within the familial and community context.[43] It has e.g. asked at what age children were free to abstain from manifestations obligated by parents,[44] and urged Member States to review practices in isolated religious communities to ensure that they did not interfere with children's rights to freedom of religion.[45]

The most well-known pronouncements on the idea that children's (religious) rights are not subject to adult discretion and can be invoked against them have emanated from the Council of Europe. In the landmark *Kjeldsen* case, Judge Kellberg held that it was 'hardly conceivable' that the ECtHR drafters had intended for children's manifestation rights to be subject to parental power (indeed, they had not)[46] and that it would be 'wrong to say that a child, who holds another philosophical conviction than his parents, must abide by their

34 Ibid., 577
35 Ibid., 577, 578, with reference to UN Doc. E/CN.4?AC.1/SR.
36 1949 speech by Cassin, ibid., 52.
37 See 2.1.1 and 2.4.
38 HRC, *General Comment No. 17: Article 24 (Rights of the Child)* (7 April 1989) (UN Doc. Unavailable), para 2, 6 (General Comment 17).
39 De Jong (2000), 581, 582 with reference Swedish delegate's statement in A/C.3/SR.2013, 83.
40 See Langlaude (2007), 118–20.
41 Hodgkin and Newell (2007), 188, 189.
42 CmRC (2016), General Comment 20, para 43.
43 See 2.3 above.
44 CmRC, *Summary Record of 355th Meeting, Panama*. UN Doc. CRC/C/SR.355 (17 March 1997), para 12.
45 CmRC, *Concluding Observations, Norway,* UN Doc CRC/C/NOR/CO/4 (29 January 2010), paras 26, 27.
46 CoE (1975–85), Vol. VIII, 4, 24.

decision'.[47] Taking a more definite stand, the CoE's 1990 recommendation on children's rights states without hesitation that 'children have rights they may independently exercise themselves – even against opposing adults'.[48]

In practice, children thus hold the rights to freedom of religion and manifestation from which 'everyone' benefits. Unlike the parental rights discussed in Chapter 2, these personal rights to freedom of religion and manifestation are (with one circumscribed exception)[49] unqualified. Hence, whilst already limited *parental* rights in respect of children are restricted by reference to children's interests, the harm-principle, the need to be age-appropriate and to follow children's growing maturity,[50] none of the instruments makes the rights of *children* subject to particular requirements that are not applicable to adults (a different question from whether special limitations might apply). Religious human rights, moreover, protect the freedom to refrain from manifestation to the same extent as the freedom to engage in manifestation.[51] This would point towards parentally coerced religious manifestations presenting an interference[52] with children's personal rights where these PCRMs are not meant to guard against State indoctrination. However, before such a conclusion can be reached, it is important to look at the challenges rights theory, competence and culture pose in respect of children's religious rights.

3.2 What do children's religious rights protect?

Whether PCRMs can be justified under the law is not merely a matter of whether human rights to freedom of manifestation have been recognised as applicable to children. The issue is not only whether or not children *have* such rights, but how we *perceive* of religious rights, and whether we hold the same perception of the religious rights of adults and children. If our perception of the rights of children is different from that of the rights of adults, it may still be possible for PCRMs to be justified under the law. Hence, it matters how we think about rights.

Two theories of rights have played a particular role in respect of the rights of children and others. They are (1) the will theory, which regards rights as advancing people's will (generally based on choice or control), and (2) the interest theory, which views rights as furthering interests. Before examining these theories, four remarks are in place. First, the will and interest theories are not the only theories that have been employed with regard to (children's) rights. Other

47 *Kjeldsen, Busk Madsen and Pedersen v Denmark* (dec), nos. 5095/71, 5920/72 and 5926/72 (21 March 1975) ECmHR, Separate opinion by judge Kellberg.

48 PACoE, *Recommendation 1121 (1990) on the Rights of Children*, Council of Europe (1 February 1990), para 5.

49 Article 14(1) CRC, but through Article 41 unqualified rights take precedence.

50 Article 5 of the 1981 Declaration (interests and harm), and Article 14(2) CRC ('evolving capacities', often referred to as age and maturity).

51 Compare McAdam (2018), 30.

52 Note the difference between interference and violation further explained in Chapter 4.

theories like those focusing on duties or harm have equally been suggested,[53] as have combined theories of rights.[54] The main debate has nonetheless been between will and interest theories. Second, the will and interest theories have been employed with respect to both legal and moral rights, and it is not always clear which writers defending one theory or the other have in mind.[55] In the area of human rights, the two are often interlinked. Tobin, for example, refers to the 'pressing need for a firm conceptual foundation and moral justification for the idea of human rights for children' within the context of existing human rights found in the CRC.[56] Third, the two theories have been employed with respect to different, albeit related questions: what are rights, on what fundamental basis do rights rest, which function(s) do rights have, who can have rights . . . ?[57] This section is concerned with the basis and function of the right to freedom of religion and manifestation, from which the question naturally flows whether children can have such rights to the same extent as adults. Fourth, both the will and interest theory exist in a more individual and collective form. The will theory e.g. generally demands that a certain person is able to exercise control or express a choice.[58] Yet some have argued that the theory originated with Kant,[59] whose normative imperative states that expressions of the will should be extendable to others so that everyone enjoys equal amounts of independence and, ultimately, rights. Similarly, the interest theory normally focuses on personal interests,[60] especially in the area of children's rights.[61] However, some theorists have taken a more collective approach, arguing that being part of a certain constituency

53 E.g. O. O'Neill, Children's Rights and Children's Lives. (1992) 6(1) *International Journal of Law and the Family* 24, 37–9; T.W. Simon, United Nations Convention on Wrongs to the Child. (2000) 8 *International Journal of Children's Rights* 1, 2, 12.

54 E.g. R. Cruft, Rights: Beyond Interest Theory and Will Theory? (2004) 23 *Law and Philosophy* 347; G. Sreenivasan, A Hybrid Theory of Claim-Rights. (2005) 25(5) *Oxford Journal of Legal Studies* 257; L. Wenar, The Nature of Rights. (2005) 33(3) *Philosophy and Public Affairs* 223.

55 Hart, Bentham, and Ross (see below), for example focus on legal rights, whereas Eekelaar is concerned with moral rights: J. Eekelaar, Personal Rights and Human Rights. (2002a) 2(2) *Human Rights Law Review* 181, 184. Langlaude (2007), 40–5 remains silent on the matter.

56 J. Tobin, Justifying Children's Rights. (2013) 21(3) *International Journal of Children's Rights* 395, 398.

57 Compare e.g. H.L.A. Hart, 'Bentham on Legal Rights', in A.W.B. Simpson (ed.), *Oxford Essays in Jurisprudence* (2nd Series). Oxford: Clarendon Press, 1973, Wenar (2005) and the essays in D. Archard and C.M. Macleod (eds), *The Moral and Political Status of Children*. Oxford: OUP, 2002, part I.

58 M.H. Kramer, 'Rights without Trimmings', in M.H. Kramer et al. (eds), *A Debate over Rights: Philosophical Enquiries*. Oxford: Clarendon Press, 1998, 69.

59 Langlaude (2007), 40; J. Timmerman, *Kant's Groundwork of the Metaphysics of Morals*. Cambridge: CUP, 2007, 68–71.

60 See H. Brighouse, 'What Rights (if any) do Children Have?', in Archard and Macleod (2002), 50, 52.

61 Ibid.; L. Ferguson, 'Not Merely Rights for Children but Children's Rights: The Theory Gap and the Assumption of the Importance of Children's Rights', in M. Freeman (ed), *The Future of Children's Rights*. Leiden: Brill, 2014, 66.

(a group, Nation State or even mankind) is sufficient to share a rights-founding interest.[62] Whilst individual conceptions tend to be dominant under both theories, their collective counterparts play a role in the debate about children's rights, as further discussed below.

(1) The will theory

The founding father of the modern will theory, H.L.A. Hart, argued that that a person has a right if he has control over another person's duty.[63] The fullest measure of control comprises three elements: (1) the right holder may waive – or not waive – the duty, (2) after (threatened) breach the right holder may enforce rights, or leave them unenforced, and (3) the right holder may waive – or not waive – the obligation to provide compensation after a breach of rights.[64] Whilst some will theorists have focused on, for example, ideas of supremacy,[65] the 'chief desideratum' for a Hartian will theorist is control.[66]

Over time, theorists started to emphasise the choice element of the will theory, whether or not specifically related to Hart's measures of control.[67] The new formulation of the will theory became that 'rights protect choices' and only those able to choose in a morally and legally significant manner could be recognised as rights holders.[68] Therefore, those unable to choose meaningfully could not have rights,[69] unless it was accepted that a proxy could choose instead.[70] A more recent account of the will theory reconciles the elements of control and choice to offer a view on children's rights that is both true to Hartian roots and (presumably) workable in practice.[71] According to Ross, a distinction should be made between power and choice under the will theory whereby:

> choices implied by a right, namely the choice to enforce a right, waive it or leave it unenforced, are surely only incidental to the possession of a right rather than constitutive of it . . .[72] the idea of a right is . . . definitionally

62 J. Raz, *The Morality of Freedom*. Oxford: Clarendon Press, 1986, 180.
63 Hart (1973), 171–201.
64 Ibid., 193.
65 See C. Wellman, *Real Rights*. New York: OUP, 1995, 7, 8.
66 M.H. Kramer, Some Doubts about Alternatives to the Interest Theory of Rights. (2013) 123(2) *Ethics* 245, 248.
67 Hart himself noted that 'in [certain] types of cases one who has a right has a choice respected by the law': in H. Ross, Children's Rights and Theories of Rights. (2013) 21(4) *International Journal of Children's Rights* 679, 682.
68 E.g. J. Griffin, 'Do Children have Rights?', in Archard and Macleod (2002), 21, 28; Tobin (2013), 402; Cowden (2016), 34.
69 Ibid.; H. Steiner, 'Working Rights', in Kramer et al. (1998), 261.
70 H.L.A. Hart, 'Legal Rights', in H.L.A. Hart, *Essays on Bentham, Studies in Jurisprudence and Political Theory*. Oxford: Clarendon Press, 1982, 184.
71 H. Ross, Children's Rights – a Defence of Hartian Will Theory. (2014) 22 *International Journal of Children's Rights* 43.
72 Ibid., 48.

> dependent upon the notion of power, but not on the notion of attendant choices that rights confer . . . rights are [thus] looked upon as being *primarily* empowering but at the same time conferring what . . . are merely *ancillary* choices.[73]

Hence, power (which is linked to control, though perhaps not entirely the same) is constitutive of rights, meaning that rights are granted where a person is empowered through the law. Choices attach to this core of power, but they are only ancillary and more concerned with the exercise of rights.[74] Whilst the exact status of choice has thus become somewhat uncertain, power, control and choice remain important to the will theory.

(2) The interest theory

The interest theory has been attributed to Jeremy Bentham who held that legal rights are based on interests or benefits to a person, since '[o]n what occasion soever the law does anything in favour of any person, it thereby conferrs [*sic*] on that person a right'.[75] A fuller account of the interest theory as such, and particularly within the context of children's rights,[76] has since been provided by MacCormick. Under the interest theory:

> what is essential to the constitution of a right is the legal (or moral) protection or promotion of one's interests as against some other person or the world at large.[77]

The interests should be determined by someone who knows what is good for the prospective rights holder, so that issues of competence do not come into play.[78]

Modern interest theorists like Kramer have argued that not simply every interest grounds a right; there must be some form of recognition of the interest in the legal system (e.g. through laws).[79] Moreover, theorists like Raz have advocated a collective approach to the interest theory. Under Raz' version of the theory, not every right is based on the overall interests of a particular person, but can be

73 Ibid., 62.

74 Ibid., 48, 62.

75 J. Bentham, 'Of the Limits of the Penal Branch of Jurisprudence', in P. Schofield (ed.), *Of the Limits of the Penal Branch of Jurisprudence (The Collected Works of Jeremy Bentham)*. Oxford: OUP, 2010, 207.

76 N. MacCormick, 'Children's Rights: A Test-Case for Theories of Rights', in N. MacCormick (ed.), *Legal Right and Social Democracy: Essays in Legal and Political Philosophy*. Oxford: OUP, 1984.

77 D.N. MacCormick, 'Rights in Legislation', in P.M.S. Hacker and J. Raz (eds), *Law, Morality, and Society: Essays in Honour of H.L.A. Hart*. Oxford: Clarendon Press, 1977, 192, quoted in Ross (2013), 684.

78 MacCormick (1984), 156.

79 M.H. Kramer, Refining the Interest Theory of Rights. (2010) 55 *American Journal of Jurisprudence* 31, 32, 33. See also Kramer (2013), 247.

linked to a broader (group) characteristic of that person.[80] In the specific case of children, for example, Hunt Federle has suggested that 'rights flow downhill', so that the characteristic of powerlessness grounds rights.[81] On the other end of the spectrum, Ferguson has equated the relevant interests with 'the [best] interests of the child', which is a purely individual determination of interests.[82] That interpretation is probably closer to traditional conceptions of the interest theory, which required rights to promote one's interests or confer a benefit on a particular person. The particulars of the interest theory are thus still under debate, but the element of interests remains central to it.

(3) Children's rights to freedom of religion and manifestation

Both interest and will theorists have argued that the other theory withholds equal rights from children. The interest theory because it allows adults to formulate interests underlying children's rights in such a paternalistic manner that the rights founded on them become inherently limited.[83] The choice theory because its traditional emphasis on agency prevents young children from having rights altogether and only allows children to gain rights as they gain the necessary competence for control or choice.[84] Translating this to PCRMs, the interest theory could encapsulate PCRMs in the child's own right to freedom of religion as serving the child's interests, whereas the will theory could sanction PCRMs as a result of children not yet having gained the competence for choice or control necessary for a right to freedom of manifestation.

The suggested inability of the will theory to account for (young)[85] children's rights to freedom of manifestation poses a real challenge to equal religious rights for parents and children.[86] However, not every will theorist would consider this a challenge that needs to be met. Some believe that infants simply cannot have rights.[87] These theorists suggest that attempts to pre-empt children's incompetence lead to adults deciding for children, and they object to characterising as 'rights' of children what are really the wishes of adults.[88] Others have tried to address the challenge by relying on proxy-mechanisms. Hart, for example, initially argued that babies could not have rights as they lacked the power of control over duties.[89] He later changed his opinion to hold

80 Raz (1986), 180.

81 K. Hunt Federle, Do Rights Still Flow Downhill? (2017) 25 *International Journal of Children's Rights* 273, 281, 282.

82 Ferguson (2014), 66.

83 Steiner (1998), 261.

84 Kramer (1998), 69.

85 Just how 'young' is a matter of debate for religious freedom competence. See also 3.3 below.

86 Langlaude (2007), 43.

87 See Steiner (1998), 261; Griffin (2002), 21, 28. Griffin's argument runs via personhood and agency, with similar results.

88 Ibid.

89 H.L.A. Hart, Are there any Natural Rights? (1955) 64(2) *Philosophical Review* 175, 181.

that young children do have rights, though they must rely on others (normally parents) to exercise control over underlying claims until they reach the competence to do so themselves.[90] Since the proxy is limited to actions the child could take if competent, and no explicit transfer of power is necessary when the child becomes competent, the right is contended to properly belong to the child and not the proxy.[91]

The proxy-system has received sharp criticism, especially from interest theorists who claim that a right is not a full right when exercised by others.[92] That critique is a little unfair, because under the interest theory adults normally decide on the interests that underpin children's rights and one could say that a proxy exercise takes place *before* the right is identified. At the same time, it is difficult to see how especially religious rights or claims can be exercised or controlled by others than the right holder themselves.[93] Since one cannot have personal convictions for another person, it is impossible to say that the right to freedom of manifestation can be exercised by others. The ECtHR has highlighted the issue in a case concerned with parents 'exercising' their children's religious rights. It found that:

> the applicant parents also filed their complaints on behalf of the applicant children. Therefore, it cannot be formally said that the applicant parents are seeking to impose their religious convictions against their children's will. Nevertheless . . . the applicant children were unable to foresee the consequences of their parents' decision . . . because of their young age.[94]

The court thus hints at it being unwarranted to say that parents can function as a proxy where children cannot yet choose meaningfully in respect of freedom of manifestation. In addition, parents who claim to do so can be seen as imposing their own religion, and this is negatively regarded by the court.

The interest theory is often considered a superior theory in the area of children's rights.[95] Based on the fact that it is enough for children to have interests for them to have rights, the emergence of children's rights and appreciation of interest theories have been able to reinforce each other. From a child-centred perspective, this is because it is believed that (young) children can only have rights under the interest theory of rights.[96] Hence, to be able to

90 Hart (1982), 184.
91 Ibid.; Ross (2013), 697–703.
92 T.D. Campbell, The Rights of the Minor: As Person, as Child, as Juvenile, as Future Adult. (1992) 6(1) *International Journal of Law, Policy and the Family* 1, 4. See also Langlaude (2007), 42.
93 E. Lester, Religious Autonomy and World Religious Education. (2004a) 31(2) *Religion and Education* 62, 63.
94 *Konrad v Germany* (dec), no. 35504/03 (2006) ECtHR ECHR 2006-XIII, at [6, 7].
95 Tobin (2013), 403.
96 W. van den Burg, 'Rechten van kinderen: enkele filosofische kanttekeningen', in C. van Nijnatten (ed.), *Kinderrechten in discussie*. Amsterdam: Boom, 1993, 69, 70.

recognise that *all* children have rights, one would have to adopt the interest theory.[97] Vice versa, the actual recognition of children's rights has reinforced acceptance of a theory that can encompass these rights.[98] In his influential essay, 'Children's Rights: A Test-Case for Theories of Rights', MacCormick states the interest theory's case. He rejects the will theory, deemed unable to account for children's rights given young children's incapacity, in favour of the interest theory of rights, able to embrace the rights of children based on interests determined by adults.[99] Although concerned with children, MacCormick's essay also highlights an adult-centred perspective on the convergence between children's rights and the interest theory. Despite arguments increasingly being made for children's inclusion in the determination of their interests,[100] the interest theory relies heavily on adult determinations of interests because 'children are not always, or even usually the best judges of what is good for them'.[101] Hence, if adults are unwilling to cede control over religious manifestation (including where they honestly think it is not good for children to have freedom), they can make religious rights inherently restricted through interest-determinations that emphasise parental control as beneficial to children.[102] Whilst this encourages a wide embrace of children's rights – including by those who would not fathom allowing children to make their own religious choices,[103] a child can 'end up having a "right" to an outcome she does not want'.[104] PCRM's are then not only justified, but made part of the child's own religious rights.

The interest theory, however, *has* to identify paternalistic interests if it wants to be able to recognise religious rights for younger children. This is because one cannot possibly have an interest in something that one cannot on any account realise.[105] Consequently, children cannot have rights based on interests for which a certain level of capacity is required that these children do not yet have.[106] Unless paternalistic interests are identified, religious 'freedom' rights are restricted to the

97 S. Brennan, 'Children's Choices or Children's Interests: Which do their Rights Protect?', in Archard and Macleod (2002), 58.
98 Tobin (2013), 403; Ross (2014), 680.
99 MacCormick (1984), 154–6, 166.
100 E.g. M.D.A. Freeman, Culture, Childhood and Rights. (2011a) 5 *The Family in Law* 15, 28, 33; Tobin (2013), 414–16.
101 MacCormick (1984), 156. See also Langlaude (2007), 45
102 See Langlaude (2007), 53–62 on young children's rights as non-interference by the State. See also P. Alderson, *Young Children's Rights: Exploring Beliefs, Principles and Practice* (2nd ed.). London: Jessica Kingsley Publishers, 2008, 103.
103 D.M. Smolin, Overcoming Religious Objections to the Convention on the Rights of the Child. (2006) 20 *Emory International Law Review* 81, 95–7.
104 Ferguson (2014), 66. See also *Re W (Contact: Joining Child as Party)* [2003] 1 FLR 681, at [16] 'The child has a right to a relationship with his father even if he does not want it.'
105 D.W. Archard, *Children, Family and the State*. Aldershot: Ashgate, 2003, 11, 12; M. Cowden, Capacity, Claims and Children's Rights. (2012) 1(4) *Contemporary Political Theory* 362, 373.
106 Cowden (2012), 373, elaborated on in Cowden (2016), chapters 5 and 6.

same extent as under the will theory, because freedom implies autonomy.[107] Some interest theorists have therefore argued that the interest theory cannot lay claim to religious rights for children.[108] Others instead criticise the insistence on autonomy considerations.[109] Langlaude, for example, argues for a 'carefully crafted right to religious freedom . . . that does not carry the usual assumptions made by children's rights authors on the capacity and autonomy of the child', but instead focuses on wider interests.[110] Yet there are three problems with Langlaude's argument. First, it can lead to the counter-intuitive result of a child being forced to manifest the parental religion as part of that child's freedom of manifestation. Authors like Eekelaar have warned against ascribing rights (interests) to incompetent children, because it is dangerous to unilaterally determine outcomes for people 'under the guise of protecting their rights'.[111] Second, the identification of paternalistic interests for children but autonomy for adults means that at some undefined point the right changes of direction from a situation in which parents can impose paternalistic interests (an inward direction) to a situation where the child now has autonomy (an outward direction).[112] This would suggest that we are concerned with two distinct human beings, as if there was no continuing line from childhood into adulthood, and the fundamental rights of children were fundamentally different from those of adults.[113] Finally, whilst Langlaude claims that autonomy plays no role under her theory, she ultimately concludes that the child's right to freedom of religion is 'based on the interest of the child to be unhindered in their growth as an independent autonomous actor'.[114]

The idea that an interest in autonomy should underpin the right to freedom of manifestation corresponds not only with what most interest theorists would argue, it is equally more congruent with how the right is effectively regarded at the international level. The ECHR judgment referenced above clearly indicates that 'children's will', or autonomous choice forms the core of the right to freedom of manifestation.[115] The emphasis on autonomy and self-determination is also apparent from some of the other documents referenced above.[116] A different interpretation of freedom of manifestation – one that emphasises paternalistic interests – flies in the face of the right's functioning. Religious rights

107 J. Eekelaar, The Emergence of Children's Rights. (1986) 6(2) *Oxford Journal of Legal Studies* 161, 170, 171.

108 E.g. Brighouse (2002), 50, 52.

109 Langlaude (2007), 45, 46; S. Langlaude, Children and Religion under Article 14 CRC: A Critical Analysis. (2008) 16 *International Journal of Children's Rights* 475, 479.

110 Ibid., 45.

111 Eekelaar (2002a), 185; 186. See also Campbell (1992), 6: paternalistic coercion with an appeal to rights is a 'dubious practice'.

112 See on the changed focus Van den Burg (1993), 69, 70.

113 Which, indeed, some authors suggest, e.g. Brennan (2002), 67.

114 Langlaude (2007), 61.

115 *Konrad v Germany* (dec), no. 35504/03 (2006) ECtHR ECHR 2006-XIII, at [6, 7].

116 See also for a CRC overview (and critique of the CmRC's emphasis on autonomy): Langlaude (2008), esp. 493.

are often invoked to perform or omit actions generally considered contrary to a person's or humankind's welfare interests (e.g. refusal of medical treatment or limiting education).[117] This is not to say that paternalistic interests should never take precedence over religious rights (further explained in Chapter 4), but that such interests are not constitutive of the right to freedom of manifestation. The CmRC clearly recognised this when it warned against paternalistic interests impeding on children's religious rights, which by logical extension were thus not themselves based on paternalistic determinations.[118]

The result of the above is that both the interest and will theory face issues regarding children's capacity related to freedom of manifestation. The will theory because of direct reliance on control or choice, and the interest theory because of the interest in autonomous choice. This means that either young children cannot have religious rights under either theory, or that both theories should find a suitable solution. One way to solve the issue is by arguing that infants do not in fact lack capacity to make decisions and take control, and that the problem is rather with adults refusing to acknowledge and value their message-conveying.[119] There is indeed research to suggest that even premature babies co-design their lives together with their carers, and that participation rights are therefore relevant to them.[120] Moreover, some people and religions see infants as naturally spiritual with the capacity for religious belief.[121] However, whilst children are in many respects more competent than adults generally admit, it would probably take a proverbial leap of faith to hold that very young children are competent regarding freedom of manifestation. It is certainly no leap that will or interest theorists have hitherto endeavoured to take.

The second solution is to adopt a more collective or general approach to a theory of rights. This is what theorists such as Raz (interest theory) and Ross (will theory) have done. Raz has argued that an interest (e.g. autonomous religious choice) can be ascribed to all nationals of a Nation State to ground a right (e.g. freedom of manifestation), even if there is no individual benefit for a particular person (e.g. a young child).[122] In a rather similar vein, Ross has argued that young children can be generally empowered, so as to ground rights under the will theory, irrespective of whether a child is able to exercise ancillary choices with respect to waiving and

117 E.g. respectively *Jehovah's Witnesses of Moscow and Others v Russia*, no. 302/02 (10 June 2010) ECtHR; *Martins Casimiro and Cerveira Ferreira v Luxembourg*, no. 44888/98 (27 April 1999) ECtHR.

118 CmRC (2006), General Comment 7, para 17.

119 J. Bridgeman, *Parental Responsibility, Young Children and Healthcare Law*. Cambridge: CUP, 2007, 10; J. Le Gal, *Les droits et libertés de l'enfant dans les institutions éducatives de la petite enfance 2003–2007*. Nantes: CFEJE de Nantes, 2009, 2, 10.

120 E.g. P. Alderson et al., 'Are Premature Babies Citizens with Rights? Provision Rights and the Edges of Citizenship', in A. Invernizzi and B. Milne (eds), *Children's Citizenship: An Emergent Discourse on the Rights of the Child*. Delhi: Krepublishers, 2011.

121 E.g. L.J. Miller *The Spiritual Child: The New Science on Parenting for Health and Lifelong Thriving*. New York, St Martin's Press, 2015, 3.

122 Raz (1986), 180.

enforcing claims.[123] Ross' approach is not collective per se, but it is of a level of generality that makes it unnecessary to consider whether a child is competent or not for the recognition of rights. Whilst perhaps not what Bentham and Hart respectively had in mind for the interest and will theory, these more general approaches overcome the hurdle of children's rights, whilst remaining true to the idea that freedom of manifestation is based on autonomous choice.

The final solution rests on a capacity construct, such as that proposed by Cowden. Whilst writing from an interest perspective, Cowden's propositions are equally relevant for the will theory, as they address capacity and competence more generally. Cowden proposes a stacked approach that distinguishes between capacity, competence and ableness. Capacity refers to the child having the internal features and skill set to potentially do a certain thing (an in principle ability).[124] Competence is the successful and intentional exercise of that capacity, i.e. the actual ability to do something.[125] Ableness refers to external conditions that allow the child to effectively exercise their competence, such as resources and opportunity.[126] In respect of children who have not yet reached the capacity required for certain rights, Cowden suggests that reliance can be placed on the concept of 'latent capacity', which is a 'pre-existing capacity that requires development or enhancement *in the agent* to become a capacity proper'.[127] Since this latent capacity is internal to the child and requires development only within the child, it can be seen as a pre-stage of capacity sufficient for the holding of rights like freedom of manifestation that normally require capacity proper. Cowden links her theoretical argument with Article 5 CRC, which references the child's 'evolving' capacities.[128] Latent capacity is thus a normative, rather than actual, capacity. It is the promise of capacity, not capacity itself. To ground a right on latent capacity implies using a construct, but constructs are not uncommon to the law. There is no reason why we would accept them in other areas,[129] but not for such a fundamental issue as children's rights. Relying on a construct or a general approach to theories of rights thus allows both will and interest theorists to embrace religious rights for children, whilst remaining true to the idea that such rights are based on self-determination and empowerment, whether expressed in terms of autonomy or control. That does, however, not mean that competence now no longer plays a role. Even if we accept that young children can have rights, the question remains when we regard children as effectively competent to exercise control or have an actual interest in religious autonomy – and what should be done with their rights whilst children are still incompetent.

123 Ross (2014), 62.
124 Cowden (2016), 42, 46.
125 Ibid., 43, 46.
126 Ibid., 45, 46.
127 Ibid., 48 (emphasis original).
128 Ibid., 50.
129 See e.g. J. Ritter and A. Mayer, Regulating Data as Property: A New Construct for Moving Forward. (2018) 16(1) *Duke Law and Technology Review* 220.

3.3 Children's competence and parental agency

Identified as an autonomy-based right, the *exercise* of the right to freedom of manifestation is commonly expressed in the form of a choice: the choice whether and how to participate, or not participate, in a religious manifestation. This would include the choice to reject PCRMs as a matter of right. Yet a number of authors have argued that children lack the competence necessary for meaningful religious choice and should consequently not be regarded as capable of relying on religious rights.[130] This raises the further issue of whether it is possible and desirable for parents to exercise religious choice for an incompetent child (parental agency).

The area of children's competence is a confusing area of law in which different terms (capacity, ability, maturity, etc.) are used interchangeably and often remain ill-defined.[131] Using Cowden's staged approach, the relevant consideration we are here concerned with is competence: the actual ability to do something i.e. the exercise of capacity, unconstrained by external conditions or ableness.[132] To be competent in respect of freedom of manifestation is to have the actual ability to choose in relation to religious manifestations, including by rejecting PCRMs. Academics do nonetheless not generally accept that the simple fact of being capable to make a choice is enough for competence. Special requirements qualify what counts as relevant choosing.[133] Simply being able to communicate a preference for a certain act or inaction is not sufficient to hold that a child possess competence with regard to freedom of manifestation.[134] Yet the bar for what counts as competent choosing is often set unreasonably high. Children must not only be able to state a choice, they must be able to reflect on underlying values, understand the consequences of their actions for themselves, others and society as a whole, they must predict outcomes and then be able to choose either wisely or rationally (preferably they should choose what adults consider serves their interests), or on the basis of a coherent value system.[135] In short, they must be able to overcome the highest level of incompetence identified by Beauchamp and Childress:

- i The inability to evidence a preference or choice;
- ii The inability to understand one's situation or relevantly similar situations;
- iii The inability to understand disclosed information;
- iv The inability to give a reason;
- v The inability to give a rational reason;

130 E.g. Griffin (2002); R. Noggle, 'Special Agents: Children's Autonomy and Parental Authority', in Archard and Macleod (2002).

131 E. Kay and M. Tisdall, Challenging Competency and Capacity? Due Weight to Children's Views in Family Law Proceedings. (2018) 26 *International Journal of Children's Rights* 159, 162–66.

132 Cowden (2016), 42–6.

133 E.g. Brennan (2002), 59; Eekelaar (2002a), 186, 187; Griffin (2002), 21; Noggle (2002), 101.

134 Brennan (2002), 59.

135 See n. 133, esp. Noggle. Eekelaar is more realistic on what should count as choosing.

vi The inability to give reasons where risk and benefit have been weighed;
vii The inability to reach a reasonable decision, as judged, for example, by a reasonable person standard.[136]

The requirements placed on children appear more concerned with ideal, rather than relevant (or realistic) choice. They go well beyond usual requirements for rights-related competence, especially keeping in mind that competence in respect of human rights does not equal a *carte blanche* for the unconstrained and full exercise of those rights. This is even apart from the fact that many religion and faith-related choices do not readily fit the mould of liberal conceptions of rationality, but are nonetheless, or perhaps especially for that reason, protected by religious rights.

If we were to require children to make ideal choices in order to be considered competent, we would be asking far more of children than we do of adults. For example, we would normally require an adult to have some stated convictions before they can invoke a right to positively manifest a religion,[137] yet in respect of imposed manifestations it is generally sufficient that the adult does not want them and there is no need to rely on convictions which specifically reject the relevant manifestation.[138] The fact that a child, as the case may be, is too immature to understand that the relevant choice has harmful consequences (an understanding many adults lack as well), or does not act on a fully coherent set of values (which many adults may not either), may be relevant in respect of limitations on the right to freedom of manifestation, but should not necessarily lead to the conclusion that a child is incompetent.

There are two more arguments that have been made in respect of children which influence the discussion of their competence. First, Freeman has argued that current conceptions of competence focus too much on objective wisdom, whilst disregarding children's 'experiential knowledge',[139] or knowledge (and competence) obtained through lived experience and familiarity with a subject.[140] For example, a child growing up in a family where a religion is manifested daily may not be able to base religious choices on objective wisdom, but could still be competent because the lived experience gave the child an understanding necessary to make a relevant choice. Secondly, authors such as

136 T. Beauchamp and J. Childress, *Principles of Biomedical Ethics*. Oxford: OUP, 2001, cited in M. Freeman, Why it Remains Important to Take Children's Rights Seriously. (2007) 15 *International Journal of Children's Rights* 5, 12.

137 E.g. a level of 'cogency, seriousness, cohesion and importance': *Eweida and Others v United Kingdom*, nos. 48420/10, 59842/10, 51671/10 and 36516/10 (2013) ECtHR, ECHR 2013, para 81.

138 E.g. *Buscarini and Others v San Marino*, no. 24645/94 (18 February 1999) ECtHR (Grand Chamber).

139 Freeman (2007), 13.

140 Kay and Tisdall (2018), 176. See also P. Alderson and M. Goodwin, Contradictions within Concepts of Children's Competence. (1993) 1(3) *International Journal of Children's Rights* 303, esp. 303–6; J. Piaget, Intellectual Evolution from Adolescence to Adulthood. Translated by J. Bliss and H. Furth. (2008) 58 *Human Development*, 40, 45, 46.

Peleg have emphasised the importance of development in respect of children's rights.[141] Competence requirements can cause a vicious circle: if children are barred from accessing and exercising their rights until they have reached a high level of competence, they also do not get the practice that is needed for them to develop such higher levels, so that ultimately they are unlikely to ever reach the high level of competence needed for access to their rights. The development and experiential knowledge arguments thereby reinforce each other: the practice advocated for under the development argument will lead to new levels of experiential knowledge that enhance competence.

It may be accepted that competence to choose requires more than simply stating a preference. Some level of understanding is essential, but not to the extent of a perfectly reasoned choice. The child must also be able to communicate the choice in some manner.[142] A useful definition of children's competence in respect of freedom of manifestation then becomes:

> A child is competent if (s)he can communicate a choice of which (s)he understands the subject.
>
> Therefore, children are competent with regard to freedom of manifestation if they are able to communicate a choice with regard to an activity (or omission thereof) which they understand is an aspect of religion or belief or a ritual.

Within the context of freedom of manifestation, this implies that children have some underlying desires or convictions, although these need not be more extensive than those required of adults. A feeling of morality can e.g. be sufficient.

This raises the question of when children reach such competence. Traditionally, the age at which children under different (mostly Western) religions were considered able to make their own religious choices has been around 7 or 8.[143] However, this age was based on a maturity stretching beyond that required for competence for freedom of manifestation: it was, and sometimes is, considered an age at which children would have the understanding to make a life-long commitment to a certain faith. Competence for freedom of manifestation arises earlier, although how early is a matter of debate.

In providing guidance on the development of religious competence, theorists have traditionally tended to place much reliance on Piagetian stage theories,[144]

141 N. Peleg, Reconceptualising the Child's Right to Development: Children and the Capability Approach. (2013) 21 *International Journal of Children's Rights* 523. See also Noggle (2002), 97, 105; Cowden (2016), 43, 46.

142 Cowden (2016), 63.

143 Group for the Advancement of Psychiatry, *How Old is Old Enough? The Ages of Rights and Responsibilities*. New York: Brunner/Mazel, 1989, 8, 9.

144 Important religion-related stage theories have been developed by Piaget, Kohlberg, Elkind, Erikson, Oser, Goldman and Fowler. See L.L. Barnes et al., Spirituality, Religion and Pediatrics: Intersecting Worlds of Healing. (2000) 104(6) *Pediatrics* 899, 900; R.W. Hood Jr. et al., *The Psychology of Religion: An Emperical Approach* (4th ed.). New York: Guilford Press, 2009, 77 ff.

despite aspects of such theories having been criticised.[145] Stage theories offer support for the idea that around 7 children come of age (without reaching genuine autonomy until adolescence), yet that religion can also be important to younger children. Children over the age of 2, for example, start to learn about religion and between the ages of 3 to 7 can obtain something akin to experiential knowledge.[146] By around the age of 4 to 5, children also start to distinguish between religious rules and manifestations belonging to the moral domain, and those that belong to the conventional domain, seeing the former as imperative, but not the latter.[147] They thus start to have convictions in respect of religion and manifestation.[148]

The early religious understanding of children is equally supported by more specific research that does not rest on stage theories. On the basis of research projects conducted in the Americas, Europe, Africa and Middle East, Coles has suggested that even young children (participants were aged 6–13) can have a deep understanding of religion and its manifestations.[149] More recent research has found that children aged 4–6 have an opinion on the effectiveness of religious rituals of their own and other religions.[150] Whereas young children were more likely to see rituals as functional rather than symbolic, they understood what the rituals were, and the religious purpose they served.[151] Children have been found to not only have an understanding of religious manifestation itself, but equally of the right to freedom of religion proper. In research with Canadian minors, Helwig found that the majority of participating 6-year-olds affirmed children's fundamental rights and judged 'restrictions on . . . religion [prayer] as wrong and outside the scope of governmental, school, and familial authority in both Canada and other countries'.[152] What is more, children's judgements in this respect 'were largely justified by general appeals to personal choice'.[153] It should nonetheless be kept in mind that much of the research related to religious competence is conducted in North America and may not be globally representative. Despite this limitation and the fact that the goal is not to pinpoint a specific set age at which children reach competence with regard to freedom of manifestation, it is possible

145 E.g. J. Fortin, *Children's Rights and the Developing Law* (3rd ed.). Cambridge: CUP, 2009, 83.

146 See n. 144.

147 L.P. Nucci, *Education in the Moral Domain.* New York: CUP, 2001, chapter 2, esp. 21; C.C. Helwig and E. Turiel, 'Children's Social and Moral Reasoning', in P.K. Smith and C.H. Hart (eds), *The Wiley-Blackwell Handbook of Childhood Social Development* (2nd ed.). Chichester: Wiley-Blackwell, 2011, 569–76.

148 See also L. Heiphetz et al., The Development of Reasoning about Beliefs: Fact, Preference and Ideology. (2013) 49 *Journal of Experimental Social Psychology* 559, 564: from age 5 upwards, children differentiate between religious and fact- or preference-based beliefs similar to adults.

149 R. Coles, *The Spiritual Life of Children.* Boston, MA: Houghton Mifflin, 1990, 19, 36.

150 A 2006 study described in R.A. Richert and P Granqvist, 'Religious and Spiritual Development in Childhood', in R.F. Paloutzian and C.L. Park (eds), *Handbook of the Psychology of Religion and Spirituality* (2nd ed.). New York: Guilford Press, 2015, 169.

151 Ibid.

152 C.C. Helwig, The Role of Agent and Social Context in Judgments of Freedom of Speech and Religion. (1997) 68(3) *Child Development* 484, p. 492.

153 Ibid., 492.

to infer that children probably reach competence in pre-school years, possibly around age 4–6. This is likely much earlier than most people would expect – or would feel comfortable to admit.[154] Yet it must be stressed that, for some while after reaching competence, it may still be justified to limit a child's right to freedom of manifestation, as further explained in the next chapter.

Even if competence arises at a young age, there is still some time during which a child is incompetent in respect of freedom of manifestation. Moreover, for a period of time after reaching competence, it may be justified to restrict the rights-exercise of children. What should be 'done' with children's rights during that time is a matter of disagreement between those favouring ideas of parental agency and those preferring notions of 'rights-in-trust'.

Under parental agency or 'stewardship', the parent serves as a proxy exercising the child's right on the child's behalf for as long as the child cannot exercise the right themselves.[155] The parent is traditionally required to act as if they were in a fiduciary relationship with the child, meaning that they must exercise rights for their children in ways they see as serving their children's interests.[156] The classic approach, which effectively works as the will theory's proxy system, has received much critique for its failure to check parental power and the absence of consideration of the child.[157] More recent accounts of agency are based on substituted judgement or hypothetical consent. The exercise of rights is still performed by parents on behalf of the child, but decisions are now based on what the future (or current)[158] child would have decided.[159] Yet, given that this future person is unknown and may be conditioned, substituted judgement must ultimately rely on some standard of the reasonable person.[160] Unless the parental choice is unreasonable, this again means that the choice (e.g. to manifest) can be imposed on an objecting, but incompetent child as an exercise of that child's right.

The alternative of 'rights-in-trust' aims to overcome the difficulties associated with parental agency by rejecting the idea that the rights of incompetent children need to be exercised at all.[161] Rights-in-trust are rights which, for as

154 See Peleg (2013), 533, 534.

155 J. Locke, *Second Treatise of Government.* London: Awnsham Churchill, 1689, para 56; B. Bennett Woodhouse and K.A. Johnson, 'The United Nations Convention on the Rights of the Child: Empowering Parents to Protect their Children's Rights', in M. Albertson Fineman and Worthington (eds), *What is Right for Children? The Competing Paradigms of Religion and Human Rights.* Farnham: Ashgate, 2009, 10.

156 Ibid.; E.S. Scott and R.E. Scott, Parents as Fiduciaries. (1995) 81(8) *Virginia Law Review* 2401.

157 M. Bryan, Parents as Fiduciaries: A Special Place in Equity. (1995) 3 *International Journal of Children's Rights* 227, 229, 230; C.E. Schneider, On the Duties and Rights of Parents. (1995) 81 *Virginia Law Review* 2477, 2480–4.

158 F. De Singly, *Comment aider l'enfant à devenir lui-même?* Paris: Armand Colin, 2009, chapter 2.

159 Eekelaar (1986), 170; M. Freeman, *The Rights and Wrongs of Children.* London: Frances Plinter, 1983, 57.

160 Freeman (1983), 57; J. Sorens, Libertarian Theory and Children's Rights. The Fiduciary Model, Rationality, Interests and the Challenge of Abortion. (2001) 61 *Philosophical Notes* 1, 4.

161 L.D. Houlgate, Three Concepts of Children's Constitutional Rights: Reflections on the Enjoyment Theory. (1999–2000) 2 *Pennsylvania Journal of Constitutional Law* 77, 80–6.

long as the child cannot exercise them him/herself, are to remain untouched.[162] The difference between rights-in-trust and agency is thus that under agency theory rights are *trusted to* parents, whereas under rights-in-trust the rights are as it were *in a trust* inaccessible to parents.

There is no requirement under rights-in-trust for parents to create a religious vacuum. Whilst the doctrine prevents parents from exercising their child's religious rights, it says nothing about the way parents should raise their children or may limit children's rights.[163] Neither is it opposed to children developing competence through practice of aspects of the right. What rights-in-trust primarily seeks to achieve is to prevent the exercise of freedom of manifestation by someone other than the right holder. As such, it prevents the curious outcome that children can be coerced into manifesting a religion as an exercise of their personal right to make autonomous religious choices. Or as the ECHR has held, where 'it would be very difficult for the applicant children to take an autonomous decision for themselves at [a young] age', this cannot justify a situation where parents 'impose their religious convictions'.[164] Consequently, incompetence per se is not enough reason for the acceptance of PCRMs.

3.4 A special place for culture?

A last objection to the full recognition of children's own right to freedom of manifestation is that such recognition clashes with 'culture'. The argument made is that culture influences the right's scope and/or the way rights should be understood and applied at a certain time or place.[165] Children's exercise of freedom of manifestation can, for example, be seen as problematic by some cultures that would more readily accept PCRMs as appropriate.[166] It is in that regard noteworthy that, whereas 'culture' is regularly invoked as a potential determinant of rights,[167] there is no one clear definition of what culture means within the human rights context.[168] Definitions in International Declarations and the literature nevertheless focus on practices and norms or values that are transmitted (often between generations) and allow for identification of, and

162 Ibid., 86.

163 Houlgate's theory is based on open futures, but these do not prevent religious upbringing per se: J. Feinberg, 'The Child's Right to an Open Future', in A. Aiken and H. LaFollette (eds), *Whose Child? Children's Rights, Parental Authority and State Power*. Totowa, NJ: Littlefield, Adams & Co., 1980, 124–53.

164 *Konrad v Germany* (dec), no. 35504/03 (2006) ECtHR ECHR 2006-XIII, at 7.

165 H. Montgomery, 'Anthropological Perspectives on Children's Rights', in M.D. Ruck et al., *Handbook of Children's Rights: Global and Multidisciplinary Perspectives*. New York: Routledge, 2017, 98.

166 Smolin (2006), 97–102.

167 P. Alston, The Best Interest Principle: Towards a Reconciliation of Culture and Human Rights. (1994) *International Journal of Law and the Family* 1, 20; Tobin (2013), 418–23.

168 CESCR, *General Comment No. 21: Right of everyone to take part in cultural life (art. 15, para 1a)*. UN Doc. E/C.12/GC/21 (21 December 2009), paras 10, 11 (General Comment 21).

with, a group.[169] The group in question can be global, like one of the seven cultural families, or local, such as a small minority within a Nation State.[170]

The elements of groups, transmission and attributed practices have prompted some reservations as to the viability of the cultural argument per se. This is because their combination presupposes a static, homogeneous and identifiable culture.[171] In reality, most cultural groups are internally diverse,[172] which means that an argument based on culture may not be more than an argument based on the dominant voices within a cultural group.[173] Generalizations about cultures can also lead to the attribution of practices or values that are not actually informed by the broader culture.[174] A resistance towards children's rights is, for example, often attributed to African culture, but the African Charter on the Rights and Welfare of the Child shows a remarkable similarity to the CRC in terms of child rights.[175] The cultural argument, moreover, tends to present culture as static, thereby preventing a culture from changing. Ordinarily, cultures are fluid and even embedded practices can change over time.[176] These arguments indicate that there are some inherent difficulties in claims based on culture, yet they do not warrant an *a priori* dismissal of the concept of culture. That would be irreconcilable with the many pronouncements, General Comments and provisions concerned with, and celebrating, culture at the international level.[177]

Human rights bodies agree that cultural practices form an important part of heritage and identity.[178] Cultural involvement has been found to be significant to children's sense of belonging.[179] The CRC, for example, highlights 'the importance of the traditions and cultural values of each people for the protection and harmonious development of the child' in its preamble. It also exhorts States to

169 E.g. UNESCO, Universal Declaration on Cultural Diversity (2 November 2001) <https://www.ohchr.org/en/professionalinterest/pages/culturaldiversity.aspx> last accessed 10 March 2019; T.S. Weisner, 'Culture, Context and Child Well-Being', in A. Ben-Arieh et al., *Handbook of Child Well-Being*. Dordrecht: Springer, 2014, 92–4; E.A. Hoebel, *The Law of Primitive Man*. Cambridge, MA: Harvard University Press, 1954, cited in B. Dababneh, Whose Role is it to Support the Child's Right to Culture in Australia? (2017) 28 *Australian Dispute Resolution Journal* 19, 21.

170 Weisner (2014), 88, 94.

171 Montgomery (2017), 107.

172 Bielefeldt (2015), Special Rapporteur's Children Report, paras 14, 77, 79(q).

173 M.D.A. Freeman, The Morality of Cultural Pluralism. (1995) 3 *International Journal of Children's Rights* 1, 10, 16 p. See also Montgomery (2017), 107.

174 See n. 172; J. Eekelaar, Children between Cultures. (2004) 18 *International Journal of Law, Policy and the Family* 178, 190.

175 Tobin (2013), 421. Contra Montgomery (2017), 109.

176 Tobin (2013), 420; Montgomery (2017), 109.

177 E.g. Articles 27 ICCPR and 30 CRC; Universal Declaration on Cultural Diversity; CESCR (2009), General Comment 21.

178 E.g. CmRC, *General Comment No. 17 (2013) on the right of the child to rest, leisure, play, recreational activities, cultural life and the arts*. UN Doc. CRC/C/GC/17 (17 April 2013), III (General Comment 17).

179 Ibid.

teach children respect for their cultural identity as part of the aims of education (Article 29 CRC). A number of international provisions further require that States do not deny the right to individuals to practice their culture.[180] Whilst these particular rights are personal rights and do not give any entitlements to cultures as such,[181] international law clearly recognises the relevance of culture within the context of rights.

Yet what is promoted is cultural pluralism or sensitivity, not cultural relativism or a cultural defence.[182] Pluralism and sensitivity require the valuing of diversity and respect for culture, but do not prioritise culture over human rights.[183] Rather, they tend to operate under the umbrella of human rights. Thereunder, pluralism and sensitivity can have some influence on the exercise of rights in practice, but this cannot result in substantial limitations on rights.[184] By contrast, cultural relativism regards human rights as simply another set of values that cannot take priority over cultural values.[185] Relativism allows for a cultural defence: human rights that are incompatible with values and practices sanctioned by a certain culture need not be adhered to.[186] It does not matter whether the cultural practices are harmful or not (in any case, the particular culture is likely to have a different perception of what harmful means), as long as the practices correspond with dominant cultural understandings.[187]

With the right not to be coerced at the heart of freedom of manifestation, arguments that seek to justify PCRMs by appealing to culture over the child's right must necessarily be rooted in cultural relativism. However, such relativism hasbeen rejected by human rights bodies in favour of sensitivity and pluralism within a human rights framework. The CmRC has, for example, stated that:

> Although [the] preservation of religious and cultural values and traditions as part of the identity of the child must be taken into consideration, practices that are inconsistent or incompatible with the rights established in the Convention are not in the child's best interests. Cultural identity cannot excuse or justify the perpetuation by decision-makers and authorities of traditions and cultural values that deny the child or children the rights guaranteed by the Convention.[188]

180 E.g. Articles 15 CESCR, 27 ICCPR and 30 CRC. See also the *European Framework Convention for the Protection of National Minorities*, ETS 157 (1 February 1998).

181 HRC, *General Comment No. 23: Article 27 (Rights of Minorities)*. UN Doc. CCPR/C/21/Rev.1/Add.5 (8 April 1994), para 3.1.

182 Tobin (2013), 419.

183 Ibid.; Freeman (1995), 7, 16 (Freeman (2011a) presents an updated version of this article).

184 Alston (1994), 19, 20; Tobin (2013), 422; Weisner (2014), 88.

185 Freeman (1995), 8, 9; Freeman (2011a), 17.

186 Tobin (2013), 419.

187 Freeman (1995), 16; Montgomery (2017), 107.

188 CmRC, *General Comment No. 14 (2013) on the right of the child to have his or her best interests taken as a primary consideration (Art. 3, para 1)*. UN Doc. CRC/C/GC/14 (29 May 2013), para 7 (General Comment 14).

The UN General Assembly, Human Rights Committee and Special Rapporteur on Freedom of Religion have equally urged States to promote cultural diversity, whilst simultaneously guaranteeing freedom of religion for children.[189] Yet the clearest expression of the international approach can probably be found in the CESCR's General Comment on the right to take part in cultural life. The document sets out all the negative and positive obligations States have to respect, protect and preserve a plurality of cultural traditions, heritage and identity, but states without reservation that 'no one may invoke cultural diversity to infringe upon human rights recognised by international law, nor to limit their scope'.[190] Like the role of parents discussed in Chapter 2, culture plays an internationally well-recognised role in the context of children's rights to freedom of manifestation. Yet like parental rights, it cannot alter or override the independent rights of the child.

Based on the above discussion, children thus hold a personal right to freedom of manifestation that is autonomy-based and not different in scope or nature from the personal religious rights of adults, or altered by culture. They reach competence with regard to this right at a relatively young age, though that does not mean that unlimited exercise follows and PCRMs are prohibited from age 5. Whilst coerced manifestation constitutes an interference with children's rights, such interference does not automatically equate to a breach or violation of rights as further explained in the next chapter.

189 See respectively, UN GA, *Resolution 67/179 on Freedom of Religion or Belief.* UN Doc. A/RES/67/179 (3 April 2013), preamble; paras 8 and 13; HRC (1989), General Comment 17, para 3; Bielefeldt (2015), Special Rapporteur's Children Report, paras 2, 67, 77.

190 CESCR (2001), General Comment 21, para 18.

4 Coerced manifestations as limitations on rights

The previous two chapters have explained that, whilst international law recognises the parental role in upbringing and gives parents a prior right to the State to choose children's education, it does not give parents a parental right to impose parentally coerced religious manifestations (PCRMs) (Chapter 2). Furthermore, there is no substantial difference between the personal rights to freedom of manifestation of parents (adults) and children; both have autonomy at their core (Chapter 3). This means that international law cannot sanction PCRMs as part of human rights. By their very coercive nature, PCRMs form an interference with children's rights to freedom of religion and manifestation. However, an interference does not automatically lead to a breach of human rights. There may be legitimate reasons for parents to interfere with a child's right, e.g. because its unfettered exercise could be dangerous to the child or undermine important competing interests the child has.[1] Giving primacy to children's rights 'does not mean . . . divesting parents of their responsibilities'.[2] Though it does mean that PCRMs must be formulated as *limitations on* children's rights, rather than as *part of* the rights of parents or children.

The right to freedom of conscience and thought, parental rights in education and the right not to be coerced in religion do not allow for limitations.[3] These rights are closely linked with indoctrination, which is prohibited, whether conducted by the State or a parent.[4] By contrast, the right to freedom of manifestation is subject to certain limitations, such as those related to health, public order and the rights and freedoms of others. These limitations apply equally to everyone, but in the case of children may contain particular content derived from the child's minority. This chapter discusses how especially the limitation ground of public order can encapsulate principles like parental authority and best interests that may justify a limited number of PCRMs.

1 M. Freeman, 'The Value and Values of Children's Rights', in A. Invernizzi and J. Williams (eds), *The Human Rights of Children. From Visions to Implementation*. Farnham: Ashgate, 2011, 31 (2011b).

2 J.-P. Rosenczveig, 'De nouveaux droits aux enfants?' (24 November 2013) *Le Monde blogs: Droit des enfants* <http://jprosen.blog.lemonde.fr/2013/11/24/de-nouveaux-droits-aux-enfants/> last accessed 10 March 2019.

3 HRC (1993), General Comment 22, para 8.

4 E.g. *Çiftçi v Turkey* (dec), no. 71860/01 (17 June 2004) ECtHR (unreported).

4.1 The public order limitation ground

Despite the absence of parental rights to impose PCRMs, it appears that there is some consensus at the international level as to a parental role in religious matters that goes beyond the mere 'convincing one's neighbour'.[5] The ECtHR has on several occasions noted the natural role of parents in the religious upbringing of their children,[6] and other treaty bodies have equally referred to parents bringing children up in a certain religion,[7] educating them about their religion[8] or involving them in manifestations.[9] Within this context, not all PCRMs need to be categorically rejected. Even if PCRMs will always constitute an interference with a child's right to freedom of manifestation, those that fall within the scope of a recognised limitation ground might be justified. Such grounds include public safety or health, public order (*ordre public*), public morals and the rights and freedoms of others. Most of these limitation grounds could encompass some forms of PCRMs. To secure public safety, for example, parents could make an unruly 7 year old attend a place of worship with them, instead of leaving them home alone.[10] Yet the most useful limitation ground within the context of PCRMs is that of public order, which can encompass broader concepts applicable to children and features as a limitation ground in respect of all previously discussed provisions on freedom of manifestation.

Public order (as a translation of the French *ordre public*)[11] refers to overarching principles that regulate societies and life within them. These principles operate at the national level, which is important because limitations on human rights are confined to those which individual States have prescribed by law.[12] The Siracusa Principles state that:

> 'public order (*ordre public*)' . . . may be defined as the sum of rules which ensure the functioning of society or the set of fundamental principles on which society is founded. Respect for human rights is part of public order.[13]

5 *Kokkinakis v Greece* no. 14307/88 (1993) ECtHR Series A 260-A, para 31.

6 See, Chapter 2, nn. 168–74 and accompanying text.

7 HRC (1989), General Comment 17, para 6; CmRC, *Summary Record of the 387th Meeting, Algeria*. UN Doc. CRC/C/SR.387 (10 September 1997), paras 14, 27.

8 CmRC, *Concluding Observations (third and fourth reports) Pakistan*. UN Doc. CRC/C/PAK/CO/3–4 (2 October 2009), paras 43–4.

9 Ibid.; CmRC, *Concluding Observations (third and fourth reports), China*. UN Doc. CRC/C/CHN/CO/3–4 (29 October 2013), para 42. See also Article 5 of the 1981 Declaration.

10 Note that 7 is traditionally the Western age of reason.

11 Due to a misunderstanding between the French and UK delegates regarding the meaning of *ordre public* (the UK delegate thought it meant public policy, but for the French delegate it referred to principles governing society), the French term was left out of the ICCPR (Commission on Human Rights, *Summary Record of the 319th Meeting*. UN Doc. E/CN.4/SR.319 (27 June 1952), 9, 12). Public order in the Covenant refers to overarching principles: Bielefeldt et al. (2016), 556.

12 Bielefeldt et al. (2016), 554; Schabas (2015), 435.

13 UN Economic and Social Council (UNESC), *Status of the International Covenants on Human Rights*. UN Doc. E/CN.4/1985/4 (28 September 1984), Annex: Siracusa Principles on the Limitation and Derogation Provisions in the International Covenant on Civil and Political Rights, para 22 (Siracusa Principles).

Public order encompasses grand societal ideals such as democracy and human rights,[14] but it equally contains more modest notions that underpin life in a certain society and determine the functioning of that society, such as recognised unions (e.g. marriage).[15]

Cases involving religious manifestation under the ECHR are nonetheless not uncommonly argued under Article 8 (family life), which, unlike freedom of manifestation (Article 9) does not contain a public order limitation. The issue was highlighted in the 'burqa ban' case of *S.A.S. v France*.[16] The ECtHR tried to remedy the lack of a public order limitation under Article 8 by incorporating important values and principles into the limitation ground of 'the rights and freedoms of others'.[17] It accepted that the rights and freedoms of others could include 'respect for the minimum set of values in an open and democratic society'[18] and guard against practices or attitudes that 'would fundamentally call into question [a value] which, by virtue of an established consensus, forms an indispensable element of community life within the society in question'.[19] This reasoning is essentially similar to a public order argument, but moulded into the cast of the rights and freedoms of others. Public order arguments would equally include reference to important principles on which a society has reached consensus, deviation from which would disrupt the society's functioning.[20] In light of *SAS v France*, where a public order limitation ground is not available a similar argument can thus potentially be made under the rights and freedoms of others, at least under the ECHR. Whether the same is true for other instruments is uncertain. The HRC decided in two subsequent cases that France could not rely on 'living together' and 'respect for the minimum set of values in an open and democratic society' under the rights and freedom of others, because the limitation ground required identification of actual rights and freedoms interfered with.[21] In light of this, and for reasons of readability, this chapter will refer to public order only.

Two overarching principles are particularly apt for the justification of PCRMs: the best interests of the child and notions of parental authority, responsibility or rights.[22] Dickens has called the latter 'parent/child "jural relation"',[23] but a sole

14 Respectively, *Refah Partisi (the Welfare Party) and Others v Turkey*, nos. 41340/98, 41342/98, 41343/98 and 41344/98 (2003) (Grand Chamber), ECHR 2003-II, para 86; *W. v United Kingdom*, no. 9749/82 (1987), ECtHR Series A 121, individual separate opinion Judge De Meyer.

15 J. Pineau, L'ordre public dans des relations de famille. (1999) 40(2) *Les Cahiers de Droit* 323, 330–2.

16 *S.A.S. v France*, no. 43835/11 (2014) ECtHR (Grand Chamber), ECHR 2014, para 117.

17 Ibid,. paras 117–22.

18 Ibid., para 82.

19 Ibid., paras 121, 122.

20 E. Erlings, 'The Government did Not Refer to it': SAS v France and Odre Public at the European Court of Human Rights. (2015) 16(2) *Melbourne Journal of International Law* 587, 596.

21 *Hebbaji v France*, no. 2807/2016 (2018) HRC. UN Doc. CCPR/C/123/D/2807/2016; *Yaker v France*, no. 2747/2016 (2018) HRC. UN Doc. CCPR/C/123/2747/2016, esp. paras 8.9, 8.10.

22 L. Gareil. *L'exercice de l'autorité parentale*. Paris: Librairie Générale de Droit et de Jurisprudence, 2004, 476.

23 B.M. Dickens, The modern function and limits of parental rights. 97 *LQR* (1981), 462 in S. Gilmore et al., 'Introduction', in Probert et al. (2009a), 3.

reference to legal relations is too narrow. It ignores that an important social element is also involved in definitions of the parent–child relationship. Whereas States would normally adopt e.g. parental authority to govern parent–child relations from a legal perspective, their choice is inspired by dominant social expectations of how parents and children should act towards each other. Therefore, it is more exact to refer to a 'principle governing parent–child relations' (PGPCR), since principles can be both social and legal.

Both PGPCRs and the best interests of the child play a vital role in the ordering of today's society. Through the first, States perform the crucial task of regulating family affairs, by determining the 'delicate balance between rights, duties, powers, responsibilities and authority'[24] in the parent–child relationship.[25] The second has become the *leitmotif* in all matters concerning children.[26] The best interests of the child have so often been invoked to justify limitations on rights that the concept itself has almost become an independent limitation ground – albeit unofficial and unwritten.[27] Both the HRC and the ECtHR have regularly relied on children's best interests to limit (religious) rights.[28] For example, in a case dealing with child abduction by a mother when the father and child had joined a separatist religious community, the ECtHR fully embraced the best interests of the child, which it noted enjoyed 'broad consensus', as the guiding principle in children's cases.[29]

The importance of PGPCRs and best interests justifies their categorization as being of public order. Consequently, PCRMs based on these principles can potentially be justified under international law, but only if the other limitation requirements are also met. A justifiable limitation must fit a limitation ground, be prescribed by (national) law and pass a necessity or proportionality test. As a general rule, limitations on human rights must be narrowly construed.[30] They must 'respond to a pressing public or social need' beyond mere policy considerations, and be proportionate to their stated aim.[31] The UDHR and ECHR require in this regard that limitations are 'necessary in a democratic society', whereas the ICCPR, 1981 Declaration and CRC simply refer to 'necessary'. However, the ICCPR's Siracusa Principles state that limitations on rights must comply with the UDHR's requirement of necessity in a democratic society in

24 Or a similar collection of attributes, depending on national definitions.

25 *Re M (A Child)* [2013] EWCA Civ 969, [27].

26 A. James and A. James, *Key Concepts in Childhood Studies.* London: Sage, 2012, 7.

27 See *Dolhamre v Sweden*, no. 67/04 (8 June 2010) ECtHR, dissenting opinion Judge Zupančič.

28 E.g. *Patera v Czech Republic*, no. 546/2000 (2002) HRC UN Doc CCPR/C/75/D/546/2000, para 7.3.

29 *Neulinger and Shuruk v Switzerland*, no. 41615/07 (2010) ECtHR (Grand Chamber) ECHR 2010, para 135. See also *Dolhamre v Sweden*, no. 67/04 (8 June 2010) ECtHR, para 111.

30 *Friend and Others v United Kingdom* (dec), nos. 16072/06 and 27809/08 (24 November 2009) ECtHR, para 41; Hodgkin and Newell (2007), 152.

31 Bielefeldt et al. (2016), 555 with reference to UN doc. E/CN.4/1985/4; Schabas (2015), 438. See also CmRC, *Concluding Observations, Democratic People's Republic of Korea.* UN Doc. CRC/C/PRK/CO/5 (23 October 2017), para 21 'limitations to the right to freedom of religion [must be] proportional and not arbitrary'.

case of a state of emergency – when the State is given most power to interfere with rights.[32] From this, it can be derived that 'necessity in a democratic society' should certainly apply when there is no emergency. Given further that the Special Rapporteur has observed that ICCPR requirements for limitations equally apply with regard to the CRC,[33] it seems that the condition for limitations to be necessary in a democratic society applies across the board to limitations on the right to freedom of manifestation.

A PCRM can thus only limit a child's religious rights if doing so is needed to preserve a democratic society. Given the endless variety of religious manifestations, what exactly would be considered necessary in a democratic society is impossible to state and depends entirely on the case. Limitations should nonetheless not contradict democratic values such as pluralism, equality, broadmindedness, human dignity, participation, tolerance and solidarity.[34] This suggests that e.g. patriarchal, unduly paternalistic and authoritarian limitations on freedom of manifestation are not easily justifiable. By contrast, pluralism is considered one of the hallmarks of a democratic society.[35] Limitations 'necessary in a democratic society' can therefore encompass minority practices as well as aspects of a particular society's culture and thereby address the concerns related to culture raised in Chapter 3.[36]

A minimum requirement for necessity is that the principle invoked under public order is itself compatible with democracy and human rights.[37] Yet even if that is the case, a specific limitation may not be necessary in a democratic society. This is especially true where an appeal to principles that are otherwise compatible with democratic values appears to be 'political expediency in disguise'.[38] For example, far-reaching conceptions of secularism form part of public order in States like France and Turkey. These conceptions have, in principle, been deemed compatible with democracy and the human rights regime.[39] Yet the HRC still ruled that the specific limitation of banning religious symbols in public schools, albeit based on secularism, was not necessary.[40]

32 UNESC (1984), Siracusa Principles, para 65.

33 Bielefeldt (2015), Special Rapporteur's Children Report, paras 38-41, 70.

34 See J. Deshmukh-Ranadive, 'Introduction', in J. Deshmukh-Ranadive (ed.), *Democracy in the Family. Insights from India*. New Delhi: Sage, 2008, 8; D.A. Gozdecka. Religions and Legal Boundaries of Democracy in Europe: European Commitment to Democratic Principles. Thesis (PhD), University of Helsinki, 2009, 54, 55; R.B. Talisse, *Democracy and Moral Conflict*. Cambridge, New York: CUP, 2009, 3, 4.

35 E.g. *Kokkinakis v Greece*, no. 14307/88 (1993), ECtHR Series A 260-A, para 31.

36 Section 3.4.

37 *Refah Partisi (the Welfare Party) and Others v Turkey*, nos. 41340/98, 41342/98, 41343/98 and 41344/98 (2003) (Grand Chamber), ECHR 2003-II, para 99.

38 S. Greer, *The Exceptions to Articles 8 to 11 of the European Convention on Human Rights*. Strasbourg, Council of Europe, 1997, 14.

39 *Sahin v Turkey*, no. 44774/98 (2005) (Grand Chamber) ECHR 2005-XI, para 144; *Singh v France*, no. 1852/2008 (2013) HR. UN Doc. CCPR/C/106/D/1852/2008, para 8.6.

40 *Singh v France*, no. 1852/2008 (2013) HRC. UN Doc. CCPR/C/106/D/1852/2008, para 8.7.

The difference between the general compatibility of concepts and specific determinations of necessity in a democratic society is also relevant for best interests and PGPCRs. Both concepts are compatible with democracy.[41] However, not every action based on a PGPCR or children's best interests is necessary to the extent that it may limit children's right to freedom of manifestation and justify PCRMs. For example, allowing parents to decide whether or not an adolescent takes religious instruction may be encompassed in the principle of parental responsibility, but the limitation would not be necessary in a democratic society. Adolescents are normally able to decide for themselves, and the parental right interferes with pluralism and tolerance. In the same vein, demanding that a teenager accompanies parents to a place of worship may be in their best interests, but not of a necessity justifying a limitation on the child's right not to manifest the parental religion. This would be especially true if the parental decision disregarded the important democratic value of participation through non-involvement of the child.

By contrast, if the objecting child was 7 years old, PGPCRs and best interests pointing to attendance at worship could be seen as providing necessary limitations on freedom of manifestation. A child that age cannot normally be left home alone, so if it is considered that worshipping overall serves this child's interests, the PCRM may be justified because the alternative would endanger the child. Furthermore, the bringing up of children with which parents are entrusted requires them to give children bearings.[42] To benefit from pluralism and participation in a democratic society, children need to have some frame of reference, often called a 'primary culture'; an initial moral framework that may or may not be religious.[43] Hence, Dillen has argued that, notwithstanding the ultimate goal of allowing children to make their own decisions, there are several reasons to allow for religious coercion as part of a primary culture (though she does not use that term).[44] First, in order to give children a positive perspective on the future, it is important that they are involved in matters that are valuable to parents.[45] Secondly, children cannot effectively make their own choices without an initial framework, because there would be no measure from which they could judge.[46] Finally, democratic values like tolerance are enhanced through the provision of an initial framework, because it gives children an idea of relativity and the importance of everyone's own moral framework.[47] There thus appear to be strong links

41 See nn. 28, 29; *Hoffmann v Austria*, no. 12875/87 (1993), ECtHR Series A 255-C.

42 E.g. CmRC (2006), General Comment 7, paras 15–21.

43 B.A. Ackerman, *Social Justice in the Liberal State*. New Haven, CT: Yale University Press, 1980, chapter 32. See also T.H. McLaughlin, Parental Rights and the Religious Upbringing of Children. (1984) 18(1) *Journal of Philosophy of Education* 75, 78. Note that Ackerman's concept of primary culture only applies to 'infants' until around the age of 5, whereas the concept is here extended to slightly older children.

44 Dillen (2006), 133.

45 Ibid.

46 Ibid.

47 Ibid., 134.

between democratic values and the provision of a primary culture, which could mean that PCRMs in that setting may be deemed necessary in a democratic society (insofar they do not endanger the child). However, much depends on the way the broader principles of PGPCRs and best interests are given shape. Some PGPCRs and best interest determinations are more likely than others to embrace PCRMs that would not ultimately be necessary in a democratic society as discussed below.

4.2 Principles governing parent–child relations

Almost every State has included in its family code a provision dealing with the relations between parents and children (its PGPCR). Though it is uncommon for such provisions to provide elaborate guidance on acceptable parenting, or even to list matters which fall within the reign of the PGPCR. Their function is to provide a mediating principle for any applicable attributes (rights, duties, powers, etc.) and the parent–child relation as a whole. The most common PGPCRs are parental rights, responsibility and authority. Parental rights gives parents near-absolute rights or power over children (i.e. simple power).[48] Parental responsibility sees child-rearing as a responsibility of parents and gives rights to parents because they have duties/responsibilities.[49] Parental authority refers to legitimate parental power. Legitimacy can be determined externally (through legislation or judgments) or internally (power is negotiated within the family).[50]

It is undisputed that all three principles encompass the religious or philosophical upbringing of children under the attributes of rights or power.[51] Parental rights therefore do not exist at the international level, but they normally do exist at the domestic level. However, what it means for parents to have a right or power in relation to children's religious upbringing at the national level depends entirely on the mediating principle which governs it. As such, the three mediating principles have an impact on the acceptability of PCRMs per se, but they equally affect the extent to which limitations on children's rights to freedom of manifestation would be considered necessary in a democratic society. The next sections discuss the three principles more fully, focusing in particular on parental responsibility and authority.

4.2.1 Parental rights

Parental rights is the oldest principle and derived (via paternal power) from *patria potestas*: the almost absolute power of fathers to rule their household.[52]

48 See 4.2.1.

49 See 4.2.2.

50 See 4.2.3.

51 See also 6.3, 7.3 and 8.3 below.

52 R. Saller, Patria potestas and the Stereotype of the Roman Family. (1986) 1(1) *Continuity and Change* 7.

The PGPCR allows parents to take decisions for children and impose their will with very little regard for the child. Parents can unilaterally determine the whole of the child's upbringing, subject only to legal duties and limits (most notably child protection and criminal law), and, if accepted in the particular jurisdiction, the autonomous decision-making of children having reached a certain level of competence (Gillick competent or mature minors).[53] Beyond this, parents do not need to involve their children in decisions regarding them, or respect children's own personality, something which has caused Liu to remark that the principle is 'outdated' and 'a misconception of the nature of the parent-child relationship'.[54]

International law has not looked favourably upon the principle of parental rights. Treaty bodies have on numerous occasions criticised the doctrine of parental rights as incompatible with (children's) human rights.[55] Moreover, the adoption of the CRC itself largely took place as a reaction to the persistence of parental rights.[56] The Convention challenges in particular 'the presumption that parents have rights of ownership over the child',[57] often formulated more benignly as children 'belonging to' parents.

With its emphasis on children as objects, rather than subjects with human rights, it is unlikely that parental rights could function as a suitable basis for necessary limitations on children's freedom of manifestation. Not only does the principle allow for a great many PCRMs beyond those necessary in a democratic society,[58] the PGPCR does not fulfil the minimum requirement of being itself compatible with human rights.

4.2.2 Parental responsibility

Parental responsibility[59] emerged in the second half of the 20th century with the dual aim of promoting equality between parents and bringing about a shift in thinking from parental rights as circumscribed by duties to parents having rights

53 *Gillick v West Norfolk and Wisbech Area Health Authority and Department of Social Security* [1986] AC 112.

54 A.N.C. Liu, *Family Law for the Hong Kong SAR*. Hong Kong: Hong Kong University Press, 1999, 216.

55 E.g. PACoE, *Recommendation 874 (1979) on a European Charter on the Rights of the Child*, Council of Europe (4 October 1979); CMCoE, *Recommendation No. R (84)4 on Parental Responsibilities*, Council of Europe (28 February 1984) and explanatory memorandum; Hodgkin and Newell (2007), 188, 189.

56 N.V. Lowe and G. Douglas, *Bromley's Family Law* (10th ed.). Oxford: OUP, 2006, 367–8.

57 G. Lansdown, 'The Evolving Capacities of the Child', in Committee on the Rights of the Child, *A Guide to General Comment 7: 'Implementing Child Rights in Early Childhood'*. The Hague: Bernhard van Leer Foundation, 2006, 151.

58 Though this depends somewhat on the exact legal framework in which parental rights operate.

59 This section reproduces parts of E. Erlings, Is Anything Left of Children's Rights? How Parental Responsibility Erodes Children's Rights Under English Law. (2016) 24(3) *International Journal of Children's Rights* 624.

because they have duties.[60] However, experience at the national and international (regional) level demonstrates that, whilst the PGPCR was initially campaigned for as a means to enhance children's status within the family,[61] the texts that have been adopted and parental responsibility's operation may not be capable of delivering better respect for children and their rights. The operative part of the CoE's leading Recommendation on Parental Responsibilities[62] does not mention children's rights or autonomy and a previously identified duty for parents to consult children did not make it into the text.[63] Instead, the recommendation gives parents powers and duties to ensure the moral and material welfare of their children.[64] Similarly, in England parental responsibility was advocated for as a means to further children's rights,[65] but by the time of its adoption the PGPCR had redirected its focus to parental rights (concomitant to duties) and children's interests (as determined by responsible parents).[66] Parental responsibility is now firmly based on parental rights and duties, and children's interests or welfare. This raises two issues from a children's rights perspective, the first related to the elements of parental responsibility and the second concerned with children's participation.

Parental responsibility justifies parental rights through the existence of parental duties and responsibility for children's welfare. Yet, the idea that rights must be instrumental to duties does not itself prevent the existence of broad parental rights.[67] Moreover, the concomitance of rights to duties creates an expectation of 'something for something'.[68] If a parent, for example, has a duty to ensure

60 See N.V. Lowe, The Meaning and Allocation of Parental Responsibility – a Common Lawyer's Perspective. (1997) 11 *International Journal of Law, Policy and the Family* 192; J. Herring, 'Parental Responsibility, Hyper-Parenting and the Role of Technology', in R. Brownsword et al. (eds), *Oxford Handbook of Law, Regulation and Technology*. Oxford: OUP, 2017 (2017a), 407.

61 Erlings (2016), 626.

62 CMCoE, *Recommendation No. R(84)4 on Parental Responsibilities*, Council of Europe (28 February 1984). See also Council of Europe, *Explanatory Report to Committee of Ministers of the Council of Europe, Recommendation Rec(2006)19 on policy to support positive parenting*, Council of Europe (13 December 2006).

63 M. Killerby, 'The Council of Europe's Contribution to Family Law (Past, Present and Future)', in N. Lowe and G. Douglas, *Family Law across Frontiers*. The Hague: Martinus Nijhoff, 1996, 19, 20.

64 Appendix, Principle 1.

65 J. Eekelaar and R. Dingwall, *The Reform of Child Care Law. A Practical Guide to the Children Act 1989*. London: Routledge, 1990, 23.

66 L. Fox Harding, 'Parental Responsibility' – A Dominant Theme in British Child and Family Policy for the 1990's. (1994) 14(1-2) *International Journal of Sociology and Social Policy* 84, esp. 94; J. Eekelaar, Parental Responsibility: State of Nature, or Nature of the State? (1991) 13(1) *Journal of Social Welfare and Family Law* 37; H. Reece, 'From Parental Responsibility to Parenting Responsibly', in M. Freeman (ed.), *Law and Sociology*. Oxford: OUP, 2006, 460, 461.

67 See e.g. Reece (2006), esp. 461; H. Reece, 'The Degradation of Parental Responsibility', in Probert et al. (2009), esp. 87.

68 E. Such and R. Walker, Young Citizens or Policy Objects? Children in the 'Rights and Responsibilities' Debate. (2005) 34(1) *Journal of Social Policy* 39, 39.

a child's education, then they should have the right to determine what that education should look like. Especially where duties are not well-defined, parental responsibility can give parents broad rights in exchange for relatively minor duties.[69] Fox Harding has additionally suggested that the introduction of parental responsibility has simply led to the reformulation of parental rights into responsibilities (e.g. the right to determine a child's education becomes a duty to do the same).[70] Parental responsibility has therefore been linked with strong parental rights,[71] especially in the area of religion.[72] Such rights are further enhanced through the nexus between responsibility, duties and welfare. Under parental responsibility, parents have rights because they have the responsibility and duty to further children's welfare. Yet as frequently remarked, the notion of welfare is largely undefined.[73] It often functions as 'a box in which everyone puts what he wants to find inside'.[74] Some parents may find children's rights inside, but that is unlikely in the case of a parent who imposes PCRMs. This does not mean that the coercing parent is not seeking to further their child's welfare. Parents who e.g. impose PCRMs in order to secure salvation are in fact so concerned with their child's (spiritual) welfare that they are willing to do anything to safeguard it.[75] Fortin aptly observes:

> Although the average parent inevitably brings up his or her children with the best of intentions, the essential subjectivity of the 'welfare' or 'best interests' test does little to persuade repressive parents to adjust their parenting style to promote children's rights more effectively . . . parents may . . . argu[e] that they are promoting their children's best interests[76]

69 Erlings (2016), 630.

70 Fox Harding (1994), 94, with reference to L. Fox Harding, Underlying Themes and Contradictions in the Children Act 1989. (1990) 15 *Justice of the Peace* 591.

71 Ibid.

72 A. McCall Smith, 'Is Anything Left of Parental Rights?', in E. Sutherland and A. McCall Smith (eds), *Family Rights, Family Law and Medical Advance*. Edinburgh: Edinburgh University Press, 1990, 9; R. Taylor, Responsibility for the Soul of the Child: The Role of the State and Parents in Determining Religious Upbringing and Education. (2015) 29 *International Journal of Law, Policy and the Family* 15, 18–21.

73 See E.E. Sutherland and L.-A. Barnes Macfarlane, 'Introduction', in E.E. Sutherland and L.-A. Barnes Macfarlane (eds), *Implementing Article 3 of the United Nations Convention on the Rights of the Child: Best Interests, Welfare and Wellbeing*. Cambridge: CUP, 2016, 11, 12. See also E.E. Sutherland, 'Article 3 of the United Nations Convention on the Rights of the Child: The Challenges of Vagueness and Priorities' in the same volume.

74 F. Dekeuwer-Défossez, Réflexion sur les Mythes Fondateurs du Droit Contemporain de la Famille. (1995) 2 *Revue Trimestrielle de Droit Civil* 249, 265.

75 See also A. Apetroaia et al., Parental Responsibility Beliefs: Associations with Parental Anxiety and Behaviours in the Context of Childhood Anxiety Disorders. (2015) 188 *Journal of Affective Disorders* 127, 131: parental anxiety (e.g. regarding salvation) creates a heightened sense of parental responsibility associated with more intrusive and less warm behaviour (e.g. PCRMs).

76 Fortin (2009), 322.

What matters for the exercise of parental responsibility is whether a parent has in good faith, 'responsibly',[77] taken a decision with regard to their child, not whether the outcome of that decision supports children's rights. If parents fulfil their legal duties, parental responsibility sanctions conceptions of welfare at odds with children's (religious) rights – and gives parents powers to enforce them. The PGPCR's emphasis on responsibility places children's rights-exercise in a precarious position when confronted with an application of parental responsibility seeking to limit it, 'since it is difficult to argue . . . that parents should be more irresponsible'.[78]

A second issue with parental responsibility is that it places the decision-making power solely in the hands of those who are responsible, i.e. parents.[79] As children are not the holders of responsibility, they therefore do not qualify for any concomitant rights.[80] Whilst parents may exercise their responsibility with love and care, nothing prevents them from doing so without the child's involvement, or agreement.[81] This is because the interaction parental responsibility governs is between parents and children's *welfare*, not between parents and children themselves. The PGPCR has been criticised as adult-centric and welfarist 'broadly conceived as something that is done to children, a view which takes little, if any, account of children's own subjectivity'.[82] Others have similarly argued that parental responsibility reduces children to 'passive recipients'[83] of parental decision-making under a PGPCR that leaves 'no room for reciprocity, interactivity and negotiation of rights and responsibilities between parent and child'.[84] Contrary to the CmRC's suggestion that children irrespective of their age are 'active social agents' and not 'passive recipients of care',[85] parental responsibility only recognises parents as actors. It thereby ignores that families are communities to which both parents and children contribute.[86]

Parental responsibility has been coined 'the modern version of parental rights'[87] (though packaged in the nicer language of care and responsibility).

77 Reece (2006), 470.
78 Fox Harding (1994), 104.
79 M. Freeman, 'Disputing Children', in S. Katz et al. (eds), *Cross Currents*. Oxford: OUP, 2000, p. 452.
80 A. James, 'Responsibility, Children and Childhood', in J. Bridgeman et al. (eds), *Responsibility, Law and the Family*. Aldershot: Ashgate, 2008, 158.
81 S. Perälä-Littunen and M.L. Böök, The Beginning and End of Parental Responsibility – Finnish Parents' Views. (2012) 43(6) *Journal of Comparative Family Studies* 925, 925: parental responsibility is hard (though not impossible) to exercise with children's involvement.
82 A. James, 'Parents: A Children's Perspective', in A. Bainham et al. (eds), *What is a Parent?* Oxford: Hart, 1999, 182.
83 Such and Walker (2005), 44; Herring (2017a), 419.
84 Such and Walker (2005), 44.
85 CmRC (2006), General Comment 7, para 16.
86 F. De Singly, 'Le statut de l'enfant dans la famille contemporaine', in F. De Singly (ed.), *Enfants, adultes. Vers une égalite de status?* Paris: Universalis, 2004a, 22; Such and Walker (2005), 48, 49.
87 Herring (2017a), 407.

It could be argued that this should not be a problem for present purposes, because the principle is used as a limitation on the child's right to freedom of manifestation. If no parental rights were included in the PGPCR, then it would not function as a *limitation* on rights. However, as noted above, limitations need to be narrow, suitable and 'necessary in a democratic society'. A principle which does not require children's participation (an essential democratic value) and gives a prominent place to parental rights may not be a fitting basis for limitations that fulfil these conditions. Moreover, as Herring argues, parenting 'is not a job to perform with responsibility; it is a relationship'.[88]

4.2.3 Parental authority

Parental authority as a PGPCR[89] is based on legitimate parental power and maintains close ties with the authoritative (or democratic) parenting style.[90] It is described by Kuhar and Reiter as:

> [A] product of family communication that is constantly *co-constructed* in the process of *interaction* between parents and children . . . Unlike power, which is associated with one-sided and situative demonstrations of assertiveness, parental authority is *relational* and requires active participation of the child in order to become a legitimate and institutionalised aspect of . . . family life. . . . While power is unilateral, authority requires mutuality.[91]

The definition highlights two important aspects of parental authority: first, parental authority refers to *legitimate* power and not simple power. Second, parental authority requires communication and participation of children who are active agents in the parent–child relation.

The legitimation of parental power can be external or internal. Through a legal framework, the State (which itself holds authority in most democracies) can provide external legitimation to exercises of parental power in the face of opposition from children.[92] Laws on neglect can e.g. legitimise parental power to take an objecting 7 year old to a place of worship to effectuate supervision. Conversely,

88 Ibid., 419.

89 Not to be confused with authority as an attribute of e.g. parental responsibility.

90 Authoritative parenting is based on high expectations, combined with high support and negotiated limits on children's autonomy. See on parenting styles: D. Baumrind, Effects of Authoritative Parental Control on Child Behavior. (1966) 37(4) *Child Development* 887; M. Pinquart and R. Kauser, Do the Associations of Parenting Styles with Behaviour Problems and Academic Achievement Vary by Culture? Results from a Meta-Analysis. (2018) 24(1) *Cultural Diversity and Ethnic Minority Psychology* 75.

91 M. Kuhar and H. Reiter, Towards a Concept of Parental Authority in Adolescence. (2013) 3(2) *C•E•P•S Journal* 135, 147, 148.

92 See A. Fives, *Evaluating Parental Power: An Exercise in Pluralist Political Theory*. Manchester: Manchester University Press, 2017, 150, 151.

States can protect children by de-legitimising parental power which children themselves could see as legitimate.[93] Children who suffer religion-related abuse, for example, sometimes consider parental actions legitimate because they believe they deserve punishment for their sins.[94] External legitimation or de-legitimation can be based on children's protection, interests or rights. Internal legitimation, by contrast, requires that those involved see the exercise of parental power as legitimate. This clearly has implications for PCRMs (which children would not normally see as legitimate), although it does not mean that manifestations can never be imposed (generally depending on the decision-making process).

Recognising someone as holding authority usually entails giving up one's own autonomy in recognition of the fact that the other person makes better decisions.[95] Most writers on parental authority therefore propose that the legitimacy of parental power lies in parents' greater knowledge, expertise and/or experience as perceived by the child.[96] In much the same way, the CmRC and Special Rapporteur have stated that '[t]he more the child himself or herself knows, has experienced and understands, the more the parent[s] . . . have to transform direction and guidance into reminders and advice and later to an exchange on an equal footing'.[97] Experience and knowledge are nonetheless not the only sources of legitimation. The fairness with which the matter is dealt, for example, could equally legitimise power, as can a context of support.[98] Power may become legitimate when its purpose is explained, the issue is discussed (or negotiated) and what Fize calls an 'authority of dialogue' is established.[99] This is particularly important in respect of PCRMs, because religiously inspired behaviour is often not founded upon knowledge (faith cannot be 'known') and religious experience is highly personal. Whilst children may consider a PCRM legitimate because parents make better decisions, it is more likely that legitimacy will be arrived at because the process of imposition was fair.

93 J. Le Gal, *Pour que nos enfants puissent apprendre ensemble: Respecter leur personne et leurs droits* (2011), 7 <http://www.meirieu.com/ECHANGES/jeanlegal.pdf> last accessed 10 March 2019.

94 B.L. Bottoms et al., Religion-Related Child Physical Abuse: Characteristics and Psychological Outcomes. (2003) 8(1–2) *Journal of Aggression, Maltreatment and Trauma* 87, 103.

95 K. E. Himma, Just 'Cause you're Smarter than me doesn't Give you a Right to Tell me What to Do: Legitimate Authority and the Normal Justification Thesis. (2007) 27(1) *Oxford Journal of Legal Studies* 121, 125.

96 M. Fize, *La democratie familiale. Evolution des relations parents-adolescents.* Paris: Presses de la Renaissance, 1998, 180; Le Gal (2011), 7; Y. Yaffe, 'Parental authority': What do we Know about the Construct? (2013) 2(9) *International Journal of Educational Research and Development* 211, 214.

97 CmRC, *General Comment No. 12 (2009) The right of the child to be heard.* UN Doc. CRC/C/GC/12 (01 July 2009), para 84 (General Comment 12); H. Bielefeldt, *Elimination of All Forms of Religious Intolerance. Interim Report of the Special Rapporteur on Freedom of Religion or Belief.* UN Doc. A/67/303 (13 August 2012b), para 32.

98 C. Mellado et al., Interactive Associations of Parental Support, Demands and Psychological Control, over Adolescents' Beliefs about the Legitimacy of Parental Power. (2018) 64 *Journal of Adolescence* 81, 85.

99 Fize (1998), 275.

To some, the idea of children considering the legitimacy of parental power may sound too abstract or could leave children 'abandoned to their autonomy'.[100] Yet, research from the social sciences suggests that neither is true. Children are not abandoned, because under parental authority, parents may need to set negotiable rules, but they still need to set rules.[101] The absence of parental control can equally lack legitimacy. Kuhn and Laird, for example found that children who experienced 'pre-mature independent decision-making' regarded this negatively.[102] Additionally, parents should also see the ultimate exercise of power as legitimate. Parental authority requires a balance that is normally brought about through communication. In fact, parental authority cannot exist without the exchange of views between parents and children.[103] To obtain legitimacy some mutual understanding must arise. This understanding is not always self-evident as children typically view parental action as no longer legitimate some time before parents do.[104] Hence parental authority's dependence on participation of the child in the decision-making process and communication between parents and children to bring mutual expectations to bear and engage in explanation, justification and possibly negotiation.

Work by influential childhood researchers has further suggested that there is nothing abstract about children considering the legitimacy of parental power.[105] Children are conscious of, and draw boundaries between, parental acts they consider legitimate and those thought of as a simple exercise of power.[106] This is the case irrespective of children's background and culture. Assadi et al., for example, found that children in highly hierarchical societies such as Iran assess the legitimacy of parental power,[107] and Yau and Smetana found the same was true for Confucian collectivist societies like China (Mainland) and Hong Kong.[108]

100 Hafen and Hafen (1996), 449.

101 Baumrind (1966), 898; Kuhar and Reiter (2013), 139, 140. See also Mellado et al. (2018), 82.

102 E.S. Kuhn and R.D. Laird, Individual Differences in Early Adolescents' Beliefs in the Legitimacy of Parental Authority. (2011) 47(5) *Developmental Psychology* 1353, 1361.

103 Fize (1998), 191, 285.

104 E.g. E. Hui, Adolescent and Parental Perceptions of Medical Decision-Making in Hong Kong. (2011) 25(9) *Bioethics* 516, 522, 526.

105 See especially the work of Tisak (M.S. Tisak, Conceptions of Parental Authority. (1986) 57(1) *Child Development* 166), Darling (e.g. N. Darling et al., Individual Differences in Adolescents' Beliefs about the Legitimacy of Parental Authority and their own Obligation to Obey: A Longitudinal Investigation. (2008) 79(4) *Child Development* 1103) and Smetana (e.g. J.G. Smetana, Parenting Styles and Conceptions of Parental Authority during Adolescence. (1995) 66(2) *Child Development* 299). Increasingly research takes place beyond the United States: Pinquart and Kauser (2018) identified 428 studies for their meta-analysis of which 161 were American studies.

106 Ibid.

107 S.M. Assadi et al. Beliefs about Parental Authority, Parenting Styles, and Parent–Adolescent Conflict among Iranian Mothers of Middle Adolescents. (2011) 35 *International Journal of Behavioural Development* 424, 173–6.

108 J. Yau and J. Smetana, Adolescent–Parent Conflict in Hong Kong and Shenzhen: A Comparison of Youth in Two Cultural Contexts. (2003) 27(3) *International Journal of Behavioural Development* 201.

Legitimacy further varied according to subject and age, indicating how parental authority's parameters are subject to change, but not the principle itself.[109] Research on parental authority further suggests that process and parenting style are important in considerations of legitimacy, including where religion is concerned.[110] Children of religious parents have e.g. been found to be most likely to consider propositions related to religious identity or values as legitimate where parents employed an authoritative or democratic parenting style.[111] This and other research further indicates a practical advantage of parental authority: children who consider an exercise of power as legitimate are more likely to comply with parental demands.[112]

Parental authority is thus legitimate power based on an involvement of, and communication with, the child, who is seen as an active agent and partner, set within the framework provided by the State. It coincides with perceptions of the family as a training ground for democratic citizenship under the CoE,[113] and the UN's description of the family as 'the smallest democracy at the heart of society'.[114] Moreover, the PGPCR's emphasis on communication and participation echoes the CmRC's statement that parents should act 'in a child-centred way, through dialogue and example, in ways that enhance young children's capacities to exercise their rights, including their right to participation (art. 12) and their right to freedom of thought, conscience and religion (art. 14)'.[115] Given the democratic values embedded in the PGPCR and its emphasis on children's own autonomy, parental authority appears to be a more promising basis for the justification of PCRMs than parental responsibility, which faces difficulties accounting for children's participation, or parental rights which requires no legitimacy for exercises of power other than parenthood. Yet whether that is indeed the case depends in large part on how the principles are executed and perceived in practice. These are matters which will be discussed in the chapters examining national frameworks that shed further light on parental authority (France, Chapter 6), parental responsibility (England, Chapter 7) and parental rights (Hong Kong, Chapter 8).

109 Ibid., 207–10.

110 M.D. Berzonsky, Identity Style, Parental Authority, and Identity Commitment. (2004) 33(3) *Journal of Youth and Adolescence* 213, 218; P.C.L. Heaven et al., Parental Styles and Religious Values among Teenagers: A Three-Year Prospective Analysis. (2010) 171(1) *Journal of Genetic Psychology* 93, 97.

111 Ibid.

112 Ibid.; Such and Walker (2005), 54; Darling (2008), 1114.

113 CmCoE, *Recommendation Rec (2002)12 of the Committee of Ministers to Member States on Education for Democratic Citizenship*, Council of Europe (16 October 2002), para 2.

114 Département de l'information des Nations Unies, *Les familles, cœur de la société*. UN Doc. DPI/1512/SOC/CON—94-34130 (September 1994). See also G.B. Melton, It's All about Relationships! The Psychology of Human Rights. (2010) 80(2) *American Journal of Orthopsychiatry* 161, 164.

115 CmRC (2006), General Comment 7, para 17.

4.3 The best interests of the child

In addition to PGPCRs, children's interests can be a legitimate reason to limit their right to freedom of manifestation. This is especially true if the PCRM is necessary to ward off harm to children. For example, a 12 year old may refuse to accompany parents on a religious pilgrimage during a school holiday. If there is no one to look after the child, leaving them home alone would be unsafe and carries a real risk for the minor to be harmed. The parents could instead be asked to forego the pilgrimage, but this may be a disproportionate limitation on their own right and undermine the child's understanding of the rights of others and the need to compromise within healthy family relationships (further discussed in the next chapter). Alternatively, the child could be taken along, despite their objections, so that the parents can look after him/her. If best interests have been prescribed by law, restricting the minor's freedom of manifestation to prioritise interests in safeguarding and family functioning could be seen as necessary in a democratic society, depending on the decision-making process. Hence, PCRMs serving the best interests of the child can sometimes take precedence over children's freedom of manifestation via the public order limitation ground. For this to happen, it is necessary to recognise that best interests can function as a limitation on rights, and that interests must have been determined in a manner compatible with public order requirements.

4.3.1 Interests as limitations

Rather than as a limitation on rights, the best interests of the child are better known as a right itself, encapsulated in Article 3 CRC. The Article states that in every action concerning children, their interests must be a primary consideration. So far, Article 3 and its underlying best interests principle have mainly received critique as being too vague and open to diametrically opposing interpretations of what is in children's interests.[116] More recently it has been argued that best interests should not be seen as a substantive or procedural right at all.[117] Kilkelly notes that no actual rights language is used in Article 3 CRC;[118] that best interests finds its origin in paternalism rather than a rights-based approach;[119] that the principle's balancing requirements sit ill with the concept of rights;[120] and that the CmRC's interpretation of best interests has focused mostly on compliance with other CRC rights, rather than offer a fully distinct right.[121] The author suggests

116 See Dekeuwer-Defossez (1995), 265; Erlings (2016), 628; Sutherland and Barnes Macfarlane (2016), 11, 12.

117 U. Kilkelly, 'The Best Interests of the Child: A Gateway to Children's Rights?', in Sutherland and Barnes MacFalane (2016), 51–66.

118 Ibid., 57.

119 Ibid., 56.

120 Ibid., 60, 61.

121 Ibid., 60. Kilkelly therefore argues that best interests can be seen as a national gateway to international rights. However, she admits that there is little evidence that they function in this way in practice (63).

that the fact that Article 3 was so readily adopted had more to do with the drafters' familiarity with best interests as already enshrined in their domestic laws, than a thorough examination of the proposed provision as a right.[122] These objections make a convincing case against the use of best interests as a right per se. Yet, they also inadvertently provide compelling reasons for the use of best interests as a limitation on the right to freedom of manifestation. Limitations must be based on domestic regulations to be 'prescribed by law'. States' familiarity with best interests indicates that the concept already forms part of the fabric of their laws, meaning that the limitation can build on an existing infrastructure. Further, the criticised open-endedness and undefined nature of best interests allows for the consideration of a wide variety of matters that are relevant to religious manifestations, including cultural considerations and ties with (religious) communities.[123] As a limitation on rights, it also does not matter that best interests flows from a paternalistic approach. Most limitations on rights are inspired by a form of paternalism. It is because of this reason that the courts scrutinise proposed limitations to see if they are necessary in a democratic society. The CmRC has, for example, held that a child's interest in socialisation should not be widely invoked to unduly restrict rights.[124] Furthermore, the balancing requirement included in best interests is a helpful characteristic, rather than a barrier. Limitations require that different positions and arguments are weighed and balanced to determine a proportionate outcome. In this respect, the CmRC's requirement that 'the best interests of a child must be assessed individually'[125] on a child-specific case-by-case basis makes the principle useful for limitations on rights (as opposed to rights themselves, which should apply similarly to all human beings). Equally, the Committee's emphasis on children's other rights in the interpretation of best interests is important,[126] because it fulfils the requirement that public order limitations must themselves be compatible with human rights. The very characteristics that make best interests questionable as a right thus make the principle very suitable as a limitation on rights. It is therefore not surprising that, as noted above,[127] international bodies have already accepted that it may sometimes be necessary in a democratic society for best interests to limit rights to freedom of manifestation. So far, they have done so in cases concerning the religious rights of parents as balanced with the interests of children,[128] but best interests would work equally well as a limitation on children's own religious rights, especially within the family context, where the principle was first developed.

122 Ibid., 53.

123 See S. Van Praagh, Religion, Custody and a Child's Identities. 35(2) *Osgoode Hall Law Journal* 309; Scolnicov (2011) (throughout).

124 CmRC (2006), General Comment 7, para 17.

125 CmRC (2013), General Comment 14, para 24.

126 Ibid., esp. paras 41–5; Kilkelly (2016), 60.

127 Under 4.1.

128 E.g. *Neulinger and Shuruk v Switzerland*, no. 41615/07 (2010) ECtHR (Grand Chamber) ECHR 2010. See also Bielefeldt (2015), Special Rapporteur's Children Report (throughout).

4.3.2 The determination of interests for public order

For best interests to be able to function as a public order limitation on rights, they must be narrowly interpreted, yet capable of encompassing a wide range of values, whilst themselves remaining compatible with human rights and other democratic principles. This calls for a reflection on how children's interests are currently established.

A common way to determine children's interests in rights literature is to identify categories of interests,[129] such as the well-known triptych of basic, developmental and autonomy interests.[130] However, since children's rights authors have traditionally adhered to the interest theory of rights, these interests are normally used as a basis to build rights on, not to limit them.[131] This makes existing interest categories difficult to use as limitations on rights. Such categories may be too broad, because they were aimed at supporting rights rather than limiting them. Conversely, categories may be too narrow because, as a result of their *raison d'être,* they tend to only include interests that can be reformulated into rights. Children have important interests that are not easily restated in terms of rights but may provide a reason to limit freedom of manifestation. This is particularly true for relational interests, which are the interests children have in developing and maintaining good relations with important people and communities in their lives.[132] The ECtHR, for example, found in a religious dispute that the child's best interests capable of limiting parental religious freedom rights in a democratic society comprised not only 'the child's interest to ensure its development in a sound environment', but also 'the child's ties with its family . . . and . . . personal relations'.[133]

More amenable concepts of best interests are included in the CmRC's General Comment 14[134] and some countries' 'welfare checklists' (lists with indicators to determine best interests),[135] used in proceedings governed by the best interests principle.[136] The former explicitly places interests within a human rights framework, by linking interests such as that to a 'holistic development' with the right to life, survival and development (Art. 6 CRC) and emphasises the in-principle priority of rights. Consequently, '[a]lthough preservation of religious and cultural values and traditions as part of the identity of the child must be taken into consideration, practices that are inconsistent or incompatible with the rights

129 See Fortin (2009), 17.

130 Eekelaar (1986), 170; 171.

131 See section 3.2.

132 The interest here goes beyond one in being preferably raised by parents (article 9 and 18 CRC) and ability to practice culture (Article 30 CRC).

133 *Neulinger and Shuruk v Switzerland*, no. 41615/07 (2010) ECtHR (Grand Chamber) ECHR 2010, para 136.

134 CmRC (2013) General Comment 14, paras 46–84.

135 E.g. s. 1(3) *Children Act* 1989, chapter 41; s. 3(2) *Children Proceedings (Parental Responsibility) Bill* 2015 (Hong Kong).

136 See for critique Sutherland (2016), 38.

established in the Convention are not in the child's best interests'.[137] Welfare checklists in turn tend to emphasise relational aspects that would be relevant to religion within the family context. Te checklist included in Hong Kong's 2015 *Children's Proceedings (Parental Responsibility) Bill* e.g. requires that regard be had to 'the nature of the relationship of the child with each of the child's parents and with other persons'.[138] Importantly also, both the General Comment and Welfare Checklists refer to 'other relevant considerations' beyond those listed and allow a certain open-endedness that can develop with attitudes in society as would be expected in a public order context.

Irrespective of their use as guidelines, nearly all interest determinations suffer from a similar defect in their use as public order limitations. Public order refers to overarching principles on which *consensus* exists in society. However, when categorisations of interests or determinations of best interests are proposed, there is virtually no evidence of inclusivity.[139] Children in particular are not normally asked for their contribution to what might be in their interests.[140] Only when their interests are included in larger socio-legal projects does there seem to be regard for children's voices, but such projects are far and few between.[141] Instead, interests are considered the prerogative of adults, especially if children's rights are to be separately considered.[142] The balance of interests itself may include children's views as a separate element, but this is not the same as including children in the determination and interpretation of all elements that make up children's interests.

If interests are to serve as a public order limitation on children's rights to freedom of religion that is necessary in a democratic society, the exclusion of children in their determination is not defensible. Even if we were to accept that interest limitations take on a paternalistic outlook, and we accept that children do not always know what is best for them,[143] children should still be involved in identifying what matters to their lives.[144] For a limitation to be necessary in

137 CmRC (2013) General Comment 14, para 57.

138 S. 3(2)(c).

139 Tobin (2013), 412.

140 J.E McIntosh, Four Young People Speak about Children's Involvement in Family Court Matters. (2009) 15(1) *Journal of Family Studies* 98, 101 'My Judge thanked me for coming but said they were capable of making [best interest] decisions without me'. See also A. Ben-Arieh and N. Tarshish, 'Children's Rights and Well-Being', in Ruck et al. (2017), 75, 76 on children's participation as a future goal.

141 E.g. U. Kilkelly, *The Rights and Legal Status of Children and Parental Responsibilities: The Views of Children and Young People*. Council of Europe, Document CJ-FA (2011) 6 (2011), 13.

142 Gareil (2004), 233, 473; D. Archard and M. Skivenes, Balancing a Child's Best Interests and a Child's Views. (2009) 17 *International Journal of Children's Rights* 1, 2.

143 See Langlaude (2007), 49, 50.

144 J. Eekelaar, The Interests of the Child and the Child's Wishes: The Role of Dynamic Self-Determinism. (1994) 8 *International Journal of Law and the Family* 42, 48; M. Freeman, *Article 3. The Best Interests of the Child: A Commentary on the United Nations Convention on the Rights of the Child*. Dordrecht: Martinus Nijhoff, 2005, 7; Tobin (2013), 412, 415.

a democratic society 'the presumption . . . must be in favour of inclusion'.[145] The interests invoked to justify PCRMs must therefore have been determined through an inclusive process. This includes hearing from children, which can be done through 'children's hearings, children's parliaments, children-led organizations, children's unions or other representative bodies, discussions at school, social networking websites, etc.'[146] In addition, research with children can provide an important impetus for the identification of interests, although Tobin rightly warns that this should be participatory research with children rather than adult-driven research on children.[147] Eventually, though, children's insights need to come together with those of others, such as parents and people working with children to ensure that deliberation is indeed inclusive. That is the case at a more general level (the interests of children as a group), but also in each individual case where the balance of interests (the best interests of the child) might provide a legitimate reason to limit a child's freedom of manifestation and impose a PCRM – if the public order limitation is narrowly construed, suitable and ultimately necessary in a democratic society. Where that is not the case and a PCRM is still imposed, a violation of the child's right emerges. That violation then prompts the question of whether – and how – children should be able to enforce their rights, discussed in the next chapter.

145 *Shindler v United Kingdom*, no. 19840/09 (07 May 2013) ECtHR, para 103.
146 CmRC (2013) General Comment 14, para 91.
147 Tobin (2013), 415.

5 Invoking and enforcing freedom of manifestation within the family

The previous three chapters looked at the legal framework that applies to parentally coerced religious manifestations (PCRMs). Under this framework, there is recognition that parents have a role to play in the religious education of their children and a right against the State to prevent the State from indoctrinating their children. Parents also have a right as individuals and parents to try to convince their children of their religion. However, they do not have a (human) right to force their children to manifest the parental religion. Unless a PCRM can be justified under a limitation ground such as public order and is necessary in a democratic society, children's rights to freedom of manifestation pose a barrier to imposed manifestation. Most PCRMs are therefore a violation of rights. This invites the question of what can be done about such violations. Should children's religious rights be enforceable within the family, and if so, how can children vindicate their rights in a meaningful way? This chapter looks at both these elements of enforcement: the potential objections against invoking and enforcing children's religious rights within the family and the use of court and alternative dispute resolution (ADR) to challenge PCRMs. Attention is further paid to the horizontal effect of human rights and States' positive obligations to ensure compliance by private parties.

Note that this chapter is principally concerned with cases that do *not* invite compulsory State intervention because they have e.g. reached the child protection threshold. The emphasis is on the situations where there is no obvious harm, but States still have a duty to protect children's freedom of manifestation.[1]

5.1 Horizontal effect and positive obligations

Human rights treaties generally impose obligations on State Parties and confer rights to individuals against States. A discussion of freedom of manifestation within the family may therefore appear without cause: human rights cannot in

1 Compare *Eweida and Others v United Kingdom*, nos. 48420/10, 59842/10, 51671/10 and 36516/10 (2013) ECtHR, ECHR 2013, para 95, where the banning of a religious necklace caused no harm of a serious nature, but breached freedom of manifestation.

principle be invoked against parents (or children). This difficulty can be remedied through reliance on the concepts of horizontal effect and positive obligations. Horizontal effect refers to a situation in which fundamental rights apply between individuals without the mediation of the State.[2] Direct horizontal effect describes a situation in which individuals can invoke fundamental rights directly against each other. Indirect horizontal effect applies where reference is made to fundamental rights, but these serve to give meaning to existing legal principles.[3] Indirect horizontal effect is readily accepted by most States and international organisations, especially where it relates to interpretations of the law in accordance with applicable rights.[4] Direct horizontal effect is more problematic, although it has been gaining slow acceptance at the international level.[5] Moreover, some States have unilaterally decided that treaties or provisions enjoy direct horizontal effect in their legal order.[6]

Of the documents containing rights to freedom of manifestation, the UDHR has full direct horizontal effect,[7] but like the 1981 Declaration, it is non-binding. Conversely, the HRC has decided that ICCPR provisions do not have direct horizontal effect as a matter of international law (though they may as a matter of national law).[8] Yet it stated in General Comment No. 17 that 'it is primarily incumbent on the family, . . . and particularly on the parents, to create conditions to promote the harmonious development of the child's personality and his enjoyment of [ICCPR] rights'.[9] This indicates that ICCPR provisions apply within the family, even if they cannot be directly enforced within that context. Direct horizontal effect of the ECHR has been accepted in cases of violations 'repugnant to the fundamental ideals of the Convention or [aimed] at the destruction of the rights and freedoms set forth therein'.[10] It is thus not sufficient for horizontal effect under the ECHR that there is a breach: the action of the individual must seek to destroy the rights of another. The ICCPR and ECHR were nonetheless adopted at a time when there was general opposition to the conferral of rights vis-à-vis individuals.[11] By the time of the CRC's drafting, this had changed and

2 D. Spielmann, *L'effet potentiel de la Convention européenne des droits de l'homme entre personnes privées*. Brussels: Bruylant, 1995, 28.
3 Ibid.
4 E.g. *Ubamaka Edward Wilson v Secretary for Security* [2012] HKEC 1757; s. 3 *Human Rights Act* 1998, chapter 42.
5 Spielmann (1995), 28.
6 E.g. France, see 6.2 below.
7 UN GA, *Resolution 53/144 Declaration on the Right and Responsibility of Individuals, Groups and Organs of Society to Promote and Protect Universally Recognised Human Rights and Fundamental Freedoms*. UN Doc A/RES/53/144 (8 March 1999).
8 HRC, *General Comment 31: Nature of the general legal obligation on States Parties to the Covenant*. UN Doc CCPR/C/21/Rev.1/Add.13 (29 March 2004), para 8.
9 HRC (1989), General Comment 17, para 6.
10 *Pla and Puncernau v Andorra*, no. 69498/01 (2004) ECtHR, ECHR 2004-VIII (Bratza J).
11 See 2.4.

it was envisaged that the CRC would have direct horizontal effect,[12] though following some objection the Convention is now silent on the matter.[13] The CmRC nevertheless seems to suggest that the CRC does enjoy horizontal effect. It has regularly enquired with States about human rights within the family,[14] and in General Comment 16 it stated that, whilst the CRC is 'principally' addressing State obligations:

> duties and responsibilities to respect the rights of children extend in practice beyond the State and State-controlled services and institutions and apply to private actors . . . [they] must meet their responsibilities regarding children's rights and States must ensure they do so.[15]

Yet even where no direct effect applies, States are still subject to positive obligations under human rights treaties. These obligations refer *inter alia* to duties of the State to protect human rights in horizontal relations, resulting in State responsibility at the international level if the State does not effectively (try to) fulfil its duties.[16] States must thus ensure that rights are protected against the actions of private individuals, for example by criminalising private behaviour which would be a violation if perpetrated by the State.[17] Positive obligations to protect rights in private relations have been accepted under all human rights mechanisms examined in Chapters 2 and 3, normally on the basis of a provision that requires the State party to 'ensure' or 'secure' rights.[18] Under the CRC, States also have a positive obligation to change negative societal attitudes towards children exercising their rights.[19] To fulfil their positive obligations, States can themselves ensure that private parties respect rights. However, this would require extensive surveillance of private relationships and interventions likely to violate other rights like privacy. It therefore appears accepted that the most feasible manner for States to ensure respect for human rights in private relations is by offering an appropriate legal framework and accompanying remedies for alleged victims of violations.[20] Positive obligations are

12 E. Verhellen, *Convention on the Rights of the Child: Background, Motivation, Strategies, Main Themes*. Antwerp: Garant, 2000, 69.

13 Detrick (1999), 90.

14 E.g. CmRC, *Summary record of the 147th meeting, Chile*. UN Doc CRC/C/SR.147 (20 April 1994), para 6.

15 Committee on the Rights of the Child, *General Comment No. 16 (2013) on State obligations regarding the impact of the business sector on children's rights*. UN Doc CRC/C/GC/16 (17 April 2013), para 8.

16 Spielmann (1995), 30.

17 E.g. *A. v United Kingdom*, no. 25599/94 (1998) ECtHR Reports 1998-VI concerning 'reasonable chastisement' amounting to inhuman and degrading treatment.

18 E.g. Articles 2 ICCPR, 2 CRC and 1 and 13 ECHR.

19 Hodgkin and Newell (2007), 178, 179.

20 *Glass v United Kingdom*, no. 61827/00 (2004) ECtHR, ECHR 2004-II, para 75; J.-F. Akandji-Kombe, *Positive obligations under the European Convention on Human Rights*. Strasbourg: Council of Europe, 2007, 16.

usually taken to be fulfilled if (1) the State has a mechanism in place that regulates possible limitations on human rights within private relations in a way that is respectful of rights *and* (2) provides individuals with remedies against private parties violating their rights under that mechanism.[21] In the case of PCRMs, the first requirement (a rights-compatible framework) can be fulfilled by States' adoption of a PGPCR that supports children's religious rights. The second requirement (a remedy) would be fulfilled if children were able to access the justice system in relation to an exercise of the PGPCR that does not respect their rights.[22] Through horizontal effect and positive obligations, children can thus rely on their right to freedom of manifestation against parents who impose PCRMs. However, not everyone thinks that children (or indeed anyone) should be able to rely on rights within the family, even if this is legally possible.

5.2 Arguments against rights within the family

Two lines of argument have been developed to oppose the application of rights within the family. The first focuses on the idea that there are superior alternatives to rights within the family and the second is based on a rejection of intra-family rights per se. Regarding the former, Van den Burgh, for example, has proposed that it would be better to focus on parental obligations than rights because a parent 'who only provides that to which his children strictly speaking have a right clearly falls short'.[23] He derives this argument from O'Neill's thesis that obligations should underpin rights, though uses it to reject rights themselves.[24] However, for children to have rights does not mean that parents only have obligations corresponding to those rights.[25] A parent may, for example, have an obligation to sign a medical consent form on behalf of a child in need of treatment, despite the child's right to manifest their religion through refusal of medical care. Parental obligations and children's rights can exist independently.

Other authors have contended that there should not be religious rights within the family because it would be better to solve religious issues through parental responsibility and children's interests.[26] Prioritising parental responsibility and interests would nonetheless not be in keeping with international law, since

21 See United Nations High Commissioner for Human Rights (UNHCHR), *Access to Justice for Children. Report of the United Nations High Commissioner for Human Rights.* UN Doc. A/HRC/25/35 (16 December 2013).

22 See Bielefeldt et al. (2016), 89, 90.

23 Van den Burg (1993), 72. See also T. Cockburn, Children and the Feminist Ethics of Care. (2005) 12(1) *Childhood* 71, 102.

24 Van den Burg (1993), 72; O'Neill (1992), 24–42.

25 Eekelaar has e.g. written on children's rights and separate parental obligations: J. Eekelaar, The Importance of Thinking that Children have Rights. (1992) 6(1) *International Journal of Law, Policy and the Family* 221 and J. Eekelaar, Are Parents Morally Obliged to Care for their Children? (1991b) 11(3) *Oxford Journal of Legal Studies* 340.

26 Smolin (2006), 97; R. Adhar, Religion as a Factor in Custody and Access Disputes. (1996) 10(2) *International Journal of Law, Policy and the Family* 177, 178. See also Mumford (1998), 135–7, 145.

both principles can account for PCRMs which international law would reject.[27] Moreover, in many jurisdictions, children's interests are considered paramount when a decision must be taken in their regard, and sometimes interests are also the stated aim of parental responsibility. Where a parent's personal religious practice only slightly impacts on the interests of a child, that parent could then theoretically be prevented from manifesting.[28] Yet if the parent, like the child, has a personal right to freedom of manifestation in the family, the protection of that right could on occasion present a stronger claim than responsibility and best interests. There are thus both child-centred and parent-centred reasons for accepting intra-family rights.

The second line of argument against religious rights within the family is that such rights are undesirable. This argument is principally divided into two strands. The first focuses on the fear that introducing rights would alter family relations from loving relationships to connections dominated by fear and confrontation (5.3.1). The second is concerned with family unity, which is said to be undermined by having and enforcing religious rights within the family (5.3.2).

5.2.1 The relationship argument

The family has traditionally been a place in which rights play a very minimal role. Still today, many commentators feel that rights have no place in familial contexts, which should instead be governed by care, affection and solidarity.[29] It is believed that rights will turn loving family relationships into cold contractual affairs, featuring continuous confrontations as its members exert their claims against each other.[30] This criticism, which has played an important role in the debate over women's rights,[31] is now regularly advanced to oppose children's rights within the family.[32] Its basic premise is that rights negatively affect relationships.

In an influential article, Waldron has attempted to reconcile the existence of intra-family rights with concerns about family relationships by proposing that rights perform a fall-back function for when problems cannot be solved through reliance on affection and mutual respect.[33] However, Waldron simultaneously

27 See Chapters 3 and 4.

28 See J. Eekelaar, Beyond the Welfare Principle. (2002b) 14(3) *Child and Family Law Quarterly* 237. Compare *F.L. v France*, ECtHR, Application No. 61162/00 with decision of 3 November 2005 (admissibility).

29 For discussion see Tobin (2013), 423–6; H. Brighouse and A. Swift, *Family Values: The Ethics of Parent–Child Relationships*. Princeton, NJ: Princeton University Press, 2014, 14; R. Ekman Ladd, 'Philosophical Perspectives on Children's Rights', in Ruck et al. (2017), 154, 157; J. Herring, *Family Law* (8th ed.). Harlow: Pearson, 2017b, 483.

30 See J. Waldron, When Justice Replaces Affection: The Need for Rights. (1988) 11(3) *Harvard Journal of Law and Public Policy* 625, 628.

31 J. M. Thomson, 'The Reform of Family Law in England', in A.G. Chloros (ed.), *The Reform of Family Law in Europe*. Deventer: Kluwer, 1978, 43.

32 See n. 29.

33 Waldron (1988), 627, 628.

proposes that rights can be actively used to challenge existing norms.[34] Moreover, the author admits that human rights cannot function as fall-backs because they are constant constraints.[35] Hence, freedom of manifestation applies constantly, and not merely when affection for their children cannot dissuade parents from imposing PCRMs. Waldron nonetheless mentions a more helpful manner to reconcile concerns for rights and relations within the family, by attributing a fall-back function to rights *assertions*. Whilst the substance of the claim may be central to family functioning, it is 'its presentation as a claim –that is, as an entitlement that one party presses peremptorily, querulously, and adversarially against the other – that would lead to our misgivings'.[36] Children having and exercising the right to freedom of manifestation need thus not interfere with family relations if children do not bring forward claims to their right every time the issue of manifestation comes up. Beckman takes this one step further by making rights secondary to virtues at the level of language.[37] Although that would certainly make the existence of rights more palatable to those opposed to them, it also deprives rights of much of their meaning and strength. As Ekman Ladd argues:

> The key here is not to eliminate the possibility of ever using the language of rights in familial relationships, but to acknowledge that it is not generally used or needed in everyday situations. Yet . . . [t]o deny children the possibility of invoking rights would be to deny them a powerful moral and legal protection.[38]

Excluding the language of rights carries the danger of reducing children's rights to mere symbolism.[39] The same is true for the enforcement of rights. Although immediate reliance on legal procedures is not desirable within the family context, the existence of such procedures may be warranted for situations where other forms of dispute resolution yield no (appropriate) results.[40] Yet it does matter *how* family members invoke rights. The Council of Europe has provided guidance in this regard. When exercising and invoking their rights, family members should:

- argue in defence of one's viewpoint;
- listen to, understand and interpret other people's arguments;
- recognise and accept differences;
- make choices, consider alternatives and subject them to ethical analysis;

34 Ibid., 641.
35 Ibid., 643.
36 Ibid., 627. See also Cockburn (2005), 83 on enabling conditions for adequate care.
37 L. Beckman, Rights, Rights-Talk, and Children. (2001) 35 *Journal of Value Inquiry* 509, 514.
38 Ekman Ladd (2017), 158
39 B. Shmueli, Love and the Law, Children Against Mothers and Fathers: Or, What's Love got to do with it? (2010) 17 *Duke Journal of Gender Law & Policy* 131, 170.
40 Ibid., 181–5. See also section 5.4 below.

- shoulder shared responsibilities; and
- establish constructive, non-aggressive relations with others.[41]

The CoE does not indicate that rights will have negative effects on family relationships, or that they should not be relied upon, but does suggest that 'living together' requires thoughtfulness in rights enforcement.[42] Hence, if family members keep adversarial rights claims and legal procedures as final remedies instead of their mode of communication, rights need not negatively impact on family relations.

Some authors nonetheless remain unconvinced: they argue that not rights discourse, but rights per se will alter relationships. Rights hang as a dark cloud over the family, altering the way in which the family interacts.[43] Parents who fear at all times that they may do something wrong, whereupon they will be pointed to their children's rights, will hesitate to show their children true love and care.[44] The insecurity further inhibits spontaneous gestures of affection that may or may not coincide with children's rights.[45] Parents could doubt their parenting skills so severely that their parenting becomes less effective.[46] For example, a religious parent whose child has a right to freedom of manifestation within the family could find themselves confused as to the acceptability of involving their child in their religion. As a result, the parent, who would have otherwise organised family activities around that religion, now refrains from doing so for fear of violating the child's right. Dillen has in this respect warned of the 'museafication' of religion, whereby the fear of coercing children leads parents to offer religion in the same detached manner as museums offer art.[47]

These arguments appear exaggerated, if only because the parent–child relationship is already regulated through child protection and other laws, and this has not seemingly resulted in desperate parents. Parents may have become more careful, and conscious of their actions in respect of children, but it is hard to see how this is problematic. As Brighouse and Swift note, 'a parent who never reflects on what she owes her children as people separate from herself is either a saint or worryingly unreflective'.[48] The issue is whether introducing rights *adversely* affects family relationships, not whether their introduction effects no change at all. There is, moreover, no support for the suggestion that

41 CmCoE, *Recommendation Rec (2002)12 of the Committee of Ministers to Member States on Education for Democratic Citizenship*, Council of Europe (16 October 2002), preamble, para 2 and Appendix under 2.

42 Ibid.

43 E. Buss 'Parental' Rights. (2002) 88 *Virginia Law Review* 635, 647–50; C. Lasch, *Haven in a Heartless World: The Family Besieged*. New York and London, 1977, 172, in Reece (2006), 482.

44 Buss (2002), 647–50.

45 Ibid.

46 Ibid.

47 Dillen (2006), 130–3.

48 Brighouse and Swift (2014), 20.

children's rights will cause parents to shy away from showing their children affection or reduce their confidence, if not competence. Laws distinguishing between 'reasonable chastisement' as acceptable punishment and child abuse, for example, could have made parents very anxious about their way of parenting, but there is no indication that parents became excessively insecure after the introduction of limits on disciplining children. In the United Kingdom, this situation would have been exacerbated by the case of *A v United Kingdom* in which the ECtHR found that the prohibition of degrading treatment applied between parents and children and was not covered by reasonable chastisement.[49] Furthermore, the English *Children Act* 1989 gave competent children access to court to challenge aspects of parental responsibility on the basis of their interests.[50] According to the above reasoning, English parents should have been feeling very insecure about their child-rearing capacities for quite a while now, but the 2010 Parental Opinion Survey found that, of 2,319 parents with children aged 0–19, 93% felt confident about their parenting.[51] As children's rights give guidance on what a constructive parent–child relationship looks like,[52] and most parents are naturally inclined to love their children,[53] the introduction of children's rights is more likely to positively, rather than negatively, affect relationships within the family.

5.2.2 The family unity argument

The second objection to the introduction of intra-family religious rights is that these rights undermine family unity.[54] Positive links between shared faith and family functioning have been well established in sociological and psychological research.[55] Sharing the same moral outlook and faith suggests that parents and children are also able to share the same communication framework, base acceptance and rejection of behaviour on standards they both recognise as

49 *A. v United Kingdom*, no. 25599/94 (1998) ECtHR, Reports 1998-VI.

50 S. 10(8).

51 Department of Education, *Parental Opinion Survey 2010*. Research Report DFE-RR061 (2010), 15, 22. Confidence levels dropped as children aged, though even in the 16+ category most parents still felt confident.

52 Tobin (2013), 424; Brighouse and Swift (2014), 20.

53 M.D.A. Freeman, Taking Children's Rights More Seriously. (1992) 6(1) *International Journal of Law, Policy and the Family* 52, 55.

54 E.g. J.E. Coons, 'The Religious Rights of Children', in J. Witte and J.D. Van der Vyver (eds), *Religious Human Rights in Global Perspective. Religious Perspectives*. The Hague: Martinus Nijhoff, 1996. See also Thomson (1978), 43; Tobin (2013), 423; Brighouse and Swift (2014), 18, 168–74.

55 See for overviews: L. Marks, Religion and Family Health: An Overview and Conceptual Model. (2006) 45(4) *Journal of Religion and Health* 603; A. Husain, An Eco-Systems Based Model for Faith-Inspired Parenting. (2013) 23(2) *Journal of Human Behaviour in the Social Environment* 159, 160, 161; D.C. Dollahite et al., Why Religion Helps and Harms Families: A Conceptual Model of a System of Dualities at the Nexus of Faith and Family Life. (2018) *Journal of Family Theory and Review* 219, 222.

valid, and share in activities that are meaningful to either side.[56] Shared faith thus facilitates dialogue and understanding. Numerous studies have furthermore suggested that participation in religious activities makes children feel good and leads to better adjustment.[57] Religious practices such as prayer have also been found to function as ways to increase togetherness and family interaction, provide support and enhance connectedness.[58] Moreover, the performance of religious manifestations by children delights parents, who have themselves often found happiness in their faith and wish for their children to find the same.[59]

However, the positive effects of shared faith and involvement in manifestations are only obtained when parents and children share more or less the same level of personal religiousness (believing) and organisational religiousness (acting).[60] The benefits of being 'united' through religion and manifestations do not seem to apply when children believe in the same religion but interpret it differently, hold a different religion or do not believe at all.[61] This is all the more true if accusatory or manipulative approaches to religious practice are employed.[62] Existing research suggests that religious dissonance places adolescents at risk of internalising (somatic complaints, depression etc.) and externalising (delinquent behaviour etc.) symptoms,[63] while coerced manifestation has been associated with drug and alcohol abuse.[64] In addition, religious dissonance tends to lead to frustration and conflict, further increased if 'normal' conflict becomes inscribed with religious meaning.[65] This further causes children to feel less affection for their parents.[66] Compulsory manifestation is moreover likely to generate

56 J. Kim-Spoon et al., Adolescents Who are Less Religious than their Parents are at Risk for Externalizing and Internalizing Symptoms: The Mediating Role of Parent–Adolescent Relationship Quality. (2012) 26(4) *Journal of Family Psychology* 636, 636–40.

57 Ibid., 636, 637. See R. Klanjšek et al., Religious Orientation, Low Self-Control, and Deviance: Muslims, Catholic, Eastern Orthodox, and 'Bible Belt' Christians. (2012) 35 *Journal of Adolescence* 671, 671, 672 for an overview.

58 J.M. Chelladurai et al., 'The Family that Prays Together . . .': Relational Processes Associated with Regular Family Prayer. (2018) 32(7) *Journal of Family Psychology* 849, 853, 855.

59 Wood Colby (1982), 64.

60 Kim-Spoon et al. (2012), 640.

61 Ibid., 638–40.

62 Chelladurai et al. (2018), 850.

63 Kim-Spoon et al. (2012), 638–40.

64 J.W. Lee et al., Family Worship Patterns and their Correlation with Adolescent Behaviour and Beliefs. (1997) 36(3) *Journal for the Scientific Study of Religion* 372, 380.

65 A. Mahoney et al., Religion and the Sanctification of Family Relationships. (2003) 44(3) *Review of Religious Research* 220, 232; A. Mahoney, Religion and Conflict in Marital and Parent–Child Relationship. (2005) 61(4) *Journal of Social Issues* 689, 699; G.M. Brelsford and A. Mahoney, Relying on God to Resolve Conflict: Theistic Mediation and Triangulation in Relations between College Students and Mothers. (2009) 28(4) *Journal of Psychology and Christianity* 291, 299.

66 C.E. Stokes and M.D. Regnerus, When Faith Divides Family: Religious Discord and Adolescent Reports of Parent–Child Relations. (2009) 38 *Social Science Research* 155, 164.

resentment and an uncooperative attitude from children,[67] while parents live in constant fear of being 'found out' by the community.[68] Based on interviews with 476 parents and adolescents, Dollahite et al. conclude that '[i]f expectations are coercive, problems arise',[69] including for intergenerational relationships, in which 'disharmony . . . may divide'.[70]

The family unity argument against rights is thus principally an argument for external unity (the family is seen as united by the outside world) since disregard for rights and imposition of PCRMs are not likely to lead to internal unity. As Blackmun J held in *Planned Parenthood of Missouri v Danforth*, it is difficult to conclude that rejecting autonomy 'will serve to strengthen the family unit . . . where the minor and the . . . parent are so fundamentally in conflict and the very existence of [the situation causing conflict] already has fractured the family structure'.[71] Treating the family as a unit when opinions are divided is likely to generate more conflict than it resolves. Conversely, acknowledging the religious rights of different family members can be a way to avoid conflict, because there is a recognition that people's claims to different practices, or lack thereof, are legitimate. Rather than being its source, rights can prevent conflict from coming into existence. This is because the existence of equal rights implies 'the principle of cooperation', not separation.[72] Lovinger et al., for example, found that children who live different religious experiences from their parents do not seek to break ties, or undermine unity, but hope for a partnership within the family.[73] An analogy could be drawn with children of divorced parents who follow the (non) religious convictions of one parent, whilst remaining connected and united – and sometimes living – with the other.[74]

Accepting religious rights within the family could actually *enhance* unity, because it requires family members to be respectful towards other members and their manifestations. It may also make children more willing to participate in such manifestations. A teenager forced to attend a place of worship will sit there sulking and perhaps trying to ruin the occasion for his/her parents, whereas a teenager who knows that they have the right not to be there, but came to please their parents, causes parents a wholly different experience much more

67 B.J. Strahan, *Parents, Adolescents, and Religion*. Corranbong: Avondale Academic Press, 1994, 11, in Lee et al. (1997), 378. See also G. Smith, *Children's Perspectives on Believing and Belonging*. London: National Children's Bureau, 2005, 18.

68 E. Tabory and S. Hazan-Stern, Bonds of Silence: Parents and Children Cope with Dissonant Levels of Religiosity. (2013) 33 *Contemporary Jewry* 171, 180.

69 Dollahite et al. (2018), 223, 229.

70 Ibid., 230.

71 *Planned Parenthood of Missouri v Danforth* (No. 74-1151) 28 US 52.

72 K. Scheiwe, Between Autonomy and Dependency: Minors' Rights to Decide on Matters of Sexuality, Reproduction, Marriage, and Parenthood. (2004) 18 *International Journal of Law, Policy and the Family* 262, 263.

73 S.L. Lovinger et al., Some Clinical Applications of Religious Development in Adolescence. (1999) 22 *Journal of Adolescence* 269, 270, 271 and 276. See also Dillen (2006), 131.

74 E.g. *Re C (A Child)* [2012] EW Misc 15 (CC).

likely to increase family unity. The existence of religious rights within the family does not mean that people will always go their separate ways without any willingness to share in the religious practices of other family members as family activities.[75] It does not mean that children cannot agree to manifest a religion they do not believe in. What it does mean is that they cannot be forced to do so unless the PCRM is covered by a limitation to their right to freedom of manifestation. It also means that a balance must be found within the family. Rights empower their holders, but part of the process of empowerment is gaining a more general awareness of rights, including the idea that others' rights must also be respected.[76] The CmRC has on various occasions emphasised that the rights of children go hand in hand with the rights of other family members and the family itself.[77] Children hold independent rights, but these 'will be especially meaningful in the context of the rights of parents and other members of the family – to be recognized, to be respected, to be promoted. And this will be the only way to promote . . . respect for the family itself'.[78] What causes family unity is mutual respect and understanding, communication and a willingness to accommodate another person's belief and practices, not the fact that every family member participates in the same practice.

Ultimately, the family unity argument is an argument about who determines that unity. Unity is based on the assumption that either everyone agrees, or when there is religious conflict a designated person (or couple) takes decisions for the family. That person is generally not the child, but the parent(s),[79] much like it used to be the husband and not the wife as described by Thomas:

> A principal reason why a wife enjoyed so few rights at common law was the doctrine of unity of the spouses, that is, that in the eyes of the law a man and his wife were one. But this did not mean that the spouses participated equally in the personality created out of them: rather, the effect of the law could be summed up by the cynical proposition that, while man and wife were one, the man was the one.[80]

Substituting 'husband' with parents and 'wife' with child turns the above into a fair representation of the family unity argument under which the parents are 'the one'. It has been argued that if 'a system of rights were to make the parent hostage to the religious preferences of children, the identity of the family would be deeply compromised'.[81] The family unity argument thus relies heavily on the idea

75 Tabory and Hazan-Stern (2013), 171.
76 M. Brandon and L. Fisher, *Mediating with Families*. Pyrmont: Thomson Reuters, 2018, 269.
77 See Hodgkin and Newell (2007), 78, 79.
78 Committee of the Rights of the Child, *Report on the Seventh Session (Geneva, 26 September–14 October 1994)*. UN Doc CRC/C/34 (8 November 1994), para 198.
79 See in this regard Article 5 of the 1981 Declaration (organisation of family life).
80 Thomson (1978), 43.
81 Coons (1996), 174.

that there should not be religious rights for *children* within the family. If unity is the concern, why not let the child decide?

5.3 Enforcing rights within the family

Enforcement of rights takes the discussion a step further. Rights enjoyment carries significant normative force and considerate assertions can bring about a more respectful situation if rights are interfered with. However, it is not always enough to invoke rights when one cannot enforce them. Particularly when it comes to children's right to freedom of manifestation, it is easy to imagine a parent prioritising a divine command over a child's temporal right that cannot be enforced. If children insist on their own competence, this can lead to parent–child conflict.[82] Yet that does not seemingly deter children who are willing to defend their freedom of manifestation, even if this leads to conflict with parents.[83] Normally such conflict will be solved or remain within the family, though some children have used the justice system to challenge limitations on their freedom of religion.[84] This raises two further questions beyond that of children having rights within the family. Should religious rights be enforceable within the family? And if so, how?

The problem of enforcement is to a large extent linked to more general perspectives on children and their rights. Children who seek to enforce their rights challenge the dominant outlook under which children's rights are exceptions to parental rights, granted along the way as children mature.[85] Children who enforce religious rights against adults already *have* rights, irrespective of whether adults think they are old and mature enough to be granted any. The question becomes one of limits on their rights, rather than their existence. Second, and most importantly, children who seek to enforce rights against adults challenge the welfare perspective that continues to underlie attitudes towards children and their rights.[86] Instead of adult determinations of what is good for children, enforcement by minors highlights children's empowerment. Such empowerment contradicts the dominant vulnerability/incompetence discourse.[87] Ultimately, enforcement by children challenges theories that locate power in adults. To allow children to enforce an autonomy-based right to freedom of manifestation takes down the most significant vestige of adult power: to

82 I. Hutchby and M. O'Reilly, Children's Participation and the Familial Moral Order in Family Therapy. (2010) 12(1) *Discourse Studies* 49, 49.

83 See sections 6.5, 7.5 and 8.5; Dollahite et al. (2018), 223.

84 E.g. Cass civ, n° 89-20878, 11 June 1991, *Bulletin* I, N° 196, 129.

85 See Taylor (2015), 18–21. See also e.g. 6.3 below.

86 H. Stalford and K. Hollingsworth, 'Judging Children's Rights: Tendencies, Tensions, Constraints and Opportunities', in H. Stalford et al., *Rewriting Children's Rights Judgments: From Academic Vision to New Practice*. Oxford: Hart, 2017, 35, 36.

87 See J. Herring, 'Vulnerability, Children and the Law', in M.D.A Freeman (ed.), *Law and Childhood Studies: Current Legal Issues*. Oxford: OUP, 2012, esp. 243–50. Herring argues that everyone is vulnerable, not that children need empowerment.

ignore the rights-claims of children as long as children are not seriously harmed. Genuine respect for children's rights would nonetheless require a possibility for children to enforce their rights. This is especially true for personal rights like freedom of manifestation. Moreover, where genuine conflict is already present and cannot be resolved within the family, the alternative of letting it simmer is unattractive in view of the negative outcomes outlined above.[88]

Still, the enforcement of rights could cause particular antagonism, because at that stage exterior mechanisms are employed. This means that the appearance of (external) family unity can no longer be upheld, and an 'outsider' is brought into the family conflict.[89] Such enforcement, rather than rights themselves, may hurt children's and parents' relational interests and undermine possibilities for families to be reunited (internally). Though instead of this being a reason to reject the enforcement of freedom of manifestation in the face of PCRMs, it is a reason to explore what processes serve families best. The discussion which needs to be held is not an adult-centred discussion of whether we are willing to compromise adults' power-hold by giving children access to enforcement mechanisms, but a family-centred one of how we can organise credible enforcement mechanisms that are able to encompass both individual rights and the value of the family where PCRMs are imposed.

5.3.1 Access to court

Rights are traditionally enforced through legal proceedings. It would therefore be logical to give children access to court when PCRMs interfere with their right to freedom of manifestation. Access to justice, including court, 'is a fundamental right in itself and an essential prerequisite for the protection and promotion of all other human rights' for children.[90] There are nonetheless two preliminary hurdles to legally challenging PCRMs, apart from whether children *should* have access to court. The first is that '[i]n most jurisdictions . . . children cannot institute legal proceedings by themselves' because the law considers them legally incompetent.[91] This incompetence is said to protect children,[92] but that concern does not seem to extend to all areas of the law. Children stand trial for offences they have committed, and some jurisdictions allow parents to apply for measures where their non-complying child is 'beyond parental control'.[93] It is therefore

88 Section 5.3.2.

89 J.L.C. Ma, The Diagnostic and Therapeutic Uses of Family Conflicts in a Chinese Context: The Case of Anorexia Nervosa. (2005) 27(1) *Journal of Family Therapy* 24, 25, 31.

90 UNHCHR (2013), para 3.

91 M. Paré and T. Chong, Human Rights Violations and Canadian Mining Companies. (2017) 21(7) *International Journal of Human Rights* 908, 919.

92 P.-B. Lebrun, *L'essentiel sur l'autorité parentale*. Paris: Ellipses, 2010, 22.

93 This can apply to failing to manifest: G.D. MacDonald, Accepting Parental Responsibility: 'Future Questioning' as a Means to Avoid Foster Home Placement of Children. (1992) 71(1) *Child Welfare* 3, 13–15.

difficult to see why children should not have access to court when parents violate rights. Moreover, children's legal incompetence is inconsistent with human rights requirements themselves. The CmRC, for example, has often warned that children should be treated as competent beings unless there is actual evidence of their incompetence.[94] Some safeguards may be called for (see below and in Chapters 6–8), but a blanket incompetence is unwarranted.

The second hurdle was introduced at the beginning of this chapter: human rights normally apply between individuals and the State unless the State accepts horizontal effect. States still retain positive obligations, but these must be enforced at the international level, including e.g. via the CRC complaints procedure if they have ratified the Third Optional Protocol. However, it would be sensible for a State to seek to acquit itself of its positive obligations by providing children with a rights-respecting framework governing PCRMs and a way to challenge violations of this framework – and thus freedom of manifestation itself. Since most States regulate religious upbringing via their civil law(s), this would mean giving children access to family or specialised children's courts. The CmRC has, for example, supported a 'right to make . . . applications to family courts' for older minors.[95] Furthermore, human rights treaties themselves obligate States to provide children with access to remedies for vindication of their rights.[96] Court features prominently amongst such remedies. Hence the UN's *Access to Justice for Children* report states:

> [A]ccess to justice refers to the ability to obtain a just and timely remedy for violations of rights as put forth in national and international norms and standards . . . It applies to civil, administrative and criminal spheres of national jurisdictions, . . . and covers all relevant judicial proceedings, affecting children . . . *Children should have the possibility to complain and initiate legal proceedings in cases of violations of their rights.*[97]

Children should additionally be empowered to use court procedures and receive free legal assistance since they 'are usually at a disadvantage when engaging with the legal system'.[98] They must be made aware of their rights and the workings of the court procedure, and receive appropriate information whilst they make

94 CmRC (2006), General Comment 7, para 16.
95 CmRC (2016), General Comment 20, para 39.
96 E.g. Articles 2 ICCPR, HRC, 4 CRC and 13 ECHR. See also HRC, *General Comment No. 31 on the nature of the general legal obligation imposed on States Parties to the Covenant*, UN Doc. CCPR/C/21/Rev.1/Add.13 (26 May 2004), para 15; Paré and Chong (2017), 908, 909.
97 UNHCHR (2013), paras 4, 58. Original emphasis in bold. See also CmCoE, *Guidelines of the Committee of Ministers of the Council of Europe on Child-Friendly Justice*, Council of Europe (17 November 2010), para 34. The previous 1996 *European Convention on the Exercise of Children's Rights*, CETS 160 (1 July 2000) gave children procedural rights within existing procedures but not a right of access to court itself.
98 UNHCHR (2013), para 58. Emphasis omitted.

their way through the system.[99] Stalford et al. have therefore argued that the right to information is three-layered and consists of 'practical and procedural information' (how does the court work?), 'foundational rights-based information' (how should it work to respect rights?) and 'agency-asserting information' (how to use this information in the child's situation?).[100]

Some jurisdictions like Australia,[101] England,[102] and South Africa[103] already allow children access to the family or children's courts to challenge an exercise of parental responsibility, albeit on the basis of best interests. In England, for example, children can apply for 'section 8 orders'[104] after having obtained leave from the High Court on the basis that the child has 'sufficient understanding to make the proposed application for the section 8 order'.[105] A child-applicant would normally receive legal aid and instruct their own lawyers.[106] Otherwise, the procedure is the same as that followed if a parent were to apply for an order upon divorce. Under section 8 proceedings, children can apply for child arrangement orders determining residence and contact, such as with a third party outside the parents' religious community.[107] Prohibited steps orders prohibit a parent from a certain exercise of parental responsibility, like making a child go through a religious rite of initiation,[108] and under specific issue orders a parent is told (or allowed, depending on who is applying) to exercise responsibility in a certain way, e.g. by sending the child to a less orthodox school than (s)he has hitherto attended.[109]

The enforcement by children of religious rights within the family could very well take place through a procedure similar to the one currently in force in England, albeit with relevant adjustments. If a child has a right to a lawyer, it makes more sense, having had the benefit of meeting the child in person, if the lawyer decides whether the child is competent to instruct them, like they do with other clients. This arrangement also provides a child with a relatively easy possibility of a 'second opinion' from another lawyer. The law can instead specify that a case is struck off the list if it appears that the child is not competent and assistance cannot help them. Lawyers should be free of charge for the child, but equally for the child's parents if they cannot afford a lawyer to ensure equal legal representation. Children can then apply for orders relating to the exercise of parental

99 Ibid., para 56.

100 H. Stalford et al., Achieving Child Friendly Justice through Child Friendly Methods: Let's Start with the Right to Information. (2017) 5(3) *Social Inclusion* 207, 212, 213.

101 65C *Family Law Act* 1975 (Cth) (No. 53, 1975, Compilation 82).

102 10(8) *Children Act* 1989.

103 14 *Children's Act* 2005 (Act 38, 2005).

104 Orders under s. 8 *Children Act* 1989.

105 10(8) *Children Act* 1989.

106 15(1) Schedule 1, *Legal Aid, Sentencing and Punishment of Offenders Act* 2012, chapter 10.

107 Previously these orders were orders for custody: *Re R (A Minor) (Religious Sect)* [1993] 2 FLR 163.

108 *Re C (A Child)* [2012] EW Misc 15 (CC).

109 *Re G (Children: Religious Upbringing)* [2012] EWCA Civ 1233.

power, similar to the orders existing under the *Children Act* 1989. Yet, whereas *Children Act* decisions are taken on the basis of children's best interests, where fundamental rights are involved limitations on these rights must be narrowly construed as explained in Chapter 4.[110] There is a very important difference between best interests as a ground for limitation under public order, if prescribed by law and necessary in a democratic society (i.e. a very narrow limit), and best interests as the principle governing the entire situation (the widest possible reach). A best interests principle may therefore not be an appropriate guideline when religious freedom is involved. Instead, a no-harm principle would be more fitting, especially since this would correspond with the threshold for limitations on parental upbringing under child protection.[111] A court can also not disregard the rights of others within the family, such as parents' personal right to freedom of religion,[112] even though important limitations on parents' rights may be justified in order to further children's autonomy, development and interests.[113] Hence, where a child makes an application to the family court for an order seeking to protect their freedom of manifestation through a particular exercise of parental power, the court should determine the case on the basis of whether the order would harm the child or unjustifiably interfere with the rights of other family members (the latter inevitably requiring a balancing exercise between rights).

Opening court procedures to disputes over religious manifestation between parents and children has some distinct advantages, other than allowing for compliance with international obligations. First, court proceedings are often described as empowering, particularly for vulnerable parties in civil matters.[114] The *Access to Justice* report e.g. links the ability to access remedies with children's empowerment.[115] Judicial procedures further guarantee formal equality, and due process rules ensure fair treatment and likely an equitable outcome.[116] Both children and parents may feel that they can benefit from a formal procedure that is concerned with 'resolving disputes about people's rights'[117] rather than advancing a policy or standpoint. Another often mentioned advantage of taking matters of social justice to court is that these issues gain public attention, and through favourable

110 J.G. Merrills, *The Development of International Law by the European Court of Human Rights* (2nd ed.). Manchester, New York: Manchester University Press, 1993, 77.

111 See also A. Daly, *Children, Autonomy and the Courts: Beyond the Right to be Heard*. Leiden: Brill Nijhoff, 2017, 10 and chapter 6.

112 As State entities, courts must uphold everyone's human rights.

113 See e.g. *Deschomets v France* (dec), no. 31956/02 (16 May 2006) ECtHR (unreported).

114 T. Grillo, The Mediation Alternative: Process Dangers for Women. (1991) 100(6) *Yale Law Journal* 1545, 1557; R. Hunter et al., 'Access to What? LASPO and Mediation', in A. Flynn and J. Hodgson (ed.), *Access to Justice and Legal Aid: Comparative Perspectives on Unmet Legal Need*. Oxford: Hart, 2017, 245.

115 UNHCHR (2013), 5, 25.

116 See A.M. Noone, ADR, Public Interest Law and Access to Justice: The Need for Vigilance. (2011) 37(1) *Monash University Law Review* 57.

117 Hunter et al. (2017), 245.

precedents change in society can be achieved.[118] A landmark judgment could e.g. be key to changing the widely held view that the imposition of PCRMs is a parental right, despite this view's inconsistency with international law. Finally, disputes are sometimes so protracted that without judicial intervention no solution can be reached.[119] Since parents may think that religious benefits are superior to exercising human rights, there is a heightened chance of conflict related to PCRMs ending in deadlock, and adjudication (or the threat thereof) necessary to overcome the impasse.

At the same time, questions may arise as to the appropriateness of court procedures to regulate religious differences within the family context. The adversarial nature of legal proceedings seems especially unconducive to (continued) family relations. Whilst rights themselves need not undermine family unity or relational interests, taking the other party to court would probably not be regarded as a constructive means to enforce rights. The initiation of legal proceedings is generally regarded as an act of hostility, engendering a climate of conflict.[120] Subsequent proceedings exacerbate this conflict as parties are required to take opposing stands and dismiss their opponent's position whilst defending their own.[121] Parents and children would have to dig in their positions vis-à-vis each other, simultaneously trying to convince the judge that the other side is 'wrong'. Rather than bringing parents and children together with a view to their continued relationship, court proceedings drive the two apart. It is therefore not surprising that the idea of children taking parents to court is often associated with 'children divorcing parents'.[122] However, custody cases in which children have continued to live with one parent whilst challenging their religious upbringing with the help of the other parent demonstrate that this need not be the inevitable result of court action.[123] In any case, if the child was no longer interested in living with the parents they would not litigate over (just) the PCRM. This does, however, not detract from the fact that the adversarial nature of court proceedings does not likely serve children's relational interests or family functioning, and may deter children from seeking remedies for PCRMs in the first place.

118 R.A.B. Bush and J.P. Folger, Mediation and Social Justice: Risks and Opportunities. (2012) 27(1) *Ohio State Journal on Dispute Resolution* 1, 5; A.J. McCammon and A.R. McGrath, Litigating Change? Social Movements and the Court System. (2015) 9(2) *Sociology Compass* 128.

119 Hunter et al. (2017), 245.

120 See H. Radovanovic, Parental Conflict and Children's Coping Styles in Litigating Separated Families: Relationships with Children's Adjustment. (1993) 21(6) *Journal of Abnormal Child Psychology* 697.

121 E.B. Langan, 'We Can Work it out': Using Cooperative Mediation – a Blend of Collaborative Law and Traditional Mediation- to Solve Divorce Disputes. (2010–2011) 30(2) *Review of Litigation* 245, 253.

122 H. Houghton-James, Children Divorcing their Parents. (1994) 16(2) *Journal of Social Welfare and Family Law* 185, 185. See also 6.6.1.

123 *Re C (A Child)* [2012] EW Misc 15 (CC; CCas civ, n° 89-20878, 11 June 1991, *Bulletin* I, N° 196, 129.

A second concern relates to the use of religious discourse in court. Legal procedures require parties to frame their arguments in non-religious terms,[124] with children's issues decided on the basis of secular laws.[125] Yet religious arguments underlie the very position of at least one of the parties (normally the parents, although a child may have their own religious views). McCrudden has therefore argued that, as the language of human rights started to take centre stage, religion found itself side-lined because it could not express itself in the language of rights.[126] Whilst a child seeking to challenge PCRMs based on freedom of manifestation benefits from legally accepted language, their parents might not. This issue is compounded if parents do not have a lawyer who can 'translate' their religious concerns into legal terms. However, children are not necessarily indifferent to the religiously motivated concerns of their parents; they may accept and value them, even if they do not share them.[127] Most importantly, they understand them. Whilst children who have received a religious upbringing may no longer agree with the outcome, they are still able to appreciate religious standards and communication frameworks.[128] Courts can at most note the existence of religious concerns, but they must dismiss them as legally irrelevant.[129] This is likely to cause parents agony and possibly generates resentment in ways unlikely to improve the family situation or even desired by the child.

Finally,[130] there is concern that giving children access to court simply shifts decision-making 'from the parents to the State', unless a child's religious right is decisive (in which case it can be 'implemented by suitable court order').[131] This carries the danger, according to some authors, that judges will decide in line with their own convictions, since neutrality is hard to achieve in religious matters.[132] Yet neutrality is also hard to achieve in other matters from which judges are not barred, such as matters related to equality like same-sex marriage. Moreover, part of the concern is based on the vagueness of the best interests principle which leaves judges considerable space to impose their own views.[133]

124 E.g. *Newcastle City Council v Z* [2005] EWCH 1490 (Fam), at [53].

125 CmRC, *Concluding Observations, Niger*. UN Doc CRC/C/NER/CO/2 (18 June 2009), para 8; CmRC, *Concluding Observations (third and fourth reports), Pakistan*. UN Doc CRC/C/PAK/CO/3-4 (15 October 2009), para 44.

126 C. McCrudden, Multiculturalism, Freedom of Religion, Equality, and the British Constitution: The JSF Case Considered. (2011) 9(1) *I•CON* 200, 207.

127 J. Lees and J. Horwath, 'Religious Parents . . . Just Want the Best for their Kids': Young People's Perspectives on the Influence of Religious Beliefs on Parenting. (2009) 23 *Children and Society* 162, 173.

128 Kim-Spoon et al. (2012), 640.

129 Unless as part of 'parents views': *Re A (Children: Conjoined Twins)* [2000] 4 All ER 961.

130 The issue of costs is purely a political matter and not discussed. Conversely, human resources may be a concern, because court access for children requires properly trained people (including lawyers and judges): UNHCHR (2013), para 57.

131 Adhar (2000), 105.

132 Ibid. See also Adhar (1996), 178; Buss (2002), 650, 654.

133 See n. 132.

If a no-harm principle in conjunction with respect for rights would apply, there is much less scope for the imposition of personal views.

More pressing is that the judge becomes a 'substitute decision-maker' for the *entire* family.[134] Whilst parents and children may be given the opportunity to explore options with the judge, it is the judge who takes the final decision on religious manifestation.[135] The family must then implement it, irrespective of its feasibility or desirability.[136] Court proceedings thus prevent the family from reaching a mutually agreeable solution themselves and taking responsibility for their own lives.[137] Sometimes this is inevitable, because the conflict is too entrenched.[138] Generally though, as Murphy and Singer note, 'courts may not be the best places for families to resolve disputes' because their essential role is not as providers of problem-solving processes, but 'adjudicators of last resort and forums for the creation and enforcement of important social norms'.[139] Using the courts to enforce religious rights may thus bring justice, but potentially little harmony or a family-friendly resolution to conflicts regarding PCRMs. It is an option that should be available to minors, because it allows them to genuinely enforce rights, set precedents and overcome disputes that cannot be solved in another manner. However, it may be useful to also consider alternative forms of dispute resolution that have been recognised as more amenable to continuing relationships and capable of enhancing family-functioning.

5.3.2 Access to mediation

Amongst the many forms of alternative dispute resolution, mediation is the most commonly employed in family disputes and therefore the form here discussed. The process is traditionally defined as one under which two or more parties in conflict voluntarily aim to reach a mutually agreeable solution with the help of a neutral third party, the mediator, under conditions of confidentiality (though changed perceptions of mediation and legal regulation such as mandatory reporting of child abuse have impacted upon the practice and principles like confidentiality).[140] Many States have explicit policies to divert family conflict from the courts to mediation services, but these policies normally exclude any reference to mediation between parents and minors.[141] Moreover, there is an

134 Daly (2017), 23.

135 P. Bonfils and A. Gouttenoire, *Droits des mineurs* (2nd ed.). Paris: Dalloz-Sirey, 2014, 723.

136 Buss (2002), 648.

137 J.C. Murphy and J.B. Singer, Moving Family Dispute Resolution from the Court System to the Community. (2016) 75(9) *Maryland Law Review Endnotes* 9, 12. Hunter et al. (2017), 239.

138 Hunter et al. (2017), 245.

139 Murphy and Singer (2016), 9.

140 R.H.M. Leung, *Hong Kong Mediation Handbook* Hong Kong: Sweet & Maxwell, 2014, 18; Brandon and Fisher (2018), 481–99.

141 Or mention it in passing only: Department of Justice, *Report of the Working Group on Mediation*. Hong Kong: Government of the Hong Kong Special Administrative Region, 2010, 21.

abundance of literature on family mediation,[142] though only a handful of authors consider parent–child mediation independently.[143] With the very recent exception of France,[144] and to a lesser extent Australia,[145] it is furthermore difficult to find any structured provision of general parent–child mediation services in practice, although individual initiatives do exist.[146] The reason for this may be quite simple: where children do not have access to court, they also do not have to be considered for alternatives to court. It is only where parents and children could face each other in court, for example in the context of children 'beyond parental control' applications, that mediation is seen as particularly relevant.[147] Given children's increased access to court, attention to ADR is nonetheless likely to increase.[148] Moreover, there is progressively more recognition of children's role as active participants in the family,[149] prompting the development of dispute resolution mechanisms that can account for this altered perception.[150] Mediation fits this new context as a mode of ADR premised on the participation of parents and children, who are both perceived as agents contributing to family processes. Additionally, the emphasis mediation places on dialogue, exchange of views and the opening of communication structures addresses the previously identified issue that PCRM-related conflict is closely linked with family functioning.

If it takes place under the right conditions, mediation is said to have a range of benefits when compared to court procedures (quicker,[151] less damaging, dealing with actual concerns rather than legal terms, promoting self-determination and communication, the outcome likely to be more durable because not imposed by a stranger, etc.).[152] The process may be especially relevant – and has been successfully used – where families face disagreement over PCRMs.[153] Mediation aims to establish, first, whether the rights assertions by children and coerced manifestations

142 Including child-inclusive mediation between adults. See e.g. J.E. McIntosh et al., Child-Focused and Child-Inclusive Divorce Mediation: Comparative Outcomes from a Prospective Study on Post-Separation Adjustment. (2008) 46(1) *Family Court Review* 105.

143 Recently especially A. Mouttet, 'France: Implications des enfants dans la mediation familiale', in J. Mirimanoff (ed.), *Médiation et jeunesse: Mineurs et mediations familiales, scolaires et penales en pays francophones*. Brussels: Larcier, 2013; Leung (2014); J.S. Tucker et al., Effectiveness of Parent–Child Mediation in Improving Family Functioning and Reducing Adolescent Problem Behaviour: Results from a Pilot Randomized Controlled Trial. (2017) 46(3) *Journal of Youth and Adolescence* 505; Brandon and Fisher (2018).

144 See 6.6.2.

145 Especially in cases of divorce via Family Relationship Centres.

146 See e.g. Mouttet (2013), 83.

147 See R.A.B. Bush, Staying in Orbit, or Breaking Free: The Relationship of Mediation to the Courts over Four Decades. (2008) 84 *North Dakota Law Review* 705.

148 See 8.5.1 below.

149 E.g. F. De Singly, 'La cause de l'enfant', in De Singly (2004b), 22; Such and Walker (2005), 48, 49.

150 E.g. CMCoE, *Recommendation Rec (2002)12 of the Committee of Ministers to Member States on Education for Democratic Citizenship*, Council of Europe (16 October 2002) discussed above.

151 Paré and Chong (2017), 919 emphasise the need for quick procedures in view of children's development.

152 Hunter et al. (2017), 247 provide an overview.

153 MacDonald (1992), 13–15; Brandon and Fisher (2018), 261, 278–87.

by parents (the manifest conflict) are perhaps prompted by deeper, underlying issues.[154] For example, as much as parents may be concerned with children's welfare, they could simultaneously experience a refusal to manifest their religion as a personal rejection by a significant person in their lives.[155] Assurances from the child that they reject the PCRMs but not their parents can then help to solve this issue. Family mediation further seeks to improve relationships between parties by changing communication patterns and family functioning, even if no agreement is eventually reached.[156] As Leung explains:

> Mediation . . . gives the family members a legitimate context for sharing their views, voicing out their opinions, expressing their needs and asking for change. They enjoy a more equal status in mediation, and are empowered to negotiate. Mediation of family disputes is therefore more than just a process of conflict resolution. It is an opportunity for the parties to learn [a] new style of communication, discussion, interaction and negotiation [that] will prepare them to deal with future disagreement and arguments.[157]

Mouttet notes that mediation may be useful for parties to get things off their chest.[158] However, the author (who ran a parent–child mediation service), emphasises that parent–child mediation can have important positive effects beyond that. The process allows parties to truly explain their feelings, be listened to without judgement and aided to understand the other party's viewpoints.[159] Parent–child mediation can thereby renew intra-family dialogue, overcome (religious) enmeshment and improve relationships as the parents and child search together for a solution to their problem.[160] Mediation's ability (even if not always the outcome) to thus bring parties closer together, rather than drive them apart, makes the process attractive for families.

Furthermore, mediation encourages parties to negotiate solutions that work for *them*, beyond the constraints of legal rules or legal language.[161] Religiously motivated arguments can be fully acknowledged (though not necessarily accepted) in PCRM-related mediation and religion is able to play a part in the solution in ways it cannot in court. For example, parties may agree to 'theistic mediation' under

154 A. Taylor, *The Handbook of Family Dispute Resolution: Mediation Theory and Practice*. San Francisco, CA: Jossey-Bass, 2002, 344, 345.
155 S. Gutstein, Family Reconciliation as a Response to Adolescent Crises. (1987) 4 *Family Process* 475, in MacDonald (1992), 5.
156 M. Roberts, *Mediation in Family Disputes: Principles of Practice*. Abingdon: Ashgate, 2008, 34, 35, but see Tucker et al. (2017), 506, 512.
157 Leung (2014), 211.
158 Mouttet (2013), 95.
159 Ibid., 88, 95, 96.
160 Ibid.
161 Roberts (2008), 34, but compare R. Field and J. Crowe, The Construction of Rationality in Australian Family Dispute Resolution: A Feminist Analysis. (2007) 27 *Australian Feminist Law Journal* 97, 98–102.

which disagreement regarding manifestation is handed over to God or another supernatural entity.[162] The parents no longer impose PCRMs, because trust is placed in God to bring the child back if God wills.[163] While the result is the same as a court deciding that a child enjoys freedom of manifestation, to frame it in religiously acceptable terms may mean that both parents and children feel taken seriously and increases the chance that the agreement will be honoured.[164] Vice versa, it is possible that during the mediation, the child voluntarily agrees to participate in the contested manifestation out of respect for parental concern and disquiet. This does not mean that the child has changed their mind on the manifestation itself, but that they are willing to do something for their parents, knowing it will bring them relief and joy. In both cases the mediation has an empowering effect on parents and children, whose concerns have been taken seriously, and who have agreed to a unique arrangement on (and in) their own terms.[165]

Mediation thus has distinct advantages to court procedures, but it equally raises concerns related to children's capacity, power and justice. Capacity to mediate is divided into legal and functional capacity.[166] Legal capacity depends on domestic legislation, though parents' engagement in mediation with their child can be taken as parental consent for the child's participation if children are otherwise legally incompetent to mediate. Children's functional capacity (their actual ability) to mediate is a matter that may cause more concern, despite Mouttet noting that children are generally more adept at mediation than their parents![167] Yet the available literature on parent–child mediation either does either not address the issue of children's capacity,[168] or rejects capacity assessments in favour of facilitating competencies.[169] Brandon and Fisher, for example, propose that parent–child mediation with children as young as 10

162 Brelsford and Mahoney (2009); G. Brelsford, Divine Alliances to Handle Family Conflict: Theistic Mediation and Triangulation in Father–Child Relationships. (2011) 3(4) *Psychology of Religion and Spirituality* 285.

163 Brelsford and Mahoney (2009), 292.

164 Roberts (2008), 34. See also e.g. C. Shelley, Beating Children is Wrong, isn't it? Resolving Conflicts in the Encounter between Religious Worldviews and Child Protection. (2013) 15(2) *Ecclesiastical Law Journal* 130, 141 (appeal to divine gift of human uniqueness).

165 *Mutatis mutandis* M. Lichtenstein, Mediation and Feminism: Common Values and Challenges. (2000) 18(1) *Mediation Quarterly* 19, 21.

166 L. Boulle and R. Field, *Australian Dispute Resolution*. Chatswood: LexisNexis Butterworths, 2017, 300.

167 Mouttet (2013), 90.

168 Though see La Maison de la Médiation, *Les médiations parent–adolescent sont désormais subventionnées par la CAF* (2018) <http://maisonmediation.fr/acc/18-blog/78-les-mediations-parent-adolescent-dans-le-referentiel-de-la-caf> last accessed 10 March 2019, on the competences of 'creativity, sensitivity, competence to negotiate and evaluate'.

169 Brandon and Fisher (2018), 261–76. See also S.H. Crawford et al., From Determining Capacity to Facilitating Competencies: A New Mediation Framework. (2003) 40(40) *Conflict Resolution Quarterly* 385.

is possible if sessions are short, the focus is narrow and terms used are more concrete.[170] Some capacity-assessment may nonetheless be warranted, because a child who does not have the capacity to mediate may be coerced into an unfair agreement. Generally, children would need to understand the mediation process and be able to take part in it, they would need to be able to express their views, understand the concerns of others, communicate appropriately and contribute to options discussed.[171] That requires 'some degree of knowledge and articulateness [and] some ability to negotiate and problem solve'[172] that at least most teenagers would have. Specific issues may nonetheless arise in parent–child mediation and further research on the concept of capacity in this context is therefore much needed.

Debates on capacity tend to be overshadowed by concerns related to power-imbalances in mediation. Whereas it was previously believed that the mediation process, its principles and the mediator's interventions were sufficient to address power-imbalances,[173] there is now recognition that this is not necessarily the case and mediators can sometimes make matters worse with their interventions.[174] Most of the power-balance debate focuses on abuse,[175] or unequal access to court.[176] Yet, where the imposition of PCRMs leads to abuse, the designated mechanism is that of child protection, not mediation. Further, if children have access to court to challenge parental behaviour, the power-imbalance no longer exists. In fact, since the prospect of court would be more problematic to parents (who cannot use their religious arguments in court) than to children, the power-balance in this respect tilts in children's favour. In general, it is a misconception to think that parents are always the more powerful party and children the weaker. During mediation, power 'may shift backwards and forwards between the adolescent and his or her parents'.[177] Parents may for example be well educated and hold the power of the purse,[178] but children wield power through control over expressions of love and affection, or in religious disputes their ability to discredit the family within the religious community.

170 Ibid., 265, 266.

171 A. Molomby, Elder Mediation. New Solution to an Aging Issue. (2013) 33(4) *The Proctor* 42, 43; M. Condell, Capacity to Mediate and the Human Right to Self-Determination: The Mediator's Responsibility! (2015) 2(1) *Journal of Mediation and Applied Conflict Analysis* 211, 220; Boulle and Field (2017), 300.

172 Boulle and Field (2017), 300.

173 E.g. J.A. Lemmon, *Family Mediation Practice*. New York: Free Press, 1985, 129–34.

174 Field and Crowe (2007) provide an overview.

175 E.g. Lichtenstein (2000), 21; Field and Crowe (2007), 114, 115; C. Piper, 'Mediation and Vulnerable Parents', in J. Wallbank. and J. Herring (eds), *Vulnerabilities, Care and Family Law*. Abingdon: Routledge, 2014, 115.

176 D. Baker, Juvenile Mediation: Innovative Dispute Resolution or Bad Faith Bargaining? (1995–6) 27 *University of Toledo Law Review* 897, 912.

177 Brandon and Fisher (2018), 264.

178 See C. Baylis and R. Carroll, The Nature and Importance of Mechanisms for Addressing Power Differences in Statutory Mediation. (2002) 14(2) *Bond Law Review* 285.

To address power-imbalance, the mediator can use a variety of interventions and also the mediation process itself may mitigate the impact of imbalances.[179] In addition, parties may be supported by a lawyer who can give them advice on their position, and help them review the mediation agreement before it is signed to see whether it is fair.[180] Other options are the appointment of a child advocate or mediator teams consisting of an adult and young person.[181] Yet power-imbalances are a natural aspect of life, and what has been negotiated on equal standing within the confines of the mediation room may look very different in the real world.[182] Some commentators have therefore suggested that mediators should only ensure a minimum power base for each party (one could call it a form of 'working power').[183] Others have argued that mediation should empower parties by supporting them to a level the party feels comfortable with, rather than trying to achieve equality.[184] In any case, as Bush notes whilst linking power and capacity:

> People cannot be forced to think more clearly, make decisions, or communicate effectively and empathetically . . . the most an intervener can do . . . is to act in ways that allow and support the parties' own intrinsic capacities . . . If this is done consistently and effectively, parties naturally find their own footing in a more constructive interaction, and then they proceed to address disputed issues effectively.[185]

It is difficult to predict how power imbalances will affect parent–child mediation without further experience and research. However, a case study by MacDonald demonstrates that even where highly religious parents seemingly wield all power within a family, parent–child mediation is feasible (and *in casu* successful).[186]

A final concern is that of justice: mediation can help the family reach compromise, but can it also help to enforce religious rights? The primary function of mediation is to problem-solve, not to safeguard rights.[187] 'Channelling' children's rights cases towards informal processes can be especially problematic as long as children are still in the process of securing recognition of their rights.[188] Doing so precludes the effectuation of change via precedent, plus mediation's lack of

179 See Bush and Folger (2012), 15–18.
180 Hunter et al. (2017), 242.
181 Taylor (2002), 347. Brandon and Fisher (2018), 266. See *mutatis mutandis* Crampton (2013), 433 on elder advocates.
182 Bush and Folger (2012), 31.
183 A. Hobbs and A. Alonzi, Mediation and Family Group Conferences in Adult Safeguarding. (2013) 15(2) *Journal of Adult Protection* 69, 75.
184 Bush and Folger (2012), 31, 40.
185 Bush (2008), 748.
186 MacDonald (1992), 14, 15.
187 Murphy and Singer (2016), 9.
188 Bush and Folger (2012), 5. See also Noone (2011), 57.

due process is said to perpetuate social injustice.[189] Mediation does indeed not produce landmark judgments, but if the mediation agreement is one that respects rights, social change can be achieved through changes in practice amongst families. Moreover, courts do not always cause social change either. It is, for example, still believed that French children cannot enjoy freedom of religion because of a 1991 judgment preventing a minor's religious conversion.[190] The argument on denial of rights and perpetuation of oppression is more concerning. Existing good practice indications, standards and guidelines may not be able to help children subjected to PCRMs. Children concerned with their religious rights could be belittled, because society deems minors enforcing their religious rights precocious. A first answer to this concern is appropriate mediator training and accreditation.[191] Rights concerns might also weigh in favour of legal assistance for parents and children,[192] although this has to be balanced with the desirability of legalising the mediation process. Most importantly, mediation should truly function as an alternative to court, operating 'in the shadow of the law'. With the knowledge that a case may end up in court when rights are not respected, there is every reason for the mediating parties to take rights duly into account. As such, mediation can be used to enforce religious rights, but not always in the same straightforward manner as court procedures, and especially not without eventual access to those procedures. In recompense, mediation presents a significantly more family-friendly means of dispute resolution, which is why the UN recognises it as a 'child-sensitive' form of access to justice.[193]

5.4 Conclusion

Where children are subjected to PCRMs, the starting point of the discussion should be the child's personal human right to freedom of manifestation. This right is based on autonomy, which means that PCRMs by their very coercive nature form an interference. Yet that does not necessarily mean that PCRMs are always out of bounds. Parents may not have a human right to impose PCRMs, but international law is not oblivious to the role parents play in religiously educating their children or the justifications that sometimes exist for coerced manifestation. Moreover, parents hold a personal right to freedom of religion, which includes a right to seek to convince their children ('others') of that religion. Where PCRMs interfere with children's freedom of manifestation, reliance can also be placed on the limitation ground of public order, which allows for limitations on the basis of principles that regulate life in society, such

189 N. Illman Meyers, Power (Im)balance and the Failure of Impartiality in Attorney-Mediated Divorce. (1995–6) 27 *University of Toledo Law Review* 853, 859, 860; Noone (2011), 6; Bush and Folger (2012), 5.

190 Cass civ, n° 89-20878, 11 June 1991, *Bulletin* I, N° 196, 129. See section 6.3.

191 UNHCHR (2013), para 57.

192 See Hunter et al. (2017), 242.

193 UNHCHR (2013), para 23, 24.

as PGPCRs and children's best interests. Those limitations must nonetheless be narrowly construed and 'necessary in a democratic society', which means that most PCRMs will not be covered and pose a violation of children's freedom of manifestation. Consequently, questions of invoking and enforcing rights arise. These questions play at various levels (international, national, family) as a result of horizontal effect and positive obligations. They also involve normative and practical aspects related to whether rights should apply within the family and whether access to justice is desirable and feasible where parents impose PCRMs. The response to both should be positive: rather than negatively affect relationships and undermine family unity, rights can strengthen a family through their emphasis on mutuality, cooperation and respect. Where rights are nonetheless denied, children should have access to justice. It is at this stage that careful consideration should be given to what mode of conflict resolution is most likely to aid families in conflict over religious manifestation. Whilst access to court should be available as a last resort, mediation offers a more family-friendly approach, capable of opening communication structures and improving family functioning. For that reason, the provision or support of, and access to parent–child mediation should be high on States' agendas.

The above discussion of approaches to PCRMs demonstrates that national law plays an important role in respect of both limitations and enforcement. Limitations on human rights are *always* based on domestic law: the human right itself forms the benchmark at the international level, but States are allowed to limit it in accordance with stated conditions. PCRMs, for example, can only play a role as a limitation on children's right to freedom of manifestation if a State gives parents the right to impose manifestations under its domestic law. Additionally, as argued in this chapter, the matter of rights enforcement is to a large extent a domestic affair. Discussions of national practice are therefore essential to considerations of human rights, especially when looking at religious human rights within the private sphere. The next three chapters willconsider the legal systems of France, England and Hong Kong, which each take distinct approaches to PCRMs governed by different conceptions of the relation between parents and children and the role of the State.

6 Parentally coerced religious manifestations in France

6.1 Introduction

Religion has historically played an important role in French society. Yet consistent with a civil law approach that focuses on the collective good shaped by legislation, the government has not shied away from regulating religious manifestations where these have impacted on the founding principles of the Republic, or the interests of its citizens. Under France's legislative framework, parentally coerced religious manifestations (PCRMs), governed by the PGPCR[1] of 'parental authority', are especially viewed with suspicion. This chapter provides an overview of parental authority as it relates to children's freedom of manifestation and PCRMs, followed by the limitations France places on parental power. It then discusses the possibilities for children to invoke and enforce their rights within the family via the (legal) justice system and mediation.

An examination of the law alone nonetheless cannot paint a complete picture of the situation related to PCRMs, or the enforcement of freedom of manifestation. Law, practice and attitudes do not always coincide (how many pedestrians wait for a green light to cross an empty road?). Moreover, when considering how to approach PCRMs and parent–child dispute resolution, the views of those concerned should play a role. Disregarding opinions 'on the ground' is not only undemocratic, but carries the danger of reaching academically valid, but practically unfeasible and unwanted conclusions. Hence, this chapter and the two that follow do not only include an overview of 'law in the books', but also draw on findings from research undertaken to gauge opinions, attitudes and practice from those concerned with PCRMs, most notably minors themselves.

The research conducted in France comprised of anonymous questionnaires distributed to students at four high schools (*collèges*) and interviews with final-year trainee teachers at a teacher training college (*institut universitaire de formation des maîtres*, now *école supérieure du professorat et de l'éducation*).[2] The decision to include teachers in the research was based on the important role schools and

1 Principle governing parent–child relations.

2 Ethics approval was obtained from the Survey and Behavioural Ethics Committee at The Chinese University of Hong Kong. Fieldwork took place in 2013.

teachers play in France, both as providers of a 'secondary Republican culture' (see 6.4.2 below) and because of their explicit role in detecting problems within the family.[3] How teachers view PCRMs and the possibility to enforce freedom of manifestation within the family is therefore key to an appreciation of the potential for challenges to imposed manifestations in France.

The interviewees were still trainee-teachers, but they had significant teaching experience and were close to sitting the national accreditation examination. For ease of reference, they will be referred to as 'teachers' or 'interviewees'. Interviewees were invited to participate in the research via a contact at the teacher training college. Seventeen – twelve male, five female – accepted the invitation.[4] All were in their twenties apart from one mature trainee. Four interviewees were on track to become elementary school teachers, with the other thirteen aiming for high school positions. The interviews were conducted in French at the teacher training college in a room somewhat removed from those were classes were held (and away from the administration of the college). They were semi-structured, exploring teachers' attitudes towards PCRMs, possibilities for intervention and support for parent–child dispute resolution in cases in which parents violated children's rights. Interviews were scheduled to last for 30 minutes, but most lasted for up to an hour due to interviewees' willingness to talk about matters they felt had been neglected during their study. As permission for recording was not given, written notes were taken and transcribed directly following the interviews. Data was later analysed through a framework analysis.

Additionally, anonymous questionnaires were distributed to students at four high schools in the same city as where the teacher training college was located: a second-tier French city, located in an otherwise mostly rural region. Conducting the research in this setting had the advantage of revealing the opinions of participants living in an urban area and of participants from the surrounding villages. The questionnaire included 29 Likert-scale questions under the headings of 'religion' and 'conflicts between parents and children'. The former related to decision-making within the family, religious manifestations (including PCRMs) and religious dispute between parents and children; the latter asked about parent–child dispute resolution, focusing on access to court and mediation. Some questions were asked twice; once in relation to a child designated as young, in elementary school or aged 8 years old and once in relation to a high school child or adolescent. Previous research by Helwig found that many respondents did not support a right to freedom of religion for children,[5] but this may have been the result of the relatively young age of Helwig's 8-year-old model child, making it

3 A role enhanced by legislation adopted upon suggestion by France's Children's Parliament: Loi No 2000-197 du mars 2000 *visant à renforcer le rôle de l'école dans la prévention et la détection des faits de mauvais traitements à enfants* in Bonfils and Gouttenoire (2014), 99.

4 One class of around 30 students and some 12 students from another course were invited to participate, leading to a response rate of around 40%.

5 Helwig (1997), 486.

useful to explore if the same views would be held vis-à-vis older children. The questions on dispute resolution did not specifically refer to religion, though from the feedback it appears that many students interpreted dispute resolution as in relation to religious conflict irrespectively. Students were also asked for personal particulars via multiple choice questions and had the possibility to contribute comments on (1) religion within the family, (2) dispute resolution within the family and (3) the questionnaire itself, including whether they had difficulty understanding the questions. The questions were discussed with a psychologist, pedagogue, several school teachers and some parents in France and other jurisdictions. They were amended following comments and pre-testing. For the research in France, the questionnaire was translated into French.

Several schools were approached for participation through the contact at the teacher training college. A number of schools declined participation, with some stating that they did not think (the enforcement of) religious rights within the family would be an appropriate topic to discuss with students in school.[6] Four schools, including one with a high number of children with an ethnic minority background and one private denominational school, agreed to participate after obtaining approval from the *parents d'élèves* (parent council). One school made students' participation subject to parental consent. The school with many minority students asked that questionnaires were completed in class and not at home as initially proposed, so that help could be offered to the students, if needed. 156 students (52% female, 48% male) with an average age of 15 (mode = 14) completed the questionnaire.[7] The majority of students held French nationality, with 13% holding the nationality of a non-European Union State. Of the students indicating whether they had a religion, two-thirds reported having a religion, while a third said they did not.[8] This was the same for their parents, though 6% of participants stated that they did not share their parents' religion. Nearly two-thirds had previously participated in religious manifestations, which in most cases (85%) was the parental religion. The questionnaire respondents will be referred to as 'surveyed children' or 'students'.

The research conducted in France is exploratory and therefore subject to limitations. It is not representative of either French students or teachers. Availability sampling was used in respect of interviewees and whilst care was taken to include a variety of schools in the questionnaire sample, access depended on a contact in France and the response rate was lower than expected. There also appeared to be some difficulties for a few students in fully understanding the concept of mediation, which may have influenced answers. Despite these limitations, the research offers compelling narratives of attitudes towards PCRMs and dispute resolution within the family from different stakeholders. The insights obtained

6 See sections 6.4.2 and 6.5 below.

7 Response rates varied greatly according to the different schools from over 90% to below 30%.

8 Students were not asked which religion they adhered to, because this was seen as inappropriate by French teachers.

are drawn upon when discussing the law in relation to horizontal effect, parental authority, the limitations on parental powers and possibilities for children to challenge PCRMs.

6.2 Horizontal effect tempered by children's incompetence

An important characteristic of the French legal system is the wide applicability of human rights, including in relations between private parties. Although it is not possible to rely on constitutional rights within the private sphere,[9] France has extended horizontal effect to the whole of the ECHR and ICCPR.[10] Consequently, both Articles 9 ECHR and 18 ICCPR apply within the parent–child relationship. These rights recognise children's freedom of manifestation and give parents a very limited right to choose children's education, but not to the point of imposing PCRMs.[11] Whether article 14 CRC and the CmRC's accompanying progressive interpretations also apply horizontally remains uncertain. This is because the horizontal effect of provisions other than those included in the ECHR or ICCPR must be decided on a case-by-case basis by each of France's three jurisdictions (constitutional, administrative and civil/criminal).[12] In a 1996 case, the *Conseil d'État* ruled within the administrative jurisdiction that Article 14 CRC would not have direct effect.[13] However, the *Cour de Cassation* has yet to pronounce itself on Article 14 in civil matters. Considering that this court has already given horizontal effect to the CRC rights to privacy, participation and development,[14] it is probable that it will also find the right to freedom of manifestation to apply horizontally.[15] Yet irrespective of whether the CRC applies

9 The entire *bloc de constitutionalité* (constitutional package), including the *1789 Déclaration des Droits de l'Homme et du Citoyen* does not have horizontal effect. The same is true for treaties that are not ratified and non-binding instruments (e.g. the UDHR or 1981 Declaration). See CE, 18 April 1951, Rec.p. 189 *Élections de Nolay.*

10 Cass crim, n° 75-90.687, 3 June 1975, *Bulletin Criminel* n° 141, 382 *Respino;* CE Assemblée, n° 107470, 19 April 1991 *Belgacem;* Cass civ, n° 89-13163, 23 October 1990, *Bulletin* I, n° 222, 158 for the ECHR and Cass civ, n° 82-11541, 26 April 1983, *Bulletin civil* n° 13 for the ICCPR. See also Bonfils and Gouttenoire (2014), 23.

11 See Chapter 2.

12 Each jurisdiction has its own supreme court, collectively known as *Les Hautes Juridictions*: the *Conseil Constitutionnel* (CC) for constitutional revision, the *Conseil d'État* (CE) for administrative matters and the *Cour de Cassation* (Cass) for all other cases. These courts need not (and do not) follow each other's decisions.

13 CE, n° 140872, 3 July 1996 *Paturel.* That the parent sought to rely on Article 14 CRC to challenge a law authorising operations without parental consent in case of urgency possibly played a role.

14 Défenseur des Droits, *Effet direct de la Convention Internationale Relative aux Droits de l'Enfant dans l'ordre juridique française* (2016) <https://www.defenseurdesdroits.fr/sites/default/files/atoms/files/ddd-tableau_effet_direct_cide.pdf> last accessed 10 March 2019, lists provisions enjoying horizontal effect. See on the establishment of possible horizontal effect Cass civ, n° 02-16336, 18 May 2005, *Bulletin* I, n° 211, 179; Cass civ, n° 02-20613, 18 May 2005, *Bulletin* I, n° 212, 180).

15 Compare Gareil (2004), 396 and Bonfils and Gouttenoire (2014), 42.

horizontally, the ECHR and ICCPR provide sufficient protection for freedom of manifestation in respect of PCRMs. This is especially true when reference is made to the principle of *laïcité* (secularism), which is a foundational principle of French society.[16] Although the principle is now often employed as a political tool against religion, historically *laïcité* connotes a positive concept, aimed at allowing people of different creeds to coexist.[17] *Laïcité* rests on three indivisible values: freedom of conscience and religion, equality before the law and State neutrality.[18] Together they provide a framework under which State neutrality serves as a means to achieve freedom of religion and equality for all.[19] 'All' includes children and *laïcité* is therefore capable of reinforcing the importance of freedom of manifestation for both parents and children, outside and within the family. Consequently, parents in France should in principle respect their child's right to freedom of manifestation, unless a limitation ground justifies a certain PCRM.

The *a priori* applicability of human rights within the family is well-established in France. It seemed supported by surveyed children, some of whom asserted in their comments that they had religious rights vis-à-vis parents. By contrast, only a small minority of interviewees used the term 'rights' to describe children's position within the family, though many described something akin to a right to freedom of manifestation. Yet even those who stated that children had rights within the family did not all think that such rights were effectively opposable to parents, either because parents had superior rights to 'bring their children up according to their culture and beliefs' or because this was simply the reality. A paradigm emerged under which the teachers agreed that, theoretically, children should be able to enjoy freedom of manifestation within the family, but most struggled to see how this could be applied in practice.

The same theory/practice divide pervades French law, but with the effect of excluding children entirely from relying on their human rights within the family. Although children are recognised as full human beings (*personnes à part entières*) and therefore holders of human rights,[20] French law makes a distinction between holding and exercising rights.[21] Those who lack competence cannot exercise or enforce rights and children are subject to a blanket legal incompetence.[22] Hence:

16 Ministère de l'Éducation, Circulaire n° 2013-144 du 6-9-2013: *Charte de la* Laïcité *à l'École*. MENE 1322761C (6 September 2013) <http://www.education.gouv.fr/pid285/bulletin_officiel.html?cid_bo=73659> last accessed 10 March 2019.

17 J. Baubérot, *Les 7 laïcites françaises – Le modele français de laïcite n'existe pas*. Paris: Éditions de la Maison des Sciences de l'Homme, 2015, 153–8.

18 Stasi (2003), 9.

19 Baubérot (2015), 153–8.

20 E.g. J. Carbonnier, *Droit civil*, 2. *La famille, l'enfant, le couple* (21st ed.). Paris: Presses Universitaires de France, 2002, 147; De Singly (2004b), 8; Gil-Rosado (2006), 6.

21 Compare Défenseur des Droits, *De la naissance à 6 ans: Au commencement des droits*. Paris: Défenseur des Droits, 2018, 7, 'every child has rights which they enjoy since birth' – it is unclear whether enjoyment equals exercise.

22 Lebrun (2010), 78. See also Gil-Rosado (2006), 14; F. Dekeuwer-Défossez, *Les droits de l'enfant. Que sais-je?* Paris: Presses Universitaires de France, 2010, 22; Bonfils and Gouttenoire (2014) (throughout).

> A minor is an incompetent . . . That incompetence prevents him from having a genuine right to act legally . . . The incapacity of a minor is deemed 'of exercise' because a minor could perfectly well be the holder of rights and obligations, but (s)he is deprived of the ability to exercise them.[23]

Whilst minors have a right to freedom of manifestation, they cannot exercise this right unless and only in such situations as exemptions to incompetence are specifically granted under the law.[24] This means that, as a rule, freedom of manifestation will not be the starting point when considering PCRMs. Instead, coerced manifestation is governed by the national PGPCR: parental authority.

6.3 Coerced manifestations under parental authority

Religious upbringing and education fall within the scope of parental authority in France and PCRMs are subject to the rules this principle imposes.[25] Parental authority has been part of the law since 1970 (when it replaced paternal power)[26] and was notably retained during a major family law overhaul in 2002/3, despite calls for the adoption of parental responsibility.[27] Two commissioned reports had compared parental authority favourably with parental responsibility on the basis that the parent–child relationship was best described as a relation based on legitimate power with two actors.[28] It was feared that parental responsibility would make parents committed to their duties, but not to their children.[29] Parental authority endured, but its definition was adjusted to reflect that the principle had evolved in a manner consistent with children's status and rights.[30] Article 371-1 *Code Civil* (Civil Code) now reads:

23 Dekeuwer-Défossez (2010), 22, 23.

24 E.g. L141-1, L141-2 and L141-3 *Code de l'Éducation* (Loi n° 2003-339 du 14 avril 2003 *portant ratification de l'ordonnance n° 2000-549 du 15 juin 2000 relative à la partie Législative du code de l'éducation (1)*) stipulate that children enjoy freedom of religion and manifestation in public and aided schools.

25 Cass civ, n° 16-12848, 20 April 2017; Bonfils and Gouttenoire (2014), 458.

26 P. Verdier and C. Sellenet, *La nouvelle authorite parentale et les actions de soutien à la parentalité* (2nd ed.). Boulogne-Billancourt: Berger-Levrault, 2016, 42.

27 P. Murat, 'L'état des devoirs legaux des parents envers leur enfant', in P. Jacques (ed.), *Être parent aujourd'hui*. Paris: Dalloz, 2010, 49. Calls resurfaced in a recent commisioned report: J.P. Rosenczveig et al., *Des nouveaux droits pour les enfants? Oui. . . dans l'interet meme des adultes et de la democratie*. Paris: La Documentation française, 2014, 75 (Rosenczveig Report).

28 I. Théry, *Couple, filiation et parente aujourd'hui, le droit face aux mutations de la famille et de la vie privee*. Paris: éd. Odile Jacob, La Documentation française, 1998, 190; F. Dekeuwer-Défossez, *Rénover le droit de la famille: Propositions pour un droit adapte aux realites et aux aspirations de notre temps*. Paris: La Documentation française, 1999, 59. See also F. Dekeuwer-Défossez, 'Droits de l'enfant et responsabilites parentales', in De Singly (2004), 33–47.

29 Gareil (2004), 255.

30 Loi n° 2002-305 du 4 mars 2002 *relative à l'autorité parentale (1)*, and later Loi n° 2013-404 du 17 mai 2013 *ouvrant le mariage aux couples de personnes de même sexe (1)*.

> Parental authority is a collection of rights and duties, with the interest of the child as its purpose.
>
> It is vested in the parents, until majority or emancipation, to protect the child's safety, health and morality, to assure his/her education and to permit his/her development, within the respect due to the identity [*personne*] of the child.
>
> The parents involve the child in decisions that concern him/her, according to his/her age and level of maturity.[31]

Although Art. 371-1 refers to some attributes, parental authority itself is strictly a 'social function, not a natural right',[32] with a focus on relation rather than prerogatives.[33] The purpose of parental authority is to promote the child's interests. This might be thought of as inviting paternalism. However, the inclusion of interests was a deliberate move away from paternalist notions of the child as vulnerable and helpless under the previous regime.[34] Autonomy, for example, is an explicit interest of the child under French law and policy.[35] The provision further requires parents to protect children, educate them and allow for their development, essentially charging parents with the task of allowing children to obtain the competence needed for autonomous rights exercise. The two commissioned reports had previously emphasised that *auctoritas* ('raising, promoting and enhancing') required parents to enhance the capabilities of their children and ensure that children reach the level of autonomy needed to sustain themselves as well as participate fully in society, including as citizens with rights.[36] Parents must, moreover, raise children with respect for their child's identity or personality,[37] a phrase introduced to balance children's duty expressed in Article 371 to 'honour and respect' their parents.[38] The requirement to respect children's personality is justiciable.[39] This is important, because

31 'L'autorité parentale est un ensemble de droits et de devoirs ayant pour finalité l'intérêt de l'enfant. Elle appartient aux parents jusqu'à la majorité ou l'émancipation de l'enfant pour le protéger dans sa sécurité, sa santé et sa moralité, pour assurer son éducation et permettre son développement, dans le respect dû à sa personne. Les parents associent l'enfant aux décisions qui le concernent, selon son âge et son degré de maturité.'

32 J.P. Rosenczveig, *Rendre justice aux enfants*. Paris: Seuil, 2018, 249.

33 Verdier and Sellenet (2016), 171.

34 Lebrun (2010), 31; Malhaurie and Fulchiron (2011), 603.

35 See 6.4.3 below and Ministère de Solidarité et de la Santé, *Dessine-moi un parent. Stratégie nationale de soutien a la parentalite 2018–2022*. Paris: Direction Générale de la Cohésion Sociale, 2018, chapters 2 and 3.

36 Dekeuwer-Défossez (1999), 59; L. Leveneur, 'renforcer l'autorite parentale et promouvoir les droits de l'enfant?', in F. Dekeuwer-Defossez and C. Choain (eds), *L'autorite parentale en question*. Villeneuve d'Ascq: Presses Universitaires de Septentrion, 2003, 51.

37 *Personne* does not translate very well into English, but identity or personality come closest.

38 F. De Singly, 'Qu'est-ce qu'un bon parent?', in Dekeuwer-Défossez and Choain (2003), 21, 23; J. Dufaux et al., *Liberté religieuse et regimes des cultes en droit français*. Paris: Éditions du CERF, 2005, 690, 691.

39 CA Riom, 21 mars 2006, inédit (unpublished available via Legifrance).

claims related to freedom of manifestation can be reformulated in terms of respect for the child's identity.[40] PCRMs are likely to fail to respect a child's identity, which means that 'coerc[ing] the manifestation of a religion to which [the child] does not adhere . . . goes contrary to the obligation of parents to respect the child's identity' and cannot therefore be sanctioned by parental authority.[41] Finally, Article 371-1 compels parents to involve their children in all decisions concerning them in accordance with their age and maturity. This phrase implements Article 12 CRC (right to participation), which requires that children should have a say in religious matters when young and take their own decisions with growing maturity.[42] The idea itself goes back to 1962 when Barbier famously argued in respect of older minors that 'what could beforehand be commanded, can now only be suggested. To guide and to orient is not to choke'.[43]

France's PGPCR emphasises that, within the parent–child relationship, children are actors who should be taken seriously. Parents are still charged with children's interests, protection and development, but parental authority is 'an accompaniment of the child towards majority',[44] rather than a stronghold of parental power. Case-law further explains that parental authority is above all a matter of mutual trust between parents and children, allowing children to develop within a context of participation based on dialogue and appropriate boundaries.[45] The Lyon Court of Appeal e.g. considered in a 2011 case that a mother raised the children in a loving atmosphere, although she had had to rely on social services for parenting advice.[46] Conversely, the father held strong principles and offered a solid education, but his views on upbringing were rigid and his behaviour authoritarian. He left his daughters little personal space and showed no trust in them. Ruling in favour of the mother, the court held:

> It appears that the educational method applied by the mother, which is based more on dialogue and confidence with regard to the girls, is fruitful and allows the two adolescents to grow while being involved with decisions that concern them, according to their age and maturity [and] with respect for their identity/personality, conform . . . article 371-1 Code Civil, while the educational method applied by the father, which is primarily based on control and a certain infantilization, does not allow for the development of the girls, even destabilizes them, places them in danger [at risk], and makes them lose self-confidence.[47]

40 Bonfils and Gouttenoire (2014), 464.

41 Ibid.

42 CmRC (2009), General Comment 12, para 84.

43 P. Barbier, Religion, puissance paternelle et modalites des funerailles d'un enfant. (1962) 1 (Doctrine) *La Gazette du Palais* 57, 58.

44 G. Raymond, *Droit de l'enfance et de l'adolescence*. Paris: Lexis Nexis Litec, 2006, 169.

45 CA Lyon, n° 09-02766, 21 February 2011; CA Versailles, n° 14/07797, 26 November 2015.

46 CA Lyon, n° 09-02766, 21 February 2011.

47 Ibid.

Through parental authority, French law gives children the power to make their own decisions as they mature. Yet in addition, the *Code Civil* grants parents ('the married couple') the right and duty to provide for the moral direction of the family and assure children's upbringing and education (Art. 213).[48] The provision's focus is on allowing the child to benefit from a shared culture between parents and children. Under Art. 213, parents are expected to give their children bearings and norms needed for stability, growth and the 'harmonious development'[49] of the child's personality.[50] Receiving direction under Art. 213 in accordance with parental authority under Art. 371-1 implies 'taking root in a family and integration into a value system',[51] much like obtaining a primary culture.[52] Parents may thus initiate their children in a religious way of life and give them a religious upbringing, but must remain within the constraints of the law when doing so.[53]

Whilst presumably unfamiliar with the *Code Civil* and its accompanying case-law, the students' responses to statements and questions touching upon parental authority appeared very much in line with the legal understanding of parental authority. Consistent with their increased involvement under Article 371-1 *Code Civil*, the students accepted that parental decisions could sometimes take precedence over their own, although less so as they grew older. Whereas two-thirds agreed that a parental decision was more important than that of an elementary school child, this dropped to 45% in case of a high school child (*collégien*). One student invoked the concepts of trust and legitimate power by stating that children 'should place . . . trust in [their] two parents, because they have most experience in life'. Furthermore, although the questionnaire did not include any statements on dialogue, notions of dialogue and communication were often referred to in the feedback section as vital to the parent–child relationship. One student, for example, suggested that 'within the family, religion must one day be the subject of a calm conversation in which parents and children talk about it'. That children's autonomy was set in a family framework like under Art. 213 *Code Civil* was reflected by equal amounts of students (just over 50%) agreeing that children had the right to make decisions for themselves, and parents had the right to take decisions for the family. If religion was involved, a distinction was made between initiation (most considered knowledge of the parental religion important) and determination (less than half thought it was 'normal' for children to have the same religion as their parents).

48 Loi n° 70-459 du 4 juin 1970 *relative à l'autorité parentale.*

49 TGI Versailles, 24 September 1962, D. 1963.52 discussed in J. Rubellin-Devichi, The Best Interests Principle in French Law and Practice. (1994) 8 *International Journal of Law and the Family* 259, 262.

50 J. Rubellin-Devichi, Les perspectives d'evolution de la famille et le droit. (1990-1) *Droit de l'Enfance et de la Famille* 91, 97 in Gareil (2004), 16.

51 Malaurie and Fulchiron (2011), 618.

52 See Chapter 4.

53 P. Chaillou, *Guide du droit de la famille et de l'enfant.* Paris: Dunod, 2003, 74; S. Delrieu and V. Zalewski, *Droit des mineurs et des majeurs proteges.* Paris: Ellipses, 2010, 40.

Answers further echoed that an important reason to allow parents to provide direction is that young children may not yet be able to make their own choices: two-thirds thought that teenagers (*jeunes adolescents*) were old enough to decide on their on their own religion, but only 10% considered that the same was true for 8 year olds. However, this difference was not replicated for coerced manifestation. When asked about the permissibility of PCRMs (here prayer), approximately a quarter (29%) of surveyed children agreed that parents could impose religious manifestations on teenagers, and the same (26%) was true for young children.[54] This could indicate a general rejection of coercion irrespective of age. Alternatively, some answers may have been influenced by some students adhering to religions which only deem manifestations compulsory for older children,[55] and perhaps the idea that with increased involvement in decisions came increased responsibility for behaviour. Generally, the students advocated for religious autonomy within the family when children did not follow their parents' religion or practised it in ways different from their parents (an issue for a number of students). As one student stated:

> It is fundamental to me that every child can choose his/her religion, if (s)he wants to be practising or not, without family constraint (*carcan familial*).

The importance of freedom of choice in religion and manifestation within the family was highlighted by the majority of surveyed children who provided comments. Some based their appeal to autonomy on the personal nature of religion, others on rights. One student, for example, noted '[m]y religion, I have chosen myself even if my parents have the same. I know a lot about other religions because I have studied them. It's my choice and I am proud to have this religion.' Another remarked 'It's a right, and yet it's not applied everywhere.' Within this context, the respondents further emphasized the importance of mutual respect within the family, agreeing in equal numbers that parents should act considerately with regard to their child's religion and children should act considerately with regard to their parents' religion, because 'everyone has the right to think differently'.

Many interviewees also supported the idea that children should be able to make their own decisions regarding manifestation, at least as children grew older. One, for example, noted that when children are young 'they only absorb, later they [are able to] choose'. There was concern that 'religion is a personal choice' and some interviewees specified that PCRMs were not acceptable. A small minority nonetheless thought that 'too much emphasis on rights' or autonomy was undesirable because it could e.g. lead to an *enfant roi* (a child

54 29% and 26% respectively. 28% agreed that religious parents had to ensure (*doivent s'assurer*) that their child attended a place of worship.

55 Although students were not asked about their religion, some mentioned it voluntarily.

obeyed by everyone). Furthermore, 'frustration is part of growing up'. Much like under the notion of parental responsibility, another interviewee stated that, because parents are responsible for their child, 'if the parents want their child to, for example, go to church, we feel that the parents hold the moral authority'. If a child were to object, 'it's ok if the parents give him/her a slap (*claque*)'.[56] Yet, whilst the majority of interviewees agreed that children had rights or should be given the autonomy to choose their own religious practice (or absence thereof), this did not mean that that they also thought that choice should be upheld where parents disagreed. Almost all were reluctant to accept that the practical consequence of doing so would mean that parents could not enjoy full power to determine the family's religious practice. One interviewee suggested that 'individual choice is the most important in religion, but . . . while children from age 15–16 will develop their own ideas, for the moment they will still manifest their parents' religion'. If parents would not listen to children, all children could do was 'stick with it until majority'.

Sticking with it until majority seems inconsistent with the principle of parental authority, whose emphasis on respect and participation sits ill with PCRMs. Yet most French writers contend that, even under the current law, parents hold broad rights to impose PCRMs and otherwise determine their child's religious upbringing and education.[57] Even if parents are required to pay attention to the age and maturity of the child:

> As a principle, the parents determine the religion of their child: this choice is imposed upon the child, as well as manifestations associated with the parental choice . . . There is thus no right to religion or absence of religion for the child.[58]

The argument for the absence of children's autonomy is based on a 1991 case in which the *Cour de Cassation* held that a minor could not convert from Catholicism to the Jehovah's Witness faith.[59] The case is often interpreted as denying freedom of religion to minors, but that conclusion need not be derived from it. The court did not state that children had absolutely no choice in matters of religious manifestation. It held that the girl in question needed to have reached majority before she could choose to join a *specific* religion, namely the Jehovah's Witness faith, which is considered a (dangerous) sect from which

56 Corporal punishment is legal in France. A. Gouttenoire, 'Les droits de l'enfant en droit français', in O. Cvejić Jančić, *The Rights of the Child in a Changing World*. Cham: Springer, 2016, 117.

57 E.g. Carbonnier (2002), 113; J. Casey, *L'enfant et sa famille*. Paris: Lexis Nexis, 2003, 163; Dufaux et al. (2005), 688; Gouttenoire (2016), 117.

58 Casey (2003), 163.

59 Cass civ, n° 89-20878, 11 June 1991, *Bulletin* I, n° 196, 129; Laroche-Gisserot (1996), 49–52; Carbonnier (2002), 113; Casey (2003), 163 ; Dufaux et al. (2005), 688; Dekeuwer-Défossez (2010), 69. For a more balanced discussion : Gil-Rosado (2006), 65–77.

French children should be kept far away.[60] Had the conversion been the other way around, the child's freedom to manifest her own religion might have been upheld. For example, in the well-known ***mineure de Versailles*** case, the court ordered that a devout Catholic girl could continue to adhere to her faith and its practices, despite her parents' conversion to Protestantism and their wish that she be raised in that religion.[61] The Jehovah's Witness case is nonetheless regarded by some of the most eminent French family lawyers as authority for the proposition that religious manifestation is a parental prerogative,[62] especially when combined with children's general incompetence.[63]

In view of the 'shocking' situation in which parents can 'force religious observance upon an adolescent who does not sincerely believe in what (s)he does',[64] a number of authors have (unsuccessfully) proposed that the government adopt a religious pre-majority.[65] More recently, the Rosenczveig Report recommended that where children are 'able to express their opinion on any matter concerning them in an intelligent manner', they should be seen as having the competence (***discernement***) to exercise their rights and make their own decisions.[66] This notion of competence is not entirely alien to freedom of manifestation under French law. In 1913 a court found that a father suffered no prejudice when his children participated in a cult, because the children had been sufficiently mature to make a 'reasoned personal choice'.[67] However, the legislator is yet to act upon the Rosenczveig Report's recommendations. In the meantime, there is increasing support for the idea that (irrespective of its uncertain status) the law on parental authority should itself be read in accordance with Article 14 CRC, which contains an element of increased competence.[68] Additionally, as also argued above, some writers have advocated for an interpretation of parental authority as opposing PCRMs where these are not necessary for children's development or protection with an appeal to the PGPCR's

60 Mission Interministérielle de Vigilance et de Lutte contre les Dérives Sectaires (Miviludes), *La Miviludes et l'arret de la Cour Européenne des Droits de l'Homme du 5 juillet 2012 concernant les Témoins de Jéhovah* (2012) <http://www.derives-sectes.gouv.fr/missions/actualites/la-miviludes-et-larrêt-de-la-cour-européenne-des-droits-de-lhomme-du-5-juillet-2> last accessed 10 March 2019.

61 TGI Versailles, 24 September 1962, D. 1963.52 (though the case was brought in child protection because of the psychological distress the girl suffered).

62 E.g. Carbonnier (2002), 113; Gouttenoire (2016), 117; Rosenczveig (2018), 264.

63 Leveneur (2003), 63.

64 P. Barbier, L'enfant, la religion et le droit. (1960) 1 (Doctrine) *La Gazette du Palais* 72, 75. See also Dekeuwer-Défossez (2010), 69.

65 E.g. Barbier (1960); Carbonnier (2002), 29; J. Hauser, Religion de l'enfant: Cacophonie chez les juges du fond. (2008) 107(3) *Revue Trimestrielle de Droit Civil* 472, 473. For critique: Malhaurie and Fulchiron (2011), 622.

66 Rosenczveig Report (2014), 11.

67 Tribunal Civil de Creil, 19 December 1913 in Dufaux et al. (2005), 689.

68 Verdier and Sellenet (2016), 77.

best interests, identity and participation requirements.[69] That would be an interpretation truer to the letter of the law, France's international obligations and the way some of its young people view the parent–child relationship, but it is likely to require legislative or judicial action to convince the Academy.[70]

6.4 Limitations on parental power

Without any clear statement to the contrary, the general opinion amongst French authors and others remains that children's religious manifestations are determined by their parents. However, the French law places important limitations upon parental power to coerce manifestations and requires children to at least reach the competence to make their own religious choices. It does so through a limiting legal framework, its education system and children's interests. Child protection equally delineates parental power in important ways, but will be discussed in section 6.5, because children can themselves initiate child protection procedures.

6.4.1 A limiting legal framework

During the French Revolution, Danton famously told the Senate 'children belong to the Republic, before belonging to their parents'.[71] In many ways, this is still the case. Parental authority is a social function 'kept in check by society'[72] and delineated by the legislator. A number of general (mostly criminal) laws that apply to the family have a bearing on religious manifestations, in particular in the following areas.

1) Vaccination

Parents are under an obligation to vaccinate their children, failing which they risk prosecution for maltreatment and having their children excluded from educational or sanitary establishments.[73] Religious convictions cannot provide an excuse for non-vaccination.[74]

69 Carbonnier (2002), 122; Dekeuwer-Défossez (2010), 69; Bonfils and Gouttenoire (2014), 464.

70 Potentially problematic is Cass civ, n° 16-12848, 20 April 2017 where a mother could have her 14-year-old son in care registered at a religious school based on parental authority and article 2P1 ECHR. However, it is unknown whether the minor was opposed and minors explicitly enjoy freedom of religion in school (see 6.4.2).

71 D. Youf, Seuils juridiques d'âge: Du droit romain aux droits de l'enfant. (2011) 11 *Sociétés et Jeunesses en Difficulté* (online) <http://journals.openedition.org/sejed/7231> last accessed 10 March 2019, 10.

72 Verdier and Sellenet (2016), 42.

73 L3111-2 *Code de la Santé Publique*, Loi n° 2017-1836 du 30 décembre 2017 *de financement de la sécurité sociale poir 2018 (1)*.

74 CE, n° 153477, 10 January 1996 *Huret*.

2) Medical treatment

Parents must allow children to undergo compulsory health checks and provide them with medical treatment,[75] regardless of whether their religion rejects medicine (or the world at large).[76] The law equally allows minors to receive medical treatment, including an abortion, without parental consent.[77] It is illegal to prevent anyone from having an abortion (including through deliberate misinformation),[78] which means that religious parents cannot force their daughter to carry a baby to term. Separately, parents also cannot rely on religious motives to prolong futile medical treatment, especially if a child is opposed.[79]

3) Harmful practices

Harmful medical or bodily interventions based on belief systems such as female circumcision are actively prosecuted,[80] although male circumcision is as yet still allowed.[81] Harmful practices like ritual scarring can be prosecuted under assault on a minor under the age of 15.[82]

4) Diet

Both the criminal and civil law require parents to feed their children 'according to their needs',[83] but these needs must be physical and not religious. Making children participate in a 'purifying' religious diet that leaves them malnourished, for example, does not meet their needs.[84]

5) Dress

Wearing any face-covering dress (e.g. a full-face veil) in public is illegal.[85] Furthermore, the wearing of religious symbols (headscarf, kippa, large cross, etc.)

75 R2132-1 *Code de la Sante Publique* and 227-15 *Code Pénal*, Loi n° 92-684 du 22 juillet 1992 *portant réforme des dispositions du code pénal relatives à la répression des crimes et délits contre les personnes* respectively.

76 Cass crim, n° 66-93627, 29 June 1967. These cases normally lead to child protection measures, but here the child had died.

77 L1111-5 and L2212-7 *Code de la Sante Publique*, Loi n° 2016-41 du 26 janvier 2016 de modernisation de notre système de santé.

78 L2232-2 *Code de la Sante Publique*, Loi n° 2017-347 du 20 mars 2017 relative à l'extension du délit d'entrave à l'interruption volontaire de grossesse.

79 CE, Juge des référés, n° 416689, 15 January 2018.

80 222-7 to 222-12 and 222-16-1 *Code Pénal*; Raymond (2006), 163; M.-T. Hermange, *Les Enfants d'Abord: 100 Propositions pour une Nouvelle Politique de l'Enfance*. Paris: La Documentation française, 2001, 127, 128.

81 Rosenczveig (2018), 127–32.

82 222-13 *Code Pénal*. See CA Rennes, n° 14-01216, 2 September 2014.

83 203 and 310 *Code Civil*; 227-15 and 227-16 *Code Pénal*.

84 M. M. 'Banyuls-sur-Mer: Les parents écroues pour avoir maltraite leurs 8 enfants', *L'Indépendent* 15 April 2009, 31.

85 Loi n° 2010-1192 du 11 octobre 2010 *interdisant la dissimulation du visage dans l'espace public*.

is not allowed in public schools.[86] This means that parents are quite limited in imposing religious dress (which was exactly the aim of the relevant laws).[87]

6) Education

Giving a child a purely religious education violates education law,[88] as explained in the next section.

7) General parental obligations

Parents cannot subtract themselves from their parental obligations in ways that 'jeopardise the health, safety, morality or education of their child'. This is, for example, the case if they make children engage in sexual acts encouraged by their religion.[89] It does not matter if the parents are themselves indoctrinated.[90] A particular offence under subtraction is 'moral abandonment' (*abandon moral*), which was found in a case in which parents had sent their son abroad to a religious cult where he received religious instruction under harsh conditions.[91]

In addition to more general provisions, the legislator has adopted a law aimed at dealing more specifically with coerced manifestations. Article 223-15-2 *Code Pénal* on the 'fraudulent abuse of ignorance or situation of vulnerability'[92] prohibits leading minors or people under severe pressure to act, or omit to act, in a way which is severely detrimental to them.[93] Although its wording is neutral, the provision was adopted with a view to sectarian practices (and now also radicalisation)[94] in which followers and their children would participate as a result of mental pressure.[95] The article's emphasis is on psychological influence or control,[96] seeking to respond to situations in which detriment is not caused *to* minors, but where a minor is manipulated or pressured into causing themselves harm through their *own* (in) actions. This is particularly relevant for PCRMs, which consist of manifestations

86 Loi n° 2004-228 du 15 mars 2004 *encadrant, en application du principe de laïcité, le port de signes ou de tenues manifestant une appartenance religieuse dans les écoles, collèges et lycées publics.*

87 See section 2.6.

88 Article 131-4 *Code de l'Éducation.*

89 CA Bourges, n° 08-00031, 17 June 2008.

90 Ibid.

91 Cass crim, n° 93-81881, 11 July 1994, *Bulletin Criminel*, n° 269, 664. In a later case no violation was found, because the child had not suffered (and a violation of the Education Act was not sought): Cass crim, n° 01-82591, 17 October 2001, *Bulletin Criminel* n° 214, 683.

92 *L'abus frauduleux de l'état d'ignorance ou de la situation de faiblesse.*

93 Loi n° 2009-526 du 12 mai 2009 *de simplification et de clarification du droit et d'allègement des procédures (1).*

94 Direction de la Protection Judiciaire de la Jeunesse (DPJJ), *Document thematique a l'appui des pratiques professionnelles: L'emprise mentale* (7 October 2016), 3.

95 C. Picard, *Rapport sur la proposition de loi tendant à renforcer la prevention et la repression des mouvements sectaires portant atteinte aux droits de l'homme et aux libertes fondamentales.* Assemblée Nationale, Doc N° 3083 (23 May 2001).

96 Cass crim, n° 03-83910; 05-82121; 12-81532, 16 October 2013.

by minors themselves. Such coerced manifestations are prohibited to the extent that they cause a minor serious detriment (which includes the simple fact of being raised in a sect); a minor subjected to them should be given access to a different life plan, including through non-religious education.[97]

6.4.2 The State's secondary culture

To the grand consternation of some fellow senators, some of Danton's famous words re-entered the Senate in 2018 when the former minister for Families, Childhood and Women's Rights declared that:

> Parents cannot deprive children of that to which they have a right. Children do not belong to their parents; their education consists of taking them beyond their home.[98]

French parents may give their children a primary religious culture in line with parental authority and direction, but they must also allow the State to give children a secondary culture, based on Republican values and in accordance with children's human rights.[99] Article L.111-2 *Code de l'Éducation* states that every child has a right to an education which complements that received within the family.[100] Hence, when asked whether they saw their role more as teaching (*enseigner*), or as educating/bringing up (*éduquer*), all interviewees responded that being a teacher implied both. Article L.111-2 further stipulates that education should allow for the child's flourishing and prepare the child for professional life, as well as the exercise of civic rights and duties in France's contemporary information and communication society.[101] It is aimed at allowing children to grow and develop their own identity, or as one of the interviewees remarked:

> The child should not take over our norms, but with the frame of reference provided, (s)he chooses his/her own values within the constraints of the law. We should sensitise students to the values of the Republic, which are universal [like] human rights.

Above all, education should conform to the principle of *laïcité*,[102] France's version of secularism described above and considered by one of the interviewees to be 'the

97 DPJJ (2016), 14.

98 Sénat Français, *Compte rendu analytique officiel du séance du 21 fevrier 2018*. 58e séance de la session ordinaire 2017–2018 (21 February 2018) (Mme Rossignol).

99 L111-1 and L111-2 *Code de l'Éducation*. See also B. Walter, *Le droit de l'enfant a être éduquer*. Paris: L'Harmattan, 2001, 52.

100 L111-2 *Code de l'Éducation*.

101 Ibid.

102 For an overview of *laïcité*'s role, legal regulation in education, guidance and educational materials: Ministère de l'Éducation nationale, de l'Enseignement supérieur et de la Recherche, *La laïcité à l'école* (2018) <http://www.education.gouv.fr/cid95865/la-laicite-a-l-ecole.html> last accessed 10 March 2019.

main rule of the game'. Jules Ferry designed the French education system to be free, secular and egalitarian so that it could be made compulsory for all children irrespective of their background.[103] Most interviewees perceived *laïcité* as an educational tool to ensure that children learned to respect each other, and with which a feeling of collectiveness irrespective of background could come into existence. Although a small minority referred to *laïcité* as exclusionary, the majority supported the principle as a positive, inclusive value, pointing out that 'laic does not mean without religion; *laïcité* accepts everyone'. At the same time, *laïcité* required that religious practice in schools would 'not disturb others' and was freely chosen. This set the school environment apart from the home environment. Whilst nearly all interviewees had been reluctant to prioritise children's freedom of manifestation over PCRMs within the family, different rules applied in school. One interviewee underlined that, if a child was forced to manifest a religion at home, at least 'within the [school], (s)he does not need to express [the religion]'. This is because the law grants children in public and aided schools an express right to freedom of manifestation,[104] including the right to exempt themselves from religious instruction.[105] Children exercise these rights independently of parental involvement, subject only to a duty of non-interference with education itself.[106]

However, *laïcité* appeared to represent something significantly greater than a principle regulating religion or a means to enhance students' unity. The accounts interviewees gave of *laïcité* in education were comprehensive and encompassing. *Laïcité* should help children to 'think for themselves'. This necessitated acquainting them with scientific knowledge and an appreciation of facts in different subjects, as well as societal values, human rights and opportunities in life. The principle was seen by some as the driver behind much of the curriculum because it required widening children's horizons. As one interviewee stated: 'the school is there to open the mind. . . a *laïque* opening of the mind'. To many interviewees there was thus an entanglement between *laïcité* and the general mission of education in France, which is to provide children with a very comprehensive education, irrespective of its mode of delivery.[107]

Since 2006, all French children must achieve a 'common base of knowledge, competence and culture' (*socle commun de connaissances, de compétences et de culture*).[108] The common base essentially translates Article 29 CRC (goals

103 Lebrun (2010), 36.

104 L141-1 and L141-2 *Code de l'Éducation*. See also CmRC, *Initial Reports of States Parties Due in 1992: France*, UN Doc CRC/C/3/Add.15 (4 June 1993), para 224; G. Gonzalez, 'L'exigence de neutralité des services publics', in G. Gonzalez (ed.), *Laïcité, liberté de religion et Convention européenne des droits de l'homme*. Brussels: Bruylant, 2006, 198.

105 Elementary schools must give children time off on a day other than Sunday to attend religious instruction outside school: L.141-3 *Code de l'Éducation*.

106 L511-1 *Code de l'Éducation*. See also Gonzalez (2006), 198.

107 In general four types are distinguished: State and aided schools, independent schools, distance education (dispersed by the state) and home-schooling.

108 Décret n° 2006-830 du 11 juillet 2006 *relatif au socle commun de connaissances et de compétences et modifiant le code de l'éducation*; Décret n° 2015-372 du 31 mars 2015 *relatif au socle commun de connaissances, de compétences et de culture*.

of education) and EU Recommendation 2006/962/EC (key competences)[109] into French law. It presents a broad education package that requires children to achieve competence across five domains: vocabulary, learning skills, citizenship, science and an understanding of the world.[110] An understanding of *laïcité* forms part of citizenship.[111] Substantively, the common base includes French, a foreign or regional language, mathematics and science (including information science), arts and physical education and four elective subjects such as economics or geography.[112] An increasingly tight system of monitoring and inspections targeting State and independent schools, distance learning and home-schooling seeks to ensure that children do indeed obtain the common base.[113] The base gives substance to the law's demand that all children receive an education that complements that received within the family and equips them with indispensable skills and knowledge. It has the potential (perchance the aim) to genuinely question the culture in which parents raise their children and allows children to reach the competence to exercise freedom of religion and challenge PCRMs. This has made the common base controversial amongst parents and communities whose convictions and practices do not align with it,[114] especially now that the common base applies in full to home-schooling and independent schools.[115] However, the *Conseil d'État* held in 2017 that the application of the common base and its monitoring in independent schools and home-schooling did not violate parental rights (to family life and in education), because both were necessary to secure the child's right to education as recognized under national and international law.[116] In implementing children's rights and advancing the aims of the Republic, the

109 European Parliament and Council Recommendation 2006/962/EC *on key competences for life-long learning* (18 December 2006).

110 Décret n° 2015-372 du 31 mars 2015 *relatif au socle commun de connaissances, de compétences et de culture*, Annexe.

111 Ministère de l'Éducation nationale, de l'Enseignement supérieur et de la Recherche, Compétences du Socle; Cycle 4 (2016) <http://cache.media.eduscol.education.fr/file/College_2016/74/6/RAE_Evaluation_socle_cycle_4_643746.pdf> last accessed 10 March 2019.

112 Ibid.; Ministère de l'Éducation nationale, de l'Enseignement supérieur et de la Recherche, *Evaluer la maîtrise du socle commun aux cycles 2, 3 et 4* (2017) <http://eduscol.education.fr/cid103803/evaluer-la-maitrise-du-socle-commun-du-cycle-2-au-cycle-4.html> last accessed 10 March 2019.

113 L131-10 *Code de l'Éducation* and Ministère de l'Éducation Nationale, Décret n° 2016-1452 du 28 octobre 2016 *relatif au contrôle de l'instruction dans la famille ou des établissements d'enseignement privés hors contrat*. See also the tightening of rules regarding the opening of independent schools: Loi n° 2018-266 du 13 avril 2018 visant à simplifier et mieux encadrer le régime d'ouverture et de contrôle des établissements privés hors contrat.

114 Ch.R.-P., 'L'état veut encadrer les écoles hors contrat et l'enseignement à domicile', *La Dépêche* 12 June 2016, <https://www.ladepeche.fr/article/2016/06/12/2363940-etat-veut-encadrer-ecoles-hors-contrat-enseignement-domicile.html> last accessed 10 March 2019.

115 Ministère de l'Éducation Nationale, Circulaire n° 2017-056 du 14 avril 2017 *relatif à l'instruction à domicile*.

116 CE, n° 406150, 19 July 2017. See for a constitutional challenge to the first common base: CC, n° 2005-512 DC, 21 April 2005 *loi d'orientation et de programme pour l'avenir de l'école*.

State thus offers children a secondary culture that places an important restriction on parental power generally and specifically to impose PCRMs unchallenged.

6.4.3 Children's interests

Children's interests officially form the purpose of parental authority and should therefore be the main limit on parental power to impose PCRMs, together with children's identity and participation.[117] In reality, children's interests concerning religious manifestation (apart from those covered by the legislative framework) are mostly considered when a case reaches the courts via custody or child protection procedures.[118] French law (or policy guidance) offers no definition of best interests, though article 373-2-11 *Code Civil* does include a list of factors that judges must take into account when pronouncing themselves upon aspects of parental authority (previous practice, the child's views, parental attitude towards responsibilities and the other parent, expert findings, welfare reports and violence between parents). The exercise of establishing a child's interests itself is purely discretionary.[119] Moreover, with French judgments generally being a page or two long, there can be no expectation of an elaborate motivation for decisions regarding best interests. As a result, the concept is highly contentious and often mocked as a hallowed, but elusive magical formula (if not worse);[120] an open notion for adults to fill.[121] This is particularly problematic in the area of religion, which is closely related to personal morals and convictions. Hence, the Rosenczveig Report identified a pressing need for further guidance and called for a public debate on children's interests in religion.[122] However, the new round of family law reform for which the report was commissioned did not go through and the report's recommendations have been shelved.[123]

Children's interests regarding religious manifestation thus remain fully discretionary, although some broad themes have emerged from decided cases. First, in line with the legislative framework, children have an interest in developing and flourishing (*se développer et s'épanouir*).[124] Religious manifestations or parenting

117 371-1 *Code Civil.*
118 Gil-Rosado (2006), 291.
119 Dekeuwer-Defossez (2010), 61; P. Verdier, De l'interet de l'enfant aux droits de l'enfant. (2009) 43(2) *Enfances et Psy* 85, 90.
120 T. Dumortier, L'interet de l'enfant: Les ambivalences d'une notion 'protectrice'. (2013) 3 *La Revue des Droits de l'Homme*, DOI 10.4000/revdh.198, 1. See O. Bourguignon, J.L. Rallu and I. Théry, *Du divorce et des enfants*, INED, 1985, 34 in Gareil (2004), 265: 'Serpent de mer juridique, écran de fumée, coquille vide, masque, protée, arlésienne juridique de la famille, tarte à la crème [judicial electric eel, smoke-screen, empty shell, mask, Protus, judicial Arlésienne of the family (something people talk about, but will never happen), cream pie (a word so often invoked, it has lost meaning)]'.
121 Dekeuwer-Défossez (1995), 265; Gareil (2004), 473.
122 Rosenczveig et al. (2014), 102.
123 Rosenczveig (2018), 254.
124 Cass civ, n°16-28010, 28 March 2018.

practices that do not allow a child to thrive physically and psychologically (including cognitively) are not in children's interests.[125] This is e.g. the case where living conditions are such to 'compromise [children's] development and psychological equilibrium'.[126] Manifestations aimed at isolation are particularly problematic.[127] As also one of the interviewees stated 'a family can imprison itself in its religion', but that would be irreconcilable with children's interests in broadening their horizon and being allowed to exercise autonomy in religion, or at least reach the competence to do so.

Secondly, children in France have an undisputable interest in not being involved in (imposed) manifestations of religious 'sects' or radicalised movements.[128] The Lyon Appeals Court has stated without ambiguity that it is 'in the best interests of the child that he be protected from any risk of sectarian influence, even minimal'.[129] The difference between parents imposing PCRMs generally and within the context of a sect was also highlighted by one of the teachers; although the interviewee was uncertain about what to do with the former, the latter clearly required action and triggered mandatory reporting procedures. The simple fact of bringing a child up within a sect can lead to child protection measures in France, especially if there are also concerns about children's development and isolation.[130] In addition the courts have on multiple occasions relied on children's interests to deny custody, residence or full access rights to parents who planned to involve their children in sectarian manifestations.[131] It was e.g. held contrary to children's interests to come into contact with any aspect or member of the Raelian movement,[132] and a Jehovah's Witness mother lost residence because the manifestations of her religion were deemed 'reprehensible'.[133] Vice versa, the interest in not being aligned with a 'sect' or engaging in its manifestations can limit children's own right to freedom of religion. It determined the outcome (no conversion until majority) in the case involving the minor wishing to convert to the Jehovah's Witness faith discussed above.[134]

Contrary to England and Hong Kong, French courts have not identified the practice of religion as generally being in (young) children's interests. There may, however, be other interests that can lead a court to order a child's religious

125 Cass civ, n° 09-66133, 20 October 2010, *Bulletin* I, n° 205.

126 Cass civ, n° 94-05024, 28 mars 1995, *Bulletin* I, n° 141.

127 *Schmidt v France* no. 35109/02 (26 July 2007) ECtHR (unreported).

128 CA Versailles, n° 14-07797, 26 November 2015; CAA Bordeaux, n° 18BX00142, 27 April 2018.

129 CA Lyon, n° 10-05167, 16 May 2011.

130 Cass civ, n° 09-66133, 20 October 2010, *Bulletin* I, n° 205; *Schmidt v France* no. 35109/02 (26 July 2007) ECtHR, paras 9, 12, 28, 69 and 86. See also Gil-Rosado (2006), 270–6.

131 See C. Courtin, La religion de l'enfant en cas de separation des parents. (2010) 1 *Actualité Juridique Famille* 29. Contra CA Reims, 27 June 2002 in Gil-Rosado (2006), 80 (a Seventh Day Adventist mother taking perfect care of her children should not lose custody).

132 Cass civ, n° 98-12338, 22 February 2000, *Bulletin* I, n° 54, 37.

133 Cass civ, n° 98-13673, 13 July 2000.

134 Cass civ, n° 89-20878, 11 June 1991, *Bulletin* I, n° 196, 129.

practice or facilitate it.[135] For example, equality of the sexes led a court to order the religious instruction of a 10-year-old girl because her brother had received it and the girl should not be deprived of the same education as her brother.[136] The case further invoked relational interests between siblings through religion. That religious practice can have this function was also recognized by the surveyed children, one of whom stated that 'it is also religion which gives sense to the family and the love conveyed between [its members]'. Another emphasised that 'in order to develop it is better to have peaceful relations with your parents', but this required the absence of 'family constraint' in religion.

What is particularly important to the courts is the opinion of the child regarding the manifestation(s) at issue. French children have a robust right to be heard in procedures concerning them.[137] Every child must be made aware of their right to be heard and if they refuse to exercise it, the judge must verify whether this is their true wish or they have been unduly influenced, for example by a sect.[138] Discernment or competence plays an important role. The right to be heard is absolute if a competent minor (around age 7–8) requests it,[139] though incompetent children should be heard as well.[140] Furthermore, where a minor is capable of instructing a lawyer (around age 13), they have a right to be represented by one, paid for by the State.[141] Whilst other arrangements can be made, it is normal practice in France for children to be heard directly by the judge in a face-to-face meeting that takes place in the judge's chambers.[142] This is something for which judges are trained.[143] In practice, it means that children can have a real influence on the decision.[144]

135 TA Dijon, n° 1502100–1502726, 28 August 2017. See E. Erlings, A way out of *laïcité*? The child's best interests as justification for religious manifestation. (2018b) 20(2) *Ecclesiastical Law Journal* 200, 202–6.

136 CA Versailles, n° 05/06909, 29 June 2006.

137 388-1 *Code Civil* and 338-1 to 338-12 *Code de Procédure Civile*, Décret n° 2009-572 du 20 mai 2009 *relatif à l'audition de l'enfant en justice*.

138 388-1 *Code Civil*; J.P. Rosenczveig, 'Le droit de l'enfant d'être entendu' (11 January 2007) *Le Monde blogs: Droit des enfants* <http://jprosen.blog.lemonde.fr/2007/01/11/le-droit-de-lenfant-detre-entendu-173/> last accessed 10 March 2019.

139 388-1 *Code de Procédure Civile*. Cass civ, n° 11-18849, 24 October 2012 *Bulletin* I, n° 212. On competence see Lebrun (2010), 91 and e.g. CA Lyon, n° 10-07933, 27 June 2011.

140 Rosenczveig (2018), 45. A guardian ad litem (*administrateur ad hoc*) may also be appointed in criminal or civil procedures to represent children's interests if they seem contrary to those of parents; Lebrun (2010), 93.

141 338-1 *Code Civil* and 9-1 Loi n° 91-647 du 10 juillet 1991 *relative à l'aide judiciaire*. See also Chaillou (2003), 112; Lebrun (2010), 93.

142 338-1 to 338-12 *Code de Procédure Civile*. Direction de l'Information Légale et Administrative, 'Divorce, séparation: Un enfant mineur peut-il être entendu par le juge?' *Gouvernement de la République française* (22 May 2018) <https://www.service-public.fr/particuliers/vosdroits/F10479> last accessed 10 March 2019.

143 Défenseur des Droits, *L'enfant et sa parole en justice. Rapport 2013 consacré aux droits de l'enfant*. Paris: La Documentation française, 2013, 54.

144 M.H., 'L'enfant a droit d'être entendu!' *Dalloz* (30 November 2012) <http://actu.dalloz-etudiant.fr/a-la-une/article/lenfant-a-droit-detre-entendu/h/aeb32c7d851865917bacc11171a840f2.html> last accessed 10 March 2019.

Children's views must be considered separately from their interests, but in cases of religious manifestation children's views and interests often merge.[145] The result is that it is virtually never in children's interests to be subjected to PCRMs. Children's interests have e.g. militated against a father seeking to impose a ritual circumcision on his objecting son,[146] or the baptism of children opposed to that manifestation.[147] Courts have on multiple occasions refused to grant residence to parents who coerced children into practising their religion,[148] and a father saw his visiting rights suspended because he forced his children to wear religious attire, restricted their activities and remained unwilling to reflect on his use of 'moral and psychological pressure'.[149] By contrast, the court decided that a Jehovah's Witness mother could take her child to religious meetings, because she gave an undertaking to respect her child's religious freedom and would not oblige him if he did not manifest a will to go.[150] Judges thus plainly consider freedom of manifestation and the absence of PCRMs to be in children's interests. However, before a court can pronounce itself on children's views, interests and rights, children should first have access to court.

6.5 Invoking and enforcing rights within the family

A 2016 survey by the *Défenseur des Droits* (ombudsman for rights) found that children's rights were not well-known and well understood in France.[151] Of the 5,117 adults who participated in the survey, 48% were incapable of spontaneously citing at least one right when asked which children's rights they knew of.[152] The other participants mostly cited protection and development rights such as education and health, with only 8% making reference to freedom of opinion and expression.[153] Furthermore, participants generally thought that protecting and upholding the rights of children was the task of judges and the government, not that of parents and the family.[154] A central role was also played by educational establishments. They presented the first port of call for people concerned about a

145 Contra Verdier (2009), 88.
146 CA Lyon, 25 July 2007, RTD civ 2008, 99.
147 Cass civ, n° 14-23724, 25 September 2015.
148 Cass civ, n° 99-19954, 19 February 2002; Cass civ, n° 98-13673, 13 July 2000; *F.L. v France* (dec), no. 61162/00 (3 November 2005) ECtHR; *Deschomets v France* (dec), no. 31956/02 (16 May 2006) ECtHR.
149 Cass civ, n° 98-14386, 24 October 2000, *Bulletin* I, n° 262, 170.
150 CA Rennes, 10 May 2007, Juris-Data no. 2007 348540. For an overview of cases I. Riasetto, Droit privé. (2011) 2011(1) *Société, Droit et Religion* 137, 142–5.
151 Défenseur des Droits, *Enquête dur l'acces aux droits* (Volume 4). Paris: Défenseur des Droits, 2017.
152 Ibid., 12.
153 Though this can be explained because 'child' (*enfant*) in French connotes a young child: ibid., 30.
154 Ibid., 16.

child's rights.[155] However, a few teachers in this book's research mentioned that they themselves did not know very well what the rights of children were.

The interviewees also held different opinions on whether children should be taught about rights within the family. Many felt that schools 'have a role in teaching about the rights of children within the family', though in practice teachers 'don't really talk about that'. Conversely, some thought that teaching about freedom of manifestation in the family was inappropriate, or contrary to *laïcité* because of the impact it could have on the home situation. The most pressing issue, according to some teachers, was nonetheless not the teaching about rights per se, but the fact that teachers in France were not expected to talk about invoking and enforcing rights with children. One interviewee suggested that information on rights enforcement should be an essential part of human rights education which 'should focus in particular on the right of children to object and complain. Children need to know what to do [where to go] when they do not agree with how they are treated.' At the same time, the interviewees emphasised that, first and foremost, religious manifestation and PCRMs were a matter for the family if the manifestations were not harmful. In line with the requirements and interpretation of parental authority, they argued that the problem needed to be solved between the child and his/her parents through communication and dialogue:

> When a child is forced to manifest a religion, the child should talk to his/her parents: there should be a dialogue within the family. . . . We [teachers] don't have the right to tell parents how to bring up their children.

The surveyed children were equally concerned with intra-family communication and dialogue as a means to address problems related to religious manifestation. Respondents echoed the interviewees in holding that (religious) conflict should preferably 'be dealt with within the family' because 'the resolution of conflicts within the family should be managed between the persons concerned'. If possible, conflict should be avoided altogether through mutual respect and freedom of religion for all family members, but students' own reality suggested that this was not always the case. Nearly a quarter of students (23%) indicated that their parents did not allow them to decide for themselves what to believe or not to believe and 13% stated that they had had fights related to religious manifestation with their parents. Once conflict had arisen, most students offering comments on parent–child conflict resolution proposed that parents and children should try to solve the issue through communication. This involved 'talking together [seated] around the table, saying everything one thinks and trying to solve the problems by mutual agreement'. However, as one student mentioned, 'parents always want to be right'. Conflicts cannot always be solved within the family

155 Ibid., 25.

and 'if [solving it together] doesn't work, one should ask for outside help', for example 'with the help of a lawyer if it is too serious.'

6.5.1 Access to court

The legal incompetence of children prevents them from taking any legally significant action, unless specifically authorised to do so.[156] As a result, children cannot challenge an exercise of parental power or PCRMs via court procedures on parental authority before a family judge (*juge aux affaires familiales* – JAF).[157] Such proceedings can only be initiated by parents or the attorney general (*Procureur de la République*).[158] Despite it being specifically envisaged by the law's drafters that children could petition the attorney general to initiate a case, the latter's decision is entirely discretionary.[159] Moreover, if the attorney takes on the case, the child does not become a party to the procedure and cannot take any action reserved for parties.[160] Children will, however, have access to their influential right to be heard and a decision in their interests.[161] Yet there is little evidence of attorney generals taking parents to court on their children's behalf, much less to challenge PCRMs. The actual situation is therefore that children do not have access to court. This situation has received critique in the literature as not genuinely respecting children as rights holders.[162] The Rosenczveig Report therefore recommended that competent children should be allowed to exercise their rights and enforce them in court.[163] That recommendation was nonetheless not included in a legislative proposal seeking to enlarge access to court in civil procedures (a proposal which itself was not adopted).[164]

The hesitancy to give children access to court was also reflected by the reaction of interviewees to the prospect of children challenging PCRMs in court. Two interviewees dismissed the idea outright, because a child could never return to their family afterwards, evoking the idea of children divorcing their parents.[165] Only one interviewee was unreservedly in favour. Importantly, this interviewee had the experience of being involved in parental divorce proceedings and, being competent, had been able to instruct their own lawyer in connection with their right to be heard. To the interviewee this had felt like

156 See e.g. CE Juge des référés, n° 375956, 12 March 2014 (exception for unaccompanied minors where fundamental rights are jeopardised).

157 But see 6.5.3 on access in child protection.

158 373-2-7 *Code Civile.*

159 S. Royale, min. del. J.O.A.N. première séance du 14 juin 2001, p. 4252 in Gareil (2004), 236.

160 Cass mixte, n° 98-18661, 9 February 2001, RJPF 2001-4/38 this is irrespective of whether they are separately represented.

161 See 6.4.3 above.

162 Dekeuwer-Défossez (2010), 72; Rosenczveig (2018), 262. See also Gil-Rosado (2006), 305.

163 Rosenczveig Report (2014), 12, 124.

164 *Proposition de loi relative à l'autorité parentale et à l'intérêt de l'enfant*, Assemblée Nationale N° 1856, 14ième Législature (2014).

165 See 5.4.1.

suing a parent (because the case essentially concerned one parent's unwillingness to accept the interviewee's wishes) and being able to do so had provided much relief. The interviewee's concern was therefore not so much with whether children should have access to court, but the difficulties minors would face in obtaining a lawyer and starting the procedure. The other interviewees did not dismiss the option of access to court completely, but they were not convinced court procedures would be of help in religious disputes, or at all. Taking parents to court was 'an extreme measure' and 'what problem would it solve? There is no reflection'. One interviewee relied on dialogue and the values children learn at school to question access to court:

> I don't know whether it would be a good idea . . . I think it is excessive: it prevents dialogue. I think dialogue is the most important, although there is often this idea of 'the parents are right, the children are wrong'. Hence it is important that the school can provide different values. [Judicial procedure may potentially only be justified in respect of] aspects that completely change a child's life.

Although 'it's a good thing that there's at least something' a fellow teacher noted, court procedures gave 'the idea of a *système a l'Americaine*. . . discussions are more important'.[166]

The surveyed children agreed that discussions within the family were the most important, but they seemed less hesitant about access to court. Although a slightly higher percentage (37%) did not think children should be able to take the case to court when parents disrespect their rights, 35% of students supported access to court (13% strongly so). Though students' comments conveyed that taking conflict outside the family was always a measure of last resort, there were no indications that court was unacceptable. In fact, access to court was the most popular amongst the different means of extra-familial dispute resolution (court, mediation, help of a known person like a teacher and help of an unknown person) mentioned in the questionnaire. This jars with current reality under which children do not have independent access to court.

Whether that situation will change potentially depends less on public opinion than external circumstances. France has ratified the CRC's Optional Protocol on individual complaints.[167] This means that children can now apply to the CmRC[168] if they feel that the State has violated their rights, including by not living up to its positive obligations to prevent parents from imposing PCRMs.[169]

166 A *procès à l'americaine* or *système à l'americaine* are terms to indicate an overuse of legal procedures to the extent that it becomes undesirable, or even ridiculous.

167 United Nations, Depository, *Status of Treaties: 11 d Optional Protocol to the CRC on a Communications Procedure* <https://treaties.un.org/pages/ViewDetails.aspx?src=IND&mtdsg_no=IV-11-d&chapter=4&clang=_en> last accessed 10 March 2019.

168 Children can also apply to the ECtHR, but the procedure is more complicated. Bonfils and Gouttenoire (2014), 778.

169 See Chapters 2 and 3, and 5.2.

International procedures require exhaustion of domestic remedies to allow a State to right the wrongs. Yet if such remedies are not available a child can apply directly to the CmRC.[170] Depending on how the CRC system will develop, this may provide the French government with an incentive to open its domestic infrastructure to children and allow domestic judges to be the first to decide – in the interests of children, taking their rights duly into account.

See also section 6.5.3 below for children's access to court in child protection.

6.5.2 Access to mediation

Mediation is well-established within the context of procedures that come before the JAF.[171] Once JAF procedures have been opened, judges have long had the power to order family mediation, including between parents and children (often in cases of alienation).[172] Yet such orders require prior access to the JAF, which children do not currently have. Some mediation organisations therefore started to offer parent–adolescent mediation as part of early individual initiatives. These have reportedly been very successful in re-establishing the parent–child relationship with attention for the parental role and children's rights.[173]

Since April 2018, however, the Family Allocations Office (Caisse d'Allocations Familiales – CAF) has funded parent–adolescent mediation for parents and children aged 13–18 in conflict.[174] This has resulted in an explosion of organisations offering parent–child mediation, as well as training courses for family mediators, because in order to offer parent–adolescent mediation, the CAF requires 28 hours of prior specialised training.[175] A mediation service open to parents and children in conflict corresponds with the propositions made in Chapter 5, that parent–child conflict, especially where it concerns parentally imposed religious manifestations, is best resolved through alternative dispute resolution rather than court.

170 CmRC, *Model Form for Submissions of Individual Communications to the Committee on the Rights if the Child under the Optional Protocol to the Convention on the Rights of the Child on a Communications Procedure* (2015), 1, 4 <https://www.ohchr.org/Documents/HRBodies/CRC/ModelCommunicationForm_en.pdf> last accessed 10 March 2019.

171 Cour de Cassation, La médiation. (Numéro hors-série) *Bulletin d'information de la Cour de Cassation* <http://www.courdecassation.fr/publications_cour_26/bulletin_information_cour_cassation_27/hors_serie_2074/mediation_8925.html#II> last accessed 10 March 2019. The Défenseur des Droits can also mediate, but complaints must be linked to State action.

172 A. van Kote, Médiation familiale: Une autre parole entre l'enfant et ses parents séparés. (2010) 93(1) *Connexions* 109, 113–17.

173 Mouttet (2013), 83 ff.

174 Caisse d'Allocations Familiales, *Référentiel national de financement partenarial des services de médiation familiale* (2018). Available at <http://www.fenamef.asso.fr/images/fichiers/Re%CC%81fe%CC%81rentielnationaldefinancementpartenarialdelaMF-V.janvier2018.pdf> last accessed 10 March 2019.

175 Ibid. Courses are e.g. offered by the Ligue Française pour la Santé Mentale, Avec des Mots Médiation and La Maison des Droits des Enfants et des Jeunes.

There are nonetheless two obstacles to challenging PCRMs via mediation in France. First, it appears that some organisations limit the scope of parent–child mediation to conflict within the context of divorce and separation,[176] despite the government's reference to a general service as good practice in its national action plan on parenthood.[177] The limitation would mean that children whose parents are not divorced remain deprived of the possibility to resolve religious conflict via mediation. Secondly, what has come to be known as the 'verticality/horizontality' divide can preclude mediation on PCRMs. The mediation process itself is horizontal: all parties are equal and their words carry equal value.[178] However, the relationship between parents and children is vertical and depending on the meaning given to that situation, parent–child mediation might be of less help to a child subjected to PCRMs as expected. One accredited mediator, for example, explains:

> According to the law, the adolescent is a child subjected to parental authority. They must be involved in decisions that concern them; They have the right to express [their opinion], but their words are not the law [they do not make the rules]. . . . Therefore, parent adolescent mediation does not cover subjects concerning a parental decision . . . Though the way the decision is carried out can be treated during the mediation.[179]

To insist that the decisions remain those of parents fails to recognise that children's development eventually leads to their own decision-making, especially in the area of religion.[180] The above interpretation of mediation's parameters would further significantly limit its use in cases of PCRMs, as these relate to a parental decision regarding religious manifestation.

Much will thus depend on how the new service of parent–adolescent mediation develops as it operates over time. To aid that development, a first step would be to make children aware of its existence and workings. French children are often not well aware of what mediation entails and that makes them 'suspicious' of a process in which the neutral third is another adult.[181] Of the surveyed children, a third expressed an interest in mediation if they were in conflict with their parents, but one of the students noted that they had found the questions on mediation difficult. Additionally, 39% thought their parents would like to

176 E.g. Ligue Française pour la Santé Mentale, *Pôle médiation familiale Formations* (2018) <https://www.lfsm.org/pole-mediation-familiale-formations-2018/> last accessed 10 March 2019.

177 Ministère de Solidarité et de la Santé (2018), 24

178 La Maison de la Médiation, *Les mediations parent-adolescent sont desormais subventionnees par la CAF* (2018) <http://maisonmediation.fr/acc/18-blog/78-les-mediations-parent-adolescent-dans-le-referentiel-de-la-caf> last accessed 10 March 2019.

179 Ibid.

180 CmRC (2009), General Comment 12, para 84.

181 Mouttet (2013), 93.

mediate with them if they had a conflict, rising to 45% if children also had access to justice. Students seemed to have more trust in the legal system securing their rights than in having their rights protected through mediation, which they potentially saw as an adult-centred process. During a follow-up visit to one of the schools, it emerged from an informal conversation with some children (who may or may not have been participants) that the more children knew about mediation, the more enthusiastic they became about the process.

Contrary to the students, the interviewees had a good grasp of the mediation process and when prompted on its use to solve parent–child conflict, they much preferred it to court access. Most teachers supported mediation as a means of dispute resolution because of its ability to re-establish communication: 'often when there is a conflict, the discussion is cut off and mediation will allow for dialogue'. Some interviewees also highlighted the benefit of genuine participation by the child and one pointed out that in mediation 'both parties must show tolerance towards each other', underlining the importance of mutual respect. Even the interviewee who had advocated access to court based on personal experience thought mediation would have been preferable, remarking that 'mediation would be more than useful. It may not be enough, but then there would always be the stick of being able to get a lawyer'. Not every interviewee thought that mediation was feasible though, either because of power-imbalances or in the specific case of PCRMs because *laïcité* would prevent the State from mingling in religious affairs. Other interviewees saw mediation as a tool to potentially avoid State interference in religious upbringing because the family would take the decision. Overall, interviewees indicated they would be happy to refer children subjected to PCRMs to mediation, especially if the alternative was court. As one interviewee explained:

> Mediation would be better, because there is discussion. . . . Power imbalances would be difficult, especially when parents are not open-minded on the topic [religion]. On the other hand, I do not think that it is better to place [parents and children] on a level of equality thanks to the justice system. In that case, the decision is eventually the decision of the judge, the judgement of a third party.

This, the interviewees suggested, would only be different if PCRMs raised child protection concerns, in which case the State had a duty to interfere and court action was appropriate.

6.5.3 Social services and child protection

Social services and child protection are the only area in France in which the rights of the child are specifically recognised. Article L-112-4 *Code de l'Action Sociale et des Familles* (Social Security/Services and Families Act)[182] states that every decision

182 Loi n° 2007-293 du 5 mars 2007 *réformant la protection de l'enfance (1).*

in these fields must be guided by 'the child's interests, their basic, physical, intellectual, social and emotional needs, *as well as their rights*' (emphasis mine). Although social services are not generally a venue to enforce rights, they may be of help in cases of parent–child conflict, where they have an explicit role to play.[183]

'Outside help' was something, the surveyed children offered, that could be sought if working things out within the family did not work, or the issue was too serious. However, one student warned, 'If one asks for outside help [in case of conflict], the child could go to a foster home', indicating that there might be some misconceptions about the consequences of seeking help. Most students did not clarify what they thought 'outside help' consisted of. Only one specifically referred to a form of social services: a psychologist (most likely the school psychologist who has an important function in treating and advising students, teachers and parents in France).[184] This may be indicative of a lack of awareness of who minors could contact if they are in conflict with their parents, as previously suggested by the interviewees.

However, interviewees themselves were unsure about what to do if there was (religion-related) conflict within the family. Many stated that they had never been taught and did not know who to refer the child to if parents imposed PCRMs. A few teachers suggested that if a child sought their help regarding PCRMs they could perhaps talk to the parents 'in the most pedagogical tone possible', but the majority noted that teachers should not interfere in family life. Nearly all teachers indicated that they would ask for advice about what to do with students whose parents imposed PCRMs that were not harmful from the director, education adviser and other support persons at school. In general, the interviewees suggested that services available to the child (and their family) would principally be the social worker (*assistant sociale*), nurse and psychologist at school, with only a few mentioning external social services, such as those offered by the department.[185]

Departmental services vary widely in the services on offer as a result of decentralisation and there is no guarantee that an appropriate service, such as family counselling, is available.[186] Moreover, the services are said to be 'flooded'[187] and do not have sufficient resources to commit to family concerns without immediate danger. Services are also voluntary and parents imposing PCRMs can thus refuse to cooperate with them.[188] Over the last few years, the focus of social services for the family has furthermore changed. Whereas services were previously seen as *accompagner la famille* (accompanying the family), they are now

183 Ministère de Solidarité et de la Santé (2018), chapters 3 and 6.

184 See V. Martin-Lavaud, *Psychologue à l'école*. Toulouse: Éditions Érès, 2017, esp. chapters 2–4.

185 A *departement* is similar to a province or county.

186 Title II of the *Code de l'Action Sociale et des Familles*, esp. L121-1 L121-2, L123-2, L123-4; L221-1, Loi n° 2002-2 du 2 janvier 2002 *rénovant l'action sociale et médico-sociale* (1). See also Dekeuwer-Défossez (2010), 91, 92.

187 Rosenczveig (2018), 244.

188 Lebrun (2010), p. 88. Although refusal can lead to loss of benefits: Dekeuwer-Défossez (2010), 92.

a *soutien à la parentalité* (support for parenthood), focusing on placing parents in a position to solve family issues themselves.[189] The lack of family focus is even more pronounced for the services at schools. These services are primarily aimed at individual treatment or counselling, advice, referral and most of all offering a listening ear (*écoute*).[190]

The teachers themselves also emphasised that their principal role in a case of coerced manifestation would be to listen to the child in a way that would make the child feel taken seriously. By contrast, if there were child protection concerns or the child was involved in a sect then action was required (though there was some confusion as to what action exactly). There are extensive mandatory reporting procedures in France which cover teachers, doctors and other professionals, who must refer a case to the child protection services if they believe a child is 'in danger' (*en danger*, roughly at risk of harm).[191] What constituted danger was broadly interpreted by the interviewees. Although simple parent–child conflict would not be enough, danger existed where there was 'symbolic violence, or that the child is hampered in his/her development'. Generally, if the PCRMs was harmful, or imposed in a harmful or violent manner, this required a report.

A report can in turn lead to child protection services (*l'Aide Sociale à l'Enfance*) applying for a child protection measure (*mesure d'assistance educative* – MAE), unless parents voluntarily accept an offer of help and supervision.[192] If the 'child's health, security, or morality are endangered, or his education or physical, emotional, intellectual or social development are seriously compromised' (the child protection threshold), Art. 375 *Code Civil* states that a variety of persons can apply to the children's judge (*juge des enfants*) for a MAE. These persons include the parents, persons in charge of the child, public prosecutor, child protection services and the minor themselves.

A notable exception to children's legal incompetence is thus every child's right to apply to court for a MAE.[193] If the procedure is opened, the minor

189 See Verdier and Sellenet (2016), 167; Ministère de Solidarité et de la Santé (2018). See also E. Bec and N. Bel, *Pratiques actuelles avec les familles: Revue de la littérature et dossier bibliographique*. Toulouse: CREAI-ORS, 2018, 3–8, 38.

190 The same applies for social services specifically aimed at young people. Ministère de Solidarité et de la Santé (2018), 24, 25.

191 L226-1 to L226-13 *Code de l'Action Sociale et des Familles.*

192 France has a very extensive system of child protection (updated in 2016) with different actors, coordinating entities and legal procedures, the description of which is beyond the scope of this book. See C. Daadouch and P. Verdier, Protection de l'enfance: Ce qui change avec la loi du 14 mars 2016 et ses onze decrets. (2017) *Délinquance, Justice et Autres Questions de Société* (online) <https://www.laurent-mucchielli.org/public/Article_Daadouch_Verdier_reforme_protection_enfance.pdf> last accessed 10 March 2019; Verdier and Sellenet (2016), 87–239. A MAE is the most commonly used mandatory child protection measure.

193 375 *Code Civil* and Cass civ, n° 94-05102, 21 November 1995, D. 1996, 420. The minor becomes a party to the procedure and may appeal decisions and go into cassation, (s)he may also demand the revision of a MAE (375-6 *Code Civil*): Cass civ, n° 92-05032, 12 July 1994, Defrenois 1995, 322. See further 1186 and 1191 *Code de Procedure Civile;* Casey (2003), 3.

automatically becomes a full party to it, and if (s)he is competent, has a right to a lawyer paid for by the State.[194] The child's parents equally have a right to a lawyer, who, if the family has insufficient means, is also paid for by the State.[195] So structured, the MAE procedure is essentially one between parents and children and it has therefore been suggested by several French writers that children who are forced to manifest a religion could apply for child protection measures to remedy the situation.[196] It is in this respect an advantage that the content of MAE's is not defined, or restricted. Judges may order whichever action or inaction they think will solve the problem (which has earned the procedure a reputation of 'domain of improvisation, personal conceptions, empirical approaches and experiments, all without criteria, limits and a precise judicial framework').[197] Two relevant conditions nonetheless apply: first, the judge must take the religious convictions of the minor and their family into account.[198] While the judge cannot pay attention to religiously motivated arguments as a result of the requirements of *laïcité*,[199] the final decision must be respectful of the religion(s) of both parents and children. Second, the judge must seek the cooperation of the family.[200] Although a decision can eventually be imposed, MAE procedures allow for a dialogue with the parties on what would constitute a feasible solution to the problem at hand.[201] These conditions make the argument that MAE procedures should be used to challenge PCRMs very attractive.

However, MAE procedures are *child protection procedures*. To use them, it is not enough that children's rights or interests are at stake.[202] A child must be, or is at the point of being, maltreated in a manner that reaches the child protection threshold. While 'danger' presents a relatively low threshold,[203] like the interviewees, the *Cour de Cassation* has held that conflict per se cannot trigger a MEA.[204] A disagreement over PCRMs without aggravating circumstances is thus not enough to reach the threshold of danger.[205] For example, in a case in which a minor challenged religious practices imposed by his father, the court held that that a MAE was only appropriate because the son objected to the

194 1187-3 *Code de Procedure Civile*. Otherwise an *administrateur ad hoc* is appointed.

195 Administration française, *Mesure d'Assistance Éducative: Conditions pour en bénéficier et procédure* (2011) <http://vosdroits.service-public.fr/particuliers/F457.xhtml> last accessed 10 March 2019.

196 S. Plana, *Le proselytisme a l'epreuve du droit prive*. Paris: l'Harmattan, 2006, 90. See also Gil-Rosado (2006), 248.

197 M. Huyette, 'L'autorite parentale face aux Mesures d'Assistance Éducative', in Dekeuwer-Défossez and Choain, (2003), 165.

198 1200 *Code de Procedure Civile*.

199 Gareil (2004), 81.

200 375-1 *Code Civil*.

201 Murat (2010), 63.

202 Dekeuwer-Défossez (2010), 96. See also Rubellin-Devichi (1994), 260.

203 See Chaillou (2003), 90–2.

204 C. Delaporte-Carré, *L'Articulation des Institutions de Protection de la Personne de l'Enfant Contre ses Parents*. Paris: Dalloz, 2008, 29, citing Cass civ, n° 87-05074, 14 February 1990.

205 Contra Delaporte-Carré (2008), 29, 30.

practices *and* the manifestations themselves were contentious.[206] Intervention may also be called for if a child suffers psychological repercussions from the conflict caused by PCRMs.[207]

Since MAE procedures are the only form of access to court for minors, some authors have suggested broadening the scope of danger for it to encompass conflict relating to the exercise of parental authority.[208] Yet that would not be an appropriate solution. Its scope is already very broad (e.g. every contravention of the legislative framework in section 6.4.1 can lead to child protection measures and where the minor applies for a MAE particular flexibility is applied).[209] The consequence of widening 'danger' further is to allow for near-discretionary State intervention and potential social engineering. Moreover, asking minors to use the child protection procedure for the protection of their religious rights requires children to victimise themselves and their families. That is incompatible with the function of human rights as a means of empowerment. Rather than extending MAE procedures, the government would do better to extend family services and access to court in family proceedings.

6.6 Conclusion

French law accords children horizontally applicable rights to freedom of manifestation under the ECHR, ICCPR and potentially CRC. These should in principle bar parents from imposing PCRMs unless justified by a limitation ground as explained in Chapters 2 and 3. However, children's legal incompetence implies that, although children have rights, they can neither exercise nor enforce these rights. PCRMs are instead governed by parental authority, which is equally contradictorily applied in the field of religion. Parental authority builds on interests, identity, involvement, trust and dialogue in ways that conform with what children and adults regard as desirable family-functioning. It is unlikely that the PGPCR would accommodate PCRMs beyond those that would be 'necessary in a democratic society'. However, religious manifestation is considered a parental prerogative in France, unaffected by the prerequisites of parental authority. Whilst this does not correspond with a reasonable explanation of the law, the argument seems pervasive amongst academics and educators. Moreover, it cannot be easily tested, because children in France do not have independent access to court in JAF proceedings.

It is the French State which poses the principal challenges to parental authority via its legislative framework limiting PCRMs and the provision of a secondary culture imbued with *laïcité*, the values of the Republic and human rights. Although

206 Cass civ, 7 July 1987 discussed in F. Moneger, Les musulmans devant le juge français. (1994) 2 *Journal du Droit International* 345. See also Plana (2006), 90.

207 Cass civ, n° 63-80 001, 7 April 1965, *Bulletin Civil* n° 258, D. 1965.704.

208 Dekeuwer-Défossez (2010), 97. Compare with Leveneur who thinks the procedure already goes too far in involving children, Leveneur (2003), 57, 58.

209 See Gil-Rosado (2006), 256–80.

the State's emphasis on reaching competence might be seen as enough by some adults, it appears that French minors also seek to exercise their rights and ultimately have them enforced. Some are themselves willing to risk conflict with parents to assert their (non-)religious convictions. To resolve this conflict, minors may now be able to engage in parent–child mediation as advocated in Chapter 5. This is a very positive development, though its use is undermined by a lack of independent access to court as a safety valve. Child protection procedures cannot fulfil that role. Children seeking to enforce their right to freedom of manifestation are not by definition victims, they are citizens of the Republic *à part entières* that want to be taken seriously by their parents and the State.

7 Parentally coerced religious manifestations in England

7.1 Introduction

English law places much emphasis on personal liberty. Yet in the case of parentally coerced religious manifestations (PCRMs), this is the liberty of parents, rather than that of children. Under England's principle governing parent–child relations (PGPCR), parental responsibility, parents are firmly put in charge of their children's religious lives until a matter comes before the courts or a child reaches a high level of competence. The former is especially important, because England is the only jurisdiction included in this book where children have independent access to court in family proceedings. This chapter looks at the way PCRMs and children's freedom of manifestation are regulated by parental responsibility and the limitations that apply to the parental right to determine a child's religion. It then considers the possibilities for children to enforce their religious rights, and for families to resolve religious conflict.

In addition to providing an overview of the law, the chapter draws on findings from research conducted in England. Like in France, anonymous questionnaires were distributed to students, although in England the students were older. Interviews in England were not held with teachers, but with representatives (not in the formal sense) of religious communities. Teachers in England do not have the same position and responsibilities as they do in France, and more importantly, education is not regulated to the same extent. In England, religion and parental convictions have very significant influence on children's education.[1] Given also the very limited role the State plays in matters of religious upbringing (explained below), comments from religious communities themselves would be more meaningful to the question of the acceptability of PCRMs.

The questionnaires distributed in England were similar to those in France, with the addition of questions on participants' religion and religious education. Due to ethics requirements,[2] only students over the age of 16 could be included in the

1 See further 7.4.1 below.

2 Ethics approval was obtained from the Survey and Behavioural Ethics Committee at the Chinese University of Hong Kong, and the ESSL, Environment and LUBS (AREA) Faculty Research Ethics Committee at the University of Leeds to which the author was attached during fieldwork in England. Fieldwork took place in late 2013.

research, as they would be able to participate without parental consent. However, many contacted schools still declined participation based on the impossibility of obtaining parental consent within the available time-frame (three months). Over a period of two months, a large number of schools was contacted, with colleagues and others actively helping to identify potential schools for participation. Often, individual teachers were enthusiastic about participation, but school committees ultimately declined. In view of the seeming impossibility to engage schools, further ethics approval was applied for to distribute the questionnaire to first-year university students, who would still have their adolescent years fresh in mind. For this purpose, the questionnaire was slightly modified, asking students to report on their experiences as a minor. During preparations for this changed research, one high school indicated they were willing to participate and also a group of local college students who attended a university information session filled out the questionnaire. Questionnaires were therefore ultimately obtained from both high school (college) and university students. They will be collectively referred to as 'students' and separately as 'college students' and 'university students'.

116[3] sixth form students filled out the questionnaire,[4] though many were aged 18 or over.[5] The majority of college students stating their gender identified as female (59%, 39% male) and three-quarters of those indicating their nationality held British nationality. A third of students indicating whether they had a religion (n = 98) stated that they had one, whilst 42% did not. Most students willing to indicate their religion reported being Christian or Muslim. Other religions mentioned were Sikhism and two small religious movements. Of the students who indicated whether their parents had a religion, a third stated they did, and another third stated they did not.[6] Christianity and Islam were most often mentioned as the parental religion, followed by Hinduism, Sikhism and Buddhism. 27% of college students indicated not sharing their parents' religion. Half of the college students reported having practised a religion, of which 60% indicated that this was their parents' religion.

In addition, 228 first-year law students participated in the research.[7] Nearly half of these students were aged 18, the others either older or did not indicate their age. Most respondents identified as female (61%, 34% male) and three-quarters held British nationality. Almost half of those willing to indicate whether they had a religion indicated that they did (46%), with virtually equal numbers stating they did not (47%). Most students having a religion mentioned they

3 One response was excluded as the respondent had not seemingly taken the questionnaire seriously.

4 The exact response rate cannot be stated with certainty as the school arranged for distribution of the questionnaire internally and it is not clear how many students were ultimately asked to participate. However, in view of the large size of the college, the response rate was probably rather low.

5 58% of the 99 students that had stated their age. Their answers have been included as these students were within a setting that was apparently still regarded as regulated by parental responsibility.

6 Wherever the numbers do not 'match up', this is because students either ticked the 'I prefer not to tell' box, or they neither agreed, nor disagreed.

7 A 72% response rate.

were Christian, followed by Muslim. Others stated they adhered to a different (Middle-) Eastern religion or smaller religious or belief movement.[8] Just over half of the university students stated that their parents had a religion, whilst 38% indicated that their parents did not. The most often referenced parental religion was Christianity, followed by Islam, five different (Middle-) Eastern religions and a smaller Western religion. 14% of university students indicated that they did not share their parents' religion. Most students reported having manifested a religion, and for 39% this was the parental religion.

Additionally, interviews were conducted with seven 'representatives' of religious communities,[9] either local religious leaders, or prominent members of the community proposed by that community. It should be stressed that a community (let alone a religion) cannot possibly be represented by one person, but the goal was to obtain a range of insights, not a definite stance from a particular denomination. Semi-structured interviews of around an hour were conducted with interviewees of one mainstream and two small Christian religions, two Middle Eastern religions and two Eastern religions. Since they often took place at places of worship and community centres where recording was not feasible, written notes were taken that were later transcribed and analysed through a framework analysis. Topics evoked in the interviews include religious obligations of parents and children, acceptability of PCRMs, possibility for the religious community to intervene in cases of PCRMs, opinions on children's access to court and parent–child mediation.

The research conducted in England was exploratory and it had some limitations. It is neither representative of English students, nor of members of the religions included. Availability sampling was used, and the response rate for college students was low. There are no denominational schools involved in the research (all contacted religious schools declined participation). Student respondents were often over the age of 18 and university participants were asked to report retrospectively on their family situation as minors. Furthermore, interviews could not be arranged with members of some of the larger religious communities in England, and it is likely that interview participants did not belong to the stricter strands of their religion, given that they agreed to participate in secular university research conducted by a woman. Its limitations notwithstanding, the research has produced persuasive accounts from different perspectives, and offers important initial insights into the appreciation of freedom of manifestation and its enforcement within the family in England. These insights are drawn upon in the discussion of the law in relation to horizontal effect, parental responsibility and its limitations, and possibilities for children to challenge PCRMs.

8 Four (Middle)-Eastern religions and three smaller religious movement were identified, but given the small numbers adhering to them, identifying the exact religions could identify the participants.

9 A 58% response rate.

7.2 Rights without horizontal effect

England has a dualist system of law, which requires that treaty provisions are implemented into domestic law before individuals can rely on them at the national level. Yet as a 'general principle, [the government] does not incorporate international treaties into domestic law'.[10] Of the instruments discussed in Chapters 2 and 3, only a limited version of the ECHR has been implemented via the *Human Rights Act* 1998 (HRA). The Act does not include Articles 1 (duty to ensure respect) and 13 (right to a remedy) ECHR, thereby excluding positive obligations to ensure respect in private relations and remedies for rights violations. Direct horizontal effect was explicitly rejected.[11] The HRA does nonetheless require that existing legislation is interpreted as far as possible in a manner compatible with the ECHR, without affecting the 'validity, continuing operation or enforcement' of legislation incompatible with Convention rights (s. 3). Moreover, as public authorities, courts should not act in a manner contrary to the Act when they decide on private disputes.[12] Consequently, the HRA gives children an exercisable right to freedom of manifestation, but they cannot rely on it within the family. The right can, however, influence open legal notions like parental responsibility, though not laws explicitly contrary to it, like the impossibility for minors under 16 to exempt themselves from religious education at school.[13]

Other treaties referred to in Chapters 2 and 3 cannot give individuals rights at the national level,[14] unless they have become part of ECHR law and are incorporated via the HRA.[15] The ECtHR has, for example, found Article 14 CRC (religious freedom) to be applicable in child abduction cases, so regard could be had to that right if a similar case arose in England.[16] However, Article 14 CRC cannot apply between parents and children within the family context, because even if the ECtHR would find the provision relevant in that respect, the HRA does not have horizontal effect. What is more, the United Kingdom has suggested that it might repeal the HRA and eventually replace it with a still

10 CmRC, *Replies of the United Kingdom of Great Britain and Northern Ireland to the List of Issues.* UN Doc. CRC/C/GBR/Q/5/add.1 (11 April 2016), para 5. The UK is also not a party to individual human rights complaints mechanisms (ICCPR, CRC, etc.), with the exception of the ECtHR whose jurisdiction is compulsory (Article 32 ECHR).

11 D. McGoldrick, The United Kingdom's Human Rights Act 1998 in Theory and Practice. (2001) 50(5) *International and Comparative Law Quarterly* 901, 936.

12 Unless sanctioned by law (s. 6 HRA).

13 S. 55 *Education and Inspections Act* 2006, chapter 4. Contrary to *CJ, JJ and EJ v Poland* (dec), no. 23380/94 (1996) ECmHR, DR 84-A, 46.

14 *The Queen (on the application of T) v The Secretary of State for Justice Birmingham Magistrates' Court* [2013] EWHC 1119 (Admin), at [23]–[32].

15 *ZH (Tanzania) v Secretary of State for the Home Department* [2011] UKSC 4, at [22]–[23]; *R. (on the application of JS) v Secretary of State for Work and Pensions* [2014] EWCA Civ 156, at [69].

16 *X v Latvia*, no. 27853/09 (2013) ECtHR (Grand Chamber), ECHR 2013, para 37.

undefined national bill of rights.[17] The future of human rights per se is thus uncertain, quite apart from their applicability within the private sphere. Yet that does not necessarily mean that people do not think they have rights within the family. Rights-talk itself was largely absent from the questionnaires and interviews. Only two college students and one interviewee stated in so many words that children had a *right* to freedom of manifestation, the latter adding that this was their personal opinion and their community had no formal standpoint on freedom of manifestation. Some participants nonetheless expressed ideas connoting the existence of religious rights within the family by emphasising children's religious decision-making power, though there was also recognition of the aspirational nature of such a right. One student, for example, expressed that they felt 'we all have a right to choose but the parents/care givers are in charge of a family'. That charge is called parental responsibility under English law and it is the PGPCR that regulates children's manifestation within the family in the absence of horizontally applicable rights.

7.3 Coerced manifestations under parental responsibility

Religious upbringing in England[18] is governed by the principle of parental responsibility.[19] The notion of parental responsibility, as parental rights based on duties in respect of children's welfare, has long formed part of the English law.[20] In *Re Agar Ellis*,[21] a case normally interpreted as having established near-absolute parental rights,[22] the court noted that: 'the rights of a father are sacred rights, because his duties are sacred duties'.[23] Courts would not likely interfere with paternal rights because fathers were trusted to naturally fulfil their duties, and it was believed to serve children's interests for them to be under paternal control.[24] The court therefore upheld a Protestant father's right to forbid contact between his Catholic daughter and her Catholic mother. However, it also ruled that, had the father attempted to change his daughter's religion, there would have been cause to intervene.[25] Shortly afterwards, the Chancery division made paternal rights and interest-determinations expressly subject to the 'responsibilities' parents owed children as part of the marital duty.[26] A century later, Lord

17 See e.g. S. Clear, UK Human Rights Act is at Risk of Repeal – Here's Why it Should be Protected. *The Conversation* (12 February 2019) <https://theconversation.com/uk-human-rights-act-is-at-risk-of-repeal-heres-why-it-should-be-protected-111368> last accessed 10 March 2019.

18 This section reproduces parts of Erlings (2016), with permission of Koninklijke Brill.

19 S. Langlaude, Parental Disputes, Religious Upbringing and Welfare in English Law and the ECHR. (2014) 9(1) *Religion and Human Rights* 1, 3–6.

20 See 4.2.2.

21 *Re Agar-Ellis, Agar-Ellis v Lascelles* (1883) LR 24 Ch. D. 317. (*Agar-Ellis*).

22 Taylor (2009), 125; Fortin (2009), 322.

23 *Agar-Ellis* (1883), at 329.

24 Ibid.

25 Ibid.

26 *Re Elderton (Infants)* (1884) LR 25 Ch.D. 220, at 220, 229.

Scarman reiterated in the landmark *Gillick* case that 'parental rights are derived from parental duty and exist only so long as they are needed for the protection of the person and property of the child'.[27] *Gillick* further established the notion of Gillick competence under which parental rights must yield to children's own decision-making where children have reached a certain (high) level of competence, discussed below.[28]

With the principle itself firmly embedded in the law, the Law Commission advised in 1988 that the adoption of parental responsibility to replace parental rights would be a linguistic change only.[29] Hogget (now Baroness Hale) has further suggested that parental responsibility reflected the reality of parenthood, and the relationship between parents and society under which society 'expects parents to bring up their own children and, so long as they meet our expectations to a reasonable standard, we will respect their right to do so'. [30] Despite the emphasis on the codification of law and practice, some change from parental rights was nonetheless anticipated: parental responsibility would make parents act more dutifully towards their children and enhance children's rights.[31] Yet the legislative debate became dominated by the idea that parental responsibility would reduce the need for State intervention in the family since responsible parents could be trusted with greater autonomy.[32] This suited the government's agenda, and soon parental responsibility came to mean parental freedom and autonomy in child-rearing.[33] Ultimately, the *Children Act* 1989 failed to 'embrace any new or revolutionary concept of children's rights'[34] (it did not even mention them).[35] The counterparts of parental responsibility would be children's welfare and parental rights.[36]

S. 3(1) *Children Act* 1989 states that parental responsibility 'means all the rights, duties, powers, responsibilities and authority which by law a parent of a child has in relation to the child and his property'. The provision is a 'non-definition',[37] referring to parental responsibility's attributes but remaining silent on its substance and functioning. The substance has now been derived from the common law: all matters previously identified as parental rights are now recognised as parental

27 *Gillick v West Norfolk and Wisbech Area Health Authority and Department of Social Security* [1986] AC 112, at 184.

28 Ibid., at 186. See 7.4.1.

29 The Law Commission, *Family Law: Review of Child Law, Guardianship and Custody. Report No. 172.* House of Commons. HC 594, Session 1987–1988 (1988), 5, 6.

30 B. Hoggett, *Parents and Children* (4th ed.). London: Sweet & Maxwell, 1993, 11.

31 Eekelaar and Dingwall (1990), 23; Eekelaar (1991a), 37, 39.

32 The Law Commission (1988), 5. See for discussion Fox Harding (1994), 85, 104.

33 Eekelaar (1991a), 38; Fox Harding (1994), 85, 104.

34 A. Bainham, *Children. The New Law.* Bristol: Family Law, 1990, 5.

35 See also J. Masson, *The Children Act 1989: Text and Commentary.* London: Sweet & Maxwell, 1990, 3. Only procedural rights for children were included.

36 Fox Harding (1994), esp. 94.

37 Masson (1990), 3.

responsibilities.[38] As to the PGPCR's functioning, there is no clear guidance, but a number of aspects that define parental responsibility have been identified since its adoption.[39] First, under parental responsibility duties are more important than rights,[40] but now that rights have been reformulated as responsibilities, the boundaries have blurred.[41] When, for example, the government proposed to monitor the education of home-schooled children, parents relied on parental responsibility to oppose what one termed 'an illegal infringement of my rights as a parent. The law says I'm responsible for my children's education.'[42] The confusion is further exacerbated where parents have been granted extensive rights in relation to vague or minimal duties.[43] Herring therefore suggests that it is easier to outline the limitations on parental power than the power itself, because parents can in principle 'make decisions about all areas of the child's life'.[44] This links to the second aspect of parental responsibility: although parental responsibility gives 'priority to children's welfare',[45] this is a welfare determined by parents.[46] As long as parents do not break the law, cause child protection concerns or disregard Gillick competence, parents are the ones to decide on children's welfare.[47] They must do so 'responsibly' (with a *bona fide* attitude),[48] but it does not matter (legally!) whether they disregard children's opinions, their rights or what society would regard as fundamental values or interests.[49] If parents e.g. sincerely believe that an authoritarian upbringing involving corporal punishment and leaving no space for children's own identity serves their welfare, then the law protects such upbringing under parental responsibility.[50] This is the case even if judges have wondered whether it is a desirable state of affairs to regard children 'as little more than the largely passive objects of more or less paternalistic parental . . . decision-making'.[51] The difficulty relates to a third characteristic of parental responsibility under the English law. Since rights attach to duties or responsibility, and children do not have either, they also do not have a claim to concomitant

38 Herring (2017b), 444 with reference to R. George, *Ideas and Debates in Family Law*. Oxford: Hart, 2012, 131. See also Lowe (1997), 195.
39 See for a more elaborate overview Erlings (2016), 626–42.
40 Freeman (2000), 452.
41 See also Fox Harding (1994), 94.
42 S. Weale, 'Home Educating Parents Object to Council's Home Visit Plans', *Guardian*, 31 December 2014 <https://www.theguardian.com/education/2014/dec/31/home-educating-parents-council-visits-westminster-london> last accessed 10 March 2019.
43 See Reece (2009), esp. 87.
44 Herring (2017b), 445.
45 Hansard Parliamentary Debates, *Child Maintenance*. HL Debates, 29 October 1990, vol. 522, cc 1695–1708, 1695.
46 E.g. Eekelaar (1991a), 38; Freeman (2000), 452; Reece (2006), 461; Erlings (2016), 628; 629.
47 Herring (2017b), 445.
48 Reece (2006), 460, 461.
49 Fortin (2009), 322.
50 *R (Williamson) v Secretary of State for Education and Employment* [2005] UKHL 15; *Re G (Children (Religious Upbringing)* [2012] EWCA Civ 1233 (*Re G*).
51 *Re Roddy (A Child) (Identification: Restriction on Publication)* [2003] EWHC 2917 (Fam), at [46].

rights within the parent–child relationship.[52] As Such and Walker explain, the relationship between rights and responsibilities is 'one of dependency' and children are excluded from responsibilities reserved for adulthood.[53] Whilst parents are 'responsible for their children' and children do not have their own responsibilities, children's rights or opinions are subordinate to those of parents, unless parents exercise their rights in a 'cruel and abusive' manner.[54]

Parental responsibility has actually made it harder for children to negotiate their position within the family and challenge parental power, because it is difficult to question responsibility.[55] The PGPCR as currently applied furthermore suggests high levels of control over children, because parental responsibility makes parents accountable for their children under English law.[56] Parents are now e.g. responsible for children's truancy or offending, in view of the expectation that those with parental responsibility are in control.[57] Herring has argued that parental responsibility is therefore increasingly leading to hyper-parenting: the micro-managing and intrusive supervision of children's lives by parents who need to control their children.[58] This leads to the merging of parents and children's identities, with the child becoming a reflection of the parent in a manner that 'overlooks the agency of children themselves' and thereby misrepresents the parent–child relationship.[59] As a result of its application, parental responsibility is said to 'perpetuat[e] the importance of parental rights whilst telling us nothing about children's rights'.[60]

In effect, parental responsibility has in many ways confused the debate about parental rights by changing the semantics, but not the underlying principles. In the 1985 *Gillick* case, Fraser LJ stated that 'most wise parents relax their control gradually as the child develops and encourage him or her to become increasingly independent'.[61] Two decades later, Munby J (as he then was) suggested that 'wise parents resist the temptation to keep their children metaphorically wrapped up in cotton wool'.[62] A linguistic change has thus occurred from parental 'control' (rights) to 'cotton wool' or concern (responsibility), yet the result is the same.[63] Although it is recognised that parents should preferably regard their children as active agents, both PGPCRs support wide parental power for parents who choose

52 Such and Walker (2005), 39, 44; James (2008), 156–8.
53 Such and Walker (2005), 44.
54 *Re K (A Child) (Secure Accommodation Order: Right to Liberty)* [2001] 1 FLR 526, at [99].
55 Fox Harding (1994), 104; Such and Walker (2005), 54.
56 Reece (2006), 463–8.
57 See K. Hollingsworth, Responsibility and rights: Children and their parents in the youth justice system. (2007) 21(2) *International Journal of Law, Policy and the Family* 190.
58 Herring (2017a), 409.
59 Ibid., 416, 417.
60 James (2008), 156.
61 *Gillick v West Norfolk and Wisbech Area Health Authority and Department of Social Security* [1986] AC 112, at 170.
62 *Local Authority X v MM (by her litigation friend, the Official Solicitor)* [2007] EWHC 2003 (Fam), at [120].
63 See also A. Bainham, 'Is Anything Now Left of Parental Rights?', in Probert et al. (2009), 23, 24.

not to be 'wise'. Ultimately, the principle of parental responsibility in England does not work very differently from that of parental rights. It is a responsibility that is exercised over the child, not with the child, and places decision-making very solidly in the hands of parents in ways that are not particularly democratic.

Contrary to the law, the surveyed students did not think that children should be the passive recipients of parental responsibility. Nearly three-quarters of both college and university students thought that children should be able to make decisions for themselves, although they also recognised that parents had the right to make decisions for the family. As one student noted, the two can go hand in hand where 'we make up our own minds and respect family wishes'. Nevertheless, children's own decision-making did not automatically imply that they could also take decisions in opposition of their parents, although college students were much more likely than university students to prioritise the decisions of both older and younger children. This difference may have been inspired by background, lived reality or values, with law students likely to have greater affinity with the law and often coming from higher socio-economic classes with more involved, but potentially also more controlling parents.[64] Less than half of the college students, compared to most university students, agreed that the decision of a parent should take precedence over that of an elementary school child. By the time children had reached high school there was significantly less endorsement of parental primacy: 21% of college students and 38% of university students would still prioritise parental decision-making. Conversely, where freedom of religion was concerned, the difference between the students was much less pronounced. This might be because many students indicated that religion was 'personal' and therefore a decision to be taken by the person concerned, though some recognised that children needed 'guidance and morals', which faith could give. A majority also thought that, where parents had a religion, it was important for children to know a lot about that religion. Furthermore, religion could 'bring a family together, so it is important parents try to give their kids the same religion as them without forcing'. This is reminiscent of the primary culture that parents bring their children into as discussed in Chapter 4. It corresponds with most students indicating that they did not think a child in elementary school was old enough to decide on their own religion.[65] By contrast, 80% of college students and 83% of university students thought that a high school child would be old enough to decide on their own religion. Moreover, one college student emphasised, once the child has made their own decision, parents should not only tolerate, but *support* their child in that decision:

> Religion should be the choice of the individual not the choice of the parents. Once the child is old enough to understand different religions and their meanings, let them make their own decision and their parents should be supportive of that. Not pressurise them into their religion.

64 See R. Sullivan, *Barriers to the Legal Profession*. London: Legal Services Board, 2010, esp. 1–4.

65 Though college students were more likely to state that elementary school children were old enough.

Such pressure, or coercion, was seen as particularly problematic in respect of religious manifestation. Whereas half of the university students had stated that children in elementary school were too young to decide on their own religion, less than a quarter thought that parents could make young children manifest the parental religion.[66] In respect of high school students, the vast majority of both college and university students rejected PCRMs: 18% of university and 10% of college students thought that parents should be allowed to impose manifestations. However, that did not mean that children who believed differently or not at all would never be willing to share manifestations with their family. As argued in Chapters 3 and 5, children can *choose* to participate in manifestations of their parents' religion. This was pointed out by one student who stated: 'My parents do not mind that I choose not to have a religion even though I do participate in activities done for my parent's [*sic*] religion'. The most important for most students was the existence of a choice and growing agency, seen as especially pertinent in the area of religion.

The English law takes the reverse approach: although parents possess extensive parental rights in general, they hold claim to particularly broad prerogatives in respect of children's religious education and upbringing. Parents have a right to *determine* (and impose) their child's religious upbringing and manifestations.[67] The determination is strengthened through the principle of parental responsibility and the rights parents hold under the HRA. Whilst it has been acknowledged that children also hold rights under the HRA, it is not until a child is Gillick competent (when parental rights yield anyway), that courts have allowed children to rely on autonomy-supporting rights that impact on parental responsibility.[68] Moreover, there is a tendency in religion-related human rights cases to focus solely on the rights of parents.[69] For example, in a case on religiously motivated corporal punishment, the House of Lords except Baroness Hale ignored the rights of children and based themselves entirely on parents' personal rights to religious freedom (Article 9 ECHR).[70] In another landmark case (*Re G*),[71] the court had to decide between the application of a mother who wished to raise

66 For college students this was 13%.

67 See n. 38; Langlaude (2014), 4 with reference to *Re J (Specific Issue Order: Child's Religious Upbringing and Circumcision)* [2000] 1 FLR 571.

68 E.g. *Re Roddy (A Child) (Identification: Restriction on Publication)* [2003] EWHC 2917 (Fam); *R (Axon) v The Secretary of State for Health* [2006] EWHC 37 (Admin). Compare with cases involving protection rights: *Re A (Children: Conjoined Twins)* [2000] 4 All ER 961; *A National Health Service Trust v D* [2000] 2 FLR 677.

69 This was pointed out by Baroness Hale in *R (Williamson) v Secretary of State for Education and Employment* [2005] UKHL 15, at [71]. See also *The Queen on the application of K v London Borough of Newham* [2002] EWHC 405 (Admin); *Re N (A Child: Jehovah's Witness)* [2011] EWHC B26 (Fam).

70 *R (Williamson) v Secretary of State for Education and Employment* [2005] UKHL 15, esp. at [35], [74]. See also Taylor (2009), 134–7. This is a misunderstanding of the law, as explained in 2.4.

71 *Re G* [2012] EWCA Civ 1233.

the children in an orthodox manner and send them to co-educational orthodox schools and the objections of the father who sought to maintain the children in the ultra-orthodox environment they had grown up in. It transpired that the children's ultra-orthodox education was entirely at odds with fundamental values such as equality of opportunity between the sexes and respect for children's views and aspirations. However, throughout the judgment, Munby LJ stressed that there was no question as to whether parents could raise and educate their children in this manner, which was their 'entitlement' under parental responsibility,[72] supported by their personal right to freedom of religion (9 ECHR). The judge added a postscript to emphasise that *Re G* was not about State intervention, in which case 'the family' could rely on ECHR Articles 8 (family life), 9 (freedom of religion) and 2P1 (parental rights in education).[73] Whereas the court thus mentioned the rights of parents and those of the family unit to support controversial exercises of parental responsibility, there was no recognition of the children having their own rights, and that some of these rights e.g. related to education, participation, information, equality and potentially freedom of religion appeared in direct conflict with parents' 'entitlement'.

In view of existing (case-)law and practice, Taylor has argued that the foundational concern under English religion-related law is parents' freedom of choice.[74] Where parents agree on religious upbringing, they may virtually impose any kind of manifestation that does not place a child at risk of significant harm (the child protection threshold).[75] Gillick competence might also play a role when children are older but, as discussed below, parents can prevent their child from ever reaching such competence. In respect of religion, parental responsibility is:

> largely concerned with parents' freedom to raise their children as they wish without State interference . . . This freedom with its roots in nineteenth-century common law, is subject to very little regulation.[76]

If anything, regulation supports parental wishes and facilitates, if not normalises, the imposition of PCRMs. The law e.g. states that only parents can exempt children under 16 from religious education and worship at school.[77] This has led to questioning and condemnation by the CmRC as contrary to children's freedom of manifestation.[78] Yet within the English context, 'the child's freedom is rarely

72 Ibid., at [39].
73 Ibid., at [93].
74 Taylor (2009), 140; Taylor (2015), 31.
75 S. Furness and P. Gilligan, *Religion, Belief and Social Work*. Bristol: Policy Press, 2010a, esp. chapters 4 and 6; Taylor (2015), 32.
76 Taylor (2009), 140.
77 S. 71 *School Standards and Framework Act* 1998, chapter 31.
78 CmRC, *Summary Record of 2114th Meeting, United Kingdom of Great Britain and Northern Ireland*. UN Doc. CRC/C/SR.2114 (27 May 2016), para 22 (Mr Kotrane); CmRC, *Concluding Observations, United Kingdom of Great Britain and Northern Ireland*. UN Doc CRC/C/GBR/CO/5 (12 July 2016), para 36.

seen behind the parent's right',[79] even if this sits ill with the idea that parental rights only exist for as long as necessary to protect the child. Decisions on manifestations and their imposition are for responsible parents to make, inspired by personal convictions and practices of their respective religions and communities.

Regarding the latter, according to the interviewees parents under all religions, bar one, were expected to bring their children into the religion as a result of explicit scriptural obligations, or informal anticipation. Parents were therefore encouraged to involve children in religious manifestations and teach them about the religion, though most interviewees added that the community as a whole also had an important role to play. Yet to most interviewees the key parental responsibility was instilling the religious values and principles of the relevant faith:

> There is an obligation to bring up children into the religion, but the most important is to impart the values which affect life . . . They are part and parcel of the faith. Parents must make them understood and use them as part of real life.

Even where communities facilitated learning about the religion through formal study, the family was seen as the 'natural school where the foundations for life are laid'. Parents could teach children informally within the context of everyday life, though they were to principally lead by example. Religious upbringing, one interviewee stated, was first and foremost 'being a role model'. Some interviewees remarked that part of the parental role (supported by the community) was also to help children who were questioning their faith and its practice. Here, interviewees emphasised the importance of communication. Especially if a child expressed a desire to give up the faith or its manifestations, one interviewee stressed that parents should talk with them: 'Try to answer questions and find out "what is the reason?"'. Parents were expected to take their children seriously and 'not say "how dare you!"'.

In the interpretation of the interviewees, none of the participating religions encouraged PCRMs. Religious manifestation could only be imposed for two reasons. First where the child had not yet reached the age of independent thinking or ability to choose and they would benefit from the discipline of manifestations and learning about a religion. Secondly, where non-participation in manifestation would be more harmful. It was e.g. not safe and 'probably illegal' to leave a young child alone as parents went to worship, so 'you take them with you and hope they enjoy'. The interviewees thus proposed a view on religious manifestation close to the framework introduced in Chapter 4, although they did not base their views primarily on children's freedom of manifestation. Interviewees' main concern was of a practical nature: children who were forced to manifest would be unhappy and look for opportunities to rebel. Eventually, PCRMs would probably make children 'turn away from the religion entirely'. Notwithstanding the primacy of practicality, interviewees also gave principled reasons for not forcing a religion and PCRMs

79 Taylor (2009), 124.

upon children. Many pointed to the idea that religion should be a voluntary choice, or if not a choice, then at least a voluntary matter. All interviewees shared the view that at some point, whether sooner or later, children would have to be allowed to make their own decisions, even if these were 'heart-breaking' to parents. Here, most interviewees drew connections with children's competence, for example:

> As they grow older, with their growing independence, they no longer need to [manifest]. The parents will say 'we'd love you to come . . . but we can't force you'.

> For a child, until he has reached the age of independent thinking, it is the parents' responsibility to guide him to the faith [through example, explanation and discipline]. After that, it is a 'choice', a personal matter.

Although one interviewee expressed some dissatisfaction at the prospect of children leaving the religion or refusing to manifest it, interviewees generally agreed that if a child had chosen not to practise, their decision should be respected. Parents should continue to propose to the child to come back, but ultimately all parents could do was 'pray for them'. However, children had to exercise their 'choice' with regard for other family members. This coincided with the requirement in some religions that children should honour their parents, even if none of the interviewees interpreted that as complete obedience. One interviewee described it more like thoughtfulness where 'if you know something bothers your parents a lot, you should at least be having that in mind'. Another interviewee suggested that there should be reciprocity of respect between parents and children. To a large extent, what the interviewees proposed was closer to the model proposed in this book than the English law as it stands, though practicality and morality played a larger role than rights. Some interviewees in fact pointed to the difference between what was allowed under the law and what would be desirable from the perspective of their religion. However, the interviewees were keenly aware of the mediation posed by individual parents and one suggested that all depended 'on how traditional the family is'. Religious communities can thus influence parents, but the final decision is theirs, subject to limitations imposed by the law.

7.4 Limitations on parental responsibility

Although parental rights and powers to determine children's religious lives are extremely broad, they are not limitless. The most important limitations are posed by children's own competence, the child protection threshold (especially where there is overlap with the criminal law) and – when public authorities like courts become involved – children's interests.[80] The latter can pose real limitations on

80 Herring (2017b), 445 identifies as possible limitations the criminal law, need for consent from another person with parental responsibility, child protection, court orders, Gillick competence and children's human rights.

parental rights to impose PCRMs but is dependent on the involvement of the State. By contrast, the effects of Gillick competence and the child protection threshold are relatively minimal.

7.4.1 Gillick competence

Under 19th-century common law, where a minor 'of sufficient age and intelligence' had 'received and formed' different religious convictions from their parents, parental rights had to yield.[81] However, during the 20th century the thought that parents controlled their children until majority came to prevail.[82] In *Hewer v Bryant*, Lord Denning challenged this perspective by holding that the common law should declare 'the legal right of a parent to the custody of a child . . . a dwindling right'.[83] Some years later, the *Gillick* case reinstated the previous position and proclaimed the legal notion of 'Gillick competence' to designate at which point children could make their own decisions.[84] Although originally decided in the medical context, *Gillick*'s scope now extends to other aspects of parental responsibility.[85] Once a child is Gillick competent, parents can no longer impose PCRMs.

In *Gillick*, a devout mother sought confirmation of her parental right to control her daughters' contraceptive treatment. Rather than confirming this right, the House of Lords established that, if a child had reached a certain level of understanding and intelligence, they would be able to make decisions in lieu of – and perchance opposition to – their parents.[86] To avoid wide interference with parental rights, the bar for Gillick competence was set high: a child would need to understand the decision, matters involved in taking it, and consequences flowing from it, and *then* be able to make a reasonable assessment of the advantages and disadvantages of the decision, or at least 'fully understand' the decision in ways going beyond a mere understanding of its nature.[87] Where the child is intending to do something harmful, the courts have allowed further inroads on Gillick competence,[88] although this is normally done by declaring a child incompetent despite clear indications to the contrary.[89]

81 *Re Besant* (1879) 11 Ch.D. 508, at 519. See also *Agar-Ellis*, 317.

82 E.g. *R v Carroll* [1931] 1 KB 317.

83 *Hewer v Bryant* [1970] 1 QB 357, at 369.

84 *Gillick v West Norfolk and Wisbech Area Health Authority and Department of Social Security* [1986] A.C. 112, at 186. See also A. Bainham, Lord Denning as a Champion of Children's Rights: The Legacy of Hewer v Bryant. (1999) 14 *Denning Law Journal* 81.

85 E.g. *Sheffield City Council v Bradford MBC* [2013] 1 FLR 1027 (place of residence); *Re S (Child as Parent: Adoption: Consent)* [2017] EWHC 2729 (consent to adoption).

86 *Gillick* (1985), at 189.

87 Ibid., at 186, 189.

88 *Plymouth Hospitals NHS Trusts v YZ* [2017] EWHC 2211 (Fam), at [12; 13].

89 E.g. *Re E (A minor) (Wardship: Medical Treatment) [1993] 1 FLR 386; An NHS Foundation Trust v A and others* [2014] EWHC 920 (Fam). See also G. Douglas, The Retreat from Gillick. (1992) 55(4) *Modern Law Review* 569; Herring (2017b), 493, 494.

Gillick competence has been subject to critique. It is, for example, not clear what exactly the test is in different contexts.[90] Gillick Competence has also been said to work as an exclusionary notion: children are often declared incompetent for the simple reason that adults disagree with their decision or think it is unwise.[91] The concept has been called unwarranted because it imposes responsibilities on children and leads to negative relational consequences.[92] Most often, though, criticism focuses on the very high threshold Gillick competence sets and how this relates to expectations of adults.[93] Courts do not normally declare children Gillick competent until they are well into their teens,[94] informed,[95] articulate[96] and with a full, rational grasp of the circumstances.[97] This contrasts with the much lower threshold set by the *Mental Capacity Act* 2005,[98] which applies to adults and requires them to understand, retain (for short periods of time) and weigh or use information, to then communicate a decision (s. 3). Adults must also be given help to understand relevant information and unwise decisions do not necessarily point to incapacity (s. 1). It is therefore significant that in *Re S*, Cobb J held that, although the *Mental Capacity Act* does not as such apply to minors, he saw 'considerable merit' in borrowing aspects from it when deciding on Gillick competence.[99] The judge proposed that the test for decision-making competence should be decision-specific and relate to a child's ability to:

a) Understand the nature and implications of the decision and the process of implementing that decision;
b) Understand the implications of not pursuing the decision;
c) Retain the information long enough for the decision-making process to take place;
d) Be of sufficient intelligence and maturity to weigh up the information and arrive at a decision;
e) Be able to communicate that decision.[100]

90 R. Wheeler, Gillick or Fraser? A Plea for Consistency over Competence in Children. (2006) 332 *British Medical Journal* 807; A. Daly, No Wight for 'Due Weight'? A Children's Autonomy Principle in Best Interest Proceedings. (2018) 26 *International Journal of Children's Rights* 61, 70–3.
91 E.g. Daly (2018), 72.
92 N. Zimmerman, Gillick Competence: An Unnecessary Burden. (2019) 25(1) *The New Bioethics* 78, 91, 92.
93 E.g. Fortin (2009), 153; E. Cave, Goodbye Gillick; Identifying and Resolving Problems with the Concept of Child Competence. (2014) 34 *Legal Studies* 103, 104, 118–21.
94 See e.g. *Re B (A 14 Year Old Boy)* [2017] EWFC B28 (Fam), at [102].
95 E.g. *Re L (Medical Treatment: Gillick Competence)* [1998] 2 FLR 810 (information had been deliberately withheld, but the child was still declared incompetent).
96 E.g. *Re Roddy (A Child) (Identification: Restriction on Publication)* [2003] EWHC 2917 (Fam), at [56].
97 E.g. *Re S (Consent to Medical Treatment)* [1994] 2 FLR 1065; *Re JA (Medical Treatment: Child Diagnosed with HIV)* [2014] EWHC 1135 (Fam). Though see *Re JS (Disposal of Body)* [2016] EWHC 2859 (Fam), at [35] for a rejection of JS' views to be 'sensible'.
98 2005, Chapter 9.
99 *Re S (Child as Parent: Adoption: Consent)* [2017] EWHC 2729, at [60].
100 Ibid., at [62].

However, Cobb J made 'an important distinction . . . between the *determination* of competence to make the decision and the *exercise* by that young person of their competent decision-making'.[101] That division is also the one argued for in Chapters 3 and 4, but the requirements for the second part are much higher under English than international law. At the exercise stage, the child would still have to demonstrate a full understanding of the essential implications, especially where the decision is 'significant and life-changing'.[102] It is thus not clear that any lower threshold now applies to children's actual decision-making. Potentially the most important outcome of *Re S* is that the judgment requires that minors are given appropriate information regarding the decision at hand to enhance their autonomous decision-making.[103]

Information was also identified as important in religious decision-making by the students. Many believed that children should be able to make an *informed* decision on religion and manifestation, which required 'access to religious information enough to make my own decision'. As one student stated: 'my parents gave me knowledge of their religion a lot and now let me decide what I believe as I grew up'. Comments on becoming acquainted with religion referred to understanding the parental, students' own and different religions, so that a genuine choice could be made on personal manifestations, or lack thereof. For one student, for example, this meant that her level of practice was higher than that of family members, which was 'a personal choice through individual research'. Parental modelling was key and could lead to a wish 'to be like them [parents] and follow their religion because they set an amazing example'. However, parents were not the only source of information about religion, or knowledge generally. Students appreciated the role of the education system in broadening their horizons. This meant that the education system had to offer something in addition to information about the parental religion. Only a quarter of the students agreed that religious parents must give their children a religious education and less than a fifth thought that schools should give children religious education in conformity with the parental religion. By contrast, nearly three-quarters agreed that children should learn about all the main religions at school, which corresponds with previous research on English children valuing learning about other religions.[104]

Information is thus crucial to religion-related decision-making generally and Gillick competence in particular. However, the implication of *Re S* is that minors must have access to understandable information when they are already making a decision, not to allow them to contemplate a decision in the first place. Gillick competence is a threshold, not a developmental exercise. Two issues are noteworthy in that respect, especially in the context of PCRMs. First, whilst Gillick competent children have the right to decide

101 Ibid., at [62(v)].
102 Ibid., at [61].
103 Ibid., at [41–3].
104 Smith (2005), 31–3.

on their own religious practice, there is no regulation of children's position *before* they reach the high level of competence required. There is e.g. no legal requirement that parents let children participate in decisions that concern them or pay regard to their opinions.[105] The law governing religious upbringing is 'leaving parents to decide how far to take the views of their children into account'.[106] Although the courts have accepted that parental rights are 'dwindling rights', the dwindling does not refer to children's increased involvement, but to the gradual increase in areas in which a child has reached Gillick competence.[107]As long as the child is not Gillick competent, parental rights apply absolutely and PCRMs may be imposed without discussion.[108] Conversely, once competence is achieved, decisions can be taken entirely by children from one day to the next.

Second, whilst Gillick competent children may take their own decisions, parents are not under any obligation to help their children reach such competence. *Re S* requires accommodation in terms of children's existing competence, but there is no expectation of a development of competence. Parents may not cause children developmental arrest ('significant harm'), but there is no requirement for them to encourage gaining competence.[109] They are instead at liberty to seek to prevent children from reaching religious competence by maintaining them in closed communities and restricting their education.[110] This is possible because the government is extremely reluctant to interfere with parental prerogatives in education. Rather than offering children a complementary education to that received in the family, education in England aims at supporting and furthering parental (religious) upbringing.[111] In return for their duty to provide their child with an education, parents hold robust rights to decide on content and provision, including in ways explicitly contrary to children's rights and unlikely to allow children to reach Gillick competence in numerous fields.[112] A plea to make educational requirements compatible with Article 29 CRC (the aims of education)[113] has

105 See Such and Walker (2005), 44; J. Eekelaar, *Family Law and Personal Life*. Oxford: OUP, 2006, 158–60.

106 Taylor (2009), 137.

107 *R (Axon) v The Secretary of State for Health* [2006] EWHC 37 (Admin), at [13], [130]; T. Jarrett, *Children: Parental Responsibility – What is it and How is it Gained and Lost (England and Wales)*. House of Commons Briefing Paper 2827 (2017), 2, 3.

108 See Fortin (2009), 322.

109 S. Gilmore, 'The Limits of Parental Responsibility', in Probert et al. (2009b), 79.

110 *R (Williamson) v Secretary of State for Education and Employment* [2005] UKHL 15; Taylor (2015), 20.

111 S. 9 *Education Act* 1996, chapter 56; L. Lundy, Family Values in the Classroom? Reconciling Parental Wishes and Children's Rights in Schools. (2005) 19 *International Journal of Law, Policy and the Family* 346; Department for Children, Schools and Families (DCSF), *Religious Education in English Schools: Non-Statutory Guidance*, DCSF-00114-2010 (2010), 5.

112 Fortin (2009), 411; D. Monk, 'Parental Responsibility and Education: Taking a Long View', in Probert et al. (2009), 164; Taylor (2015), 20, 26.

113 G. Badman, *Report to the Secretary of State on the Review of Elective Home Education in England*. House of Commons HC610 (2009), 8, 10.

been rejected,[114] despite the British government not having made a reservation to that provision. Under English law:

> the party with the keenest personal interest . . . is . . . the parent of the child. . . . the child may or may not share that interest. But the parent has a statutory duty.[115]

That statutory duty is very limited. Parents must ensure that their child receives 'efficient' education that is suitable to the child's age, ability, aptitude and special educational needs.[116] If they fail to do so, a local authority can issue an attendance order.[117] Efficient education is not defined, but case-law has determined that children must obtain skills in reading, writing and arithmetic,[118] and that parents must prepare children for a life in their own religious community, while enabling them to adopt *some* other form of life in later years.[119] In 2010, eight hours a week of home tuition in mathematics and English were deemed sufficient.[120] Moreover, since home-schooling parents are not required to register their child, education authorities may not know of their existence and are thus prevented from monitoring their education altogether.[121] This is extremely problematic from the perspective of children's rights and competence.[122]

Parents can also choose to send their children to independent schools, free schools and academies, which are subject to the Independent Schools Regulations.[123] These schools enjoy significant educational freedom, although the current regulations impose stricter educational requirements than was previously the case.[124] Under the old regulations a school delivering its classes in

114 House of Commons; Children, Schools and Families Committee, *The Review of Elective Home Education: Government Response to the Committee's Second Report of Session 2009–2010*. House of Commons HC 423 (2009–2010) (2010), 14.

115 *A. v Headteachers and Governors of Lord Grey School* [2006] UKHL 14, at [16].

116 S. 7 *Education Act* 1996.

117 Ibid., s. 437.

118 *Harrison and Harrison v Steevenson* (1982) QB (DC) 729/81.

119 *R v Secretary of State for Education and Science ex parte Talmud Torah Machzikei Hadass School Trust* (1985) QB Times 12 April 1985 per Woolf J. The last requirement means that parents must give children an *awareness* of the fields of knowledge open to children: House of Commons; Children, Schools and Families Committee (2010), 12.

120 *JR17 for Judicial Review (Northern Ireland)* [2010] UKSC 27, at [103]. The Northern Irish provision includes the same wording as s. 7 of the English Education Act.

121 A 2017 Private Member's Bill proposed registration, but 2018 draft government guidance confirms the current framework: D. Foster, *Home Education in England*. House of Commons Library Briefing Paper 5108 (23 May 2018), 13–17.

122 See Children's Commissioner (A. Longfield), *Skipping School: Invisible Children*. London: Children's Commissioner for England, 2019, 14.

123 *Education (Independent Schools Standards) Regulations* 2014, No. 3283 (5 January 2015).

124 Children must receive 'experience' in linguistic, mathematical, scientific, technological, human and social, physical and aesthetic and creative education, so that they obtain skills in speaking, listening, literacy and numeracy (Regulation 2). Experience is a very low threshold and can be embedded within religious instruction. Compare House of Commons, Children, Schools and Families Committee (2010), 12.

a foreign language and only offering English and mathematics as non-religious subjects passed the inspection.[125] That would now no longer be the case – which explains why the inspectorate found nearly a quarter of independent faith schools inadequate at its last inspection.[126] Moreover, the Regulations require that independent schools 'actively promot[e] the fundamental British values of democracy, the rule of law, individual liberty, and mutual respect and tolerance of those with different faiths and beliefs'. However, this requirement is aimed at fighting fundamentalism and radicalisation, not at allowing children to receive competence in religious matters.[127] It also does not mean that children should not partake in the religious ethos and practice of the school or be encouraged to think about freedom of manifestation. Only where children are educated in public or aided schools are they taught the national curriculum, which envisages a comprehensive education that leads to children obtaining a wide knowledge base.[128] That knowledge could lead them to question certain manifestations. Beyond this there is limited investment in leading children to Gillick competence regarding religious manifestation. Whilst religious education forms part of the curriculum, there is some evidence that teachers are wary to approach religious matters from a critical perspective or discuss freedom of religion at all.[129] Active citizenship and education on rights have generally been considered in need of improvement in England.[130] Moreover, the obligatory daily act of worship in schools and religious education from which only parents can exempt children reinforces the normalcy of imposed manifestation.[131] This reflects that the English education system was designed to support parental religious upbringing, something that is hard to reconcile with enhancing children's competence to take their own religious decisions. Ultimately, Gillick competence is thus an important, but effectively restricted limitation on parental rights that depends on a high threshold which children may never reach, and below which a child does not have a right to participation at the national level.

125 Fortin (2009), 421, 422.

126 Ofsted, *The Annual Report of Her Majesty's Chief Inspector of Education, Children's Services and Skills 2017/18*. House of Comments Document HC 1707 (2018), 62.

127 Taylor (2015), 28–31. See also C. Vincent, Cohesion, Citizenship and Coherence: Schools' Responses to the British Values Policy. (2018) *British Journal of Sociology of Education*, DOI 10.1080/01425692.2018.1496011, esp. 2, 10.

128 Information on the different curricula that apply per school stage is available at <https://www.gov.uk/government/collections/national-curriculum> last accessed 10 March 2019.

129 Ofsted, *Transforming Religious Education. Religious Education in Schools 2006–09*. Ofsted Document 090215 (2010), para 21; Ofsted, *Religious Education: Realising the Potential*. Ofsted Document 130068 (2013), esp. 10, 14.

130 CmRC, *Concluding Observations, United Kingdom of Great Britain and Northern Ireland*. UN Doc CRC/C/GBR/CO/5 (12 July 2016), paras 33, 73.

131 S. 71 *School Standards and Framework Act* 1998. Minors in sixth form (over the age of 16) can exempt themselves: s. 55 *Education and Inspections Act* 2006.

7.4.2 The child protection threshold

Under English law, parental rights exist for children's welfare, but this is quite different from parents having to exercise their rights in ways that enhance or correspond with children's interests or welfare. English parents are not under a legal obligation to heed their children's interests, whether determined by themselves or society.[132] In some cases, the government even accommodates religious precepts it deems contrary to children's welfare by e.g. making vaccinations optional,[133] or exempting places of worship from the prohibition on serving alcohol to minors.[134] The limitation the law poses on the exercise of parental discretion in religious upbringing is that parents cannot cause their child 'significant harm'. This threshold serves two functions: it indicates the boundaries of parental powers to impose PCRMs and it signals the point at which the State can forcefully intervene in the family to protect children through care or supervision orders.[135] In addition, parents have to abide by the criminal law, which specifically prohibits female circumcision,[136] and contains a more general provision on the causing of unnecessary suffering or injury to health to a person under 16 that may apply to harmful PCRMs.[137] The provision was for example breached when a parent took his sons to a religious festival where they practised flagellation.[138] This is apart from non-specific criminal provisions like false imprisonment that may e.g. apply where a parent restrains their child in an unacceptable manner to effectuate a manifestation.[139] By contrast, the criminal law (or child protection standard) does not prevent parents from reasonably chastising their children to enforce compliance with manifestations.[140]

132 Gilmore (2009b), 79.

133 *Re C (A Child) (Immunisation: Parental Rights)* [2003] EWHC 1376 (Fam); *Re B (A Child: Immunisation)* [2018] EWFC 56.

134 Schedule 1, s. 9 *Licensing Act* 2003, chapter 17 (though no child under 5 may be served alcohol: s. 119 *Children's Act* 1908, chapter 67). See also DCSF, *Use of Alcohol among Children and Young People*. Research Report DCSF-RW043 (2008), 23.

135 Ss. 33 and 35 *Children Act* 1989. Under a care order, a child is removed from the family. A supervision order requires a social worker to 'advise, assist and befriend' the child. See also Herring (2017b), 634–7. Note that local authorities also have the possibility to apply for specific issue or prohibited steps orders, or wardship based on impairment of interests. However, there are no cases known to the author where authorities have applied for such orders in instances that did not also meet the child protection threshold.

136 Ss. 1, 2 *Female Genital Mutilation Act* 2003, chapter 31. See also *Re B and G (Children) (No. 2)* [2015] EWFC 3, distinguishing between male ('tolerated') and female (prohibited) circumcision at [60]–[64].

137 S. 1 *Children and Young Persons Act* 1933, chapter 12: anyone who has the custody or care of a person under 16 commits an offence if (s)he 'wilfully assaults, ill-treats, neglects, abandons, or exposes him, or causes or procures him to be assaulted, ill-treated, neglected, abandoned, or exposed, in a manner likely to cause him unnecessary suffering or injury to health'.

138 *R v Syed Mustafa Z* [2008] EWCA 2847.

139 *R v Mohammed Moqbular Rahman* (1985) 81 CR App. R. 349; *Re: M* [2016] EWHC 1658 (Fam), at [8].

140 See *R (Williamson) v Secretary of State for Education and Employment* [2005] UKHL 15.

The issue of harm to children and their protection was especially important to interviewees. Although interviewees did not think that parents should impose PCRMs, they were hesitant about State regulation unless abuse was involved and/or the manifestations were harmful. One interviewee held a strong opinion regarding legal limits, stating that 'except in total extremis, the law does not have any role to play in children's upbringing'. Others noted that it was important to make a distinction between what one interviewee called 'disciplinary mode' and abuse. Parents could be 'stern' when children were young and ask that they attend a place of worship in the same way they could ask a child to go to school, but they could not cause them harm. One interviewee pointed out that on this matter it was important to determine whether a parent had their child's interests at heart, or 'emotions have taken over common sense'. Another suggested that 'parents should use their God-given intelligence to see what is harmful'. Ultimately, one interviewee concluded:

> Protecting children is appropriate, but to what point you should be protecting them is difficult to determine. The idea is to be protecting children from harm. Going to [a place of worship or religious education] isn't going to cause harm. [The religion's] ideology does not cause harm. – Other things could be harmful, for example the refusal of blood transfusions. At that point it would be reasonable to protect the child.

The interviewees were not in favour of wide regulatory powers for the State, but this should be seen in the context where many thought that the religious community could act as a buffer-zone and protect the child without involvement of the State. Where parents harmed children, someone had to step up, possibly well before a child would suffer significant harm and the national child protection threshold would be met.

The case of *Re G*, discussed above, demonstrates that the English law tolerates a very significant gap between what society would consider serves children's interests, and what it expects of parents exercising parental responsibility. Since parents are responsible for their children, the law cannot impose limitations on PCRMs until the high threshold of 'significant harm' from ill-treatment or the impairment of health or development is met.[141] The harm must be the result of a lack of care below that which can reasonably be expected of a parent, but under English law it is unlikely that a parent 'faithfully striving to follow the teachings of one of the great religions' is acting unreasonably.[142] Depending on which religions are 'great' and what the approach to other religions should be, the limit of child protection may thus leave parents considerable scope to impose a wide variety of PCRMs. In fact, it seems that today courts are especially attuned to the inculcation of harmful religious beliefs (a 'violation to the

141 S. 31 *Children Act* 1989.

142 *Newcastle City Council v Z* [2005] EWHC 1490 (Fam), at [56].

mind instead of the body'),[143] rather than practice itself,[144] with a combination of indoctrination and harmful practice seen as especially problematic.[145]

The English courts have held that parents can raise their children in the ways of 'unusual or militant religions',[146] as long as they are 'legally and socially acceptable'[147] and the militancy does not amount to extremism.[148] It is nonetheless interesting that, whilst the State has taken steps to protect children from Islamic extremism,[149] it does not appear equally willing to enforce the protection limit where parents raise children in religions described as obnoxious and dangerous, seeking to isolate and brainwash children, using children as tools, and from which the children should be kept far away.[150] This reflects not only some questionable bias,[151] but also that the law is willing to view certain practices as controversial and genuinely harmful, though not significantly so. It corresponds with the often-quoted finding by Hedley J that parenting which is barely adequate and inconsistent, causing children disadvantage and harm and leading to very unequal consequences for children must be tolerated in a diverse society (at least an English one).[152]

The HRA has further strengthened the idea that the State should not interfere with upbringing unless circumstances are particularly critical, because 'the spectre of Article 8 of the ECHR [right to family life] hangs over us all'.[153] Yet, the spectre of children's rights *also* hangs over everyone and a reluctance to intervene in family life has led to ECHR condemnation for failure to adequately protect children.[154] Despite being known to social services, children have died of exorcism,[155] a radical religious regime,[156] or have been murdered after challenging religious

143 *London Borough of Tower Hamlets v B* [2015] EWHC 2491 (Fam), at [29]; *A Local Authority v A Mother, A Father, J (A child) (by her child's guardian)* [2018] EWHC 2054.

144 E.g. *Re: M* [2016] EWHC 1658 (Fam). See also Shelley (2013).

145 *N (A Child: Section 37: Interim Care Order)* [2014] EWFC 53, at [81].

146 *B (A Child) (Care Proceedings: Appeal)* [2013] UKSC 33, at 28, quoting *Re L (A Child) (Care: Threshold Criteria)* [2007] 1 FLR 2050.

147 *Re M (Children: Transgender Parent)* [2017] EWCA Civ 2164, at [52] quoting *Re R (A Minor)* [1993] 2 FLR 163.

148 *Re M (Children)* [2014] EWHC 667 (Fam), at 23.

149 See n. 143. See also policy measures described in Baroness Hale of Richmond, Freedom of Religion and Freedom from Religion. (2017) 19 *Ecclesiastical Law Journal* 3, 6; 7.

150 *Re B and G (Minors) (Custody)* [1985] FLR 134, at [134].

151 See Baroness Hale of Richmond (2017), 12.

152 *Re L (A Child) (Care: Threshold Criteria)* [2007] 1 FLR 2050, at [50]. See also *Leicester City Council v AB* [2018] EWHC 1960 (Fam), at [13].

153 *MA, SA and HA (Children, by their Children's Guardian) v MA, HA, The City and County of Swansea* [2009] EWCA 853, at [54].

154 E.g. *A. v United Kingdom* no. 25599/94 (1998) ECtHR Reports 1998-VI; *Z and Others v United Kingdom*, no. 29392/95 (2001) ECtHR (Grand Chamber) ECHR 2001-V. But see changes under new policy leading to premature action: J. Dickens and J. Masson, The Courts and Child Protection Social Work in England: Tail Wags Dog? (2016) 46(2) *British Journal of Social Work* 355.

155 House of Commons Health Committee, *The Victoria Climbié Inquiry Report*. House of Commons Doc. HC570, 6th Report, Session 2002–03 (2003).

156 See *Birmingham City Council v AG* [2009] EWHC 3720 (Fam).

and cultural practices imposed by parents.[157] This is partly the result of an inability to adequately monitor children. Parents can e.g. refuse health checks for their children,[158] and they need not allow anyone to see their child or enter their home unless such person possesses a court order.[159] Moreover, there is no mandatory reporting duty regarding suspected harm.[160] Yet even where cases are identified, there is a hesitance to interfere with religious upbringing,[161] despite a government campaign to sensitise frontline workers to the idea that religious practices can cause harm that reaches the child protection threshold.[162] Considering that the threshold is already set high and allows for the imposition of PCRMs that are truly harmful, but not significantly so, this is concerning. Equally concerning is that, whilst the threshold itself applies to all children, protection orders can only be applied for in respect of children aged 16 and under.[163] Those aged 16–18 are still entitled to services and protection,[164] but the State can no longer forcefully intervene through child protection. Hence a significant age group in respect of PCRMs, those most likely to have formed different views on religious manifestations, remains unprotected from significantly harmful PCRMs, or manifestations which are imposed in a significantly harmful manner.[165] This is so unless they take matters into their own hands and seek voluntary help from social services, or take parents to court in civil proceedings.[166] In the latter case, moreover, the court decides not on the basis of the child protection threshold, but children's interests.

7.4.3 Children's interests

As noted above, there is an important difference between what the law allows parents to decide for their children and what 'British society' would consider

157 *R (On the Application of Ahmed) v HM Coroner South and East Cumbria* [2009] EWHC 1653 (Admin).

158 National Health Service, *Newborn Screening* (2018) <https://www.nhs.uk/conditions/pregnancy-and-baby/newborn-screening/#newborn-physical-examination> last accessed 10 March 2019.

159 See Fortin (2009), 551–6; DCSF, *Elective Home Education. Guidelines for Local Authorities.* DCSF (2013).

160 HM Government, *Reporting and Acting on Child Abuse and Neglect.* London, 2018a, 5.

161 S. Furness and P. Gilligan, Social Work, Religion and Belief: Developing a Framework for Practice. (2010b) 40(7) *British Journal of Social Work* 2185, 2195; S. Furness and P. Gilligan, 'It Never Came Up': Encouragements and Discouragements to Addressing Religion and Belief in Professional Practice –What do Social Work Students have to Say? (2014) 44(3) *British Journal of Social Work* 763.

162 E.g. National Working Group on Child Abuse Linked to Faith or Belief, *The National action plan to tackle child abuse linked to faith or belief.* Department for Education DFE-00094 -2012 (2012).

163 S. 31(3) *Children Act* 1989. See also House of Commons Education Committee, *Children First: The Child Protection System in England.* House of Commons. HC137, 4th Report, Session 2012–13 (2012), paras 73–9.

164 HM Government, *Working Together to Safeguard Children.* Document DFE-00195-2018 (2018b), 102. See 7.5.3.

165 See *R (On the Application of Ahmed) v HM Coroner South and East Cumbria* [2009] EWHC 1653 (Admin).

166 See 7.5.1 below.

serves children's interests.[167] The difference is laid bare in situations where children's interests *must* be considered. These situations are invariably dependent on involvement of the State, normally via the courts. In all private law proceedings, children's interests constitute a 'paramount consideration',[168] trumping all other considerations.[169] Interests are to be determined on a case-by-case basis, and in their formulation courts are helped by a welfare-checklist which refers to a number of matters associated with children's lives.[170] The checklist contains no reference to children's rights, but as public authorities, courts must decide as far as possible in ways that uphold human rights, including those of children.[171]

When determining children's interests in matters of religion, courts apply the 'secular effects doctrine':[172] they are not allowed to judge religions per se, but must instead concentrate on the secular outcomes of beliefs and practices.[173] The latter includes the inculcation of children with certain values, so the boundary is not clear-cut.[174] Judges must further determine interests according to 'the normal standards of society' at the time they decide on the case.[175] In *Re M (Children)* the court emphasised that when deciding on children's interests in a religion-related case:

> the function of the judge . . . is to act as the 'judicial reasonable parent,' judging the child's welfare by the standards of reasonable men and women today, 2017, having regard to the ever changing nature of our world including, crucially for present purposes, *changes in social attitudes*, and always remembering that the reasonable man or woman is receptive to change, broadminded, tolerant, easy-going and slow to condemn. We live, or strive to live, in a tolerant society. We live in a democratic society subject to the rule of law. We live in a society whose law requires people to be treated equally and where their human rights are respected.[176]

The court's reasonable parent is a considerably more liberal one than that of the law generally,[177] and with much greater regard for children's own religious

167 *Re M (Children: Transgender Parent)* [2017] EWCA Civ 2164, at [48].

168 S. 1(1) *Children Act* 1989. In other procedures interests are a primary consideration: *ZH (Tanzania) v Secretary of State for the Home Department* [2011] UKSC 4.

169 *J v C* [1970] AC 668, at 710. For critique and alternatives, see e.g. S. Choudhry and H. Fenwick, Taking the Rights of Parents and Children Seriously: Confronting the Welfare Principle under the Human Rights Act. (2005) 25(3) *Oxford Journal of Legal Studies* 453.

170 S. 1(3) *Children Act* 1989: children's wishes, needs, effect of changed circumstances, child's background, possible harm, capabilities of parents and powers available to the court.

171 *Re M (Children: Transgender Parent)* [2017] EWCA Civ 2164, at [99].

172 Taylor (2015), 23.

173 *Re G* [2012] EWCA Civ 1233, at [35, 36; 43].

174 See e.g. *N (A Child: Section 37: Interim Care Order)* [2014] EWFC 53; *A Local Authority v A Mother, A Father, J (A Child) (by her child's guardian)* [2018] EWHC 2054.

175 *Re R (A Minor) (Religious Sect)* [1993] 2 FLR 163, at 172; *Re G* [2012] EWCA Civ 1233, at [51].

176 *Re M (Children: Transgender Parent)* [2017] EWCA Civ 2164, at [60].

177 See Langlaude (2014), 2.

autonomy and the need to gain the competence to exercise autonomous decision-making.[178] Herring has suggested that a 'consistent theme in the approach of the courts is that although parents can involve the child in religious activities, the child should be left to decide their religion for themselves'.[179]

English courts generally consider it to be in children's interests to have *a* religion.[180] In *Re C*, for example, a child with secular birth parents could be adopted by a highly observant couple, as it was not in the child's interests 'to replicate the religious void in her parental home'.[181] Judges tend to regard religious experience and shared practice as important to children.[182] A related interest is for a child to have a religious community that supports them.[183] That interest was equally recognised by the interviewees who emphasised the importance of community that religion could bring to children. This was not just related to engaging in religious practices. Most communities had a venue where family activities were organised and children could engage in non-religious pastimes with others that were 'important even for children who are not particularly interested in religion'. In addition, the majority of interviewees underlined that the discipline religions, their practices and moral codes brought served young (and older) children's interests. The interest of discipline was echoed by some of the students, who highlighted that religion would provide minors with a moral framework and rules for living, which, some pointed out, had been beneficial to them personally. Contrary to France and Hong Kong the discipline aspect is not normally one that the English courts emphasise. What the courts do pay attention to are other interests that were also identified by some students and interviewees: that children receive a moderate religious upbringing, learn about other religions (and the world) and are eventually allowed to decide for themselves.

Under the English law, children are thought to benefit from being brought up and participating in multiple faiths where there is more than one faith in the (separated) family.[184] However, the emphasis is on 'experiencing' the faith: if the religions are incompatible, parents can e.g. be prevented from religious instruction.[185] Children's interests dictate that they grow up with 'balanced views',[186] or as Langlaude states: '[t]he courts approve of religious upbringing as long as it

178 See *Re G* [2012] EWCA Civ 1233, at [80].
179 Herring (2017b), 553.
180 *Re C (A Child)* [2012] EW Misc 15 (CC).
181 *Re C (Adoption: Religious Observance)* [2002] 1 FLR 1119.
182 *Re N (A Child: Religion: Jehovah's Witness)* [2011] EWHC B26 (Fam); *Re C (A Child)* [2012] EW Misc 15 (CC); *Re A (Children)* Case No. FD13P01649 (4 November 2014) unreported.
183 *Re M (Children: Transgender Parent)* [2017] EWCA Civ 2164, at [131].
184 *Re S (Specific Issue Order: Religion: Circumcision)* [2004] EWHC 1282 (Fam). *Re T and M (Minors)* [1995] ELR 1 in S. Gilmore, The Nature, Scope, and Use of the Specific Issue Order. (2004) 16(4) *Child and Family Law Quarterly* 367, 383.
185 *Re N (A Child: Religion: Jehovah's Witness)* [2011] EWHC B26 (Fam), at [89]–[91].
186 F. Burton, *Family Law* (2nd ed.). Milton Park: Routledge, 2015, 372.

does not go "too far"'.[187] This is especially true because the courts have increasingly made it clear that children should be raised in such a way that they have a range of options available to them when they grow up,[188] including their own religious choices when they are able to make them.[189] The courts will not automatically ascribe the parents' religion to children where there is a dispute concerning religion.[190] Consequently, courts have been reluctant to sanction manifestations that are irrevocable like male circumcision,[191] controversial like vaccination,[192] or illegal such as female circumcision,[193] as well as manifestations restricting children's education.[194] Furthermore, indoctrination into a single faith,[195] particularly when coupled with social isolation and/or inculcation with intolerant values towards other faiths,[196] is generally considered contrary to children's interests.[197] At the start of the 21st century, children's interests indicate moderation, tolerance and broadmindedness, but also 'great attention to the wishes of a child old enough to be able to express sensible views on the subject of religion, even if not old enough to take a mature decision',[198] and ultimately that mature decision itself.

Children's interests can thereby further a child's freedom of manifestation, as was the case in *Re C (A Child)*.[199] C, a 10-year-old Jewish girl by birth who lived with her secular Jewish mother, wished to convert to the Church of England like her father. C had herself contacted the minister to ask about baptism classes, prompting her mother to seek an order prohibiting both baptism and conversion.[200] Taking into account in particular C's interest in being involved in a religion, but also her Jewish heritage, the court ordered that C could take the baptism, but needed to wait until 16 for full conversion.[201] C's case is of interest to this book on PCRMs, even if C *wanted to manifest* the religion of one of her parents.

187 Langlaude (2014), 30.
188 *Re G* [2012] EWCA Civ 1233.
189 *Re S (Specific Issue Order: Religion: Circumcision)* [2004] EWHC 1282 (Fam.); *Re S (Minors) (Access: Religious Upbringing)* [1992] 2 FLR 313 (the *guardian ad litem* was charged to help children aged 11 and 13 think about their religion).
190 See e.g. *J (A Minor) (Prohibited Steps Order: Circumcision)* [2000] 1 FLR 571.
191 *J (A Minor) (Prohibited Steps Order: Circumcision)* [2000] 1 FLR 571; *X Local Authority v C, M, A (A Child) by her Guardian Miss Williams* (3 March 2015) Unreported, at [74]. See also *AT v FS & Anor* (27 May 2011) Unreported, at [26] on preference for medically rather than ritually performed circumcision.
192 *Re C (A Child) (Immunisation: Parental Rights)* [2003] EWCA Civ 1148.
193 *Re N (A Child)* [2006] EWCA Civ 947: a s. 8 order had to remind a father not to circumcise his daughter.
194 *Re G* [2012] EWCA Civ 1233, at [43]. Attention should also be paid to the wishes of parents.
195 *Carol Lena Wright v Stephen Wright* [1980] 2 FLR 276.
196 *Hewison v Hewison* [1977] Fam Law 207; *M v H (A Child: Educational Welfare)* [2008] 2 FCR 280; *Re M (Children)* [2014] EWHC 667 (Fam).
197 *Re M (Children: Transgender Parent)* [2017] EWCA Civ 2164.
198 *Re G* [2012] EWCA Civ 1233, at [43].
199 *Re C (A Child)* [2012] EW Misc 15 (CC).
200 Ibid., at [14].
201 Ibid., at [38]–[51].

This is because the court affirmed C's ability to choose her own religious practice whilst continuing to live with the parent whose practice she rejected. Moreover, the court took an approach under which C's interests presented a limitation on her freedom of manifestation in the manner advocated in Chapter 4, since under international law children enjoy a right to convert at a younger age than 16.[202] The interests protected were C's Jewish heritage, of which she did not know a lot,[203] and the fostering of relations with her Jewish grandparents.[204] The judge in particular wanted to give C the opportunity to become better acquainted with her mother's religion before making a final choice and therefore placed a limit on C's freedom of religion without denying its exercise altogether. If this case had been one of freedom of manifestation as limited by interests (as proposed in Chapter 4), this limitation might have been regarded as necessary in a democratic society, although the six-year gap to learn about her mother's religion was potentially disproportionate.

In light of the above, it is unlikely that, where a child is mature enough to take their own decision, courts will uphold the parental right to impose PCRMs.[205] The courts may limit children's autonomous decision-making where their interests dictate it, but in general, it is explicitly in children's interests that they reach the competence to decide on their own religious practice and parents should not impose their own.

7.5 Invoking and enforcing rights within the family

Whilst the law allows parents to impose a wide range of PCRMs and force their religion in disregard of children's own views and participation, this was not the everyday experience of most students. Three-quarters of college students stated that their parents allowed them to decide on their own religion and 85% of university students agreed that their parents had done so when they were minors. Given the state of the law, these percentages are high, but it should be noted that all college students were over the age of 16 and university students reported back on minority up to age 18. The students were also asked whether they had had 'fights' with their parents over religious manifestation to indicate a higher level of conflict than simple disagreement: 13% of college students and 11% of university students had, with levels increasing substantially where students were not religious but had religious parents.[206] Treating the family unit as one for the

202 See for a comparable case involving a 12 year old: *Rupprecht v Spain* (dec), no. 38471/10 (19 February 2013) ECtHR.

203 *Re C (A Child)* [2012] EW Misc 15 (CC), at [66].

204 Ibid., at [35].

205 See *Re S (Minors) (Access: Religious Upbringing)* [1992] 2 FLR 313: the court expressed doubts about a 'fervent' religious parent; *Re A and D (Children) (Care Proceedings: Religious Upbringing)* [2010] EWCH 2503 (Fam): a Local Authority cannot be blamed for failing to sustain the religious persuasion of the birth family if a child in care has himself decided to follow a different faith.

206 To 38% and 23% respectively.

purposes of religion, as the law does, seemingly cannot prevent the actual existence of religious conflict where children are willing to stand up for their own personal choice.

Where conflict arose in the family, the students emphasised that it should first and foremost be 'solved within the family'. Many made reference to the importance of communication, discussion, talking things through and arguing or debating with parents. Additionally, empathy was 'key'. As summarised by one student: 'family conflicts are best resolved by communicating & understanding each other'. Where these conflicts related to religion, it was also offered that issues could be 'resolved through religion', whereas another student suggested that respect for different religions would prevent conflict from occurring in the first place, because 'if there is respect in a family, religion does not matter/cause conflict'. A large majority of college and university students agreed that parents should act considerately with regard to their child's religion and children with regard to their parent's religion, though there was greater support amongst both groups of students for the former. Perhaps it was considered that parents should be extra supportive of their children as they found their way through life. If not, it would mean that students required more respect than they were willing to give, which would be hard to reconcile with equal rights within the family.

The interviewees echoed the importance of solving religion-related conflict within the family circle. Most thought it was unlikely that PCRMs would occur within their community. Should a case nonetheless arise, all interviewees thought that this should principally be a matter for the family to resolve. Moreover, two interviewees explicitly stated that they thought forced manifestation was a relational, rather than religious issue, although one in which the religious community could play a role. One remarked 'I can imagine people [in the community] talking with the [parent], but relational failures are not religious'. Except for this interviewee, all interviewees suggested that, if there was a problem related to religious manifestation that could not be solved within the family, the religious organisation would, or should, be the first port of call for both parents and children. Some interviewees explained that their religions had permanent mechanisms of dispute resolution in place that would offer children a platform to have their voice heard first, potentially followed by mediation or counselling, or an intervention similar to parent education. Other interviewees referred to the possibility of religious leaders or pastoral workers offering help *ad hoc*. The aim of intervention, interviewees said, was not to turn the child around, but to find his/her reasons for rejecting the manifestation and to reconcile the family. Moreover, one interviewee remarked, by the time the parents contacted the community it was often too late to change a child's mind, but parents themselves could be helped 'to get their head around it'. As also another interviewee explained, 'religious settings do not always protect parents' in case of religious conflict, 'now they often protect the child'. The question is whether the child would accept to be helped by the community in a case of PCRMs, and what to do where the conflict cannot be solved within either the family or community circle.

7.5.1 Access to court

Whether children's access to court procedures would be the appropriate solution for a religious conflict that got out of hand was doubted by students and interviewees alike. Access to court already forms part of the law, but a number of university students (who were commencing law students) expressed their reservations about the idea. One, for example, stated that 'court action to solve family problems is a ridiculous idea unless to do with child abuse or something very serious'. A classmate thought that in general 'dispute resolution to solve religious problems is poppycock'. Another noted that much depended on the child's culture and in their culture 'it would reflect on me poorly if I took my parents to court'. If access to court should be granted at all – and a third of both college and university students thought it did[207] – it should be a measure of last resort after 'all other means of resolution [are] exhausted'.

As previously discussed in Chapter 5, English children have access to court to challenge the exercise of parental responsibility in private law proceedings.[208] The procedure, often referred to as a 's. 8 procedure' in reference to the provision which sets out possible orders, has been advocated abroad as one allowing children to enforce their (religious) rights against the wishes of their parents.[209] However, s. 8 procedures are not procedures to enforce rights, but designed to regulate aspects of parental responsibility. They can only be used to dispute PCRMs because religious upbringing forms part of the latter. Freedom of manifestation itself can only be indirectly enforced through the court's obligation to interpret the law in accordance with the HRA (ss. 3, 6).

S. 8 orders can be granted in respect of children under 16,[210] making the procedure solely relevant for children up until that age. Before applying for an order, a minor must obtain leave from the High Court, which should be granted if the minor has 'sufficient understanding to make the proposed application'.[211] Leave is always discretionary,[212] and there is no accessible record of a court having previously granted it where parents were not separated.[213] In a rare case where a minor sought orders against her non-divorced parents, the court considered that one issue (whether she could go on an overseas holiday with her friend's family) was too trivial and another (whether she could move in with that family) should be resolved by the minor and her parents without the involvement of the court.[214] The court noted that granting leave would give the child an advantage over her

207 College students were nonetheless more likely to 'strongly agree' that such access should exist.
208 Ss. 8; 10(8) *Children Act* 1989.
209 See Dekeuwer-Défossez (2010), 72.
210 Unless exceptional circumstances apply: s. 9(7) *Children Act* 1989.
211 S. 10(8) Children Act 1989.
212 *Warwickshire County Council v M* [2007] EWCA Civ 1084, especially at [24].
213 This might be because courts have applied reporting restrictions. In *Re CT* (1993) 2 FLR 278 the child applied against adoptive parents to live with family members.
214 *Re C (A Minor) (Leave to Seek Section 8 Order)* [1994] 1 FLR 26.

parents, but even if that were true, neither the matter of advantage, nor that of triviality provide valid reasons to deny leave. In any case, what might seem trivial to a court can be of great importance to a child,[215] and – as also the research in England suggests – if the family were able to sort out their difficulties, the matter would most likely not have appeared in court.[216] Over the years, the High Court has denied leave for a number of reasons unrelated to children's maturity,[217] and it has been suggested that the leave requirement be dispensed with altogether.[218] Yet the issue may be resolved by an interpretation of the law that is truer to the text. In the recent case of *JS (Disposal of Body)* the court focused on the child's maturity, even if what she suggested she would apply for (cryopreservation) might have struck the Court as curious.[219]

If leave is granted, children can apply for child arrangement (residence and contact), specific issue (positive exercise of parental responsibility), or prohibited steps (restraint on the exercise) orders as explained in Chapter 5. Prohibited steps orders would be particularly relevant in the case of PCRMs, because they can instruct a parent to refrain from an exercise of parental responsibility such as imposing religious manifestations.[220] When applying for a s. 8 order, the child becomes a party to the procedure, and, depending on their own and family finances, is appointed a lawyer through legal aid.[221] Parents must normally pay for their own lawyer,[222] which is problematic in cases where religious claims may need translation into legal terms. The fact that the child becomes a party nonetheless does not automatically give them the right to attend court,[223] or give evidence.[224] While children may make submissions and have a right to be heard, it is within the judge's discretion to decide on attendance and giving evidence, guided by notions of welfare and harm.[225] Although it is expected that, where a child made the application, judges would allow their presence and hear their evidence directly, it is possible that a child challenging a PCRM will only have the opportunity to instruct a lawyer, but not participate in the actual court process. That would undoubtedly give the child and parents the impression that the child's claim is not (to be) taken too seriously. Conversely, there is the danger

215 See Herring (2017b), 505 who nonetheless wonders if court is appropriate.

216 The nature of an application is (only) relevant where leave is sought by a third party: s. 10(9) *Children Act* 1989.

217 See Herring (2017b), 504–6.

218 By Booth J, to the opposition of practitioners: The Advisory Board on Family Law: Children Act Sub-Committee, *Making Contact Work*. London: Lord Chancellor's Department, 2002, 73.

219 *JS (Disposal of Body)* [2016] EWHC 2859 (Fam), at [9], [31]. The application was ultimately granted.

220 See *Re S (Specific Issue Order: Religion: Circumcision)* [2004] EWHC 1282 (Fam); *Re C (A Child)* [2012] EW Misc 15 (CC).

221 15(1) Schedule 1, *Legal Aid, Sentencing and Punishment of Offenders Act* 2012. (LASPO).

222 Unless there are allegations of e.g. child abuse or domestic violence: LASPO Schedule 1.

223 *A City Council v T* [2011] EWHC 1082 (Fam).

224 *P.-S. (Children)* [2013] EWCA Civ 223, at [35–41].

225 Ibid; *Cambra v Jones* [2014] EWHC 913. See also: Working Party of the Family Justice Council, *Guidelines in Relation to Children Giving Evidence in Family Proceedings*, FJC11/01/04 (2011).

that, if children were automatically allowed to give evidence and attend court, it may become more difficult for them to obtain leave.

S. 8 procedures are not aimed at enforcing children's rights, but at defining the interests of the minor concerned.[226] A minor therefore cannot claim directly that (s)he has a right to freedom of manifestation and the PCRM has violated it. In the baptism and conversion case discussed above, for example, freedom of religion evidently played an important role, but at no point does the judgment refer to the child's right, or the concept more generally. That the child should be allowed to make her own religious decision merely formed part of her 'ascertainable wishes and views' as an aspect relevant to her interests.[227] To challenge PCRMs under s. 8, a minor must thus demonstrate how *not* practising the parental religion under imposition better serves their interests than doing so. The parents must show that forcing their child to manifest their religion better serves the child's interests than not doing so. Basing arguments on interests might be harder for parents because the English courts can only accept secular arguments regarding children's interests.[228] Conversely, there appears to be a recognised interest to have at least *a* religion,[229] so that if the minor were to argue in favour of a complete absence of religion that might be controversial. Yet with no known cases of minors challenging PCRMs under s. 8, one can only speculate on the outcome.

In this regard, one of the interviewees remarked that they would not know many 12-year-olds who understood the *Children Act* sufficiently to be able to take their parents to court over PCRMs. Neither did they think that court action would be helpful unless there was harm. All interviewees but one accepted that access to court should exist as an ultimate remedy, but they did so reluctantly and expressed the hope that it would 'not come to that'. A significant problem the interviewees identified was the 'contentious' nature of court procedures.[230] Several noted that, as a consequence, court action was perhaps only relevant if there was a 'complete breakdown of communication and ability to discuss'. Where that was not the case, access to court could do more harm than good to the family, as one interviewee summarised:

> If a child was in distress, coerced or manipulated and that [court order] was the only way they felt they could protect themselves . . . There is of course the worry of the harm and damage done to the family relationship . . . , but that works both ways, because if parents are abusive then it [intervention] is a Godsend. But if it is a loving family and the child is rebellious, then it would drive a wedge between parents and children. It is best used as a last resort.

226 Fortin (2009), 291, 292. See also *Re G* [2012] EWCA Civ 1233, at [43].

227 *Re C (A Child)* [2012] EW Misc 15 (CC), at [51].

228 *Newcastle City Council v Z* [2005] EWCH 1490 (Fam), at [53].

229 *Re C (Adoption: Religious Observance)* [2002] 1 FLR 1119; *Re C (A Child)* [2012] EW Misc 15 (CC).

230 See also 7.5.2 below.

Contrary to the English High Court (on leave applications), the interviewees suggested that not the nature of the conflict, but the state of the parent–child relationship determined whether court action was appropriate. They appeared to acknowledge that even a 'trivial' issue could become the cause for a complete breakdown of the parent–child relationship. However, they emphasized that, if the relationship could be saved, then that should be attempted.

In addition to s. 8 procedures, where minors believe that their interests are compromised because of PCRMs, they can apply for an order under the court's inherent jurisdiction, or wardship as an aspect thereof.[231] Inherent jurisdiction applications normally relate to a single act (often authorisation of medical treatment),[232] whereas wardship transfers the whole of parental responsibility to the court, which means that the court is charged with every aspect of the child's upbringing, including religious. The inherent jurisdiction and wardship are old jurisdictions and courts have limited their use since the *Children Act* 1989 introduced s. 8 orders.[233] This is because the threshold is low (best interests) whereas the consequences are far-reaching (the jurisdiction is 'limitless').[234] However, within the context of challenging PCRMs,[235] the applications remain important for two reasons. First, wardship is relevant if religion pervades a way of life and objection was made to all aspects of life with religious connotation;[236] the child lives within the confines of a religious sect;[237] or is overseas (e.g. on the way to joining a foreign fundamentalist organisation).[238] Wardship has also been used in a case in which a minor himself joined a religious movement and his carer sought to obtain his return home.[239] This is important, because it demonstrates that explicit recognition of children's freedom of manifestation would not leave parents empty-handed where they truly oppose autonomous decision-making because they feel it harms children's interests. Secondly, minors over 16 cannot be the subject of s. 8 orders regulating parental responsibility (or child protection orders).[240] It may be expected that minors sufficiently mature and willing to challenge PCRMs would be older and the

231 Rules 12.3 and 12.37 *Family Procedure Rules* 2010 No. 2955 (L17). See also: Herring (2017b), 504.

232 E.g. *Re S (a Minor) (Medical Treatment)* [1993] 1 FLR 376; *A Local Authority v M, T (By his Children's Guardian)* (8 February 2018) (unreported).

233 S.M. Cretney and J.M. Masson, *Principles of Family Law* (6th ed.). London: Sweet & Maxwell, 1997, 706.

234 *Re W (A Minor) (Medical Treatment: Court's Jurisdiction)* [1993] Fam 64.

235 See *Re P (A Minor)* [1986] 1 FLR 272: application for an abortion against religiously motivated wishes of parents (this would now fall under *Gillick* competence).

236 *Mutatis mutandis Re M (Children: Transgender Parent)* [2017] EWCA Civ 2164.

237 *Re L (Minors) (Wardship: Jurisdiction)* 1974 1 WLR 250; *Re B and G (Minors) (Custody)* [1985] Fam Law 58.

238 E.g. *Re Y (Wardship) (No 2)* [2015] EWHC 2099; *A Local Authority v HB* [2017] EWHC 1437 (Fam). See also Baroness Hale of Richmond (2017), 7.

239 *Kelly v British Broadcasting Corporation* [2001] Fam 59.

240 Ss. 9(7); 31(3) *Children Act* 1989.

inherent jurisdiction and wardship are their only means of access to court. It is noteworthy, though, that the jurisdictions are protective jurisdictions with decisions taken on the basis of children's interests. They are not designed to empower children or enforce their rights. Neither is there an obligation to seek the cooperation of the family. If parties look for conflict resolution rather than adjudication, ADR might be a better option.

7.5.2 Access to mediation

English family court proceedings are notoriously adversarial.[241] They 'ought to be but usually are not problem-solving courts'.[242] The adversarial nature is based on a long-standing tradition that emphasises parties' ability to defend their rights and question their opponent, but usually leads to the pitting of parties against each other and a focus on 'winning' rather than cooperating.[243] Some recent pilots have therefore sought to test alternative (therapeutic) ways of case settlement within the public law system.[244] The private law system, specifically where s. 8 orders are concerned, has long diverted cases to family mediation as a more family-friendly means of dispute resolution.[245] Parent–child mediation is nonetheless not widely available in England. This can be explained because children's limited practical access to court may not encourage their consideration for ADR. Second, legal aid for mediation is means-tested and whilst children may qualify for it, their parents might not.[246] Given that mediation is voluntary, there may not be many parents willing or able to pay high mediation fees to allow their children to contest PCRMs that parents consider serve their interests. Most importantly, whilst the law generally requires parties involved in s. 8 procedures to have attempted mediation before bringing the case to court, this requirement is waived where one of the parties is a minor.[247] There is thus no infrastructure under which children are automatically referred to mediation if they take a case against their parents to court. Neither is there a permanent structure offering parent–child mediation independently of court procedures, and very little evidence of individual initiatives.

This stands in stark contrast with the significantly more positive views interviewees expressed towards mediation as compared to court, albeit sometimes

241 See P. Welbourne, Adversarial Courts, Therapeutic Justice and Protecting Children in the Family Justice System. (2016) 28 *Child and Family Law Quarterly* 205.

242 Sir J. Munby, 'Changing Families: Family Law Yesterday, Today and Tomorrow – A View from South of the Border', *Edinburgh Law School Lecture* (20 March 2018), 10 <https://www.judiciary.uk/wp-content/uploads/2018/03/speech-pfd-changing-families-edinburgh.pdf> last accessed 10 March 2019.

243 J. Jolowicz, Adversarial and Inquisitorial Models of Civil Procedure. (2003) 52(2) *International Comparative Law Quarterly* 281, 282–9; Welbourne (2016), 205–8.

244 Welbourne (2016), 212–18; Munby (2018), 10.

245 See Hunter et al. (2017).

246 15(1) Schedule 1, *Legal Aid, Sentencing and Punishment of Offenders Act* 2012.

247 Rule 3.8(n) of the *Family Procedure Rules* 2010.

premised on the need to give parent–child mediation further thought where interviewees had not previously considered it. In general, interviewees were enthusiastic about mediation in cases of PCRMs. Some communities themselves offered parent–child mediation and interviewees noted that, if they became involved in matters of PCRMs, this had the double advantage of allowing the organisation to support the child and keeping the child 'on board'. At least two communities had successfully mediated between parents and children in the past and one interviewee mentioned involvement in two cases concerning children objecting to religious rules: one in which the outcome had been in favour of the child, the other in which it had not been, because the child wished to take a course of action likely to cause this minor harm. Within the context of PCRMs, some interviewees deemed of significance that using the religious organisations' own facilities (including *ad hoc*) would ensure that the person mediating was well-versed in the religion. The familiarity of the mediator with the relevant religion appeared a real concern. One interviewee, for example, feared that a secular mediator might be opinionated. Another interviewee stated that lack of knowledge could lead to a 'poorly negotiated agreement' based on 'wrong assumptions'. However, it was also appreciated that, if a child was forced to manifest, the relevant person within the religious community might be 'the last person' a child would contact. Therefore, if parents and children were in genuine conflict and they agreed on a secular mediator, rather than court, then, as one interviewee indicated, the community would 'support mediation, even if it was secular: whatever would support the family'.

The students' views on mediation were more mixed: 39% of college students and 29% of university students agreed that if they were in conflict with their parents they would (have) like(d) to solve the problem through mediation.[248] Two outcomes were of particular interest: fewer university students were interested in mediation than not, whereas the reverse was true for college students. Moreover, university students were less likely to support mediation than access to court, whilst college students favoured mediation over court. Part of the difference might be explained by the university students' greater affinity with legal procedures, but it is plausible that feasibility equally played a role. Most university students reported that they did not think their parents would be willing to solve intra-family conflict through mediation. By contrast, college students were more confident that their parents would accept to mediate with them. Even if children could otherwise take the case to court, a quarter of university students still did not think their parents would agree to mediate. The idea that parents would not be interested in mediation may have made the university students less willing to regard mediation as an option themselves, but this is a matter for further research. It is at least notable that mediation did not elicit the same questioning comments from students as access to court had.

248 26% and 47% respectively indicated that they did not.

7.5.3 Social services

Local authorities have a duty to promote the welfare of children and offer services to children who are 'in need',[249] meaning that a child must need services to maintain a 'reasonable standard' of health and development.[250] Where PCRMs are not harmful and the question is principally one of children's rights, it is therefore not certain that social services in England are available at all. However, there are further difficulties with the use of social services. First and foremost, social services are not aimed at allowing children to enforce their rights and parents need not engage with them.[251] Social workers may also be hesitant to intervene where a child seeks to enforce their freedom of manifestation in view of general attitudes,[252] and the many cases that have been brought against local authorities alleging they disrespected parental religious rights.[253] Irrespectively, there simply may not be the resources to spend on cases that present no obvious risks to children. Several authors have noted that England's austerity measures have had the effect of drastically curtailing preventative services, and reduced timelines for care proceedings are prompting social workers to focus on gathering evidence for such procedures, rather than effectively working with families to resolve issues.[254] Social services are thus unlikely to be of help to children seeking to question PCRMs.

For many interviewees, it was nonetheless not the government, but the community itself that could provide social services to families in need. Interviewees e.g. mentioned forms of pastoral care or counselling that could help. However, they realised that where family issues related to PCRMs, children might not see contacting the religious community as a viable option. None of the students referenced religious organisations or social services as avenues for help in case of family conflict. A majority stated that, if they were in conflict with their parents, they would not seek the help of an unknown third party, but rather someone they and their parents knew well, like a teacher at school. Although the statement applied wider than just to teachers (one student e.g. stated that other family

249 S. 17 *Children Act* 1989; s. 11 *Children Act* 2004, chapter 31.

250 S. 17(10) *Children Act* 1989. Moreover, there is no right to a certain service: *R (G) v Barnet LBC; R (W) v Lambeth LBC; R (A) v Lambeth LBC* [2003] UKHL 57.

251 See S. Collings and L. Davies, 'For the Sake of the Children': Making Sense of Children and Childhood in the Context of Child Protection. (2008) 22(2) *Journal of Social Work Practice* 181. Children can only express views on their wish to engage: *Re T (Judicial Review: Local Authority Decisions Concerning Child in Need)* [2003] EWCH 2515 (Admin).

252 Furness and Gilligan (2010b) and (2014).

253 E.g. *Re P (A Minor) (Residence Order: Child's Welfare)* [1999] 3 WLR 1164; *Newcastle City Council v Z* [2005] EWHC 1490 (Fam). These cases focus on authorities' obligation not to cause a child in their care to be brought up in a different religious persuasion as that of parents (s. 33(6)(a) *Children Act* 1989).

254 E.g. Dickens and Masson (2016); Welbourne (2016); M. Higgins, Child Protection Social Work in England: How Can it Be Reformed? (2017) 47(2) *British Journal of Social Work* 293, 298, 299.

members could play a role), if schools are amongst the first places where minors seek outside help, then it would be helpful for the government to reconsider the role of schools under its legislative and family support framework.

7.6 Conclusion

In the *Williamson* case, the House of Lords quoted the English Law Commission's statement that 'the child is not the child of the state'.[255] This is true, but it seems that under English law the child is so firmly the child of their parents, that there is very little space for the child being their own. Whilst this is a general outcome of the English application of parental responsibility, parental prerogatives are particularly well-established in religious education and upbringing. The right to freedom of manifestation that children have by virtue of the HRA does not apply to the family circle, and the thresholds for limitations on parental rights (Gillick competence and significant harm) are so high that parents retain a very wide scope to impose PCRMs. The majority of these, combined with the absence of an intra-family right to participation, are unlikely to be necessary in a democratic society. Indeed, England has already been found to violate children's freedom of manifestation under the CRC. Moreover, society itself has moved on from the antiquated law on which the regulation of religious upbringing is based, and there is some indication in favour of a legal (and educational) framework that respects children's increasing autonomy. The courts themselves have found such development to be desirable when called upon to determine children's interests. It is therefore significant that (subject to leave) England allows children access to court to challenge PCRMs on the basis of interests. Yet court procedures are adversarial and not everyone thinks they are an appropriate venue for families in conflict. This makes it unfortunate that children and their families do not have access to alternative forms of dispute resolution offered by the State, whether or not in consultation with religious communities where PCRMs are concerned. Advocating for further services in a time of austerity may be as difficult as it is essential, but taking one step at the time, the government could start with redefining the power-balance within families in a way that respects children's rights.

255 *R (Williamson) v Secretary of State for Education and Employment* [2005] UKHL 15, at [72].

8 Parentally coerced religious manifestations in Hong Kong

8.1 Introduction

The Hong Kong Special Administrative Region ('Hong Kong' or 'HKSAR') is a common law jurisdiction under the 'one country, two systems' framework,[1] even if certain aspects of its policy (especially educational) are more reflective of a civil approach. Hong Kong still retains 'parental rights' as its PGPCR,[2] though law reform to replace the principles of parental rights and authority, guardianship and custody (parental rights) with the notion of 'parental responsibility' has long been underway.[3] In anticipation of this reform, Hong Kong's judiciary has already begun to carefully reference the idea of parental responsibility,[4] or at least call for its speedy adoption.[5] Yet the first draft of new legislation governing the parent–child relationship, the 2015 *Children Proceedings (Parental Responsibility) Bill* ('the Bill'), has yet to be introduced to the Legislative Council (Hong Kong's 'parliament'). This chapter will provide an overview of the current PGPCR as it applies to parentally coerced religious manifestations (PCRMs) and discuss the reform proposal. It then outlines potential limitations on parental rights to impose manifestations, followed by an examination of possibilities for Hong Kong children to enforce their rights.

The examination of the law is further informed by social research conducted in the HKSAR. As the law in Hong Kong is in a state of flux, the empirical research included interviews with family law experts, as well as questionnaires for children

1 In 1997 Hong Kong was returned to China (which has a civil law tradition), but a treaty was signed to secure the continuation of the common law for another 50 years. For further exploration: J.C. Oliveira and P. Cardinal (eds), *One Country, Two Systems, Three Legal Orders: Perspectives of Evolution*. Berlin: Springer-Verlag, 2009.

2 Principle Governing Parent–Child Relations (see 4.2). S. 4 *Guardianship of Minors Ordinance*, chapter 13 (17 February 1977).

3 Law Reform Commission of Hong Kong (HKLRC), *Report: Child Custody and Access* Hong Kong, Law Reform Commission of Hong Kong 2005, 285 (Custody Report). Recommendations for reform date back to the 1990s: Liu (1999), 241.

4 See e.g. *HHML v RYD* [2012] HKEC 1592, at [26].

5 Most authoritatively *PD v KWW* [2010] 4 HKLRD 191, at [51, 81].

and mirror questionnaires for parents.[6] Conducting interviews with legal experts in family law was especially relevant because the future acceptability of PCRMs and possibilities for dispute resolution in Hong Kong depend largely on legislative reform and its interpretation. Interviews were envisaged to be semi-structured and take place in person, but this proved unfeasible for some interviewees. Therefore, two 'interviews' were conducted via e-mail correspondence and one partly via e-mail and partly in person. Interviewees were asked to comment on the concept of parental responsibility, possibilities for State intervention in matters of religion, children's access to court, and parent–child mediation in Hong Kong, with answers analysed through a framework analysis. Availability sampling was used to recruit five participants (two female, three male) involved in different aspects of legal practice: two lawyers primarily practising family law, one family lawyer who also practises extensively in ADR, one academic, and one judge who equally acts as a mediator. Two participants were born and raised in Hong Kong, the others hold (long-term) permanent residence. They will hereafter be referred to as 'interviewees' or 'lawyers'.

In addition to interviews, anonymous questionnaires were distributed to sixth-form students and their parents. The questionnaire for students was the same as the one distributed in France and England and asked about views regarding decision-making and religious manifestation within the family, as well as parent–child dispute resolution. Parents received a mirror questionnaire (e.g. instead of asking about conflict with parents, the questionnaire asked about conflict with children).[7] Both questionnaires were pre-tested and translated (a bilingual version was distributed). Subsequently, 45 schools located in different areas of Hong Kong, and representing a variety of school types and religious backgrounds, were contacted by letter,[8] with other schools approached via contacts in accordance with Hong Kong's network culture, but without success. Schools cited lack of time or seeing no particular advantage to the school as reasons for declining. Follow-up visits in person were undertaken to six schools, one of which agreed to participate. The participating school is run by a Christian church and located on a public housing estate in a more developed part of a 'rural' area of Hong Kong.[9]

Eighty-eight students aged between 16 and 18 (mode = 17)[10] participated in the research.[11] Of these students, 84% held Hong Kong nationality or permanent

6 Ethics approval was obtained from the Survey and Behavioural Ethics Committee at the Chinese University of Hong Kong. Fieldwork took place during 2013–14.

7 Distributing mirror questionnaires to parents had also been envisaged for the research in France and England but proven to be unfeasible either because schools would not be willing to participate if the research was expanded in this manner, or because it was simply not practically possible within the time-frame.

8 Consisting of a cover letter, information about the research and a reply slip with pre-stamped envelope. The advantage of using paper over email was that letters could be signed and stamped and presented on paper with the university's letter head, satisfying the cultural need for 'authority'.

9 As explained in section 8.3, its profile (common to Hong Kong education) made the school an ideal venue.

10 One student was 15, two students reported being over the age of 18.

11 This constituted a 40% response rate.

residence, 65% identified as female and 27% as male. Most students stated they were Christians, others were Buddhist or Taoist. The most often mentioned parental religion was Christianity, followed by Buddhism and Taoism. Nearly two-thirds replied that their parents had a religion, while a third stated their parents did not. Many students followed their parents' religion, but 18% of students indicated that their parents had a religion which they did not share. Some four out of five of students reported having manifested a religion, which was the parental religion in only half of the cases.

Sixty-five parents filled out the mirror questionnaire.[12] These were distributed independently from the questionnaires for students, meaning that there was not a complete overlap. Of the parents (37% of whom identified as male and 57% female), 90% held Hong Kong nationality or permanent residence. Most parents were between 40 and 50 years old, with the majority having one or two children, which were typically aged between 10 and 25 years old. 43% of parents reported having a religion, 40% said they had none. Nearly all religious parents indicated that they were Christian, with one adhering to an oriental religion and five declining to state their religion. All parents willing to indicate their child's religion stated that their child was Christian. Overall, a third reported that (all) their child(ren) had a religion, with another third stating their child(ren) did not have a religion – 8% noted that only one or several of their children had a religion. 17% of parents stated that their child (or some of their children) did not share the parental religion. Two-thirds thought their child had ever practised a religion, but again only half replied that this had been the parental religion. The parents and students (children) will be collectively referred to as 'respondents', and separately as 'surveyed parents' and 'surveyed children'.

Overall, the research in Hong Kong was exploratory in nature and subject to limitations. The most important of these is the research's non-representative nature, caused primarily by a lack of response.[13] There may have also been some socially acceptable answering. Language formed a barrier, hindering possibilities for engagement and requiring reliance on translations by third parties. Finally, interviews were based on availability sampling, and the need for some to be conducted via e-mail prevented real-time interaction. Notwithstanding these limitations, the research in Hong Kong provides important insights into freedom of manifestation within the family and dispute resolution from multiple stakeholders, notably including parents and minors. These are further discussed throughout the text below, in combination with the law in relation to the horizontal effect of human rights, parental rights and their limitations, and the enforcement of religious rights within Hong Kong families.

12 A 30% response rate.

13 Compare Wong et al., who contacted 600 Hong Kong schools of which 11 agreed to participate, resulting in 235 questionnaires. D.K.F. Wong et al., Is Parental Control Beneficial or Harmful to the Development of Young Children in Hong Kong? (2018) *Journal of Child and Family Studies* DOI https://doi.org/10.1007/s1082, 4.

8.2 Rights without horizontal effect

Hong Kong has a dualist system of law, and international treaties must therefore be implemented before they can have effect in the domestic legal order.[14] So far, the only treaty examined in Chapter 2 that has been implemented is the ICCPR, which has been incorporated through the *Hong Kong Bill of Rights Ordinance* (BORO).[15] Under the BORO, s. 8 (Article 15), children hold the same right to freedom of manifestation as enshrined in Article 18 ICCPR.[16] Initially, it was envisaged that the BORO would enjoy horizontal effect,[17] but this was ultimately rejected.[18] Therefore, children cannot now legally rely on a right to freedom of manifestation within the parent–child relationship. Nevertheless, that does not mean that Hong Kong children themselves – or indeed their parents – consider that they either do not or should not have horizontally applicable religious rights. Most respondents in the Hong Kong research simply seemed to take for granted that human rights applied within the family circle, whether they agreed with the existence of such rights or not.

Where treaty provisions are not implemented, or do not enjoy horizontal effect, judges in the HKSAR should nonetheless interpret existing laws as far as possible in accordance with relevant international provisions.[19] Human rights can thus inform, but not determine family law practice. Judges may also rely on international provisions to develop the law within their competences.[20] Moreover, international law can seep into case-law through reliance on English precedent under the common law. This has even led to the HKSAR 'implementing' provisions of treaties to which it is not a member, such as the ECHR which English judges regularly reference.[21] Finally, as public authorities, judges themselves are

14 Article 39, *The Basic Law of the Hong Kong Special Administrative Religion of the People's Republic of China*, Order No. 26 of the President of the People's Republic of China (4 April 1990) (hereafter 'The Basic Law'). W.P. Lung, International Law Before the Courts of the Hong Kong Special Administrative Region of the People's Republic of China – Twenty Years On. (2018) *Asian Journal of International Law* DOI 10.1017/S2044251318000024, 5.

15 Chapter 383 (6 June 1997). See for discussion: J.M.M. Chan, Hong Kong's Bill of Rights: Its Reception of and Contribution to International and Comparative Jurisprudence. (1998) 47 *International and Comparative Law Quarterly* 306, 307.

16 The BORO reproduces Article 18 in its entirety.

17 P. Dykes, 'The Hong Kong Bill of Rights 1991: Its Origin, Content and Impact', in J. Chan, and Y. Ghai (eds), *The Hong Kong Bill of Rights: A Comparative Approach*. Hong Kong: Butterworths, 1993, 45.

18 A. Byrnes, 'The Hong Kong Bill of Rights and Relations between Private Individuals', in Chan and Ghai (1993), 83. See also *A Solicitor v The Law Society of Hong Kong* [2004] HKCA 122, at [99]–[107].

19 *Ubamaka Edward Wilson v Secretary for Security* [2012] HKEC 1757, per Ribeiro PJ, at [43].

20 See *R v N* [2009] HKFC 15, in which Chu J relied *proprio motu* on Article 12 CRC at [21], [38].

21 E.g. in *Mabon v Mabon* [2005] EWCA Civ 634 explicit reference was made to Articles 8 ECHR (family life) and 12 CRC (right to be heard). Through heavy reliance on this case in *S v Z* [2007] HKFAMC 34, these Articles have also shaped the HKSAR's law.

bound by human rights (at least under the BORO), as are other State bodies.[22] This was emphasised by the interviewees, who seemed to favour some form of horizontal effect of human rights within the family, or at least a very thorough application of positive obligations with '[t]he starting point [being] the recognition that children are individuals with human rights' – and the endpoint being that the State should protect these. Yet that is not necessarily a position that is widely shared by Hong Kong's legal institutions in respect of unimplemented treaties such as the CRC (to which the interviewees referred extensively). The Hong Kong Law Reform Commission (HKLRC), for example, appears to suggest that unimplemented treaties do not carry any legal, but merely moral obligations for the HKSAR, with the government being under 'a moral obligation, as far as practicable, to . . . comply with the United Nations Convention on the Rights of the Child'.[23] This statement demonstrates an incorrect view of human rights law. The HKSAR's obligations under the CRC are legal obligations (albeit international), and unless the CRC provisions state so explicitly, the obligation to comply with the rights therein is not limited to what the HKSAR considers 'practicable' but applies in full. However, the HKLRC's view, which is also that of the Community Legal Information Centre,[24] would explain why the CmRC has urged the Hong Kong government so forcefully to implement the CRC.[25] Until that time, and an express granting of horizontal effect, religious rights do not apply horizontally and children's religious manifestation is regulated by the principle of parental rights.

8.3 Coerced manifestations under parental rights

In Hong Kong, religious upbringing is governed by the principle of parental rights included in s. 3(1) *Guardianship of Minors Ordinance* (GMO).[26] The GMO does not give a definition of the principle of parental rights, its attributes or the way parental rights should be exercised under the laws of Hong Kong,[27] but as a British colony, it was assumed that the English common law would give meaning to parental rights.[28] This has indeed been the case, and the principle now

22 *A Solicitor v The Law Society of Hong Kong* [2004] HKCA 122, at [99], [108].

23 HKLRC (2005), Custody Report, 16.

24 Community Legal Information Centre, 'Children's Constitutional Rights (2014–18)', *The University of Hong Kong* <http://familyclic.hk/en/topics/Child-and-youth-affairs/Childrens-protection-and-welfare/Childrens-constitutional-rights/> last accessed 10 March 2019.

25 See CmRC, *Concluding Observations, China (including Hong Kong and Macau Special Administrative Regions)*. UN Doc CRC/C/CHN/CO/2 (24 November 2005), paras 6, 7; CmRC, *Concluding Observations (third and fourth reports), China*. UN Doc CRC/C/CHN/CO/3-4 (29 October 2013), paras 7 and 11.

26 *PD v KWW* [2010] 4 HKLRD 191, at [32]; Law Reform Commission, Custody Report (2005), 19, 21; K. Hotten et al., *The Hong Kong Family Court Practice*. Hong Kong: LexisNexis, 2015, 383.

27 *C v S* [2017] HKCFI 1968, at [44].

28 See Liu (1999), 211–17.

incorporates the full list of parental rights (including that to control upbringing and decide on children's education and religion) identified at common law, supplemented by rights recognised in legislation.[29]

Parental rights have generally been described as the 'bundle of rights and duties and authority [here in the authoritarian sense] of a parent towards a child'.[30] The principle is one-directional: it is exercised by a parent over a child until the child reaches the age of legal majority (18 in Hong Kong).[31] Children remain wholly without decision-making power during this time, because the Hong Kong courts have not yet publicly accepted the concept of Gillick competence (a level of competence that allows minors to take their own decisions, overriding parental rights).[32] The research in Hong Kong nonetheless suggests that this may no longer correspond with attitudes towards the parent–child relationship, or family practice.[33] The vast majority of both surveyed parents and children indicated that children should have the right to make decisions for themselves. Only 3% of surveyed parents reported that they did not think children should have the right to take decisions for themselves.[34] At the same time, a substantial majority of respondents agreed that parents had the right to take decisions for the family. Moreover, parents were less willing than children to give priority to children's decisions over their own,[35] especially where younger children were concerned (66% thought that a parental decision took priority over that of an elementary school child, compared with 43% of student respondents). Yet as children grew older, most parents became more willing to give children greater power, though not quite to the extent of surveyed children: a third of surveyed parents would prioritise a high school child's decision over their own (an equal number would not), compared to nearly half (43%) of surveyed children. This suggests a balance between family direction provided by parents and support for children's autonomous decision-making in ways contrary to the current state of the law, which grants children no decision-making power at all.

The only aspect of the Gillick decision that the HKSAR courts have transposed into the law of Hong Kong is the idea that parental rights are derived from duties.[36] As previously discussed in the case study on England, this does

29 HKLRC, Custody Report (2005), 19 quoted in *C v S* [2017] HKCFI 1968, at [47].

30 HKLRC, Custody Report (2005), 18.

31 S. 2 *Age of Majority (Related Provisions) Ordinance*, chapter 410 (1 October 1990).

32 See *Gillick v West Norfolk and Wisbech Area Health Authority and Department of Health and Social Security* [1985] UKHL 7 discussed in 5.4.1. There is some evidence that *Gillick* competence has been proposed in the medical area: Food and Health Bureau, *E-Health Record: Continuity of Care for You*. HKSAR Government (December 2011), 54 <https://www.gov.hk/en/residents/government/publication/consultation/docs/2012/eHealth.pdf> last accessed 10 March 2019.

33 Supporting e.g. S.M. Chan et al., Chinese Parenting in Hong Kong: Links among Goals, Beliefs and Styles. (2009) 179(7) *Early Child Development and Care* 849, 854.

34 It is possible that parents and students holding more traditional views were disproportionately represented amongst those declining to participate.

35 This is consistent with previous research by Hui (2010), 522, 526.

36 *PD v KWW* [2010] 4 HKLRD 191, at [44].

not in itself mean that parental rights cannot be formidable.[37] Derived from legal duties that do not appear to go beyond the absence of maltreatment,[38] Hong Kong's PGPCR gives parents 'the right to control almost every aspect of the child's upbringing'.[39] Traditionally, control was considered a caring attribute of parenting in Chinese societies, because it was linked with a high responsiveness to the needs of children.[40] Yet parenting styles in Hong Kong have evolved.[41] Parents now prioritise authoritative parenting,[42] with an accompanying shift in values from familism to personal growth.[43] Vice versa, research suggests that Hong Kong children nowadays respond best to parenting that focuses on care and autonomy.[44] The continued emphasis on parental rights and control over children is therefore no longer appropriate and the PGPCR has been heavily criticised as sanctioning a notion of parental ownership over children,[45] a criticism that also many of the interviewees brought up.

Since religious upbringing is governed by parental rights,[46] Hong Kong parents hold near-absolute power to determine children's religious manifestations and impose PCRMs.[47] Whilst it has been held that it would bear testimony of 'sensible, rational and commendable parenting' if parents adopted a 'balanced and open approach to . . . religious education and faith',[48] parents are legally free to impose PCRMs until the child's majority. Whether this is also still socially

37 Liu (1999), 217.

38 See e.g. *GKLJ v WE a.k.a. WFYE* [2018] HKFC 19.

39 Liu (1999), 211. Liu was extensively quoted by the HKLRC in their 2005 custody report.

40 R.K. Chao, Beyond Parental Control and Authoritarian Parenting Style: Understanding Chinese Parenting through the Cultural Notion of Training. (1994) 65 *Child Development* 1111, 1112, 1113; Wong et al. (2018), 1–3. Fung et al. found that there is now a null relationship between control and family functioning: J. Fung et al., Perceived Social Change, Parental Control, and Family Relations: A Comparison of Chinese Families in Hong Kong, Mainland China and the United States. (2017) 8 *Frontiers in Psychology* 1671, 1681.

41 Exceptions such as academic control granted: see Wong et al (2018).

42 D.Y.F. Ho and T.K. Kang, Intergenerational Comparisons of Child-Rearing Attitudes and Practices in Hong Kong. (1984) 20(6) *Developmental Psychology* 1004, 1011; K.W. Chan and S.M. Chan, Hong Kong Teacher Education Students' Goal Orientations and their Relationship to Perceived Parenting Styles. (2007) 27(2) *Educational Psychology* 157, 168; Chan et al. (2009), 854. See also *PD v KWW* [2010] 4 HKLRD 191, at [46].

43 D.T. Shek, A Longitudinal Study of Hong Kong Adolescents' and Parents' Perceptions of Family Functioning and Well-Being. (1998) 159(4) *Journal of Genetic Psychology* 389; D.T. Shek, Hong Kong Chinese Parent's Perceptions of the Ideal Child. (1999a) 133(3) *Journal of Psychology* 291, 298, 300; and D.T. Shek, Perceptions of Family Functioning among Chinese Parents and their Adolescent Children. (1999b) 27(4) *American Journal of Family Therapy* 303, 310.

44 S.S.-Y. Ngai et al., The Effects of Parenting Behaviour on Pro-Social Behaviour of Chinese Adolescents in Hong Kong. (2018) 87 *Children and Youth Services Review* 154, 160.

45 Liu (1999), 216.

46 See *CLP v CSN (Formerly Known as HTY or HTYZ) and Another* [2016] 5 HKLRD 530, at [4.3].

47 Article 37 of the Basic Law also gives parents the right to 'raise a family freely', but this relates to the right to procreate and foster in view of Mainland China's one child policy: *Gurung Deu Kumari v Director of Immigration* [2010] 5 HKLRD 219, at [54].

48 *H v H* [2002] HKEC 1123, at [34].

acceptable or desired is a different matter. As one research participant noted: 'Even [if] you think that your parents have the right to rule you, you may not [be] happy with that'. Most surveyed parents did not think parental power over religious decisions should last until a child's majority. Whilst one respondent remarked that 'correct belief is vital', another parent pointed out that:

> Religious belief should be decided individually. It is great if all the family members have the same religious belief, but if not, we cannot force each other.

However, parents again made a clear distinction between younger and older children: relatively few surveyed parents (17%) thought an 8 year old was old enough to decide on their own religion, but that increased to two-thirds where a high school student was concerned. At the same time, parent respondents indicated that parents should remain invested in their children's religious education and the majority agreed that it was normal for children to know a lot about their parents' religion, if their parents had one. Here surveyed parents made a distinction between the duty of parents to *ensure* religious practice (which nearly half accepted) and the permissibility to *impose* such practice. Less than a quarter of parents responded that they thought parents should be able to impose a religious manifestation (prayer) on a young child and only a handful (8%) felt the same in respect of a high school child. Rather than coerce children, one respondent explained, 'parents should set an example for their children in [the] practice of religion and encourage children to participate together'.

The difference between encouragement and imposition was reflected by the views of surveyed children, although they more forcefully rejected PCRMs than surveyed parents did. Nearly half of surveyed children indicated that it was important for children to know about their parents' religion and over two-thirds considered it normal that parents would involve their children in religious manifestations. However, only a few thought that parents should be at liberty to impose a religious manifestation on either a young child (8%) or high school child (5%). Surveyed children seemed to be especially opposed to the coercive element, because when asked about age of discretion, more than a quarter indicated that an 8 year old would not be old enough to decide on their own religion (though only 3% found the same to be true for a high school child). As one respondent explained, children's autonomy and parental guidance could go together:[49]

> My family has a religious background . . . but my parents don't force me to believe in any religion, they let me choose myself and they guide me [while remaining] by my side.

49 See Ngai (2018), 160, noting that autonomy is the key factor leading to positive outcomes in Hong Kong adolescents, without discounting appropriate control.

The openness towards children's own religious decision-making may have been somewhat influenced by participants' lived reality: a fifth of surveyed children did not share the parental religion. This may have in part been caused by a discrepancy between the parental religion (or absence thereof) and the Christian denomination of the participating school, to which children may have converted whilst attending. Historically, welfare services and education in Hong Kong have been almost exclusively provided by Christian religious organisations,[50] actively supported by the colonial government which deemed religion the best weapon against rising communism.[51] Most people using the services were, and are, not themselves committed Christians as the main religions in Hong Kong are Buddhism and Taoism.[52] Yet families engage in manifestations of Christianity to remain in good standing with the religious organisation or school.[53] Additionally, Chen has argued, some parents deliberately send their children to a religious school, the faith of which they do not share, because they want their children to be provided with a strong moral framework.[54] The fact that the religious instruction and practices are not those of the household is taken for granted.[55] As a result, children are often forced to manifest a religion which neither they nor their parents adhere to[56] – or conversely adopt the school's religion contrary to parental intention.

The example of schools indicates a peculiarity of the Hong Kong context where parents may legally impose religious manifestations of a faith other than their own. Such PCRMs are lawful, because under the laws of Hong Kong, children do not hold a right to oppose freedom of manifestation to their parents.[57] Whereas pupils in aided schools officially have a right not to 'attend religious instruction or to participate in any religious observances',[58] under the principle of parental rights this becomes a right for parents. Hence, in Hong Kong's latest round of State reporting under the CRC where coerced manifestation in schools

50 B.H.K. Luk, 'Religion in Hong Kong History', in L. Pui-Tak, *Colonial Hong Kong and Modern China*. Hong Kong: Hong Kong University Press, 2005, 40.

51 B.K.F. Leung, 'Church, State and Education', in M. Bray and R. Koo, *Education and Society in Hong Kong and Macau*. Dordrecht: Springer, 2005, 102.

52 Research Office, Legislative Council Secretariat, *Fact Sheet Religious Facilities in Hong Kong*, FS01/17-18 (8 December 2017), 4.

53 Ibid.

54 R.H.M. Cheng, Moral Education in Hong Kong: Confucian-Parental, Christian-Religious and Liberal-Civic Influences. (2004) 33(4) *Journal of Moral Education* 533, 542, 543.

55 Ibid., 543.

56 CmRC, *Combined Third and Fourth Reports of the People's Republic of China under the Convention on the Rights of the Child – Part Two: Hong Kong Special Administrative Region*, UN Doc CRC/C/CHN-HKG/2 (25 October 2012), para 156.

57 This interpretation rests on the BORO, s. 8 (Article 15) stating that parents (but not children) have a right to educate their children in accordance with their convictions.

58 S. 20 *Code of Aid for Primary Schools* (September 1994); and s. 20 *Code of Aid for Secondary Schools* (September 1994). Available at <http://www.edb.gov.hk/en/sch-admin/regulations/codes-of-aid/> last accessed 10 March 2019.

was explicitly discussed,[59] the government underscored that children's religious manifestation is a parental prerogative and that PCRMs may be imposed. Although the HKSAR noted that all Hong Kong residents have a right to freedom of religion under the Basic Law, it did not indicate how the HKSAR would facilitate this right for children, other than by emphasising parental rights. The government contented that parents were adequately informed about the religious character of denominational schools in Hong Kong and that:

> [C]hildren may also withdraw from religious education in school with the consent of their parents. Conversely, parents may request schools to provide opportunity for their children to observe religious rituals.[60]

Or in the words of the Undersecretary for Constitutional and Mainland Affairs: children's rights in Hong Kong are protected within a 'family focus', with primacy given to the family and the promotion of 'family core values'.[61] In the eyes of the HKSAR, a child's freedom of manifestation is thus above all a freedom enjoyed by the child's parents, in the expectation that children will follow or obey parents, failing which parents can simply impose PCRMs under parental rights. Yet this may change if the legislator adopts the 2015 draft legislation aiming to abolish the parental rights PGPCR.

8.3.1 The parental responsibility proposal

In 1995, the HKLRC was asked to present proposals for law reform in the area of family law.[62] A decade later, it produced the 2005 Child Custody and Access Report, which recommended, *inter alia*, that the government replace its PGPCR of parental rights with parental responsibility and adopt related provisions found in the *Children Act* 1989 and *Children (Scotland) Act* 1995.[63] The proposal received a warm welcome from the legal community,[64] but was opposed by various interest groups and NGOs.[65] In response, the government entered a further

59 See n. 56.

60 Ibid., para 158.

61 Hong Kong Information Services Department, 'HK Committed to Protecting Children's Rights' (27 September 2013) <http://www.news.gov.hk/en/record/html/2013/09/20130927_113306.shtml> last accessed 10 March 2019.

62 A. Scully-Hill, A Critical Evaluation of the Draft Children Proceedings (Parental Responsibility) Bill. (2016) 46 *Hong Kong Law Journal* 387, 388.

63 HKLRC (2005) Custody Report, 200–5.

64 C. Remedios, The Enhancement and Protection of Children's Rights. (2010) 2 *International Family Law Journal* 145, 145, 148; Hotten et al. (2015), 380.

65 Y.K. Lau, 'Family Impact Analysis of the Proposed Legislation – Children Proceedings (Parental Responsibility) Bill in Hong Kong', The 16th World Conference of the International Society of Family Law, Amsterdam, 25–9 July 2017, 3. For arguments for and against see K. Lynch, Reform of Family Justice: Children's Dispute Resolution in Hong Kong. (2016) 17 *Cardozo Journal of Conflict Resolution* 909, 918. A common objection is that parental responsibility endures after divorce and thereby presents a tool for abusive ex-partners to 'cause trouble' via their children.

decade of consultations. During this time calls for reform increased exponentially and 'Hong Kong's judges [took] the unusual step of indicating their support for [reform]'.[66] Even more unusually, some judges simply resorted to referencing the idea of parental responsibility in their judgments and/or incorporated other HKLRC recommendations, such as the use of a welfare checklist to determine children's interests.[67] Finally, in 2015, the Labour and Welfare Department published the *Children Proceedings (Parental Responsibility) Bill* with the expectation of tabling it in the following year or 2017.[68] S. 4 of the Bill states that parents have parental responsibility, which is explained in s. 5 as follows.

> **5. Meaning of parental responsibility**
>
> (1) In this Ordinance – parental responsibility . . . means the responsibilities specified in subsection (2) and the rights specified in subsection (3).
> (2) The responsibilities are the responsibilities of a parent –
>
> (a) to safeguard and promote the child's health, development and best interests;
> (b) to provide direction and guidance to the child in a manner appropriate to the stage of development of the child;
> (c) if the child is not living with the parent, to maintain personal relations and direct contact with the child on a regular basis; and
> (d) to act as the child's legal representative, but only in so far as meeting the responsibilities is practicable and in the child's interests.
>
> (3) The rights are the rights of a parent –
>
> (a) to have the child living with the parent or otherwise regulate the child's residence;
> (b) to control, direct or guide the child's upbringing in a manner appropriate to the stage of development of the child;
> (c) if the child is not living with the parent, to maintain personal relations and direct contact with the child on a regular basis; and
> (d) to act as the child's legal representative.

Despite the Department's intentions, the tabling of the Bill is yet to happen, because further consultation on the Bill's provisions demonstrated that many consulted stakeholders remained opposed to reform.[69] It was therefore decided

66 Scully-Hill (2016), 389.

67 See e.g. *SMM v TWM* [2010] 4 HKLRD 37, at [27]; *HHML v RYD* [2012] HKEC 1592, at [26]; or *PCY v CYW (Custody, Care and Control)* [2009] HKFLR 382, at [18].

68 The full text of the Bill is available here: <https://www.lwb.gov.hk/parentalresponsibility_consult/doc/Draft_Bill_(Eng).pdf> last accessed 10 March 2019.

69 Legislative Council Panel on Welfare Services, *Follow-up on the Law Reform Commission Report on Child Custody and Access and Related Support Measures*. Legislative Council Paper No. CB(2)981/17-18(03) (12 March 2018), 1.

'not to introduce the proposed legislation into the [Legislative Council] at this stage',[70] but first promote parental responsibility via 'public education and support measures'.[71] In the meantime, a number of judgments have allowed the proposed legislative provisions to influence decisions related to parental rights.[72] Failing further action by the government, it will therefore be interesting to see whether the judiciary will ignore the Law Society's advice against the 'implementation of parental responsibility by case law' and take the lead.[73]

As lawyers with an expertise in family law, all interviewees had been involved in matters related to the adoption or functioning of parental responsibility and some had previously advocated for legislative reform. They fully supported the shift from parental rights to parental responsibility,[74] since 'the terminology of custody denotes the right to own something. Parental responsibility shifts the focus', that is 'parents should . . . be seen as having "duties and obligations" towards children – rather than "parental rights" over them'. However, one interviewee pointed to the issue discussed in Chapter 4 that the change would require more than merely 'switching labels'. This is a real concern in view of the Law Society's remark that 'parental responsibility does not change the existing rights and responsibilities of the parents, but re-emphasises their role',[75] and the Bill's stated aim to reform and consolidate 'the law relating to responsibilities and rights of parents for children'.[76] Most interviewees themselves described parental responsibility as something that is done to the child. They talked about making parents more sensitive to the needs of children, and elevating the child's position within the family, yet their focus was on what parents owe to children, not on how parents and children could both contribute to the parent–child relationship. This echoes descriptions in the literature of the new parental-responsibility model being 'child-centric',[77] but not necessarily child-inclusive, a position reflected in Scully-Hill's description of the Bill:

> The conceptual framework of the Bill requires a shift from a relationship founded on parental rights and authority over the child to a relationship based on responsibilities owed by parents to the child, with parents being able to

70 Ibid.

71 Government of the HKSAR, *Budget 2018–19. Head 141 – Government Secretariat: Labour and Welfare Bureau* (28 February 2018), 470 <https://www.budget.gov.hk/2018/eng/pdf/head141.pdf> last accessed 10 March 2019.

72 E.g. *C v S* [2017] HKCFI 1968, at [41]-[50]; *L v L* [2017] 5 HKLRD 629, at [59]; *R, MJ v OAM, a.k.a. R, AO* [2018] HKFC 131, at [29].

73 The Law Society of Hong Kong, *Law Society's Submissions* [to consultation on a joint parental responsibility model] (24 April 2012), 14 <https://keithhotten.files.wordpress.com/2012/05/law-society-response-to-child-custody-consultation.pdf> last accessed 10 March 2019.

74 One interviewee's opinion on this subject remains unknown.

75 The Law Society of Hong Kong (2012), 6.

76 See the Bill's preamble.

77 Lynch (2016), 915; Scully-Hill (2016), 392. See also Hong Kong Family Law Association, *The HKFLA's Response to the Child Custody and Access Consultation Paper 2011*. Legislative Council Paper No. CB(2) 1548/12-13(02) (30 April 2012), 13.

> exercise rights over the child only insofar as these fulfil the parents' responsibilities to the child and not for any other purpose. This shift, therefore, is to a child-centric justification for parental rights.[78]

Interviewees nonetheless emphasised the importance of children's rights. Such rights would e.g. include respect for the child's right to be heard and freedom of manifestation. When prompted about children's participation and the exercise of children's rights vis-à-vis parents, the interviewees suggested that parental responsibility could encompass these aspects. One interviewee stated that participation would be part of parental responsibility, which the interviewee understood as including a responsibility to 'ensure as far as possible that the rights of the children [including to participation] are respected and realised [and] provide additional advantages and opportunities for personal growth and fulfilment'. Notably, though, the proposed Bill makes no reference to children's rights generally, or participation in the parent–child relationship in particular.[79] Parental responsibility in the Bill only 'implicitly recognizes the human rights of the child'.[80] This reflects the tension within a society where ideas of participation and children's rights are 'alien' to traditional local culture, but parents nowadays are much less traditional, as the interviewees suggested.

The tension is equally demonstrated in the way parental responsibility is explained in the Bill. Parental responsibility consists of both parental responsibilities and parental rights, though only the former have been made subject to the restriction of being 'practicable and in the child's interests'. Moreover, there is no indication of how and by whom practicability and interests are to be determined. Even so, the new provision could improve the position of children when compared with parental rights. This is especially true because parents are required to not only safeguard, but also promote their child's health, development and best interests (note the difference between promoting 'best interests' and limitations based on 'interests'). Furthermore, parental rights to control, direct or guide the child's upbringing must be exercised in ways appropriate to children's stage of development. This extra guidance could mean that Hong Kong might avoid the pitfalls of the English legislation, whose lack of description of parental responsibility has simply resulted in a reformulation of rights to responsibilities. However, given Hong Kong's great reliance on English law and the close connection that already exists between rights and responsibilities,[81] real progress remains uncertain. Much will

78 Scully-Hill (2016), 392.

79 See *mutatis mutandis* Freeman's critique on the HKLRC's report: M. Freeman, Reforming the Law of Child Custody and Access: A Comment (2005) 35 *Hong Kong Law Journal* 29, 29.

80 Hong Kong Family Law Association (2012), 16.

81 Both legally and in practice: some parents already interpret their responsibilities as legitimation for being in charge of their child's life: A.T.Y. Chan and S.-K. Lee, Education Plans, Personal Challenges and Academic Difficulties: An Empirical Study on Self-Disclosure among Post-90s Teens in Hong Kong. (2014) 19(4) *International Journal of Adolescence and Youth* 468.

depend on interpretation of the Bill, which, if left to Chu J, will hopefully mean that a 'shift in focus from parental rights and authorities to parental responsibility *and rights of the child* is likely to take place in not too distant future'.[82]

8.4 Limitations on parental rights

For as long as the Bill has not been adopted, the PGPCR of parental rights continues to apply to the parent–child relationship and the governing of PCRMs within that relationship. Whilst this means that parental powers 'cannot be underestimated',[83] some limitations on parental control over children and religious manifestations do apply within the Hong Kong context. The main limitations on PCRMs are based on the child protection threshold, educational requirements and children's interests, as discussed below.[84]

8.4.1 The child protection threshold

Within the privacy of the family, parental rights to impose PCRMs are subject only to the constraints of child protection (on the basis of child abuse) and the criminal law. The law does not specify parental responsibilities other than to not maltreat a child – and even that obligation only follows indirectly from the law related to minors.[85] There is no legislation in place which curbs PCRMs or religious manifestation, unless concerned with public order in the sense of security and orderly conduct.[86] Rather, the government facilitates parental decision-making on religion-related issues like vaccination.[87]

General criminal law provisions, such as that prohibiting persons to cause a child in their care 'unnecessary suffering or injury' under s. 27 *Offences Against the Person Ordinance*, do apply to religious upbringing and manifestations.[88] S. 27 has a low threshold: in 2013 a father was convicted for slapping his daughter on the cheek without having a clear educational purpose.[89] If parents acted on religious motives, PCRMs causing children unnecessary suffering or injury would

82 *C v S* [2017 HKCFI 1968, at [41] (emphasis mine).

83 Liu (1999), 217.

84 Due to ethical constraints, these limitations were mainly discussed with interviewees.

85 Especially s. 34 *Protection of Children and Juveniles Ordinance*, chapter 213 (30 June 1997) and s. 27 *Offences Against the Person Ordinance*, chapter 212 (30 June 1997).

86 See P. Kapai, 'Freedom of Conscience and Religious Belief', in J. Chan and C.L. Lim, *Law of the Hong Kong Constitution* (2nd ed.). Hong Kong: Sweet & Maxwell, 2015, 24.103–24.150; HRC, *Response to the List of Issues Presented by the Human Rights Committee on 16 March 2012 Hong Kong*, Unedited Advance Version (2013), 24.

87 Vaccination is not mandatory: Department of Health, Family Health Service Child Health, Child Health (2014) <http://www.fhs.gov.hk/english/main_ser/child_health/child_health.html> last accessed 10 March 2019. However, most schools do not accept unvaccinated children.

88 See also s. 26 'exposing a child whereby life is endangered'.

89 *HKSAR v Lau On Shek* [2014] HKEC 231, at [32]–[35].

likely constitute a breach of the provision,[90] but there is no precedent to confirm this. Moreover, other than convict their parent or bind them over for a limited period of time, there is very little that the criminal law can do for a coerced minor.

By contrast, the child protection standard is directly related to parental rights, but the threshold seems much higher, at least in practice. The law itself is flexible and could cover a range of PCRMs, if so interpreted. S. 34(2) *Protection of Children and Juveniles Ordinance* (PCJO) states that 'a child in need of care and protection' concerns a minor who requires care or protection and has been or is being assaulted, ill-treated, neglected or sexually abused; his/her health, development or welfare has been, is or appears likely to be neglected or avoidably impaired; or the minor is beyond control to the extent that harm may be caused to him/herself or others. How the section should be interpreted remains a bit of a mystery: child protection cases are strictly confidential and writing on the standard is therefore limited.[91] Judicial interpretations can only be gleaned from remarks made in other cases, such as custody cases. In one of these cases, Chan J suggested that the English standard on the likelihood of harm applied to Hong Kong.[92] However, whilst the law in Hong Kong uses significantly less stringent wording than its English counterpart, its practical application sets a threshold that exceeds not only the English standard, but also the criminal threshold. The difference is highlighted in *F v L* where a 6 year old was caned to such extent by his father that he required hospital treatment and was kept for observation for ten days.[93] The father was bound over under the criminal law, but the Social Welfare Department decided at a child protection meeting that the case had been one of 'discipline' and not abuse.[94] Even where the 'extent of molestation' poses 'a real risk to the physical and psychological wellbeing of the child' the Department may decide that no abuse has taken place and the child protection threshold is not met.[95]

It may seem as if child protection legislation offers no limit at all on parental rights in Hong Kong, and in part that can be explained by continued adherence to a culture of 'familism', where priority is given to family unity over child protection.[96] The reluctance to set boundaries may nonetheless

90 See *Secretary for Justice v Lam Lui Yin* [2007] 1 HKLRD 248, at 254; *HKSAR v Lam Wai Man* [1999] 3 HKLRD 855, at 860. Religious motivation constitutes deliberate conduct: *Shum Kwok Sher v HKSAR* (2005) 5 HKCFAR 381, at [85].

91 P.L.S. Ip, Child Abuse and Neglect in Hong Kong. (2000) 5 *Hong Kong Journal of Paediatrics* 61; Hotten et al. (2015), 356–64.

92 *CLL v SW* [2013] HKEC 38, at [24–49].

93 *F v L* [2007] HKFC 22, at [6].

94 Ibid. See also *NAV v JTMW* [2017] HKFC 24, at [35].

95 *GKLJ v WE a.k.a. WFYE* [2018] HKFC 19, at [134], [135].

96 H.M. Chan, Informed Consent Hong Kong Style: An Instance of Moderate Familism. (2004) 29(2) *Journal of Medicine and Philosophy* 195; E. Hui, Parental Refusal of Life-Saving Treatments for Adolescents: Chinese Familism in Medical Decision-Making Re-Visited. (2008) 22(5) *Bioethics* 286. See also P.W.S. Leung et al., Attitudes and Child Abuse Reporting Behaviours among Hong Kong GPs. (2011) 28 *Family Practice* 195.

be driven by a lack of resources allowing for intervention once abuse is confirmed, rather than a view of parental rights as limitless. Hong Kong registers less than 1,000 child abuse cases per year out of a population of 7 million,[97] but its child protection units are chronically understaffed and under-resourced.[98] As a result, only the severest of cases are labelled as involving abuse. The caned child case may thus not necessarily suggest a receptiveness to (religious) adages such as 'spare the rod, spoil the child', but reflect a resource allocation in favour of children whose life is endangered over those suffering physical injury.[99]

The resource issues were also highlighted by one of the interviewees who argued that circumscribing parental rights on the basis of children's rights would first and foremost require a resource commitment by the government. In general, the interviewees advocated for a much lower threshold to finding a child in need of care and protection than is currently the case. They equally observed that there were limits to parental rights in religious upbringing. One interviewee suggested that the State should intervene if PCRMs crossed the line of children's rights because:

> the true yardstick must be the rights accorded to children at international or domestic law, including common law. To the extent that the manifestations forced upon children do not comply with these rights, the State has a duty to intervene to protect the children.

Although most interviewees noted that PCRMs contrary to children's rights required limitations on parental rights, they made a difference between older and younger children in terms of focus. In the case of younger children, the interviewees emphasised that limitations should target the imposition of irreversible actions and harm, whereas in the case of older children, some interviewees suggested that interference with rights protecting autonomy could constitute maltreatment. Intervention in such cases would 'not [be] a question of interference with the family structure, as the rights of parents to determine the upbringing of children must be in accordance with and subject to the rule of law'. These opinions stand in stark contrast with practice, but they are relatively well-aligned with what is written in the Social Welfare Department's *Procedural Guide on Handling Child*

97 C.W. So et al., A Local Review of Child Abuse in Hong Kong. (2018) 25(6) *Hong Kong Journal of Emergency Medicine* 350, 351, 354.

98 Hotten et al. (2015), 357. See also Y.C. Chan and G.L.T. Lam, Unravelling the Rationale for a One-Stop Service under the Family and Child Protection Services Units in Hong Kong. (2005) 48(4) *International Social Work* 419.

99 Compare P. Chiu, 'In Hong Kong, Most Child Abuse Victims Suffer at Hands of Parents', *South China Morning Post*, 15 January 2018 <https://www.scmp.com/news/hong-kong/law-crime/article/2128210/when-care-turns-cruelty-hong-kong-most-child-abuse-victims> last accessed 10 March 2019.

Abuse Cases.[100] This policy guide outlines different types of harm and recognises as psychological abuse the absence of 'developmentally appropriate autonomy through extreme over-involvement, intrusiveness and/or dominance'.[101] The guide further stipulates that children must be protected regardless of their religion and that 'superstitious' belief can lead to abuse or neglect.[102] Under the legal and policy framework, there is thus scope to use the child protection standard to limit parental rights to impose certain PCRMs, but in Hong Kong's reality there is a tolerance for upbringing that clearly contravenes this framework.[103]

8.4.2 Schooling

Education is the principal means through which the government limits parental rights in Hong Kong. Parents are under an obligation to send their child to a registered school.[104] Where they fail to do so, the government can issue an attendance order, followed by a conviction if parents do not comply with the order.[105] Private schools – including religious ones – can be set up and run with the approval of the government,[106] but home-schooling is prohibited unless there is a reasonable excuse, generally related to the child's mental or physical health.[107] Parental (religious) convictions cannot officially provide a 'reasonable excuse', although there is evidence that in practice the government tolerates various forms of home-schooling under an *ad hoc*, unofficial home-schooling policy.[108] Yet wherever that is the case, the Education Bureau actively monitors the curriculum and the child to ensure that children receive a comprehensive education.[109] This preoccupation with a wide-ranging education reflects the official standpoint as to why home-schooling is banned. According to the government:

100 Social Welfare Department, *Procedural Guide on Handling Child Abuse Cases* (Revised 2015, last updated July 2018). Hong Kong: Social Welfare Department, 2015. Available at <https://www.swd.gov.hk/storage/asset/section/1447/en/Procedural_Guide_for_Handling_Child_Abuse_Cases(Revised_2015)_updated_201807_Eng.pdf> last accessed 10 March 2019.

101 Ibid., 13.

102 Ibid., 1 and 8.

103 Compare *Naziya Aslam v Rafaqat Ali* [2004] HKCA 91: the welfare officer saw no issues with children being raised in an ultra-patriarchal, traditional and religious environment where arranged child marriage was the norm.

104 Ss. 78 *Education Ordinance*, chapter 279 (1 June 2001) and 74(1) *Education Ordinance*, chapter 290 (1 January 2005).

105 *HKSAR v Pun Chi Fai and Another* [2010] HKCFI 1719.

106 Ss. 10–13 *Education Ordinance*.

107 Hong Kong Legislative Council, *Official Report of Proceedings*. 1971–72 Session. 18 August 1971, 855 (The Hon. Chung Sze-Yuen); Hong Kong Legislative Council, *Official Report of Proceedings. 1978–79 Session*, 25 April 1979, 794–5 (The Honourable K.W.J. Topley, Director of Education).

108 E. Erlings, Don't Ask, Do(n't) Tell? Homeschooling in Hong Kong. (2018c) *Asian Journal of Law and Society* DOI 10.1017/als.2018.13, 8.

109 Ibid.; J. Steimle 'Home-Schooling in Hong Kong', *South China Morning Post*, 7 October 2014 <http://www.educationpost.com.hk/resources/education/141007-edu-insights-home-schooling-in-hong-kong> last accessed 24 August 2015 [the website no longer exists].

> school education provides children with a broader and more structured formal curriculum as well as rich learning experiences, and creates an environment where students can interact and exchange ideas among peers and with teachers. All these are essential for the all-round development of children in the areas of ethics, intellect, physique, social skills and aesthetics.[110]

In schools, the requirement of a broad education is enforced through the *Education Ordinance* and *Education Regulations* (parts of) which apply to all government, aided and independent schools.[111] Every school's curriculum and timetable must be approved and no school may engage in instruction or activities which the Permanent Secretary for Education deems 'in any way prejudicial to the welfare of the pupils or to their education generally'.[112] For example, the teaching of creationism is prohibited in courses on natural sciences.[113] Further, the Education Bureau clarified in 2017 that all government and private schools receiving subsidies would be bound by stated Key Learning Areas that include a range of subjects and skills ranging from science education to liberal studies.[114] Unaided private schools should either offer a recognised overseas national curriculum (or International Baccalaureate), or otherwise provide 'quality' education.[115] This means that schools in Hong Kong must provide a relatively broad and comprehensive curriculum that offers children large amounts of secular knowledge and skills in ways that may be at odds with religious precepts valued by parents. Moreover, the Social Welfare Department classifies it as child abuse to deprive a child of such education.[116]

The same was suggested by one of the interviewees: lack of education could constitute an irreversible action requiring child protection. Most interviewees highlighted the idea of increased competence that would eventually allow a child to take their own decisions on religious manifestations. Such competence requires education. This was recognised by the aforementioned interviewee who emphasised the importance of receiving a comprehensive education, and thus gaining the competence needed for personal choice. In this way autonomy and

110 Hong Kong Legislative Council, *Allow Children to Receive Education at Home*, LEGCO Question No. 17 (Written reply), Wednesday 14 February 2014 (The Honourable M.-K. Cheung).

111 *Education Regulations*, chapter 279A (1 January 2005).

112 R. 92 and 98, *Education Regulations*.

113 D. Cyranoski, Hong Kong Evolution Curriculum Row. (2009) 457 *Nature* 1067, 1067.

114 Hong Kong Legislative Council, *Classification of Primary and Secondary School Subjects as Compulsory and Independent Compulsory Subjects*, LEGCO Question No. 11 (Written reply), Wednesday 29 November 2017 (Secretary for Education, Mr Kevin Yeung).

115 Education Bureau, 'International Education in Hong Kong – A Prospectus', *HKSAR* (15 June 2015) <https://www.edb.gov.hk/en/student-parents/ncs-students/useful-school-list/international-school.html> last accessed 10 March 2019. International Schools Hong Kong, 'Private Independent Schools Offering Non-Local Curriculum', Education Bureau (7 December 2018) <https://internationalschools.edb.hkedcity.net/private_independent_schools.php?lang=en> last accessed 10 March 2019.

116 Social Welfare Department (2015), 4, 16 and 19.

(lack of) education were linked, because the interviewee noted that 'children's autonomy should be respected', but only once they were able to make decisions.

Though education must be comprehensive, the HKSAR cannot interfere with religious instruction and practices in schools.[117] For example, the government may not ban morning prayer or religious instruction,[118] even if that instruction undermines the teaching in other topics such as science, as long as it is separately provided.[119] The 'constitutional' prohibition of interference in schools' religious practices combined with parental rights has resulted in a *laissez-faire* attitude towards the religious environment schools create.[120] Within this environment (as noted above) religious manifestations can legally be imposed on children. Hence, although manifestations of religion that prevent attendance at school or receipt of a broad education cannot be justified by parental rights, this does not necessarily mean that the school environment offers a counterbalance to religious coercion. Through its education system, the HKSAR offers secondary *knowledge* that may lead some children to question PCRMs, but it does not offer children a secondary culture free of PCRMs.[121]

8.4.3 Children's interests

In 2012, following CmRC critique that the government did not take children's interests seriously enough,[122] the HKSAR pledged to make them paramount in all actions and decisions concerning children.[123] Yet, the Committee noted with concern that the government had not shown how it could do so, as the principle was not legally embedded and the HKSAR had no infrastructure for promoting it (the latter having changed only somewhat with the establishment of a Children's Commission[124]).[125] If the 2015 Bill became the law, this would

117 Articles 137 and 141(3) *Basic Law*.

118 *The Catholic Diocese of Hong Kong Also Known as the Bishop of the Roman Catholic Church in Hong Kong Incorporation v Secretary for Justice* [2011] HKCFA 71, at [76–92].

119 Ibid., at [89], [101]. See also M.Y. Wong, 'Religious Education in a Multi-Religious Context', in M. Sivasubramaniam and R. HayHoe (eds), *Religion and Education: Comparative and International Perspectives*. Oxford: Symposium Books, 2018, 151–66, 154, 163.

120 CmRC, Combined Third and Fourth Reports of the People's Republic of China under the Convention on the Rights of the Child – Part Two: *Hong Kong Special Administrative Region*, UN Doc CRC/C/CHN-HKG/2 (25 October 2012), paras 156–8.

121 Compare with France, section 6.4.2.

122 CmRC, *Concluding Observations, China (including Hong Kong and Macau Special Administrative Regions)*. UN Doc CRC/C/CHN/CO/2 (24 November 2005), para 6.

123 CmRC, Combined Third and Fourth Reports of the People's Republic of China under the Convention on the Rights of the Child – Part Two: *Hong Kong Special Administrative Region*, UN Doc CRC/C/CHN-HKG/2 (25 October 2012), para 105.

124 The Commission on Children was established in 2018, but it remains to be seen how effective it will be given its status and mandate: D. Mok, 'Hong Kong Gets a New Children's Commission', *South China Morning Post*, 1 June 2018 <https://www.scmp.com/news/hong-kong/community/article/2148725/hong-kong-gets-new-childrens-commission> last accessed 10 March 2019.

125 CmRC, *Concluding Observations (third and fourth reports), China*. UN Doc CRC/C/CHN/CO/3-4 of 29 October 2013, paras 8–11, 32 and 19.

change and parents would have to protect and promote their children's interests if practicable. Until that time a consideration of children's interests within the parent–child relationship is limited to court proceedings in Hong Kong. Consequently, there is a significant discrepancy between the religious situation of children who have, and who have not, come in contact with the courts, because judges do not always think PCRMs are in children's interests.

When deciding on a case involving children and their parents, Hong Kong courts must treat the child's interests – and not parental rights – as their paramount consideration.[126] To determine children's interests, the law invites courts to pay particular attention to the welfare report (if any) written in respect of the child, and children's views, which should be given due consideration 'if, having regard to the age and understanding of the minor and to the circumstances of the case, it is practicable to do so' (s. 3(1) GMO). If a PCRM would not otherwise attract judicial attention, children aiming to protect their right to freedom of manifestation should therefore do so via their right to be heard. Moreover, in some cases, which explicitly include religious conflict, a child may be separately represented by a lawyer or guardian *ad litem*.[127]

The hearing of children in Hong Kong often happens indirectly,[128] but judges appear to be open to listening to children and taking their views into account. Courts start to effectively hear children from the ages of 7–9 years old,[129] although it is considered good practice to seek the views of young children who have an 'understanding' but are not 'mature'.[130] When children are over 15, judges are no longer at liberty not to hear them, or lightly disregard their views.[131] However, courts cannot obligate a minor to present their views and where children's views have been unduly influenced, the judge is allowed to give them less weight.[132] The weight given to children's views is further balanced by other factors. Although the only other guidance mentioned in statute is the welfare report, judges have long

126 S. 3(1) GMO and *H and N*, [2012] 5 HKLRD 498, at [21]. See also ss. 48C *Matrimonial Causes Ordinance*, chapter 179 (30 June 1997); 10, 18 and 19 *Matrimonial Proceedings and Property Ordinance*, chapter 192 (4 July 1997); 8(1)(b) *Adoption Ordinance*, chapter 290 (25 January 2006): S. 8(1)(b). The best interests principle applies to wardship (*K v K* [1996] HKCFI 683, at [8] on religious upbringing), but different standards may apply in Hague applications (compare *Re P* [2004] 1 HKLRD 815 and *K v K* [2007] HKEC 141).

127 Chief Justice, *Guidance on Separate Representation for Children in Matrimonial and Family Proceedings*, PDSL6 (2012), para 15.

128 Judges can meet with children to confirm views, not to gather evidence: Chief Justice, *Guidance on Meeting Children*, PDSL5 (2012), para 2.

129 *Ong Constantino Erminda v Chau Shui Hing (No. 2)* [1989] 1 HKC 246, at [84] (9 year old); *Y v L* [1998] HKFAMC 1, at [36] (9 year old); and *S v Z* [2007] HKFAMC 34, at [1], [68] (11 and 13 years old). See also *K v K* [1996] HKCFI 683, at [1] and [35] on religion specifically (7 and 10 years old).

130 HKLRC (2005), Custody Report, 197. See e.g. *ZJ v XWN* [2018] 3 HKLRD 644, at [32].

131 *C v C*, Civil Appeal Action No. 44 of 1988 in Liu (1999), p. 252; *Re W (An Infant)* [1971] HKLR 219; *C v C* [2006] HKFLR 1 (also discusses practical aspects of ignoring views: the child had voted with his feet). See also *P v P* [2004] HKFAMC 4, discussed below.

132 See respectively *Re Kwok Micah* MP 3040/1984 at [16]; *M v H* [2006] HKEC 830, at [76], [95].

started using welfare checklists (lists of indicators) to determine children's interests.[133] In the past, these often consisted of the checklist from the English *Children Act*, or the one proposed by the HKLRC in the Custody Report.[134] However, a number of recent cases have relied on the checklist included in the 2015 Bill,[135] which mentions children's views alongside their needs, circumstances, relationship with parents, background and characteristics, risk of harm, family violence, parenting capacity, maintenance of personal relations, powers of the court and 'any other fact or circumstance the court thinks is relevant',[136] though not children's rights.

The fact that children's interests are paramount, combined with heavy reliance on English case-law, has resulted in a take on interests in religion which is very similar to that in England. Parental convictions cannot interfere with the autonomous determination of interests,[137] but judges normally defer to them in respect of children 'too young to have intelligent views of their own'.[138] Practising a religion, or several, has been held to serve the interests of young children. In *MJS v AS*, for example, the court ordered that a father could take his 6-year-old daughter with him to his place of worship as the mother was apparently not involving the child in her own religion.[139] If the mother changed her mind, it was in the child's interests to practise both religions.[140] By contrast, it is not taken to serve children's interests to be raised in a rigid religious manner, or in a way which fosters intolerance, especially not in Hong Kong, where many people of different backgrounds live together. In *K v K*,[141] both parents shared the same religion, but the father was very dogmatic, whereas the mother was more liberal. After having heard the children on their preference (in favour of the mother),[142] Seagroatt J granted custody to the mother because:

> The child's welfare within the wider community in which a variety of religious cultures are followed and practiced with mutual tolerance and recognition of human rights . . . is the most important aspect.[143] . . . [the children] should follow and observe their faith in a more modern, liberal and cosmopolitan context.[144]

133 Doing so is voluntary: *ZJ v XWN* [2018] 3 HKLRD 644, at [25].
134 See e.g. *YSL v TL* [2009] HKEC 37, at [14]; *PCY v CYW (Custody, Care and Control)* [2009] HKFLR 382, at [18]; *WHLH v CKW* FCMC1415/2009 (25 August 2011), at [25], [26]; *TPL v WYY* [2012] HKEC 1520, at [21].
135 See e.g. *L v L* [2017] 5 HKLRD 629, at [59]; *G, by his next friend Chan Liu Luna v BVR and Others* [2018] HKCFI 816, at [27].
136 S. 3(2) *Children Proceedings (Parental Responsibility) Bill.*
137 *C v C* [1977–9] HKC 363, at [13].
138 *Re W., An Infant* [1971] HKCFI 29; HCAD 264/1970 (4 June 1971), at [3] (the 'infant' was 17 and taken to have intelligent views of his own).
139 *MJS v AS* [2012] HKEC 1030, at [61–4].
140 Ibid., at [64]. For a cultural equivalent: *LWY v HM* [2016] HKFC 78.
141 *K v K* [1996] HKCFI 683. See also *KB v MS* [2016] HKFC 28.
142 Ibid., at [35].
143 Ibid., at [34]. See also *Naziya Aslam v Rafaqat Ali* ([2004] HKEC 358, at [45].
144 Ibid., at [31].

Hong Kong's unique context may thus weigh in favour of a more moderate religious upbringing, in terms of both values and manifestation. This might perhaps also explain why research participants, whether respondents or interviewees, seemed so favourable towards an open religious atmosphere within the family that focused on encouragement rather than imposition. A number of respondents also noted that a key question was whether a religion had a 'positive influence' on a child or the family. The interviewees in turn agreed that parents could raise their child in their religion, but that such upbringing should not interfere with children's interests related to absence of harm and appropriate decision-making. The interest in not being harmed through PRCMs applied across the board, that to appropriate decision-making was intertwined with children's right to freedom of manifestation (and for one interviewee with the notion of Gillick competence). As children grew older, their interests and rights required that they should be allowed to make their own religious choices. One interviewee, for example, considered that when children would 'become aware' at age 12–15, they should also have a right to freedom of manifestation exercisable within the family. At that stage, PCRMs would contravene their interests.

The Hong Kong Family Court has expressly dealt with PCRMs in a case in which Chan J set out the evolving interests of children in respect of religion and manifestation. In *P v P*,[145] the parents initially raised their children in a rigidly religious manner dictated by the father. The children were e.g. forbidden from accessing 'inappropriate' material and activities.[146] Disobedience was severely punished. Following divorce, the mother adopted a more liberal parenting practice, which led the father to apply for sole custody. Notably, the children suggested in the welfare report that their father imposed PCRMs, and that they preferred living with their mother.[147] Refusing sole custody to the father, Chan J set out the approach Hong Kong courts should take when confronted with coerced religious practice. Noting that teaching and guidance would be more sensitive to children's needs than rigid imposition of religiously motivated restrictions, the judge held:

> [allowing] children more freedom in doing their own things, in particularly with the elder children, . . . is not a bad thing at all as when children grow older and more mature, it is only natural that they seek more independence and the right to make their own decisions.[148]
>
> In fact discipline is essential for the proper and healthy growth and development of all children. But when it is too strict or rigid and to be applied across the board for all the children irregardless [*sic*] of their age, needs or level of maturity, it becomes improper, unhealthy and can be counter-productive.[149]

145 *P v P* [2004] HKFC 4.
146 Ibid, at [106].
147 Ibid, at [170].
148 Ibid., at [122].
149 Ibid., at [148].

PCRMs in respect of older children are thus in principle contrary to their interests. Yet this does not mean that parents cannot question children's behaviour which contradicts the parental religion, and guide, but not coerce, their children accordingly.[150] That in itself forms part of parents' own right to freedom of religion, as it can be included in the idea of 'convincing one's neighbour'.[151] In respect of younger children, the discipline that manifestations offer, and the moral framework that religion itself provides, are seen as positive, even if they include PCRMs which are not harmful. To a large extent, the judge's approach corresponds with argument proposed in Chapters 4 and 5; that PCRMs may form part of children's primary culture, and that everyone in the family enjoys human rights to freedom of religion and manifestation. However, at present interests are still primarily seen as a means to limit *parental* rights to determine a child's religious manifestations, rather than a restriction on children's rights to determine their own. Moreover, as *P v P* demonstrates, as long as a case does not come to court, or another form of dispute resolution, best interests are not legally applicable to religious upbringing. Access to dispute resolution is therefore crucial, but not readily available.

8.5 Invoking and enforcing rights within the family

Irrespective of the state of the law, the vast majority of surveyed children claimed that their parents allowed them to decide on their own religion, or absence thereof. Most respondents had positive experiences in respect of freedom of religion and manifestation within the family, especially where 'family members respect [their] choice'. However, this was not the case for all families. The prevalence of conflict was high: 19%[152] of surveyed children stated that they had had conflicts related to religious manifestation with their parents and 12%[153] of surveyed parents reported religion-related conflict with their children. As one of the surveyed children stated '[t]his is an important topic for me, because I am currently facing conflicts caused by religion and religious activities'.

These outcomes not only suggest that intra-family religious conflict is a genuine issue in Hong Kong, but also that Hong Kong children are not afraid of invoking their rights or autonomy within the family, even if that leads to conflict. Although certainly not all surveyed children would actively oppose parents in ways contrary to cultural expectations of filial piety,[154] one wondered:

150 Ibid., at [120].

151 See *Kokkinakis v Greece*, no. 14307/88 (1993) ECtHR Series A 260-A, para 31. This equally applies under other instruments, such as the ICCPR; HRC (1993), General Comment 22.

152 27% if parents had a religion, but the child did not, and 33% if the child had a religion, but parents did not.

153 0% if parents had a religion, but the child did not, yet 60% if the child had a religion, but parents did not.

154 See Fung et al. (2017), 1682.

> Keeping the peace with parents, just everyone avoiding the confrontation between beliefs. Is that positive to everyone's life and belief? Or is it just delaying the resolving of the problem?

This willingness to openly challenge parents takes on added significance in view of the emphasis on family harmony within Hong Kong society.[155] At the same time, surveyed parents and children stressed the importance of non-adversarial ways of resolving disputes in the family. Some respondents suggested that religion itself could bring a solution, because '[i]deally grace and power from God is the best way, even for family conflicts'. The majority of parents and children also thought it was important that parents and children showed respect towards each other's religion or absence thereof. One surveyed child relied on the proverb 'some like carrots, some like cabbage' to underscore that everyone had their own preference and this should be respected within the family. Most often, though, respondents commented that religion-related conflict within the family could be solved through communication and 'dialogue between [family] members'. Yet this required an exercise of the parental role that stands in significant contrast with the concept of parental rights. Rather than rely on near-absolute power and control, one of the surveyed parents argued:

> Parents should listen to their children's feelings and ideas, and try to understand their difficulties as if they [parents] were standing in their shoes, and do everything to help and support them. They shouldn't be stubborn, making the problem worse, or refuse to compromise and cause conflicts.

However, '[c]onflict between people can be resolved by communication only when both sides are willing to do so' and that is not always the case. It is therefore relevant to consider whether children can enforce freedom of manifestation via the courts, mediation, or social services in Hong Kong if their parents continue to impose PCRMs.

8.5.1 Access to court

> A traditional Chinese family will not resolve family conflicts by legal proceedings.

This statement appeared not only true for a traditional Chinese family, but equally for modern families in Hong Kong. Although most respondents suggested that children's rights within the family should be respected and children should be able to rely on these rights vis-à-vis their parents, there was very little support for giving children access to court to enforce these rights. In the Hong Kong context court procedures signify the complete breakdown of

155 S. Kavikondola et al., Structure and Validity of Family Harmony Scale: An Instrument for Measuring Harmony. (2016) 28(3) *Psychological Assessment* 307, 307, 308.

harmony and are considered disgraceful.[156] They make all parties involved lose face, including those who bring the case.[157] As a well-known proverb states 'in death avoid hell, in life avoid law courts'.[158] Court proceedings, especially in family cases, should only feature as a 'measure of last resort', but otherwise be avoided at all costs.[159] It is therefore unsurprising that only 16% of children and a handful of parents (6%) thought children should be allowed to enforce their rights in court, although the majority of surveyed children also did not expressly reject access to court.[160]

At the moment, however, children in Hong Kong do not have independent access to court procedures that would allow them to enforce their human rights and oppose PCRMs. Relevant procedures can only be instigated by the Director of Social Welfare (child protection and custody),[161] parents (custody)[162] or any other adult who thinks a child's interests are compromised (wardship).[163] Children can petition the Director to bring a child protection or custody application,[164] but unless a PCRM causes very significant harm, it is unlikely that valuable resources would be devoted to protecting a child's right to freedom of manifestation. Additionally, custody orders can only be made within divorce proceedings. These limitations are unfortunate, because the juvenile court may 'order [a child's] parent or guardian to enter into recognizance to exercise proper care and guardianship'[165] in child protection proceedings and the family court can direct parties to attend counselling, parent education or another form of intervention in child-related disputes.[166] Both would be useful orders where coerced manifestations take place within the family context.

The main procedure through which PCRMs can currently be challenged is wardship under the court's inherent jurisdiction. The jurisdiction can be invoked where a child's interests are endangered and, if they are so found to be, the court

156 See G. Kaufmann-Kohler and F. Kun, Integrating Mediation into Arbitration: Why it Works in China. (2008) 25(4) *Journal of International Arbitration* 479, 480, 481.

157 Ibid. Losing face is a form of embarrassment, or dishonour.

158 K. Chan et al., Attitudes towards Advertising by Lawyer's [sic] amongst Hong Kong Consumers. (2012) 2(2) *Asian Journal of Business Research* 75, 78.

159 *FHY v GJS* [2008] HKFC 11, at [83].

160 Many were undecided.

161 S. 34(1) PCJO (the Director can authorise another person and a police officer may also apply) and 10(1) GMO respectively.

162 S. 10(1) GMO.

163 S. 26 *High Court Ordinance*, chapter 4 (1 July 1997). The juvenile court may also issue a Care and Protection order *ex officio*, but the family court may not until the 2015 Bill becomes law. *R, MJ v OAM a.k.a. R, AO* [2018] HKFC 131, at [5].

164 *Mutatis mutandis* (involving a grandmother) *CLP v CSN (Formerly Known as HTY or HTYZ) and Another* [2016] 5 HKLRD 530, at [7.3].

165 34(1)(c) PCJO. Other options are appointing the Director as legal guardian, taking the child into care, or placing him/her under supervision.

166 Chief Justice, *Children's Dispute Resolution*, PD 15.13 (2016), para 12(x).

is free to take any action necessary to safeguard the child's interests.[167] Wardship fulfils a broad function in the HKSAR, since it is also the only means through which a non-custodial parent can challenge aspects of upbringing by a former spouse. Its *de facto* function is therefore somewhat like custody proceedings. For example, in a case in which the custodial parent (mother) decided to move a child from a denominational to a State school, the father had to ward his child to be able to object.[168] Children can likewise use wardship to object to PCRMs,[169] but because they have no independent access to court, they must apply with the help of a 'next friend' (an adult with an interest in the child).[170] The next friend can be anyone, such as an elder sibling or a teacher, but it may be difficult for children in Hong Kong to find a person willing to challenge PCRMs when no great harm is involved. If a next friend is found, there is a chance that children will be successful in challenging PCRMs, because wardship proceedings must be decided on the basis of children's best interests.[171] However, the goal of wardship is protection, not regulation.[172] Wardship officially transfers all parental rights to the court so that the court may protect a vulnerable child in ways 'not confined to proposals and submissions of the parties'.[173] Its function, wide discretion and guiding principles mean that it is not truly a means to 'enforce' freedom of manifestation. Yet it is the only channel children currently have to oppose PCRMs, and this is why one of the interviewees suggested that children should be made better aware of the fact that they had rights to freedom of manifestation, which they could enforce through wardship proceedings.

In the future, the situation could change. Under s. 29(1)(b) of the 2015 *Children Proceedings Bill*, children can at any time apply for leave of the court to subsequently apply for a children's order in the family court (similar to s. 8 procedures in England). The court has discretion to grant leave if a child has 'sufficient understanding to make the proposed application for which leave is being applied' (s. 30(1)). This formulation may become problematic because it could potentially allow for considerations beyond children's competence to influence the decision,[174] but at the very least it opens a window to court access. Moreover, the Bill introduces a range of new orders that are relevant to PCRMs. These include child arrangement orders (with whom the child is to live, spend time or have contact),

167 S. 26 *High Court Ordinance*. See also *Rules of the High Court*, chapter 4A (1 July 1997), Order 90, r. 3.

168 *Wong Chiu Ngar Chi v Wong Hon Wai, Linus* [1987] HKCA 257, at [5].

169 Wardship has previously been used to protect an incompetent child against parents who invoked their convictions to refuse a life-enhancing operation: *Director of Social Welfare v Lam Kwok-wah* [1988] 1 HKLR 206.

170 *Rules of the High Court*, Order 80, r. 2.

171 *K v K* [1996] HKCFI 683, at [8].

172 *Re LB (Wardship: Costs)* [2012] 1 HKLRD 266, at 272; *Re Y* (Minors) [1984] HKLR 204, at 207.

173 *G, by his next friend Chan Lui Luna v BVR and Others* [2018] 4 HKC 518, at [29]. See also *L v L* [2017] 5 HKLRD 629, at [41]–[51].

174 See Herring (2017), 504–6 in the English context.

prohibited steps orders (prohibiting certain exercises of parental responsibility), specific issue orders (providing direction on the exercise of parental responsibility) and orders depriving parents of (specific) parental rights and responsibilities (s. 28(1)). Although the guiding principle will again be the interests of the child and not their rights (s. 3(1)), the jurisdiction is not protective and therefore potentially more amenable to rights enforcement.

Whether access to court to enforce rights is a positive development was nonetheless doubted by one of the interviewees. Although this interviewee supported State intervention and highlighted the importance of hearing children and giving them separate representation, they were hesitant to give children themselves the opportunity to challenge parental behaviour. If children were given access to court (or mediation), the interviewee remarked, 'the immediate concern would be the extent to which this would . . . possibly damage the parent child relationship'. A second interviewee noted that the idea of children having access to court to challenge PCRMs necessitated further thought. The majority of interviewees were nonetheless either moderately or strongly in favour of access to court for children seeking to defend their rights within the parent–child relationship. However, most thought that unrestricted access to court would be unfeasible or inappropriate for children. Although 'children should not be denied access to justice just because they are a child', there had to be 'appropriate safeguards', for example related to children's competence. The main problem identified by the interviewees in regard to implementing access to court in Hong Kong was not of a principled, but a practical nature: a lack of financial and human resources to conduct procedures and the absence of an appropriately trained judiciary. If such problems could be overcome, 'children should be empowered to advocate for themselves, including in the courts where necessary'.

8.5.2 Access to mediation

Mediation has often been promoted in Hong Kong as a culturally sensitive means of dispute resolution in a society that is extremely litigation averse.[175] In 2007 the HKSAR's Chief Executive endorsed mediation as a means to 'alleviate conflict and foster harmony' in inter-personal conflicts.[176] Since then, the government has facilitated its practice through e.g. the adoption of a *Mediation Ordinance*.[177] The main drivers behind family mediation in Hong Kong have nonetheless been the judiciary and community organisations: the former advocating for the use of mediation

175 Though mediation itself might need some culturally inspired adjustments: H. H. Irving, *Family Mediation: Theory and Practice with Chinese Families*. Hong Kong: Hong Kong University Press, 2002.

176 D. Tsang's 2007–08 Policy Address quoted in Department of Justice, Civil Division, *Bills Committee on Mediation Bill*. Legislative Council Document No. CB(2)732/11-12(01) (3 January 2012), 2.

177 Chapter 620 (1 January 2013).

and the latter being its principal providers.[178] In *FHY v GJS*, Chu J held that parties in children's cases should mediate first since litigation 'will no doubt increase acrimony and hostility'.[179] Parties could turn to '[community] organizations where charges for mediation are low'.[180] Even where there are great differences between parties' positions, mediation might not be futile, as the process could change participants' attitudes.[181] Parties in family cases are now required to attempt mediation or risk adverse cost orders, unless there is a reasonable explanation.[182] If both applicants are legally aided, court-connected mediation is available.[183] Where this is not the case, the judiciary has set up a mediation information centre and Family-Mediation Co-ordinator's Office to conduct pre-mediation consultations and help parties to find a private or community mediator.[184] Children, however, are excluded from this infrastructure for the simple reason that they currently do not have access to court. This was duly recognised by one of the interviewees. Notably, none of the interviewees referred to mediation on their own account, but when prompted they considered it to be preferable to court in cases of (religious) parent–child conflict, where there was no abuse. Some interviewees nonetheless pointed out that mediation related to religious manifestations and PCRMs might be more challenging than other mediations unless the 'religious element' could be replaced with another subject matter. Although in religion-related cases mediation could still help to 'recognise the position of the other party', if the parties were 'entrenched in their values/ideas' a real solution could not be reached through mediation. Conversely, one interviewee noted that mediation related to PCRMs would not be fundamentally different from other types of mediation, and that in any case 'communication is a good thing no matter what the issue'. The possibility to restore communication was exactly what made most interviewees favour mediation over court 'no matter how intense the conflict'. Whereas court would be a 'nuclear bomb' (though sometimes a necessary one), mediation could enhance family functioning. As one interviewee explained:

> Mediation between children and parents is highly desirable. . . . Mediation would not only help parents and their children communicate, it would help parents learn how to be more sensitive. . . . there's a great need for it.

178 N. Alexander, 'Hong Kong: Mediation and the Future of Dispute Resolution', in S.P. Stobbe (ed.), *Conflict Resolution in Asia: Mediation and Other Cultural Models*. Lanham, MD: Lexington, 2018, 192, 193; Y.-K. Lee and A. Lakhani, The Case for Mandatory Mediation to Effectively Address Child Custody Issues in Hong Kong. (2012) 26(3) *International Journal of Law, Policy and the Family* 327, 333–5.

179 [2008] HKFC 11, at [83].

180 Ibid. For other cases: Lee and Lakhani (2012), 333–5.

181 Alexander (2018), 186, 187 for a discussion of cases.

182 Chief Justice, *Family Mediation*, PD 15.10 (2012), para 1.5. See also Chief Justice, *Mediation*, PD 31 (2014), para 5.

183 Alexander (2018), 193.

184 Hong Kong Judiciary, *Mediation Co-ordinator's Offices* <https://mediation.judiciary.hk/en/mcos.html#fmco> last accessed 10 March 2019.

That need is not presently met through the justice system and one interviewee noted that mediators might currently be 'uncomfortable' when faced with children. Yet as Scully-Hill has argued, once the 2015 Bill is adopted, Hong Kong must strengthen its 'existing commitment to recourse to ADR in family law disputes. This would require training and employing more family mediators to utilise, where suitable, child-focused and child-inclusive mediation'.[185] In general, though, most interviewees thought parent–child mediation was feasible, despite potential differences in power between parents and children. Some interviewees stated that the mediator could balance power, others instead, or in addition, placed emphasis on the child being old and competent enough to mediate. It is in this regard useful that the *Mediation Ordinance* does not require mediated outcomes to be legally binding, so that e.g. questions related to children's capacity to enter into mediation contracts do not feature in Hong Kong.[186] Again, the main problem envisaged was a lack of resources, although one interviewee remarked that the resource problem would be less pertinent in respect of mediation, than in respect of access to court, and another that mediation in general had less formal access hurdles.

Consistent with cultural expectations and previous research,[187] both surveyed parents and children were significantly more likely to accept parent–child mediation than litigation. Whereas few respondents thought children should have access to court to enforce their rights, a third (34%) of surveyed children and an even larger group of surveyed parents (43%) stated that they would consider using mediation if they were in conflict with respectively their parent(s) or child. There was nonetheless some scepticism as to whether the other party would be willing to engage in mediation (and this may have influenced own willingness): children in particular underestimated the willingness of parents to mediate with their children. Yet, as one of the surveyed parents stated, conflicts are best solved through 'a discussion in peace', which is something mediation can provide through its moderated communication.

That parent–child mediation is in fact feasible and capable of improving parent–child relationships has been demonstrated by the Parental Conflict Mediation Centre (previously the Parent-Child Mediation Centre).[188] Since 2008, the Hong Kong Federation of Youth Groups, a local community organisation, has operated a parent–child mediation service on a Yuen Long housing estate. Free mediation is offered in cases of unresolvable conflict related to a variety of issues, including personal attitudes and alleged disrespect.[189] The

185 Scully-Hill (2016), 402; Chinese University of Hong Kong, *A Study on Family Mediation Services in Hong Kong*. Hong Kong: Central Policy Unit of the HKSAR, 2017, 182–4.

186 Alexander (2018), 192.

187 Hong Kong Polytechnic University, *Evaluation Study on the Pilot Scheme on Family Mediation (Commissioned)*. Legislative Council Paper No. CB(2)1381/03-04(01) (January 2004), 3, 15.

188 See Hong Kong Mediation Centre, Spotlight: Mediation Week 2016: Mediation Carnival. (2016) 12 *Mediator's Voice* 7, 8.

189 Hong Kong Federation of Youth Groups, HKFYG Parent Support Network. (2017) 9(3) *Youth Hong Kong* 18, 18.

mediators are said to have the skills to prevent power-imbalances from negatively affecting the mediation, which is itself reportedly effective in solving disputes and restoring communication.[190] In the absence of access to the official mediation structure, it would thus be helpful to expand the service to other (community) organisations that already offer mediation or youth services (though where mediation concerns PCRMs it should be considered that a large number of community organisations are religious and therefore potentially not the most suitable venues). However, although the government has described the Centre's existence as a positive development,[191] no plans or subsidies have been forthcoming to offer parent–child mediation more widely.[192] Mediation thus remains out of reach for most families in conflict.

8.5.3 Social services

Family problems in Hong Kong tend to be diverted to social services, at least as a matter of policy. A network of 67 Integrated Family Service Centres is operated by the Social Welfare Department and subsidised NGOs to provide services under three banners: family resources unit, family support unit and family counselling unit.[193] The Centres themselves decide on the services they offer from a wide range of options.[194] This is because '[t]he government always prescribes the integrated family service centres as a panacea for a full spectrum of individual and family needs' and the Centres simply do not have the capacity to cover all.[195] Most services offered have little bearing on parent–child conflict or the issue of PCRMs, except for parent education and counselling services, though neither constitute a means to effectively enforce religious rights or genuinely challenge parental behaviour. The effectiveness of parent education programmes has been questioned (some parents used the course as proof that they knew how to parent when children disagreed with them),[196] and trials to improve outcomes are ongoing.[197] In any case, a parent imposing PCRMs might not think they need a parenting course. Counselling services would be more helpful to parents and

190 Personal visit to the Mediation Centre (an interview was not possible). Also ibid., 18, 19.

191 Department of Justice (2010), 21.

192 Most organisations face funding issues just to offer existing services: Alexander (2018), 193.

193 Social Welfare Department, *Integrated Family Service Centre* (January 2016) <https://www.swd.gov.hk/doc/family/IFSC/IFSC%20Leaflet%20(Traditional%20Chinese%20and%20English)_Jan%202016.PDF> last accessed 10 March 2019.

194 Consultant Team Department of Social Work and Social Administration, University of Hong Kong, *Building Effective Family Services: Review on the Implementation of the Integrated Family Service Centre Service Mode.* LC Paper No. CB(2)1619/09-10(01) (2010), 19.

195 Lau (2017), 11.

196 S.-M. To and T.-S. Chan, Searching for the Meaning of Parenthood: An Existential Approach to Parent Education in the Hong Kong-Chinese Context. (2013) 56 *International Social Work* 467, 476.

197 E.g. S.M. To et al., Supporting Parents in Late Modernity through Parent Education: A Mixed Methods Study in Hong Kong. (2018) 18(2) *Journal of Social Work* 164, 168, 181.

children in conflict over religion, but often Centres do not have resources left for parent–child counselling beyond crisis intervention.[198] A shortage of financial and human resources is a persistent issue and it is therefore not surprising that a number of interviewees referred to it. In general, it seemed that only one interviewee, the one who in principle was opposed to access to court and mediation, had confidence in the HKSAR's ability to intervene otherwise. Moreover, most of the surveyed children indicated that, if they had a conflict with parents, they would not ask an unknown person for help, but rather someone they knew well, such as a teacher at school (this was the same for parents). Schools already play a role in providing social services and this role is set to increase further with a budget commitment aimed at employing at least one social worker per school, although the focus is on primary schools and the prevention of abuse.[199] Additionally, teachers are expected under the 'whole school approach' to not only look after students' academic performance, but guide students in their whole person development.[200] Yet whilst teachers have indicated that they would be willing to play a greater social role, they have neither the training, nor the time to do so.[201]

Where social services and schools cannot take up the task, children's rights and welfare services in Hong Kong are often the domain of NGOs, charities and religious organisations (who operate many of the previous two).[202] Yet children's rights are not charitable affairs and children may not see religious organisations as the forum of choice to challenge PCRMs. This would especially be the case in Hong Kong where manifestations may be intimately linked with services or education obtained from the organisation. Hence, it remains uncertain to what extent social services may aid a child coerced to manifest the parental religion.

8.6 Conclusion

Although children in Hong Kong officially have a right to freedom of manifestation, that right does not apply within the family (or seemingly at all, if contrary to parental wishes). In the absence of direct effect with appropriate limitations,

198 M. Yuen et al., Professional Counselling in Hong Kong. (2014) 92(1) *Journal of Counselling and Development* 99, 101.

199 K. Cheung, 'Budget 2018: More Resources for Hong Kong Primary Schools; Aim of One Social Worker per School', *Hong Kong Free Press*, 28 February 2018 <https://www.hongkongfp.com/2018/02/28/budget-2018-resources-hong-kong-primary-schools-aim-one-social-worker-per-school/> last accessed 10 March 2019.

200 The whole school approach initially focused on the integration of special needs students but has expanded significantly beyond that. See Education Bureau (2011) *Whole School Approach to Guidance and Discipline* <http://www.edb.gov.hk/en/teacher/student-guidance-discipline-services/principles-guidelines/whole-school-approach-to-guidance-discipline/index.html> last accessed 10 March 2019.

201 S.K.Y. Lam and E.K.P. Hui, Factors Affecting the Involvement of Teachers in Guidance and Counselling as a Whole-School Approach. (2010) 38(2) *British Journal of Guidance and Counselling* 219, 227, 228.

202 K.S. Ng, Religion and Social Welfare in Hong Kong: An Overview. (2014) 14 *Research Journal of Graduate Students of Letters* 249, 249.

the HKSAR should provide a rights-respecting framework to regulate manifestations and opportunities to challenge rights violations as argued in Chapter 4. Yet Hong Kong does neither. Despite significant changes in society and indications that the population is now largely in favour of accommodating children's (religion-related) decision-making within the family, the applicable PGPCR remains that of parental rights. Moreover, there are very few limitations that apply to parental rights in Hong Kong. This is especially true in a unified family, where parental rights are mostly subject to educational requirements for lack of resources to enforce e.g. the child protection threshold. The broad education children receive can allow them to reach the competence that many adults (and some children) think they need in order to be able to make their own decisions regarding religious manifestation. However, for the law to recognise the value of increased competence – and to otherwise catch up with legal and societal expectations – reform is needed, whether via the proposed Bill or through an activist judiciary, which for long has been the driving force behind change in the government's absence.

What cannot change without the government's support is access to a justice system that allows for the challenging of PCRMs. Within the family, children already defend their position, even if that leads to conflict. However, once such conflict, or the PCRM, becomes untenable, children have nowhere to go beyond the protective jurisdictions – and even then they need an adult to initiate action. The proposed Bill envisages access to court, but it is uncertain when, or if, it will be adopted. Moreover, a sole focus on court procedures would not be culturally appropriate, or indeed conducive to the parent–child relationship, as also argued in Chapter 5. Within Hong Kong, there is far more support for alternative dispute resolution such as mediation. Limited practice moreover shows that parent–child mediation is feasible, potentially even where the dispute relates to religious manifestation. Rolling out a parent–child mediation network will nonetheless require political will and resources. The HKSAR has plenty of the latter,[203] what it needs now is a little more of the former.

203 F. Moriarty 'Hong Kong's Nearly HK$2tr Fiscal Reserves Should be Spent, to Benefit the People Who Own Them', *South China Morning Post*, 21 July 2017 <https://www.scmp.com/business/global-economy/article/2085785/hong-kongs-nearly-hk2tr-fiscal-reserves-should-be-spent> last accessed 10 March 2019.

9 Conclusion

An often quoted saying in law and religion literature is that 'a family that prays together, stays together'. This book demonstrates that the situation is more nuanced than that popular phrase suggests. Religion and religious practice can work as an important binding factor in the family, but practice can become divisive where it is imposed. An increasing number of research studies suggests that coerced manifestations have negative outcomes for both children's well-being and the family as a whole. PCRMs may give the impression of family unity to the outside world, but they commonly lead to internal conflict and resentment that impact on true togetherness. Moreover, coerced manifestations are often (though not always) a violation of the child's right to freedom of manifestation. States should protect that right, but in reality they often give preference to parental rights whilst preventing children from exercising or enforcing their own. In doing so, they not only ignore their international obligations, but they are not actually helping families, because a family culture based on respect for everyone's rights is of value to both parents and children.

The primacy of parental rights is generally based on the idea that international law grants parents a human right to decide on their children's religious manifestations, including where this leads to PCRMs. The existence of that right is virtually never questioned. A thorough examination of international law nonetheless reveals that a parental right to impose PCRMs does not exist as part of international human rights. It was neither intended by the drafters when human rights instruments were first negotiated, nor has it subsequently been accepted by treaty bodies and other organs. Whilst there is due recognition of the primacy of parents vis-à-vis the State, this does not amount to a license to impose religious manifestations on children. As a consequence, in any discussion on PCRMs, the child's own human right to freedom of manifestation should be the starting point. That right, irrespective of one's theoretical, practical or cultural outlook, should be seen as informed by autonomy. It is a right for the child to decide on their own religious practice, based on personal convictions – and for that reason cannot be practised by others for the child. However, this does not mean that there are no limits to children's autonomous decision-making. Freedom of manifestation is a right that can be limited on the basis of, for example, principles governing parent–child relations or children's best interests under the public order limitation ground. These principles already form part of the national laws of States and are meant to develop with (or replaced on the basis of) changes in society. This allows for a principled approach to children's rights where the core of freedom of manifestation remains unchanged, but limitations develop as society does. Yet for any limitation to be acceptable as a restriction on the child's right, it must not only be prescribed by (national) law and serve a recognised limitation ground, the limitation must be proportionate or necessary in a democratic society. The fact that a PGPCR is generally accepted as compatible with human rights does not mean that all parental rights a State may ascribe to it would thereby also be necessary.

The above limitation framework is often intertwined with the way States fulfil their positive obligations to ensure children's rights in their jurisdiction. Most States do not grant children horizontally applicable and enforceable rights to freedom of manifestation in the family. In general, they combine both protection of religious rights and limitations on them within their PGPCR (parental authority, responsibility, rights, etc.). Doing so does not relieve States of their positive obligation to ensure children's rights to freedom of manifestation as found under international law. States can meet this positive obligation by devising a rights-respecting framework at the national level that governs PCRMS within the family, and giving children access to enforcement mechanisms where parents overstep the boundaries of that framework and violate children's rights. The regulation of the power-balance between parents and children at the national level is thus crucial to respect for children's human right to freedom of manifestation.

However, the case studies show a general reluctance at domestic levels to fully respect children's rights irrespective of the jurisdiction's mediating principles and available infrastructure for the protection of rights. None of the jurisdictions allow children to directly rely on their human rights within the family circle: where human rights apply horizontally, children cannot rely on them, and where children can rely on human rights these do not apply between private parties. Coerced manifestations are instead governed by PGPCRs. These invariably establish children's religious manifestation as a matter for parental decision-making, seemingly unaffected by the requirements of the PGPCR itself, though the case studies do suggest that some PGPCRs are better able to protect children's rights and offer 'necessary' limitations on their freedom of manifestations than others. It matters whether a PGPCR is principally seen as demarcating spheres of power over children between parents and the State, or whether it is regarded as balancing power between parents and children – and to what extent the principle is itself based on democratic values such as participation. However, this difference is of no importance when religious manifestation is seen as an exception to the general rules of an otherwise rights-respecting PGPCR.

The primacy of parental rights is not entirely unabridged in the jurisdictions examined, but the restrictions set by the law do not lead to States fully supporting the child's right. In France, for example, the State places much emphasis on the need to circumscribe parental power through State intervention and on children reaching competence to exercise their rights, but a blanket legal incompetence prevents children from ultimately taking their own decisions. By contrast, in England, Gillick competent children can take their own decisions, but there is no infrastructure to allow children to reach competence and the State is extremely reluctant to intervene in the family on behalf of the child. In Hong Kong, there is limited emphasis on children reaching competence, no possibility for competent children to take their own decisions and very restricted intervention in the family, though this might change through the adoption of new legislation. The ultimate result is that it is legally very difficult for children to oppose PCRMs in any jurisdiction. Yet that does not mean that children do not do so in reality, or that full parental power to impose PCRMs is generally regarded as desirable.

The research included in this book indicates that children do in effect challenge parental determinations of manifestation and defend their own choices, even if that leads to family conflict. Moreover, it suggests that religious manifestation as a parental prerogative might no longer be what society expects of families and the law. Amongst research participants there was much greater support for allowing children to gradually develop competence and ultimately take their own religion-related decisions, without abrogating the parental role in giving children bearings or the State's role in protecting children. Religion was regarded as personal, and although especially some interviewees hesitated at the thought that the consequence of allowing children to decide would be to limit the rights of parents, there was recognition that doing so would be more respectful of children's rights and children themselves. Importantly, States have recognised this themselves when called upon to make decisions for children, normally via the family courts. Family procedures in France, England and Hong Kong are based on PGPCRs but decided with reference to children's interests. They paint a wholly different picture from the parental prerogative that the domestic law otherwise supports. Courts in all three jurisdictions gave primacy to children's increasing autonomy (including the development of autonomy) and indirectly the protection of their religious rights, irrespective of whether they were judging with regard to parental authority, responsibility or rights. However, most of these cases were custody cases between parents, because children do not normally have access to court at the national level. Where they do, access may be subject to e.g. leave requirements which allow courts to decline intervention in an 'intact' family (insofar as that can be said of a family whose members take each other to court). That leads to the curious conclusion that children often have to rely on warring parents in high-conflict divorces to have their right to freedom of manifestation protected at the national level. It also points to the importance of the second strand of States' positive obligations: to provide children with a remedy for when parents violate their rights.

An important discussion included in this book – and hopefully furthered by those who read it – relates to possibilities for children to enforce their right to freedom of manifestation where parents impose PCRMs. Currently, if enforcement of children's human rights is considered at all, it is normally suggested (or rejected) that children gain access to court. Court procedures *are* important, and children should have access to them as an ultimate remedy, but they are more likely to further divide families than bring them closer together. States should therefore consider adopting a more family-centred approach to dispute resolution where children's rights to freedom of manifestation are violated through PCRMs. This could mean that, in addition to access to court, they offer procedures such as mediation, which is a means of ADR already firmly embedded in family law for its promise to open lines of communication and improve family functioning. Court could then be reserved for cases that cannot be otherwise solved. At the moment, States rarely offer both. In England, for example, children have access to court (at least in theory), but not mediation, whereas in France steps have recently been taken in the mediation field, but children cannot initiate family law proceedings. In Hong Kong access to court will depend on the adoption of new legislation: at the moment children have no means of dispute resolution at all that they can initiate independently. This is despite some indications in the research that children in all three jurisdictions are willing to stand up for their rights, and participants considered that, where conflict could not be resolved within the family, court or mediation might offer alternatives. In principle, though, participants stressed that families themselves should be encouraged to solve their problems through communication, understanding and respect, showing regard for all family members and their religious practices or absence thereof. For a family to work that way it is imperative that children are themselves seen as actors in the parent–child relation, and their claim to religious rights considered legitimate. This brings the discussion full circle with the need for States to effectively protect children's rights to freedom of manifestation in the parent–child relation via their national framework, so as to meet their international commitments under human rights regimes. There is still a lot of work for States and families to do in this regard, but as a French teenager once told the author: *On n'a pas des droits pour rien!* We don't have rights for nothing!

Bibliography

Books and book chapters

Ackerman, B.A., *Social Justice in the Liberal State*. New Haven, CT: Yale University Press, 1980

Adhar, R.J., 'Children's Religious Freedom, Devout Parents and the State', in P.W. Edge and G. Harvey (eds), *Law and Religion in Contemporary Society*. Aldershot: Ashgate, 2000

Adhar, R. and I. Leigh, *Religious Freedom in the Liberal State*. Oxford: OUP, 2005

Akandji-Kombe, J.-F., *Positive Obligations under the European Convention on Human Rights*. Strasbourg: Council of Europe, 2007

Alderson, P., *Young Children's Rights: Exploring Beliefs, Principles and Practice* (2nd ed.). London: Jessica Kingsley Publishers, 2008

Alderson, P. et al., 'Are Premature Babies Citizens with Rights? Provision Rights and the Edges of Citizenship', in A. Invernizzi and B. Milne (eds), *Children's Citizenship: An Emergent Discourse on the Rights of the Child*. Delhi: Krepublishers, 2011

Alen, A. and W. Pas, 'The UN Convention on the Rights of the Child's Self-Executing-Character', in E. Verhellen (ed.), *Monitoring Children's Rights*. The Hague: Kluwer, 1996

Alexander, N., 'Hong Kong: Mediation and the Future of Dispute Resolution', in S.P. Stobbe (ed.), *Conflict Resolution in Asia: Mediation and Other Cultural Models*. Lanham, MD: Lexington Books, 2018

Arajärvi, P., 'Article 26', in A. Eide and T. Swineheart (eds), *The Universal Declaration of Human Rights: A Commentary*. Oslo: Scandinavian University Press, 1992

Arajärvi, P., 'Article 26', in G.S. Alfredsson and A. Eide (eds), *The Universal Declaration of Human Rights: A Common Standard of Achievement*. The Hague: Martinus Nijhoff, 1999

Archard, D. and C.M. Macleod (eds), *The Moral and Political Status of Children*. Oxford: OUP, 2002

Archard, D.W., *Children, Family and the State*. Aldershot: Ashgate, 2003

Bainham, A., *Children. The New Law*. Bristol: Family Law, 1990

Bainham, A., 'Is Anything Now Left of Parental Rights?', in R. Probert et al. (eds), *Responsible Parents and Parental Responsibility*. Oxford: Hart, 2009

Baubérot, J., *Les 7 laïcités françaises: Le modèle français de laïcité n'existe pas*. Paris: Éditions de la Maison des Sciences de l'Homme, 2015

Ben-Arieh, A. and N. Tarshish, 'Children's Rights and Well-Being', in M.D. Ruck et al., *Handbook of Children's Rights: Global and Multidisciplinary Perspectives*. New York: Routledge, 2017

Bennett Woodhouse, B. and K.A. Johnson 'The United Nations Convention on the Rights of the Child: Empowering Parents to Protect their Children's Rights', in M. Albertson Fineman and K. Worthington (eds), *What is Right for Children? The Competing Paradigms of Religion and Human Rights*. Farnham: Ashgate, 2009

Bentham, J., 'Of the Limits of the Penal Branch of Jurisprudence', in P. Schofield (ed.), *Of the Limits of the Penal Branch of Jurisprudence (The Collected Works of Jeremy Bentham)*. Oxford: OUP, 2010

Bielefeldt, H. et al., *Freedom of Religion or Belief: An International Law Commentary*. Oxford: OUP, 2016

Bonfils, P. and A. Gouttenoire, *Droits des mineurs* (2nd ed.). Paris: Dalloz-Sirey, 2014

Bossuyt, M.J., *Guide to the Travaux Préparatoires of the International Covenant on Civil and Political Rights*. Dordrecht: Martinus Nijhoff, 1987

Boulle, L. and R. Field, *Australian Dispute Resolution*. Chatswood: LexisNexis Butterworths, 2017

Brandon, M. and L. Fisher, *Mediating with Families*. Pyrmont: Thomson Reuters, 2018

Brems, E., 'Article 14: The Right to Freedom of Thought, Conscience and Religion', in A. Alen et al. (eds), *A Commentary on the United Nations Convention on the Rights of the Child*. Dordrecht: Martinus Nijhoff Publishers, 2006

Brennan, S., 'Children's Choices or Children's Interests: Which do their Rights Protect?', in D. Archard and C.M. Macleod (eds), *The Moral and Political Status of Children*. Oxford: OUP, 2002

Bridgeman, J., *Parental Responsibility, Young Children and Healthcare Law*. Cambridge: CUP, 2007

Brighouse, H., 'What Rights (if any) do Children Have?', in D. Archard and C.M. Macleod (eds), *The Moral and Political Status of Children*. Oxford: OUP, 2002

Brighouse, H. and A. Swift, *Family Values: The Ethics of Parent–Child Relationships*. Princeton: Princeton University Press, 2014

Bueren, G. van, *The International Law on the Rights of the Child*. Dordrecht: Martinus Nijhoff Publishers, 1995

Bueren, G. van, 'Children's Rights: Balancing Traditional Values and Cultural Plurality', in G. Douglas and L. Sebba (eds.), *Children's Rights and Traditional Values*. Aldershot: Dartmouth, 1998

Burg, W. van den, 'Rechten van kinderen: Enkele filosofische kanttekeningen', in C. van Nijnatten (ed.), *Kinderrechten in discussie*. Amsterdam: Boom, 1993

Burton, F. *Family Law* (2nd ed.). London: Routledge, 2015

Byrnes, A., 'The Hong Kong Bill of Rights and Relations between Private Individuals', in J. Chan and Y. Ghai (eds), *The Hong Kong Bill of Rights: A Comparative Approach*. Hong Kong: Butterworths, 1993

Carbonnier, J., *Droit Civil*, 2. *La famille, l'enfant, le couple* (21st ed.). Paris: Presses Universitaires de France, 2002

Chaillou, P., *Guide du droit de la famille et de l'enfant*. Paris: Dunod, 2003

Casey, J., *L'enfant et sa famille*. Paris: Lexis Nexis, 2003

Coles, R., *The Spiritual Life of Children*. Boston, MA: Houghton Mifflin, 1990

Coons, J.E., 'The Religious Rights of Children', in J. Witte and J.D. Van der Vyver (eds), *Religious Human Rights in Global Perspective: Religious Perspectives*. The Hague: Martinus Nijhoff, 1996

Council of Europe, *Collected Edition of the 'Travaux Préparatoires' of the European Convention on Human Rights*. The Hague: Martinus Nijhoff, 1975–85

Cretney, S.M. and J.M. Masson, *Principles of Family Law* (6th ed.). London: Sweet & Maxwell, 1997

Cowden, M., *Children's Rights: From Philosophy to Public Policy*. Basingstoke: Palgrave Macmillan, 2016

Daly, A., *Children, Autonomy and the Courts: Beyond the Right to be Heard*. Leiden: Brill Nijhoff, 2017

Dekeuwer-Défossez, F., 'Droits de l'enfant et responsabilités parentales', in F. De Singly (ed.), *Enfants, adultes. Vers une égalité de status?* Paris: Universalis, 2004

Dekeuwer-Défossez, F., *Les droits de l'enfant. Que sais-je?* Paris: Presses Universitaires de France, 2010

Delaporte-Carré, C., *L'articulation des institutions de protection de la personne de l'enfant contre ses parents*. Paris: Dalloz, 2008

Delrieu, S. and V. Zalewski, *Droit des mineurs et des majeurs protégés*. Paris: Ellipses, 2010

Deshmukh-Ranadive, J., 'Introduction', in J. Deshmukh-Ranadive (ed.), *Democracy in the Family. Insights from India*. New Delhi: Sage, 2008

Detrick, S.L., *A Commentary on the United Nations Convention on the Rights of the Child*. The Hague: Martinus Nijhoff, 1999

Dillen, A., *Geloof in het Gezin? Ethiek, opvoeding en gezinnen vandaag*. Leuven: Lannoo, 2006

Dorsch, G. von, *Die Konvention der Vereinten Nationen über die Rechte des Kindes*. Berlin: Duncker & Humblot 1994

Dufaux, J. et al., *Liberté religieuse et régimes des cultes en droit français*. Paris: Éditions du CERF, 2005

Dykes, P., 'The Hong Kong Bill of Rights 1991: Its Origin, Content and Impact', in J. Chan and Y. Ghai (eds), *The Hong Kong Bill of Rights: A Comparative Approach*. Hong Kong: Butterworths, 1993

Eekelaar, J. and R. Dingwall, *The Reform of Child Care Law. A Practical Guide to the Children Act 1989*. London: Routledge, 1990

Eekelaar, J., *Family Law and Personal Life*. Oxford: OUP, 2006

Eide, A., 'The Non-Inclusion of Minority Rights: Resolution 217C (III)', in G.S. Alfredsson and A. Eide (eds), *The Universal Declaration of Human Rights: A Common Standard of Achievement*. The Hague: Martinus Nijhoff, 1999

Ekman Ladd, R., 'Philosophical Perspectives on Children's Rights', in M.D. Ruck et al. (eds), *Handbook of Children's Rights: Global and Multidisciplinary Perspectives*. New York: Routledge, 2017

Evans, C., *Freedom of Religion under the European Convention on Human Rights*. Oxford: OUP, 2001

Evans, M.D., *Religious Liberty and International Law in Europe*. Cambridge: CUP, 1997

Feinberg, J., 'The Child's Right to an Open Future', in A. Aiken and H. LaFollette (eds), *Whose Child? Children's Rights, Parental Authority and State Power*. Totowa, NJ: Littlefield, Adams & Co., 1980

Ferguson, L., 'Not Merely Rights for Children But Children's Rights: The Theory Gap and the Assumption of the Importance of Children's Rights', in M. Freeman (ed.), *The Future of Children's Rights*. Leiden: Brill, 2014

Fives, A., *Evaluating Parental Power: An Exercise in Pluralist Political Theory*. Manchester: Manchester University Press, 2017

Fize, M., *La démocratie familiale. Evolution des relations parents-adolescents*. Paris: Presses de la Renaissance, 1998

Fortin, J., *Children's Rights and the Developing Law* (3rd ed.). Cambridge: CUP, 2009

Freeman, M., *The Rights and Wrongs of Children*. London: Frances Plinter, 1983

Freeman, M., 'Disputing Children', in S. Katz et al. (eds.), *Cross Currents*. Oxford: OUP, 2000

Freeman, M., *Article 3. The Best Interests of the Child: A Commentary on the United Nations Convention on the Rights of the Child*. Dordrecht: Martinus Nijhoff, 2005

Freeman, M., 'The Value and Values of Children's Rights', in A. Invernizzi and J. Williams (eds), *The Human Rights of Children. From Visions to Implementation*. Farnham: Ashgate, 2011b

Furness, S. and P. Gilligan, *Religion, Belief and Social Work*. Bristol: Policy Press, 2010a

Gareil. L., *L'exercice de l'autorité parentale*. Paris: Librairie Générale de Droit et de Jurisprudence, 2004

Gil-Rosado, M.-P., *Les libertés de l'esprit de l'enfant dans les rapports familiaux*. Paris: Défrenois, 2006

Gilmore, S. et al., 'Introduction', in R. Probert et al. (eds), *Responsible Parents and Parental Responsibility*. Oxford: Hart, 2009a

Gilmore, S., 'The Limits of Parental Responsibility', in R. Probert et al. (eds), *Responsible Parents and Parental Responsibility*. Oxford: Hart, 2009b

Gonzalez, G., 'L'exigence de neutralité des services publics', in G. Gonzalez (ed.), *Laïcité, liberté de religion et Convention européenne des droits de l'homme*. Brussels: Bruylant, 2006

Gouttenoire, A., 'Les droits de l'enfant en droit français', in O. Cvejić Jančić, *The Rights of the Child in a Changing World*. Cham: Springer, 2016

Greer, S., *The Exceptions to Articles 8 to 11 of the European Convention on Human Rights*. Strasbourg, Council of Europe, 1997

Griffin, J., 'Do Children have Rights?', in D. Archard and C.M. Macleod (eds), *The Moral and Political Status of Children*. Oxford: OUP, 2002

Hamilton, C., *Family, Law and Religion*. London: Sweet & Maxwell, 1995

Hart, H.L.A., 'Bentham on Legal Rights', in A.W.B. Simpson (ed.), *Oxford Essays in Jurisprudence* (2nd series). Oxford: Clarendon Press, 1973

Hart, H.L.A., 'Legal Rights', in H.L.A. Hart, *Essays on Bentham, Studies in Jurisprudence and Political Theory*. Oxford: Clarendon Press, 1982

Helwig, C.C. and E. Turiel, 'Children's Social and Moral Reasoning', in P.K. Smith and C.H. Hart (eds), *The Wiley-Blackwell Handbook of Childhood Social Development* (2nd ed.). Chichester: Wiley-Blackwell, 2011

Herring, J., 'Vulnerability, Children and the Law', in M.D.A Freeman (ed.), *Law and Childhood Studies: Current Legal Issues*. Oxford: OUP, 2012

Herring, J., 'Parental Responsibility, Hyper-parenting and the Role of Technology', in R. Brownsword et al. (eds), *Oxford Handbook of Law, Regulation and Technology*. Oxford: OUP, 2017a

Herring, J., *Family Law* (8th ed.). Harlow: Pearson, 2017b

Hodgkin, R. and P. Newell, *Implementation Handbook for the Convention on the Rights of the Child* (3rd ed.). New York: United Nations Children's Fund, 2007

Hoggett, B., *Parents and Children* (4th ed.). London: Sweet & Maxwell, 1993

Hood, R.W., Jr, et al., *The Psychology of Religion: An Emperical Approach* (4th ed.). New York: Gilford Press, 2009

Hotten, K. et al., *The Hong Kong Family Court Practice*. Hong Kong: LexisNexis, 2015

Hunter, R. et al., 'Access to What? LASPO and Mediation', in A. Flynn and J. Hodgson, *Access to Justice and Legal Aid: Comparative Perspectives on Unmet Legal Need*. Oxford: Hart, 2017

Irving, H. H., *Family Mediation: Theory and Practice with Chinese Families*. Hong Kong: Hong Kong University Press, 2002.

James, A., 'Parents: A Children's Perspective', in A. Bainham et al. (eds), *What is a Parent?* Oxford: Hart, 1999

James, A., 'Responsibility, Children and Childhood', in J. Bridgeman et al. (eds), *Responsibility, Law and the Family*. Aldershot: Ashgate, 2008

James, A. and A. James, *Key Concepts in Childhood Studies*. London: Sage, 2012

Jong, C.D. de, *The Freedom of Thought, Conscience and Religion or Belief in the United Nations (1946–1992)*. Antwerp: Intersentia–Hart, 2000

Joseph, S. and M. Castan, *The International Covenant on Civil and Political Rights. Cases, Materials, and Commentary* (3rd ed.). Oxford: OUP, 2013

Kapai, P., 'Freedom of Conscience and Religious Belief', in J. Chan and C.L. Lim, *Law of the Hong Kong Constitution* (2nd ed.). Hong Kong: Sweet & Maxwell, 2015

Kilkelly, U., *The Child and the European Convention on Human Rights*. Aldershot: Ashgate, 1999

Kilkelly, U., 'The Child's Right to Religious Freedom in International Law: The Search for Meaning', in M.A. Fineman and K. Worthington (eds), *What is Right for Children? The Competing Paradigms of Religion and Human Rights*. Farnham: Ashgate, 2009

Kilkelly, U., 'The Best Interests of the Child: A Gateway to Children's Rights?', in E. Sutherland and L.-A. Barnes MacFalane, *Implementing Article 3 of the United Nations Convention on the Rights of the Child: Best Interests, Welfare and Well-being*. Cambridge: CUP, 2016

Killerby, M., 'The Council of Europe's Contribution to Family Law (Past, Present and Future)', in N. Lowe and G. Douglas (eds), *Family Law across Frontiers*. The Hague: Martinus Nijhoff, 1996

Kramer, M.H., 'Rights without Trimmings', in M.H. Kramer et al. (eds), *A Debate over Rights: Philosophical Enquiries*. Oxford: Clarendon Press, 1998

Langlaude, S., *The Right of the Child to Religious Freedom in International Law*. Leiden: Martinus Nijhoff, 2007

Langlaude Doné, S. and J. Tobin, 'Article 14: The Right to Freedom of Thought, Conscience and Religion', in J. Tobin (ed.), *The UN Convention on the Rights of the Child*. Oxford: OUP (forthcoming)

Lansdown, G., 'The Evolving Capacities of the Child', in Committee on the Rights of the Child (ed.), *A Guide to General Comment 7: 'Implementing Child Rights in Early Childhood'*. The Hague: Bernhard van Leer Foundation, 2006

Laroche-Gisserot, F., *Les droits de l'enfant*. Paris: Dalloz 1996

Lebrun, P.-B., *L'essentiel sur l'autorité parentale*. Paris: Ellipses, 2010

Lemmon, J.A., *Family Mediation Practice*. New York: Free Press, 1985

Lerner, N., 'Toward a Draft Declaration against Religious Intolerance and Discrimination', in Y. Dinstein, *Israel Yearbook of Human Rights 1981*. Tel Aviv: Tel Aviv University, 1981

Lerner, N., *Religion, Secular Belief and Human Rights* (2nd ed.). Boston, MA: Martinus Nijhoff, 2012

Lester, A. and D. Pannick, *Human Rights Law and Practice*. London: Butterworths, 1999

Leung, B.K.F., 'Church, State and Education', in M. Bray and R. Koo (eds), *Education and Society in Hong Kong and Macau*. Dordrecht: Springer, 2005

Leung, R.H.M., *Hong Kong Mediation Handbook*. Hong Kong: Sweet & Maxwell, 2014

Leveneur, L., 'Renforcer l'autorité parentale et promouvoir les droits de l'enfant?', in F. Dekeuwer-Defossez and C. Choain (eds), *L'autorité parentale en question*. Villeneuve d'Ascq: Presses Universitaires de Septentrion, 2003

Liu, A.N.C., *Family Law for the Hong Kong SAR*. Hong Kong: Hong Kong University Press, 1999

Locke, J., *Second Treatise of Government*. London: Awnsham Churchill, 1689

Lowe, N.V. and G. Douglas, *Bromley's Family Law* (10th ed.). Oxford: OUP, 2006

Luk, B.H.K., 'Religion in Hong Kong History', in L. Pui-Tak, *Colonial Hong Kong and Modern China*. Hong Kong: Hong Kong University Press, 2005

McAdam, M., *Freedom from Religion and Human Rights Law*. New York: Routledge, 2018

McCall Smith, A., 'Is Anything Left of Parental Rights?', in E. Sutherland and A. McCall Smith (eds), *Family Rights, Family Law and Medical Advance*. Edinburgh: Edinburgh University Press, 1990

MacCormick, N., 'Children's Rights: A Test-case for Theories of Rights', in N. MacCormick (ed), *Legal Right and Social Democracy: Essays in Legal and Political Philosophy*. Oxford: OUP, 1984

MacDonald, A., *The Rights of the Child in Law and Practice*. Bristol: Family Law, 2011

Malhaurie, P. and H. Fulchiron, *La Famille*. Paris: Defrénois, 2011

Martin-Lavaud, V., *Psychologue à l'école*. Toulouse: Éditions Érès, 2017

Masson, J., *The Children Act 1989: Text and Commentary*. London: Sweet & Maxwell, 1990

Merrills, J.G., *The Development of International Law by the European Court of Human Rights* (2nd ed.). Manchester, New York: Manchester University Press, 1993

Miller, L.J., *The Spiritual Child: The New Science on Parenting for Health and Lifelong Thriving*. New York: St Martin's Press, 2015

Monk, D., 'Parental Responsibility and Education: Taking a Long View', in R. Probert et al. (eds), *Responsible Parents and Parental Responsibility*. Oxford: Hart, 2009

Montgomery, H., 'Anthropological Perspectives on Children's Rights', in M.D. Ruck et al., *Handbook of Children's Rights: Global and Multidisciplinary Perspectives*. New York: Routledge, 2017

Morsink, J., *Universal Declaration of Human Rights: Origins, Drafting and Intent*. Philadelphia, PA: University of Pennsylvania Press, 1999

Mouttet, A., 'France: Implications des enfants dans la médiation familiale', in J. Mirimanoff (ed.), *Médiation et jeunesse: Mineurs et médiations familiales, scolaires et pénales en pays francophones*. Brussels: Larcier, 2013

Mowbray, A., *Cases and Materials on the European Convention on Human Rights*. Oxford: OUP, 2007

Murat, P., 'L'état des devoirs légaux des parents envers leur enfant', in P. Jacques (ed.), *Être parent aujourd'hui*. Paris: Dalloz, 2010

Murdoch, J., *Protecting the Right to Freedom of Thought, Conscience and Religion under the European Convention on Human Rights*. Strasbourg: Council of Europe, 2012

Noggle, R., 'Special Agents: Children's Autonomy and Parental Authority', in D. Archard and C.M. Macleod (eds), *The Moral and Political Status of Children*. Oxford: OUP, 2002

Nowak, M., *U.N. Covenant on Civil and Political Rights: CCPR Commentary*. Kehl; N. P. Engel, 1993

Nucci, L.P., *Education in the Moral Domain*. New York: CUP, 2001

Oliveira, J.C. and P. Cardinal (eds), *One Country, Two Systems, Three Legal Orders: Perspectives of Evolution*. Berlin: Springer-Verlag, 2009

Partsch, K.J., 'Freedom of Conscience and Expression, and Political Rights', in L. Henkin (ed.), *The International Bill of Rights. The Covenant on Civil and Political Rights*. New York: Columbia University Press, 1981

Piper, C., 'Mediation and Vulnerable Parents', in J. Wallbank. and J. Herring (eds), *Vulnerabilities, Care and Family Law*. London: Routledge, 2014

Plana, S., *Le prosélytisme à l'epreuve du droit privé*. Paris: l'Harmattan, 2006

Raz, J., *The Morality of Freedom*. Oxford: Clarendon Press, 1986

Reece, H., 'From Parental Responsibility to Parenting Responsibly', in M. Freeman (ed.), *Law and Sociology*. Oxford: OUP, 2006

Reece, H., 'The Degradation of Parental Responsibility', in R. Probert et al. (eds), *Responsible Parents and Parental Responsibility*. Oxford: Hart, 2009

Richert, R.A. and P. Granqvist, 'Religious and Spiritual Development in Childhood', in R.F. Paloutzian and C.L. Park (eds), *Handbook of the Psychology of Religion and Spirituality* (2nd ed.). New York: Guilford Press, 2015

Roberts, M., *Mediation in Family Disputes: Principles of Practice*. Farnham: Ashgate, 2008

Rosenczveig, J.P., *Rendre justice aux enfants*. Paris: Seuil, 2018

Schabas, W., *The European Convention on Human Rights: A Commentary*. Oxford: OUP, 2015

Scolnicov, A., *The Right to Religious Freedom in International Law. Between group Rights and Individual Rights*. London: Routledge, 2011

Singly, F. De, 'Qu'est-ce qu'un bon parent?', in F. Dekeuwer-Defossez and C. Choain (eds), *L'autorité parentale en question*. Villeneuve d'Ascq: Presses Universitaires de Septentrion, 2003

Singly, F. De, 'Le statut de l'enfant dans la famille contemporaine', in F. De Singly (ed.), *Enfants, adultes. Vers une égalité de status?* Paris: Universalis, 2004a

Singly, F. De, 'La cause de l'enfant', in F. De Singly (ed.), *Enfants, adultes. Vers une égalité de status?* Paris: Universalis, 2004b

Singly, F. De, *Comment aider l'enfant à devenir lui-meme?* Paris: Armand Colin, 2009

Smith, G., *Children's Perspectives on Believing and Belonging*. London: National Children's Bureau, 2005

Spielmann, D., *L'effet potentiel de la Convention européenne des droits de l'homme entre personnes privées*. Brussels: Bruylant, 1995

Stalford, H. and K. Hollingsworth, 'Judging Children's Rights: Tendencies, Tensions, Constraints and Opportunities', in H. Stalford et al., *Rewriting Children's Rights Judgments: From Academic Vision to New Practice*. Oxford: Hart, 2017

Steiner, H., 'Working Rights', in M.H. Kramer et al. (eds), *A Debate over Rights: Philosophical Enquiries*. Oxford: Clarendon Press, 1998

Sutherland, E.E., 'Article 3 of the United Nations Convention on the Rights of the Child: The Challenges of Vagueness and Priorities', in E.E. Sutherland and L.-A. Barnes Macfarlane (eds), *Implementing Article 3 of the United Nations Convention on the Rights of the Child: Best Interests, Welfare and Wellbeing*. Cambridge: CUP, 2016

Sutherland, E.E. and L.-A. Barnes Macfarlane, 'Introduction', in E.E. Sutherland and L.-A. Barnes Macfarlane (eds), *Implementing Article 3 of the United Nations Convention on the Rights of the Child: Best Interests, Welfare and Wellbeing*. Cambridge: CUP, 2016

Tahzib, B.G., *Freedom of Religion or Belief. Ensuring Effective International Legal Protection*. The Hague: Martinus Nijhoff, 1996

Talisse, R.B., *Democracy and Moral Conflict*. Cambridge, New York: CUP, 2009

Taylor, A., *The Handbook of family Dispute Resolution: Mediation Theory and Practice*. San Francisco, CA: Jossey-Bass, 2002

Taylor, R., 'Parental Responsibility and Religion', in R. Probert et al. (eds), *Responsible Parents and Parental Responsibility*. Oxford: Hart, 2009

Thomson, J. M., 'The Reform of Family Law in England', in A.G. Chloros (ed.), *The Reform of Family Law in Europe*. Deventer: Kluwer, 1978

Timmerman, J., *Kant's Groundwork of the Metaphysics of Morals*. Cambridge: CUP, 2007

Veerman, P.E., *The Rights of the Child and the Changing Image of Childhood*. Dordrecht: Martinus Nijhoff, 1992

Verdier, P. and C. Sellenet, *La nouvelle authorité parentale et les actions de soutien à la parentalité* (2nd ed.). Boulogne-Billancourt: Berger-Levrault, 2016

Verhellen, E., *Convention on the Rights of the Child: Background, Motivation, Strategies, Main Themes*. Antwerp: Garant, 2000

Verheyde, M., 'Article 28: The Right to Education', in A. Alen et al. (eds), *A Commentary on the United Nations Convention on the Rights of the Child*. Dordrecht: Martinus Nijhoff Publishers, 2006

Walter, B., *Le droit de l'enfant à être éduqué*. Paris: L'Harmattan, 2001

Weisner, T.S., 'Culture, Context and Child Well-being', in A. Ben-Arieh et al., *Handbook of Child Well-Being*. Dordrecht: Springer, 2014

Wellman, C., *Real Rights*. New York: OUP, 1995

Wiener, M., 'Interpretation of the 1981 Declaration through the Mandate Practice of the United Nations Special Rapporteur on Freedom of Religion or Belief', in M.D. Evans et al., *The Changing Nature of Religious Rights under International Law*. Oxford: OUP, 2015

Wong, M.Y., 'Religious Education in a Multi-religious Context', in M. Sivasubramaniam and R. HayHoe (eds), *Religion and Education: Comparative and International Perspectives*. Oxford: Symposium Books, 2018

Articles

Adhar, R., Religion as a Factor in Custody and Access Disputes. (1996) 10(2) *International Journal of Law, Policy and the Family* 177

Alderson, P. and M. Goodwin, Contradictions within concepts of children's competence. (1993) 1(3) *International Journal of Children's Rights* 303

Alston, P., The Best Interest Principle: Towards a Reconciliation of Culture and Human Rights. (1994) *International Journal of Law and the Family* 1

Apetroaia, A., et al., Parental Responsibility Beliefs: Associations with Parental Anxiety and Behaviours in the Context of Childhood Anxiety Disorders. (2015) 188 *Journal of Affective Disorders* 127

Archard, D. and M. Skivenes, Balancing a Child's Best Interests and a Child's Views. (2009) 17 *International Journal of Children's Rights* 1

Assadi, S.M., et al., Beliefs about Parental Authority, Parenting Styles, and Parent–Adolescent Conflict among Iranian Mothers of Middle Adolescents. (2011) 35 *International Journal of Behavioural Development* 424

Bainham, A., Lord Denning as a Champion of Children's Rights: The Legacy of Hewer v Bryant. (1999) 14 *Denning Law Journal* 81

Baker, D., Juvenile Mediation: Innovative Dispute Resolution or Bad Faith Bargaining? (1995–6) 27 *University of Toledo Law Review* 897

Barbier, P., L'Enfant, la religion et le droit. (1960) 1(Doctrine) *La Gazette du Palais* 72

Barbier, P., Religion, puissance paternelle et modalites des funerailles d'un enfant. (1962) 1(Doctrine) *La Gazette du Palais* 57

Barnes, L.L., et al., Spirituality, Religion and Pediatrics: Intersecting Worlds of Healing. (2000) 104(6) *Pediatrics* 899

Baumrind, D., Effects of Authoritative Parental Control on Child Behavior. (1966) 37(4) *Child Development* 887

Baylis, C. and R. Carroll, The Nature and Importance of Mechanisms for Addressing Power Differences in Statutory Mediation. (2002) 14(2) *Bond Law Review* 285

Beckman, L., Rights, Rights-Talk, and Children. (2001) 35 *Journal of Value Inquiry* 509

Berzonsky, M.D., Identity Style, Parental Authority, and Identity Commitment. (2004) 33(3) *Journal of Youth and Adolescence* 213

Bottoms, B.L., et al., Religion-Related Child Physical Abuse: Characteristics and Psychological Outcomes. (2003) 8(1–2) *Journal of Aggression, Maltreatment and Trauma* 87

Brelsford, G.M. and A. Mahoney, Relying on God to Resolve Conflict: Theistic Mediation and Triangulation in Relations between College Students and Mothers. (2009) 28(4) *Journal of Psychology and Christianity* 291

Brelsford, G., Divine Alliances to Handle Family Conflict: Theistic Mediation and Triangulation in Father–Child Relationships. (2011) 3(4) *Psychology of Religion and Spirituality* 285

Bryan, M., Parents as Fiduciaries: A Special Place in Equity. (1995) 3 *International Journal of Children's Rights* 227

Bush, R.A.B., Staying in Orbit, or Breaking Free: The Relationship of Mediation to the Courts over Four Decades. (2008) 84 *North Dakota Law Review* 705

Bush, R.A.B. and J.P. Folger, Mediation and Social Justice: Risks and Opportunities. (2012) 27(1) *Ohio State Journal on Dispute Resolution* 1

Buss, E., 'Parental' Rights. (2002) 88 *Virginia Law Review* 635

Campbell, T.D., The Rights of the Minor: As Person, as Child, as Juvenile, as Future Adult. (1992) 6(1) *International Journal of Law, Policy and the Family* 1

Cave, E., Goodbye Gillick; Identifying and Resolving Problems with the Concept of Child Competence. (2014) 34 *Legal Studies* 103

Chan, H.M., Informed Consent Hong Kong Style: An Instance of Moderate Familism. (2004) 29(2) *Journal of Medicine and Philosophy* 195

Chan, J.M.M., Hong Kong's Bill of Rights: Its Reception of and Contribution to International and Comparative Jurisprudence. (1998) 47 *International and Comparative Law Quarterly* 306

Chan, K., et al., Attitudes towards Advertising by Lawyer's [sic] amongst Hong Kong Consumers. (2012) 2(2) *Asian Journal of Business Research* 75

Chan, S.M., et al., Chinese Parenting in Hong Kong: Links among Goals, Beliefs and Styles. (2009) 179(7) *Early Child Development and Care* 849

Chan, K.W. and S.M. Chan, Hong Kong Teacher Education Students' Goal Orientations and their Relationship to Perceived Parenting Styles. (2007) 27(2) *Educational Psychology* 157

Chan, Y.C. and G.L.T. Lam, Unravelling the Rationale for a One-Stop Service under the Family and Child Protection Services Units in Hong Kong. (2005) 48(4) *International Social Work* 419

Chan, A.T.Y. and S.-K. Lee, Education Plans, Personal Challenges and Academic Difficulties: An Empirical Study on Self-Disclosure among Post-90s Teens in Hong Kong. (2014) 19(4) *International Journal of Adolescence and Youth* 468

Chao, R.K., Beyond Parental Control and Authoritarian Parenting Style: Understanding Chinese Parenting through the Cultural Notion of Training. (1994) 65 *Child Development* 1111

Chelladurai, J.M., et al., 'The Family that Prays Together . . .': Relational Processes Associated with Regular Family Prayer. (2018) 32(7) *Journal of Family Psychology* 849

Cheng, R.H.M., Moral Education in Hong Kong: Confucian-Parental, Christian-Religious and Liberal-Civic Influences. (2004) 33(4) *Journal of Moral Education* 533

Choudhry, S. and H. Fenwick, Taking the Rights of Parents and Children Seriously: Confronting the Welfare Principle under the Human Rights Act. (2005) 25(3) *Oxford Journal of Legal Studies* 453

Cockburn, T., Children and the Feminist Ethics of Care. (2005) 12(1) *Childhood* 71

Collings, S. and L. Davies, 'For the Sake of the Children': Making Sense of Children and Childhood in the Context of Child Protection. (2008) 22(2) *Journal of Social Work Practice* 181

Condell, M., Capacity to Mediate and the Human Right to Self-determination: The Mediator's Responsibility! (2015) 2(1) *Journal of Mediation and Applied Conflict Analysis* 211

Courtin, C., La religion de l'enfant en cas de séparation des parents. (2010) 1 *Actualité Juridique Famille* 29

Crawford, S.H., et al., From Determining Capacity to Facilitating Competencies: A New Mediation Framework. (2003) 40(40) *Conflict Resolution Quarterly* 385

Cruft, R., Rights: Beyond Interest Theory and Will Theory? (2004) 23 *Law and Philosophy* 347

Cullen, H., Education Rights or Minority Rights? (1993) 7 *International Journal of Law and the Family* 143

Cowden, M., Capacity, Claims and Children's Rights. (2012) 1(4) *Contemporary Political Theory* 362

Cyranoski, D., Hong Kong Evolution Curriculum Row. (2009) 457 *Nature* 1067

Dababneh, B., Whose Role is it to Support the Child's Right to Culture in Australia? (2017) 28 *Australian Dispute Resolution Journal* 19

Daly, A., No Wight for "Due Weight"? A Children's Autonomy Principle in Best Interest Proceedings. (2018) 26 *International Journal of Children's Rights* 61

Darling, N., et al., Individual Differences in Adolescents' Beliefs about the Legitimacy of Parental Authority and their own Obligation to Obey: A Longitudinal Investigation. (2008) 79(4) *Child Development* 1103

Dekeuwer-Défossez, F., Réflexion sur les mythes fondateurs du droit contemporain de la famille. (1995) 2 *Revue Trimestrielle de Droit Civil* 249

Dickens, J. and J. Masson, The Courts and Child Protection Social Work in England: Tail Wags Dog? (2016) 46(2) *British Journal of Social Work* 355

Dollahite, D.C., et al., Why Religion Helps and Harms Families: A Conceptual Model of a System of Dualities at the Nexus of Faith and Family Life. (2018) *Journal of Family Theory and Review* 219

Douglas, G., The Retreat from Gillick. (1992) 55(4) *Modern Law Review* 569

Dumortier, T., L'intérêt de l'enfant: Les ambivalences d'une notion 'protectrice'. (2013) 3 *La Revue des Droits de l'Homme*, DOI 10.4000/revdh.198

Dwyer, J.G., Equality between Adults and Children: Its Meaning, Implications, and Opposition. (2013) 2013(4) *Michigan State Law Review* 1007

Eekelaar, J., The emergence of Children's Rights. (1986) 6(2) *Oxford Journal of Legal Studies* 161

Eekelaar, J., Parental Responsibility: State of Nature, or Nature of the State? (1991a) 13(1) *Journal of Social Welfare and Family Law* 37

Eekelaar, J., Are Parents Morally Obliged to Care for their Children? (1991b) 11(3) *Oxford Journal of Legal Studies* 340

Eekelaar, J., The Importance of Thinking that Children have Rights. (1992) 6(1) *International Journal of Law, Policy and the Family* 221

Eekelaar, J., The Interests of the Child and the Child's Wishes: The Role of Dynamic Self-Determinism. (1994) 8 *International Journal of Law and the Family* 42

Eekelaar, J., Personal Rights and Human Rights. (2002a) 2(2) *Human Rights Law Review* 181

Eekelaar, J., Beyond the Welfare Principle. (2002b) 14(3) *Child and Family Law Quarterly* 237

Eekelaar, J., Children between Cultures. (2004) 18 *International Journal of Law, Policy and the Family* 178

Erlings, E., 'The Government did Not Refer to it': SAS v France and Ordre Public at the European Court of Human Rights. (2015) 16(2) *Melbourne Journal of International Law* 587

Erlings, E., Is Anything Left of Children's Rights? How Parental Responsibility Erodes Children's Rights Under English Law. (2016) 24(3) *International Journal of Children's Rights* 624

Erlings, E., A Way Out of *Laïcité*? The Child's Best Interests as Justification for Religious Manifestation. (2018b) 20(2) *Ecclesiastical Law Journal* 200

Erlings, E., Don't Ask, Do(n't) Tell? Homeschooling in Hong Kong. (2018c) *Asian Journal of Law and Society* DOI 10.1017/als.2018.13

Field, R. and J. Crowe, The Construction of Rationality in Australian Family Dispute Resolution: A Feminist Analysis. (2007) 27 *Australian Feminist Law Journal* 97

Fox Harding, L., 'Parental Responsibility' – A Dominant Theme in British Child and Family Policy for the 1990's. (1994) 14(1–2) *International Journal of Sociology and Social Policy* 84

Fung, J., et al., Perceived Social Change, Parental Control, and Family Relations: A Comparison of Chinese Families in Hong Kong, Mainland China and the United States. (2017) 8 *Frontiers in Psychology* 1671

Furness, S. and P. Gilligan, Social Work, Religion and Belief: Developing a Framework for Practice. (2010) 40(7) *British Journal of Social Work* 2185

Furness, S. and P. Gilligan, 'It Never Came Up': Encouragements and Discouragements to Addressing Religion and Belief in Professional Practice –What do Social Work Students have to Say? (2014) 44(3) *British Journal of Social Work* 763.

Freeman, M.D.A., Taking Children's Rights More Seriously. (1992) 6(1) *International Journal of Law, Policy and the Family* 52

Freeman, M.D.A., The Morality of Cultural Pluralism. (1995) 3 *International Journal of Children's Rights* 1

Freeman, M., Reforming the Law of Child Custody and Access: A Comment. (2005) 35 *Hong Kong Law Journal* 29

Freeman, M., Why it Remains Important to Take Children's Rights Seriously. (2007) 15 *International Journal of Children's Rights* 5

Freeman, M.D.A., Culture, Childhood and Rights. (2011a) 5 *The Family in Law* 15

Gilmore, S., The Nature, Scope, and Use of the Specific Issue Order. (2004) 16(4) *Child and Family Law Quarterly* 367

Grillo, T., The Mediation Alternative: Process Dangers for Women. (1991) 100(6) *Yale Law Journal* 1545

Hale of Richmond, Baroness, Freedom of Religion and Freedom from Religion. (2017) 19 *Ecclesiastical Law Journal* 3

Hauser, J., Religion de l'enfant: Cacophonie chez les juges du fond. (2008) 107(3) *Revue Trimestrielle de Droit Civil* 472

Heaven, P.C.L., et al., Parental Styles and Religious Values among Teenagers: A Three-Year Prospective Analysis. (2010) 171(1) *Journal of Genetic Psychology* 93

Hafen, B.C. and J.O. Hafen, Abandoning Children to their Autonomy: The United Nations Convention on the Rights of the Child. (1996) 37(2) *Harvard International Law Journal* 449

Hart, H.L.A., Are there any Natural Rights? (1955) 64(2) *Philosophical Review* 175

Heiphetz, L., et al., The Development of Reasoning about Beliefs: Fact, Preference and Ideology. (2013) 49 *Journal of Experimental Social Psychology* 559

Helwig, C.C., The Role of Agent and Social Context in Judgments of Freedom of Speech and Religion. (1997) 68(3) *Child Development* 484

Higgins, M., Child Protection Social Work in England: How Can it be Reformed? (2017) 47(2) *British Journal of Social Work* 293

Himma, K. E., Just 'Cause you're Smarter than me Doesn't Give you a Right to Tell me What to Do: Legitimate Authority and the Normal Justification Thesis. (2007) 27(1) *Oxford Journal of Legal Studies* 121

Ho, D.Y.F. and T.K. Kang, Intergenerational Comparisons of Child-Rearing Attitudes and Practices in Hong Kong. (1984) 20(6) *Developmental Psychology* 1004

Hobbs, A. and A. Alonzi, Mediation and Family Group Conferences in Adult Safeguarding. (2013) 15(2) *Journal of Adult Protection* 69

Hollingsworth, K., Responsibility and Rights: Children and their Parents in the Youth Justice System. (2007) 21(2) *International Journal of Law, Policy and the Family* 190

Hong Kong Federation of Youth Groups, HKFYG Parent Support Network. (2017) 9(3) *Youth Hong Kong* 18

Hong Kong Mediation Centre, Spotlight: Mediation Week 2016: Mediation Carnival. (2016) 12 *Mediator's Voice* 7

Houghton-James, H., Children Divorcing their Parents. (1994) 16(2) *Journal of Social Welfare and Family Law* 185

Houlgate, L.D., Three Concepts of Children's Constitutional Rights: Reflections on the Enjoyment Theory. (1999–2000) 2 *Pennsylvania Journal of Constitutional Law* 77

Hui, E., Parental Refusal of Life-Saving Treatments for Adolescents: Chinese Familism in Medical Decision-Making Re-Visited. (2008) 22(5) *Bioethics* 286

Hui, E., Adolescent and Parental Perceptions of Medical Decision-Making in Hong Kong. (2011) 25(9) *Bioethics* 516

Hunt Federle, K., Do Rights Still Flow Downhill? (2017) 25 *International Journal of Children's Rights* 273

Husain, A., An Eco-Systems Based Model for Faith-Inspired Parenting. (2013) 23(2) *Journal of Human Behaviour in the Social Environment* 159

Hutchby, I. and M. O'Reilly, Children's Participation and the Familial Moral Order in Family Therapy. (2010) 12(1) *Discourse Studies* 49

Illman Meyers, N., Power (Im)balance and the Failure of Impartiality in Attorney-Mediated Divorce. (1995–6) 27 *University of Toledo Law Review* 853

Ip, P.L.S., Child Abuse and Neglect in Hong Kong. (2000) 5 *Hong Kong Journal of Paediatrics* 61

Jolowicz, J., Adversarial and Inquisitorial Models of Civil Procedure. (2003) 52(2) *International Comparative Law Quarterly* 281

Kaufmann-Kohler, G. and F. Kun, Integrating Mediation into Arbitration: Why it Works in China. (2008) 25(4) *Journal of International Arbitration* 479

Kavikondola, S., et al., Structure and Validity of Family Harmony Scale: An Instrument for Measuring Harmony. (2016) 28(3) *Psychological Assessment* 307

Kay, E. and M. Tisdall, Challenging Competency and Capacity? Due Weight to Children's Views in Family Law Proceedings. (2018) 26 *International Journal of Children's Rights* 159

Kim-Spoon, J., et al., Adolescents Who are Less Religious than their Parents are at Risk for Externalizing and Internalizing Symptoms: The Mediating Role of Parent–Adolescent Relationship Quality. (2012) 26(4) *Journal of Family Psychology* 636

Klanjšek, R., et al., Religious Orientation, Low Self-Control, and Deviance: Muslims, Catholic, Eastern Orthodox, and "Bible Belt" Christians. (2012) 35 *Journal of Adolescence* 671

Van Kote, A., Médiation familiale: Une autre parole entre l'enfant et ses parents séparés. (2010) 93(1) *Connexions* 109

Kramer, M.H., Refining the Interest Theory of Rights. (2010) 55 *American Journal of Jurisprudence* 31

Kramer, M.H., Some Doubts about Alternatives to the Interest Theory of Rights. (2013) 123(2) *Ethics* 245

Kuhar, M. and H. Reiter, Towards a Concept of Parental Authority in Adolescence. (2013) 3(2) *C•E•P•S Journal* 135

Kuhn, E.S. and R.D. Laird, Individual Differences in Early Adolescents' Beliefs in the Legitimacy of Parental Authority. (2011) 47(5) *Developmental Psychology* 1353

Lam, S.K.Y. and E.K.P. Hui, Factors Affecting the Involvement of Teachers in Guidance and Counselling as a Whole-School Approach. (2010) 38(2) *British Journal of Guidance and Counselling* 219

Langan, E.B., 'We Can Work it out': Using Cooperative Mediation – a Blend of Collaborative Law and Traditional Mediation – to Solve Divorce Disputes. (2010–11) 30(2) *Review of Litigation* 245

Langlaude, S., Children and Religion under Article 14 CRC: A Critical Analysis. (2008) 16 *International Journal of Children's Rights* 475

Langlaude, S., Parental Disputes, Religious Upbringing and Welfare in English Law and the ECHR. (2014) 9(1) *Religion and Human Rights* 1

Lee, J.W., et al., Family Worship Patterns and their Correlation with Adolescent Behaviour and Beliefs. (1997) 36(3) *Journal for the Scientific Study of Religion* 372

Lee, Y.-K. and A. Lakhani, The Case for Mandatory Mediation to Effectively Address Child Custody Issues in Hong Kong. (2012) 26(3) *International Journal of Law, Policy and the Family* 327

Lees, J. and J. Horwath, 'Religious Parents . . . Just Want the Best for their Kids': Young People's Perspectives on the Influence of Religious Beliefs on Parenting. (2009) 23 *Children and Society* 162

Lester, E., Religious Autonomy and World Religious Education. (2004a) 31(2) *Religion and Education* 62

Leung, P.W.S., et al., Attitudes and Child Abuse Reporting Behaviours among Hong Kong GPs. (2011) 28 *Family Practice* 195

Lichtenstein, M., Mediation and Feminism: Common Values and Challenges. (2000) 18(1) *Mediation Quarterly* 19

Lovinger, S.L., et al., Some Clinical Applications of Religious Development in Adolescence. (1999) 22 *Journal of Adolescence* 269

Lowe, N.V., The meaning and allocation of parental responsibility – a common lawyer's perspective. (1997) 11 *International Journal of Law, Policy and the Family* 192

Lundy, L., Family Values in the Classroom? Reconciling Parental Wishes and Children's Rights in Schools. (2005) 19 *International Journal of Law, Policy and the Family* 346

Lung, W.P., International Law Before the Courts of the Hong Kong Special Administrative Region of the People's Republic of China – Twenty Years on. (2018) *Asian Journal of International Law* DOI 10.1017/S2044251318000024

Lynch, K., Reform of Family Justice: Children's Dispute Resolution in Hong Kong. (2016) 17 *Cardozo Journal of Conflict Resolution* 909

Ma, J.L.C., The Diagnostic and Therapeutic Uses of Family Conflicts in a Chinese Context: The Case of Anorexia Nervosa. (2005) 27(1) *Journal of Family Therapy* 24

McCrudden, C., Multiculturalism, Freedom of Religion, Equality, and the British Constitution: The JSF Case Considered. (2011) 9(1) *I•CON* 200

MacDonald, G.D., Accepting Parental Responsibility: "Future Questioning" as a Means to Avoid Foster Home Placement of Children. (1992) 71(1) *Child Welfare* 3

McGoldrick, D., The United Kingdom's Human Rights Act 1998 in Theory and Practice. (2001) 50(5) *International and Comparative Law Quarterly* 901

McIntosh, J.E., Four Young People Speak about Children's Involvement in Family Court Matters. (2009) 15(1) *Journal of Family Studies* 98

McIntosh, J.E., et al., Child-Focused and Child-Inclusive Divorce Mediation: Comparative Outcomes from a Prospective Study on Post-Separation Adjustment. (2008) 46(1) *Family Court Review* 105

McLaughlin, T.H., Parental Rights and the Religious Upbringing of Children. (1984) 18(1) *Journal of Philosophy of Education* 75

Mahoney, A., et al., Religion and the Sanctification of Family Relationships. (2003) 44(3) *Review of Religious Research* 220

Mahoney, A., Religion and Conflict in Marital and Parent–Child Relationship. (2005) 61(4) *Journal of Social Issues* 689

Marks, L., Religion and Family Health: An Overview and Conceptual Model. (2006) 45(4) *Journal of Religion and Health* 603

Mellado, C., et al., Interactive Associations of Parental Support, Demands and Psychological Control, over Adolescents' Beliefs about the Legitimacy of Parental Power. (2018) 64 *Journal of Adolescence* 81

Melton, G.B., It's All about Relationships! The Psychology of Human Rights. (2010) 80(2) *American Journal of Orthopsychiatry* 161

Molomby, A., Elder Mediation. New Solution to an Aging Issue. (2013) 33(4) *The Proctor* 42

Moneger, F., Les musulmans devant le juge français. (1994) 2 *Journal du Droit International* 345

Mumford, S.E., The Judicial Resolution of Disputes Involving Children and Religion. (1998) 47(1) *International and Comparative Law Quarterly* 117

Murphy, J.C. and J.B. Singer, Moving Family Dispute Resolution from the Court System to the Community. (2016) 75(9) *Maryland Law Review Endnotes* 9

Ng, K.S., Religion and Social Welfare in Hong Kong: An Overview. (2014) 14 *Research Journal of Graduate Students of Letters* 249

Ngai, S.S.-Y., et al, The Effects of Parenting Behaviour on Pro-Social Behaviour of Chinese Adolescents in Hong Kong. (2018) 87 *Children and Youth Services Review* 154

Noone, A.M., ADR, Public Interest Law and Access to Justice: The Need for Vigilance. (2011) 37(1) *Monash University Law Review* 57

O'Neill, O., Children's Rights and Children's Lives. (1992) 6(1) *International Journal of Law and the Family* 24

Paré, M. and T. Chong, Human Rights Violations and Canadian Mining Companies. (2017) 21(7) *International Journal of Human Rights* 908

Peleg, N., Reconceptualising the Child's Right to Development: Children and the Capability Approach. (2013) 21 *International Journal of Children's Rights* 523

Perälä-Littunen, S. and M.L. Böök, The Beginning and End of Parental Responsibility – Finnish Parents' Views. (2012) 43(6) *Journal of Comparative Family Studies* 925

Phillips, B. and P. Alderson, Beyond 'Anti-Smacking': Challenging Violence and Coercion in Parent–Child Relationships. (2003) 11(2) *International Journal of Children's Rights* 175

Piaget, J., Intellectual Evolution from Adolescence to Adulthood. Translated by J. Bliss and H. Furth. (2008) 58 *Human Development*, 40

Pineau, J., L'ordre public dans des relations de famille. (1999) 40(2) *Les Cahiers de Droit* 323

Pinquart, M. and R. Kauser, Do the Associations of Parenting Styles with Behaviour Problems and Academic Achievement Vary by Culture? Results from a Meta-Analysis. (2018) 24(1) *Cultural Diversity and Ethnic Minority Psychology* 75

Praagh, S. van, Religion, Custody and a Child's Identities. 35(2) *Osgoode Hall Law Journal* 309

Radovanovic, H., Parental Conflict and Children's Coping Styles in Litigating Separated Families: Relationships with Children's Adjustment. (1993) 21(6) *Journal of Abnormal Child Psychology* 697

Remedios, C., The Enhancement and Protection of Children's Rights. (2010) 2 *International Family Law Journal* 145

Riasetto, I., Droit privé. (2011) 2011(1) *Société, Droit et Religion* 137

Ritter, J. and A. Mayer, Regulating Data as Property: A New Construct for Moving Forward. (2018) 16(1) *Duke Law and Technology Review* 220

Ross, H., Children's Rights and Theories of Rights. (2013) 21(4) *International Journal of Children's Rights* 679

Ross, H., Children's Rights – a Defence of Hartian Will Theory. (2014) 22 *International Journal of Children's Rights* 43

Rubellin-Devichi, J., The Best Interests Principle in French Law and Practice. (1994) 8 *International Journal of Law and the Family* 259

Saller, R., Patria Potestas and the Stereotype of the Roman Family. (1986) 1(1) *Continuity and Change* 7

Schneider, C.E., On the Duties and Rights of Parents. (1995) 81 *Virginia Law Review* 2477

Scott, E.S. and R.E. Scott, Parents as Fiduciaries. (1995) 81(8) *Virginia Law Review* 2401

Scheiwe, K., Between Autonomy and Dependency: Minors' Rights to Decide on Matters of Sexuality, Reproduction, Marriage, and Parenthood. (2004) 18 *International Journal of Law, Policy and the Family* 262

Scolnicov, A., The Child's Right to Religious Freedom and Formation of Identity. (2007) 15(2) *International Journal of Children's Rights* 251

Scully-Hill, A., A Critical Evaluation of the Draft Children Proceedings (Parental Responsibility) Bill. (2016) 46 *Hong Kong Law Journal* 387

Shek, D.T., A Longitudinal Study of Hong Kong Adolescents' and Parents' Perceptions of Family Functioning and Well-Being. (1998) 159(4) *Journal of Genetic Psychology* 389

Shek, D.T., Hong Kong Chinese Parents' Perceptions of the Ideal Child. (1999a) 133(3) *Journal of Psychology* 291

Shek, D.T., Perceptions of Family Functioning among Chinese Parents and their Adolescent Children. (1999b) 27(4) *American Journal of Family Therapy* 303

Shelley, C., Beating Children is Wrong, isn't it? Resolving Conflicts in the Encounter between Religious Worldviews and Child Protection. (2013) 15(2) *Ecclesiastical Law Journal* 130

Shmueli, B., Love and the Law, Children Against Mothers and Fathers: Or, What's Love got to do with it? (2010) 17 *Duke Journal of Gender Law and Policy* 131

Simon, T.W., United Nations Convention on Wrongs to the Child. (2000) 8 *International Journal of Children's Rights* 1

Smetana, J.G., Parenting Styles and Conceptions of Parental Authority during Adolescence. (1995) 66(2) *Child Development* 299

Smolin, D.M., Overcoming Religious Objections to the Convention on the Rights of the Child. (2006) 20 *Emory International Law Review* 81

So, C.W., et al., A Local Review of Child Abuse in Hong Kong. (2018) 25(6) *Hong Kong Journal of Emergency Medicine* 350

Sorens, J., Libertarian Theory and Children's Rights. The Fiduciary Model, Rationality, Interests and the Challenge of Abortion. (2001) 61 *Philosophical Notes* 1

Sreenivasan, G., A Hybrid Theory of Claim-Rights. (2005) 25(5) *Oxford Journal of Legal Studies* 257

Stalford, H., et al., Achieving Child Friendly Justice through Child Friendly Methods: Let's Start with the Right to Information. (2017) 5(3) *Social Inclusion* 207

Stokes, C.E. and M.D. Regnerus, When Faith Divides Family: Religious Discord and Adolescent Reports of Parent–Child Relations. (2009) 38 *Social Science Research* 155

Such, E. and R. Walker, Young Citizens or Policy Objects? Children in the 'Rights and Responsibilities' Debate. (2005) 34(1) *Journal of Social Policy* 39

Tabory, E. and S. Hazan-Stern, Bonds of Silence: Parents and Children Cope with Dissonant Levels of Religiosity. (2013) 33 *Contemporary Jewry* 171

Taylor, R., Responsibility for the Soul of the Child: The Role of the State and Parents in Determining Religious Upbringing and Education. (2015) 29 *International Journal of Law, Policy and the Family* 15

Tigchelaar, J. and M. Jonker, How is a Decision Made in Parental Religious Disputes? An Analysis of Determining Factors in Dutch and European Court of Human Rights Case Law. (2016) 12(2) *Utrecht Law Review* 24

Tisak, M.S., Conceptions of Parental Authority. (1986) 57(1) *Child Development* 166

To, S.-M. and T.-S. Chan, Searching for the Meaning of Parenthood: An Existential Approach to Parent Education in the Hong Kong-Chinese Context. (2013) 56 *International Social Work* 467

To, S.M., et al., Supporting Parents in Late Modernity through Parent Education: A Mixed Methods Study in Hong Kong. (2018) 18(2) *Journal of Social Work* 164

Tobin, J., Justifying Children's Rights. (2013) 21(3) *International Journal of Children's Rights* 395

Tucker, J.S., et al., Effectiveness of Parent-Child Mediation in Improving Family Functioning and Reducing Adolescent Problem Behaviour: Results from a Pilot Randomized Controlled Trial. (2017) 46(3) *Journal of Youth and Adolescence* 505

Verdier, P., De l'intérêt de l'enfant aux droits de l'enfant. (2009) 43(2) *Enfances et Psy* 85

Vincent, C., Cohesion, Citizenship and Coherence: Schools' Responses to the British Values Policy. (2018) *British Journal of Sociology of Education*, DOI 10.1080/01425692.2018.1496011

Waldron, J., When Justice Replaces Affection: The Need for Rights. (1988) 11(3) *Harvard Journal of Law and Public Policy* 625

Welbourne, P., Adversarial Courts, Therapeutic Justice and Protecting Children in the Family Justice System. (2016) 28 *Child and Family Law Quarterly* 205

Wenar, L., The Nature of Rights. (2005) 33(3) *Philosophy and Public Affairs* 223

Wheeler, R., Gillick or Fraser? A Plea for Consistency over Competence in Children. (2006) 332 *British Medical Journal* 807

Wong, D.F.K., et al., Is Parental Control Beneficial or Harmful to the Development of Young Children in Hong Kong? (2018) *Journal of Child and Family Studies* DOI https://doi.org/10.1007/s1082

Wood Colby, K., When the Family does Not Pray Together: Religious Rights within the Family. (1982) 5 *Harvard Journal of Law and Public Policy* 39

Yaffe, Y., 'Parental Authority': What do we Know about the Construct? (2013) 2(9) *International Journal of Educational Research and Development* 211

Yau, J. and J. Smetana, Adolescent–Parent Conflict in Hong Kong and Shenzhen: A Comparison of Youth in Two Cultural Contexts. (2003) 27(3) *International Journal of Behavioural Development* 201

Youf, D., Seuils juridiques d'âge: Du droit romain aux droits de l'enfant. (2011) 11 *Sociétés et Jeunesses en Difficulté* (online) <http://journals.openedition.org/sejed/7231>

Yuen, M., et al., Professional Counselling in Hong Kong. (2014) 92(1) *Journal of Counselling and Development* 99

Zimmerman, N., Gillick Competence: An Unnecessary Burden. (2019) 25(1) *The New Bioethics* 78

UN Reports

Amor, A., *Report Submitted by the Special Rapporteur on Freedom of Religion or Belief.* UN Doc. E/CN.4/2002/73 (14 March 2002)

Bielefeldt, H., *Report of the Special Rapporteur on Freedom of Religion or Belief.* UN Doc. A/HRC/16/53 (15 December 2010)

Bielefeldt, H., *Report of the Special Rapporteur on Freedom of Religion or Belief: Mission to the Republic of Moldova.* UN Doc. A/HRC/19/60/Add.2 (27 January 2012a)

Bielefeldt, H., *Elimination of All Forms of Religious Intolerance. Interim Report of the Special Rapporteur on Freedom of Religion or Belief.* UN Doc. A/67/303 (13 August 2012b)

Bielefeldt, H., *Report of the Special Rapporteur on Freedom of Religion or Belief.* UN Doc. A/HRC/22/51 (24 December 2012c)

Bielefeldt, H., *Interim Report of the Special Rapporteur on Freedom of Religion or Belief.* UN Doc. A/70/286 (5 August 2015) ('Special Rapporteur's Children Report')

Jahangir, A., *Civil and Political Rights, Including the Question of Religious Intolerance.* UN Doc. E/CN.4/2006/5 (9 January 2006a)

Jahangir, A., *Civil and Political Rights, Including the Question of Religious Intolerance: Mission to France (18–29 September 2005).* UN Doc. E/CN.4/2006/5/Add.4 (8 March 2006b)

Shaheed, A., *Report of the Special Rapporteur on Freedom of Religion and Belief.* UN Doc. A/HRC/34/50 (17 January 2017)

Shaheed, A., *Report of the Special Rapporteur on Freedom of Religion and Belief.* UN Doc. A/HRC/37/49 (28 February 2018)

Singh, K., *Report of the Special Rapporteur on the Right to Education: Protecting the Right to Education Against Commercialization.* UN Doc. A/HRC/29/30 (10 June 2015)

United Nations High Commissioner for Human Rights, *Access to Justice for Children. Report of the United Nations High Commissioner for Human Rights.* UN Doc. A/HRC/25/35 (16 December 2013)

Other reports

Advisory Board on Family Law: Children Act Sub-Committee, *Making Contact Work.* London: Lord Chancellor's Department, 2002

Badman, G., *Report to the Secretary of State on the Review of Elective Home Education in England.* House of Commons HC610 (2009)

Bec, E. and N. Bel, *Pratiques actuelles avec les familles: Revue de la littérature et dossier bibliographique.* Toulouse: CREAI-ORS, 2018

Chinese University of Hong Kong, *A Study on Family Mediation Services in Hong Kong.* Hong Kong: Central Policy Unit of the HKSAR, 2017

Children's Commissioner (A. Longfield), *Skipping School: Invisible Children.* London: Children's Commissioner for England, 2019

Consultant Team Department of Social Work and Social Administration, University of Hong Kong, *Building Effective Family Services: Review on the Implementation of the Integrated Family Service Centre Service Mode.* LC Paper No. CB(2)1619/09-10(01) (2010)

Défenseur des Droits, *L'enfant et sa parole en justice. Rapport 2013 consacré aux droits de l'enfant.* Paris: La Documentation française, 2013

Défenseur des Droits, *Enquête dur l'accès aux droits*, vol. 4. Paris: Défenseur des Droits, 2017

Défenseur des Droits, *De la naissance à 6 ans: Au commencement des droits.* Paris: Défenseur des Droits, 2018

Dekeuwer-Défossez, F., *Rénover le droit de la famille: Propositions pour un droit adapté aux réalités et aux aspirations de notre temps.* Paris: La Documentation française, 1999

Department for Children, Schools and Families, *Use of Alcohol among Children and Young People.* Research Report DCSF-RW043 (2008)

Department for Children, Schools and Families, *Religious Education in English Schools: Non-Statutory Guidance,* DCSF-00114-2010 (2010)

Department for Children, Schools and Families, *Elective Home Education. Guidelines for Local Authorities.* Department for Children, Schools and Families, 2013

Department of Education, *Parental Opinion Survey 2010.* Research Report DFE-RR061 (2010)

Department of Justice, *Report of the Working Group on Mediation.* Hong Kong: Government of the Hong Kong Special Administrative Region, 2010

Department of Justice, Civil Division, *Bills Committee on Mediation Bill.* Legislative Council Document No. CB(2)732/11-12(01) (3 January 2012)

Direction de la Protection Judiciaire de la Jeunesse, *Document Thématique a L'Appui des Pratiques Professionnelles: L'Emprise Mentale* (7 October 2016)

Food and Health Bureau, *E-Health Record: Continuity of Care for You.* HKSAR Government (December 2011) <https://www.gov.hk/en/residents/government/publication/consultation/docs/2012/eHealth.pdf>

Foster, D., *Home Education in England.* House of Commons Library Briefing Paper 5108 (23 May 2018)

Gal, J. Le, *Les droits et libertés de l'enfant dans les institutions éducatives de la petite enfance 2003–2007.* Nantes: CFEJE de Nantes, 2009

Group for the Advancement of Psychiatry, *How Old is Old Enough? The Ages of Rights and Responsibilities.* New York: Brunner/Mazel, 1989

Hermange, M.-T. *Les enfants d'abord: 100 propositions pour une nouvelle politique de l'enfance.* Paris: La Documentation française, 2001

Hong Kong Family Law Association, *The HKFLA's Response to the Child Custody and Access Consultation Paper 2011.* Legislative Council Paper No. CB(2) 1548/12-13(02) (30 April 2012)

HM Government, *Reporting and Acting on Child Abuse and Neglect.* London, 2018a

HM Government, *Working Together to Safeguard Children.* Document DFE-00195-2018 (2018b)

Hong Kong Polytechnic University, *Evaluation Study on the Pilot Scheme on Family Mediation (Commissioned).* Legislative Council Paper No. CB(2)1381/03-04(01) (January 2004)

House of Commons Health Committee, *The Victoria Climbié Inquiry Report.* House of Commons Doc. HC570, 6th Report, Session 2002–03 (2003)

House of Commons, Children, Schools and Families Committee, *The Review of Elective Home Education: Government Response to the Committee's Second Report of Session 2009–2010.* House of Commons HC 423 (2009–10) (2010)

House of Commons Education Committee, *Children First: The Child Protection System in England.* House of Commons. HC137, 4th Report, Session 2012–13 (2012)

Jarrett, T. *Children: Parental Responsibility – What is it and How is it Gained and Lost (England and Wales).* House of Commons Briefing Paper 2827 (2017)

Kilkelly, U., *The Rights and Legal Status of Children and Parental Responsibilities: the views of Children and Young People.* Council of Europe, Document CJ-FA (2011) 6 (2011)

Law Commission, *Family Law: Review of Child Law, Guardianship and Custody. Report No. 172.* House of Commons. HC 594, Session 1987–88 (1988)

Law Reform Commission of Hong Kong, *Report: Child Custody and Access* Hong Kong: Law Reform Commission of Hong Kong, 2005

Legislative Council Panel on Welfare Services, *Follow-up on the Law Reform Commission Report on Child Custody and Access and Related Support Measures.* Legislative Council Paper No. CB(2)981/17-18(03) (12 March 2018)

Ministère de Solidarité et de la Santé, *Dessine-moi un parent. Stratégie nationale de soutien à la parentalité 2018–2022.* Paris: Direction Générale de la Cohésion Sociale, 2018

National Working Group on Child Abuse Linked to Faith or Belief, *The National Action Plan to Tackle Child Abuse Linked to Faith or Belief.* Department for Education DFE-00094-2012 (2012)

Ofsted, *Transforming Religious Education. Religious Education in Schools 2006–09.* Ofsted Document 090215 (2010)

Ofsted, *Religious Education: Realising the Potential.* Ofsted Document 130068 (2013)

Ofsted, *The Annual Report of Her Majesty's Chief Inspector of Education, Children's Services and Skills 2017/18.* House of Comments Document HC 1707 (2018)

Picard, C., *Rapport sur la Proposition de Loi Tendant à Renforcer la Prevention et la Répression des Mouvements Sectaires Portant Atteinte aux Droits de l'Homme et aux Libertés Fundamentales.* Assemblée Nationale, Doc. No. 3083 (23 May 2001)

Rosenczveig, J. P., et al, *Des nouveaux droits pour les enfants? Oui. . . dans l'intérêt même des adultes et de la démocratie.* Paris: La Documentation française, 2014

Stasi, B., *Commission de Réflexion sur l'Application du Principe de Laïcité dans la République: Rapport au Président de la République.* Paris: La Documentation française, 2003

Sullivan, R., *Barriers to the Legal Profession*. London: Legal Services Board, 2010
Théry, I., *Couple, filiation et parenté aujourd'hui, le droit face aux mutations de la famille et de la vie privée*. Paris: éd. Odile Jacob, La Documentation française, 1998

Guidelines

CmCoE, *Guidelines of the Committee of Ministers of the Council of Europe on Child-Friendly Justice*, Council of Europe (17 November 2010)
CmRC, *Model Form for Submissions of Individual Communications to the Committee on the Rights of the Child under the Optional Protocol to the Convention on the Rights of the Child on a Communications Procedure* (2015) <https://www.ohchr.org/Documents/HRBodies/CRC/ModelCommunicationForm_en.pdf>
Council of the European Union, *EU Guidelines on the Promotion and Protection of Freedom of Religion or Belief*. Luxembourg: Foreign Affairs Council, 2013
Social Welfare Department, *Procedural Guide on Handling Child Abuse Cases* (Revised 2015, last updated July 2018). Hong Kong: Social Welfare Department, 2015
Working Party of the Family Justice Council, *Guidelines in Relation to Children Giving Evidence in Family Proceedings*, FJC11/01/04 (2011)

Newspaper articles

Ch.R.-P., 'L'état veut encadrer les écoles hors contrat et l'enseignement à domicile' *La Dépêche*, 12 June 2016 <https://www.ladepeche.fr/article/2016/06/12/2363940-etat-veut-encadrer-ecoles-hors-contrat-enseignement-domicile.html> last accessed 10 March 2019
Cheung, K., 'Budget 2018: More Resources for Hong Kong Primary Schools; Aim of One Social Worker per School' *Hong Kong Free Press*, 28 February 2018 <https://www.hongkongfp.com/2018/02/28/budget-2018-resources-hong-kong-primary-schools-aim-one-social-worker-per-school/> last accessed 10 March 2019
Chiu, P., 'In Hong Kong, Most Child Abuse Victims Suffer at Hands of Parents', *South China Morning Post*, 15 January 2018 <https://www.scmp.com/news/hong-kong/law-crime/article/2128210/when-care-turns-cruelty-hong-kong-most-child-abuse-victims> last accessed 10 March 2019
M.M., 'Banyuls-sur-Mer: les parents écroués pour avoir maltraité leurs 8 enfants', *L'Indépendent*, 15 April 2009
Mok, D., 'Hong Kong Gets a New Children's Commission', *South China Morning Post*, 1 June 2018 <https://www.scmp.com/news/hong-kong/community/article/2148725/hong-kong-gets-new-childrens-commission> last accessed 10 March 2019
Moriarty, F., 'Hong Kong's Nearly HK$2tr Fiscal Reserves Should be Spent, to Benefit the People Who Own Them', *South China Morning Post*, 21 July 2017 <https://www.scmp.com/business/global-economy/article/2085785/hong-kongs-nearly-hk2tr-fiscal-reserves-should-be-spent> last accessed 10 March 2019
Steimle, J., 'Home-Schooling in Hong Kong', *South China Morning Post*, 7 October 2014 <http://www.educationpost.com.hk/resources/education/141007-edu-insights-home-schooling-in-hong-kong> last accessed 24 August 2015 [the website no longer exists]
Weale, S., 'Home Educating Parents Object to Council's Home Visit Plans', *Guardian*, 31 December 2014 <https://www.theguardian.com/education/2014/dec/31/home-educating-parents-council-visits-westminster-london> last accessed 10 March 2019

Other

Département de l'information des Nations Unies, *Les familles, cœur de la société*. UN Doc. DPI/1512/SOC/CON–94-34130 (September 1994)

Gozdecka, D.A., 'Religions and Legal Boundaries of Democracy in Europe: European Commitment to Democratic Principles'. Thesis (PhD), University of Helsinki, 2009

Lau, Y.K., 'Family Impact Analysis of the Proposed Legislation – Children Proceedings (Parental Responsibility) Bill in Hong Kong', The 16th World Conference of the International Society of Family Law, Amsterdam, 25–9 July 2017

Research Office, Legislative Council Secretariat, *Fact Sheet Religious Facilities in Hong Kong*, FS01/17-18 (08 December 2017)

Websites

Administration française, *Mesure d'Assistance Éducative: conditions pour en bénéficier et procédure* (2011) <http://vosdroits.service-public.fr/particuliers/F457.xhtml> last accessed 10 March 2019

Caisse d'Allocations Familiales, *Référentiel national de financement partenarial des services de médiation familiale* (2018) <http://www.fenamef.asso.fr/images/fichiers/Re%CC%81fe%CC%81rentielnationaldefinancementpartenarialdelaMF-V.janvier2018.pdf> last accessed 10 March 2019

Clear, S., 'UK Human Rights Act is at Risk of Repeal – Here's Why it Should be Protected', *The Conversation* (12 February 2019) <https://theconversation.com/uk-human-rights-act-is-at-risk-of-repeal-heres-why-it-should-be-protected-111368> last accessed 10 March 2019

Community Legal Information Centre, 'Children's Constitutional Rights (2014–2018)', *The University of Hong Kong* <http://familyclic.hk/en/topics/Child-and-youth-affairs/Childrens-protection-and-welfare/Childrens-constitutional-rights/> last accessed 10 March 2019

Cour de Cassation, 'La Médiation' (Numéro hors-série) *Bulletin d'information de la Cour de Cassation* <http://www.courdecassation.fr/publications_cour_26/bulletin_information_cour_cassation_27/hors_serie_2074/mediation_8925.html#II> last accessed 10 March 2019

Daadouch, C. and P. Verdier, 'Protection de l'enfance: Ce qui change avec la loi du 14 mars 2016 et ses onze décrets' (2017) *Délinquance, Justice et Autres Questions de Société* (online) <https://www.laurent-mucchielli.org/public/Article_Daadouch_Verdier_reforme_protection_enfance.pdf> last accessed 10 March 2019

Défenseur des Droits, *Effet direct de la convention internationale relative aux droits de l'enfant dans l'ordre juridique française* (2016) <https://www.defenseurdesdroits.fr/sites/default/files/atoms/files/ddd-tableau_effet_direct_cide.pdf> last accessed 10 March 2019

Department of Health, Family Health Service, *Child Health* (2014) <http://www.fhs.gov.hk/english/main_ser/child_health/child_health.html> last accessed 10 March 2019

Direction de l'Information Légale et Administrative, 'Divorce, séparation: Un enfant mineur peut-il être entendu par le juge?' *Gouvernement de la République française* (22 May 2018) <https://www.service-public.fr/particuliers/vosdroits/F10479> last accessed 10 March 2019

Education Bureau (2011) *Whole School Approach to Guidance and Discipline* <http://www.edb.gov.hk/en/teacher/student-guidance-discipline-services/principles-guidelines/whole-school-approach-to-guidance-discipline/index.html> last accessed 10 March 2019

Education Bureau, 'International Education in Hong Kong – A Prospectus', *HKSAR* (15 June 2015) <https://www.edb.gov.hk/en/student-parents/ncs-students/useful-school-list/international-school.html> last accessed 10 March 2019

Gal, J. Le, *Pour que nos enfants puissent apprendre ensemble: Respecter leur personne et leurs droits* (2011) <http://www.meirieu.com/ECHANGES/jeanlegal.pdf> last accessed 10 March 2019

Government of the HKSAR, *Budget 2018–19. Head 141 – Government Secretariat: Labour and Welfare Bureau* (28 February 2018) <https://www.budget.gov.hk/2018/eng/pdf/head141.pdf> last accessed 10 March 2019

Hong Kong Information Services Department, *HK Committed to Protecting Children's Rights* (27 September 2013) <http://www.news.gov.hk/en/record/html/2013/09/20130927_113306.shtml> last accessed 10 March 2019

Hong Kong Judiciary, *Mediation Co-ordinator's Offices* <https://mediation.judiciary.hk/en/mcos.html#fmco> last accessed 10 March 2019

International Schools Hong Kong, 'Private Independent Schools Offering Non-Local Curriculum', *Education Bureau* (7 December 2018) <https://internationalschools.edb.hkedcity.net/private_independent_schools.php?lang=en> last accessed 10 March 2019

Law Society of Hong Kong, *Law Society's Submissions* [to consultation on a joint parental responsibility model] (24 April 2012) <https://keithhotten.files.wordpress.com/2012/05/law-society-response-to-child-custody-consultation.pdf> last accessed 10 March 2019

Ligue Française pour la Santé Mentale, *Pôle médiation familiale Formations* (2018) <https://www.lfsm.org/pole-mediation-familiale-formations-2018/> last accessed 10 March 2019

Maison de la Médiation, *Les Médiations Parent-Adolescent Sont Désormais Subventionnées par la CAF* (2018) <http://maisonmediation.fr/acc/18-blog/78-les-mediations-parent-adolescent-dans-le-referentiel-de-la-caf> last accessed 10 March 2019

M.H. 'L'enfant a droit d'être entendu!', *Dalloz* (30 November 2012) <http://actu.dalloz-etudiant.fr/a-la-une/article/lenfant-a-droit-detre-entendu/h/aeb32c7d851865917bacc11171a840f2.html> last accessed 10 March 2019

Ministère de l'Éducation nationale, de l'Enseignement supérieur et de la Recherche, *Compétences du Socle; Cycle 4* (2016) <http://cache.media.eduscol.education.fr/file/College_2016/74/6/RAE_Evaluation_socle_cycle_4_643746.pdf> last accessed 10 March 2019

Ministère de l'Éducation nationale, de l'Enseignement supérieur et de la Recherche, *Evaluer la maîtrise du socle commun aux cycles 2, 3 et 4* (2017) <http://eduscol.education.fr/cid103803/evaluer-la-maitrise-du-socle-commun-du-cycle-2-au-cycle-4.html> last accessed 10 March 2019

Ministère de l'Éducation nationale, de l'Enseignement supérieur et de la Recherche, *La laïcité à l'école* (2018) <http://www.education.gouv.fr/cid95865/la-laicite-a-l-ecole.html> last accessed 10 March 2019

Mission Interministérielle de Vigilance et de Lutte contre les Dérives Sectaires (Miviludes), *La Miviludes et l'Arrêt de la Cour Européenne des Droits de l'Homme du 5 juillet 2012 Concernant les Témoins de Jéhovah* (2012) <http://www.derives-sectes.gouv.fr/missions/actualites/la-miviludes-et-larrêt-de-la-cour-européenne-des-droits-de-lhomme-du-5-juillet-2> last accessed 10 March 2019

Munby, J., 'Changing families: Family law yesterday, today and tomorrow – a view from south of the border', *Edinburgh Law School Lecture* (20 March 2018) <https://www.judiciary.uk/wp-content/uploads/2018/03/speech-pfd-changing-families-edinburgh.pdf> last accessed 10 March 2019

National Health Service, *Newborn Screening* (2018) <https://www.nhs.uk/conditions/pregnancy-and-baby/newborn-screening/#newborn-physical-examination> last accessed 10 March 2019

Organisation of Security and Co-operation in Europe, *Toledo Guiding Principles on Teaching about Religions and Beliefs in Public Schools* (2007) <https://www.osce.org/odihr/29154?download=true> last accessed 10 March 2019

Rosenczveig, J.-P., 'Le droit de l'enfant d'être entendu' (11 January 2007) *Le Monde blogs: Droit des enfants* <http://jprosen.blog.lemonde.fr/2007/01/11/le-droit-de-lenfant-detre-entendu-173/> last accessed 10 March 2019

Rosenczveig, J.-P., 'De nouveaux droits aux enfants?' (24 November 2013) *Le Monde blogs: Droit des enfants* <http://jprosen.blog.lemonde.fr/2013/11/24/de-nouveaux-droits-aux-enfants/> last accessed 10 March 2019

Social Welfare Department, *Integrated Family Service Centre* (January 2016) <https://www.swd.gov.hk/doc/family/IFSC/IFSC%20Leaflet%20(Traditional%20Chinese%20and%20English)_Jan%202016.PDF> last accessed 10 March 2019

United Nations, Depository, *Status of Treaties: 11 d Optional Protocol to the CRC on a Communications Procedure* <https://treaties.un.org/pages/ViewDetails.aspx?src=IND&mtdsg_no=IV-11-d&chapter=4&clang=_en> last accessed 10 March 2019

Index

For Product Safety Concerns and Information please contact our EU representative GPSR@taylorandfrancis.com
Taylor & Francis Verlag GmbH, Kaufingerstraße 24, 80331 München, Germany

www.ingramcontent.com/pod-product-compliance
Ingram Content Group UK Ltd.
Pitfield, Milton Keynes, MK11 3LW, UK
UKHW022021180926
475701UK00005B/972

9780367727000